MW01252843

LIBRARY OF SECOND TEMPLE STUDIES

84

formerly the Journal for the Study of the Pseudepigrapha Supplement Series

Editor
Lester L. Grabbe

Editorial Board
Randall D. Chesnutt, Philip R. Davies,
Jan Willem van Henten, Judith M. Lieu,
Steven Mason, James R. Mueller,
Loren T. Stuckenbruck, James C. VanderKam

Founding Editor
James H. Charlesworth

LAND OR EARTH?

A Terminological Study of Hebrew ʾ*ereṣ*
and Aramaic ʾ*araʿ* in the Graeco-Roman Period

SHIZUKA UEMURA

t&t clark

GUELPH HUMBER LIBRARY
205 Humber College Blvd
Toronto, ON M9W 5L7

Published by T&T Clark International
A Continuum imprint
The Tower Building, 11 York Road, London SE1 7NX
80 Maiden Lane, Suite 704, New York, NY 10038

www.continuumbooks.com

All rights reserved. No part of this publication may be reproduced or transmitted in any form or by any means, electronic or mechanical, including photocopying, recording or any information storage or retrieval system, without permission in writing from the publishers.

© Shizuka Uemura, 2012

Shizuka Uemura has asserted his right under the Copyright, Designs and Patents Act, 1988, to be identified as the Author of this work.

British Library Cataloguing-in-Publication Date
A catalogue record for this book is available from the British Library.

ISBN: HB: 978-0-567-65142-6

Library of Congress Cataloging-in-Publication Data
A catalog record for this book is available from the Library of Congress.

Typeset by Free Range Book Design & Production Limited
Printed and bound in Great Britain

To my father and my late mother, and to Kiyoko

With many thanks and love

CONTENTS

Abbreviations

AB	Anchor Bible
ABD	David Noel Freedman (ed.), *The Anchor Bible Dictionary* (New York: Doubleday, 1992)
APAT	E. Kautzsch (ed. and trans.), *Die Apokryphen und Pseudepigraphen des Alten Testaments* (2 vols; Darmstadt: Wissenschaftliche Buchgesellschaft, 1994)
ATD	Das Alte Testament Deutsch
BA	*Biblical Archaeologist*
BASOR	*Bulletin of the American Schools of Oriental Research*
BDB	F. Brown, S. R. Driver and C. A. Briggs, *Hebrew and English Lexicon of the Old Testament with an Appendix Containing the Biblical Aramaic* (Oxford: Clarendon Press, 1952)
BHS	*Biblia hebraica stuttgartensia*
BR	*Bible Review*
BSac	*Bibliotheca Sacra*
BWANT	Beiträge zur Wissenschaft vom Alten und Neuen Testament
BZAW	Beihefte zur *ZAW*
CAD	Ignace I. Gelb *et al.* (eds), *The Assyrian Dictionary of the Oriental Institute of the University of Chicago* (Chicago: Oriental Institute, 1964–)
CBQ	*Catholic Biblical Quarterly*
CBQMS	*Catholic Biblical Quarterly*, Monograph Series
CII	*Corpus inscriptionum iudaicarum*
CPI	*Corpus papyrorum iudaicarum*
CSCO	Corpus scriptorum christianorum orientalium
DJD	Discoveries in the Judaean Desert
DSD	*Dead Sea Discoveries*
DSSC	M. G. Abegg Jr (ed.), *The Dead Sea Scrolls Concordance, Vol. 1: The Non-Biblical Texts from Qumran* (2 vols; Leiden: E.J. Brill, 2003)
DSSHAG I	J. H. Charlesworth (ed.), *The Dead Sea Scrolls: Hebrew, Aramaic, and Greek Texts with English Translations, Vol. 1: Rule of the Community and Related Documents* (Tübingen: J.C.B. Mohr; Louisville: Westminster/John Knox Press, 1994)
DSSHAG II	J. H. Charlesworth (ed.), *The Dead Sea Scrolls: Hebrew, Aramaic, and Greek Texts with English Translations, Vol. 2: Damascus*

	Document, War Scroll and Related Documents (Tübingen: J.C.B. Mohr; Louisville: Westminster/John Knox Press, 1995)
DSSSE	F. García Martínez and E. J. C. Tigchelaar (eds & trans), *The Dead Sea Scrolls: Study Edition* (2 vols; Leiden: E.J. Brill, 1997–8)
HAE	J. Renz and W. Röllig, *Handbuch der althebräischen Epigraphik* (3 vols; Darmstadt: Wissenschaftliche Buchgesellschaft, 1995)
HJP	E. Schürer, *The History of the Jewish People in the Age of Jesus Christ (175 B.C.–A.D. 135), A New English Edition* (G. Vermes *et al.* rev. and eds; 3 vols; Edinburgh: T&T Clark, 1973–87)
HTR	*Harvard Theological Review*
HUCA	*Hebrew Union College Annual*
IEJ	*Israel Exploration Journal*
JAOS	*Journal of the American Oriental Society*
JBL	*Journal of Biblical Literature*
JJS	*Journal of Jewish Studies*
JPSV	*Jewish Publication Society Version*
JQR	*Jewish Quarterly Review*
JSOT	*Journal for the Study of the Old Testament*
JSOTSup	*Journal for the Study of the Old Testament*, Supplement Series
JSS	*Journal of Semitic Studies*
KAI	H. Donner and W. Röllig, *Kanaanäische und aramäische Inschriften* (3 vols; Wiesbaden: Harrassowitz, 1962–4)
LBDJ	La Bible de Jérusalem
LSJ	H. G. Liddell, Robert Scott and H. Stuart Jones, *Greek–English Lexicon* (Oxford: Clarendon Press, 9th edn, 1968)
NRSV	New Revised Standard Version
NTS	*New Testament Studies*
OTP	James Charlesworth (ed.), *Old Testament Pseudepigrapha*
PAAJR	*Proceedings of the American Academy of Jewish Research*
PEQ	*Palestine Exploration Quarterly*
RB	*Revue biblique*
RevQ	*Revue de Qumran*
RSV	Revised Standard Version
SBLMS	SBL Monograph Series
SC	Sources chrétiennes
Sem	*Semitica*
SJOT	*Scandinavian Journal of the Old Testament*
TAD	B. Porten and A. Yardeni, *Textbook of Aramaic Documents from Ancient Egypt* (4 vols; Jerusalem: The Hebrew University, 1986–99)
TDNT	Gerhard Kittel and Gerhard Friedrich (eds), *Theological Dictionary of the New Testament* (trans. Geoffrey W. Bromiley; 10 vols; Grand Rapids: Eerdmans, 1964–)
TDOT	G. J. Botterweck and H. Ringgren (eds), *Theological Dictionary of the Old Testament*

TJD	A. Yardeni, *Textbook of Aramaic, Hebrew and Nabataean Documentary Texts from the Judaean Desert and Related Material* (2 vols; Jerusalem: The Hebrew University, 2000)
TLOT	E. Jenni and C. Westermann (eds), *Theological Lexicon of the Old Testament* (trans. M. E. Biddle; 3 vols; Peabody, MA: Hendrickson Publishers, 1997)
TZ	*Theologische Zeitschrift*
VD	*Verbum domini*
VT	*Vetus Testamentum*
WMANT	Wissenschaftliche Monographien zum Alten und Neuen Testament
ZAW	*Zeitschrift für die alttestamentliche Wissenschaft*
ZB	Zürcher Bibel
ZDPV	*Zeitschrift des deutschen Palästina-Vereins*

Preface

This book is a revised version of my dissertation, 'The Term *'eretz/'ara'* in Palestinian Jewish Literature of the Greco-Roman Period: A Philological Study', submitted to the Hebrew University of Jerusalem in 2005.

I am profoundly grateful to my supervisor, Prof Daniel R. Schwartz, for his constant support, advice and assistance in every stage of my work on the dissertation. He closely followed my progress on it, carefully read and commented on its drafts, and continuously encouraged me in my study.

I also owe thanks to my other teachers and friends for their assistance and advice on my dissertation. Emeritus Prof Sara Japhet, Emeritus Prof Doron Mendels and Prof Michael Stone of the Hebrew University gave me valuable suggestions on the direction of my dissertation at an early stage. Emeritus Prof Israel Ephal and Prof Moshe Taube of the Hebrew University offered valid remarks regarding their expert fields. Prof Harris G. Ives of Ibaraki Christian University read the entire manuscript and carefully improved my English. Prof Steven Fassberg of the Hebrew University and Prof Akio Tsukimoto of Rikkyo University thoroughly commented on the dissertation. Prof Tsukimoto introduced me to Emeritus Prof Philip Davies of the University of Sheffield, who presented my dissertation to Prof Lester L. Grabbe of the University of Hull.

I owe special thanks to Prof Grabbe for reading and commenting on my manuscript, and constantly providing me with advice on the revision. He recommended this work in the series Library of Second Temple Studies, and proposed the title of this book.

I would like to express also my deep sense of gratitude to Emeritus Prof Takashi Onuki and Prof Hiroshi Ichikawa for their advice and suggestions during my years at the University of Tokyo, and to Prof Isaiah Gafni for his encouragement during my years at the Hebrew University.

By dedicating this book to my parents and my wife, I wish to thank them for their constant support, encouragement, patience, and love, without which my study would never have been possible.

Chapter 1

Introduction

1.1. Main Problems Treated in this Study

The Hebrew term ארץ (*ʾereṣ*) and its Aramaic equivalent ארע (*ʾaraʿ*) have several meanings in ancient Jewish literature, such as: the earth as opposed to heaven, the earth on which human beings and animals are living (i.e., world), dry land as opposed to sea (or water), ground, soil, field, estate, territory, country, and the Land of Israel (= the Land). It is, however, not always clear in which sense the term is used in any particular passage. Above all, it is not easy at first glance to determine whether it signifies the earth or the Land. Moreover, it is expected that there might be a shift in meanings over time. The main subject of our study is to clarify the different usages of the term *ʾereṣ/ʾaraʿ* in the Jewish literature of Palestine.

The period treated in the research extends over approximately 460 years of Jewish history: from the conquest of Judaea by Alexander the Great to the aftermath of the destruction of the Second Temple, that is, the Graeco-Roman period (*c*. 333 BCE–132 CE).

The diversity of the numerous usages of the term *ʾereṣ/ʾaraʿ* occasionally obscures its precise referent. Despite recent efforts to describe the concept of Land, there is no systematic study of the term's uses in Jewish literature of the period we are analysing. Accordingly, our primary purpose is the philological clarification of uses of the term *ʾereṣ/ʾaraʿ* in Palestinian Jewish literature of the Graeco-Roman period, which we hope to achieve by:

1) determining the sense of the term in relevant passages – especially whether it means the earth or the Land
2) tracing the development of its uses according to the process of time.

It is to be hoped that clarification of the term and its usage will contribute, in turn, to the clarification of the relevant concepts as well. It is a basic term of the Creation theology. It could be utilized in a universal eschatology, since the end of the world implies the beginning of a new Creation. Therefore, it tends to be a basic term in a universal soteriology. It is also an essential term of the Land theology. The idea of the Promised Land was inclined to be a continuous national hope, which hence could be employed in an eschatological soteriology. Moreover, the two soteriologies, universal and territorial, could be combined with each other, since in both the very same term, *ʾereṣ/ʾaraʿ*, played a fundamental role, and the territory of the Promised Land had not been unanimously defined in the Bible. This means that the development of the term's usages can reveal a shift of worldviews over time, in particular, concerning eschatological soteriologies. This is important insofar as it bespeaks a possibility that universal soteriology may be an expression of national soteriology. Still, we must remind ourselves of an aspect of Second Temple Judaism, namely, sectarianism. It involves universalism in its frequent application of cosmic eschatology; it also concerns nationalism, for it tends to individualize humankind and makes a distinction within the nation. The contradictions between such ideologies as universalism and territorialism, and those between universalism and individualism on the one hand and nationalism on the other, may not be mutually exclusive. We shall contemplate the relationships of these ideologies and shift of worldviews as far as our term is concerned.

In this respect, it should be considered how such a shift of worldviews effected a change in uses of related terms and brought forth a new usage and replacement of their uses. To mention an important example: there is an expression ירש את הארץ 'to take possession of *ʾereṣ*' which frequently occurs in ancient Jewish literature. In the Bible it forms a part of the promise of the Land which will be possessed by Israel. In post-biblical literature, however, it can formulate a promise of a (new) earth which will be possessed by the righteous (Jews). Still, we can find a similar expression 'to take possession of the world (עולם)' from the first century CE on. In rabbinic literature we know normal uses of העולם הזה 'this world' and העולם הבא 'the world to come', and special attention to ארץ ישראל 'the Land of Israel', phrases which are not so familiar in the preceding periods. Thus, we can discern an extension of the biblical Land theology into a universal eschatology, on the one hand, a change of the term used and an emergence of new usage and replacement, on the other. The development of our term's usages has intimate relationships to a shift of worldviews. In short, our goal is to investigate an aspect of a shift of Jewish worldviews by observing changes in usages of the related terms.

1.2. Status of Research

Although its centrality in the Bible is apparent, the concept of Land in the post-biblical period was a factor neglected by Christian scholars until a few decades ago.[1] It is not only because their concerns have been governed by Christian doctrines, as W. D. Davies points out.[2] Rather, it is, at least partly, because there is a consensus that post-biblical Judaism was spiritualized to such an extent that the Jews most certainly understood the biblical concept of Land in a universal or

1. Thus W. D. Davies 1974: 3–5; 1982: xvi–xviii. Buber (1952) is a pioneer study dedicated to the Land theology from the Bible to the Zionist.

2. W. D. Davies 1974: 3–5; cf. Sasse 1978b: 677 n. 1: 'We cannot deal with the meanings of γῆ which have no bearing on the theological understanding of the NT.'

eschatological sense.[3] Recently, however, the abiding importance of the concept of Land as real territory through the post-biblical period has been re-examined from the theological,[4] politico-historical[5] and socio-historical[6] point of view. The coexistence of spiritualization on the one hand, and the significance of the concept of national Land on the other, would be a result of the diversity of Judaism in the period. Admitting that the problem of diversity and unity of Second Temple Judaism is well recognized by scholars,[7] this issue as related to the concept of Land still needs further exploration.

A fundamental step in explaining variety of understandings of Land is to investigate the term which expresses the concept. Although there have been efforts to discern the referent of our term in certain passages,[8] there has not been much philological research of the term as used in the post-biblical period. Thus, to focus on the two main scholars in this field, Davies does not examine the term *ʾereṣ* philologically, contenting himself with a reference to Rost's 1934 study – which, however, does not deal with post-biblical literature.[9] Similarly, despite his recognition that the term *ʾereṣ* or *hāʾāreṣ* was 'the traditional designation for the land',[10] Wilken does not attempt to seek further its application in Jewish literature. Even as for the biblical usages of the term, few systematic studies have been given,[11] whereas many books and articles have been dedicated to the Creation theology[12] and the Land theology in the Bible,[13] two central biblical theologies in which the term plays a significant role. In sum, this fundamental task for a better understanding of the concept remains almost untouched. Our research will inquire, from the philological point of view, whether, and to what extent, it is true that the term *ʾereṣ/ʾaraʿ* became spiritualized in the Second Temple period and afterward.

3. Davies himself is well aware of this point; W. D. Davies 1974: 104–29; 1982: 53–115. For further literature on universalism and spiritualization in this period concerning the Land, see e.g., Sasse 1978b: 677; Weinfeld 1984; generally, see Schwartz 1992: 1–26.

4. Heinemann 1948; Betz 1970; W. D. Davies 1974, 1982; Weinfeld 1984; Amaru 1981, 1986, 1994; Primus 1986; Wilken 1992; Safrai Z. and Ch. Safrai 1993.

5. Rappaport 1967, 1986; Applebaum 1986; Mendels 1987.

6. Sarason 1986; Gafni 1981, 1997.

7. See generally S. A. Cohen 1990; Goodblatt 1994; Hezser 1997.

8. E.g., Bergman and Ottosson 1977: 393–5; Hanhart 1983; Schwartz 1986.

9. Rost 1965 (originally 1934).

10. Wilken 1992: 265 n. 41.

11. Rost's 1934 article is still a single full-scale study of the term; further surveys can be found in major lexicons and dictionaries; e.g., Bergman and Ottosson 1977.

12. E.g., von Rad 1936; W. H. Schmidt 1967; Stadelmann 1970; Westermann 1971; Rüterswörden 1993; articles in Anderson (ed.) 1985; Davies and Clines (eds) 1998; and Reventlow and Hoffman (eds) 2002; for further bibliography, see Russell 1996: 13–18.

13. E.g., Weber 1971; Diepold 1972; von Waldow 1974; Rendtorff 1975; Brueggemann 1977; Emerton 1982; Schweid 1985; Townsend 1985; Orlinsky 1986; E. W. Davies 1989; Whitelam 1989; C. J. H. Wright 1990 esp. pp. 3–23; Wittenberg 1991; Boorer 1992; Weinfeld 1993; Habel 1995; articles in Eckert, Levinson and Stöhr (eds) 1970; Strecker (ed.) 1983; Evans and Cusack (eds) 1987; and Johnston and Walker (eds) 2000; for further bibliography, see Janzen 1992.

1.3. Methodology

Our sources are all Jewish works composed in Hebrew or Aramaic originating in Palestine from the period that remain in our hands in original forms or translations. The methodology to be employed in the research is the philological analysis of the term in its literary context and the historical consideration of its uses in relation to time. Granting that we are to discern every connotation of it, our primary concern is to examine if the term signifies the earth or the Land, and to trace the historical development of its uses in relation to these two meanings. We intend to survey all the occurrences of our term, to categorize them, and then to discuss the problematic ones. Our analysis of the term's meaning will proceed first of all from its usage in each given context.

In the case of those books whose original Hebrew or Aramaic version is lost and survive in translation(s) alone, we must work on hypothetical restoration of the original wording. Fortunately, we can usually know the equivalent for our term in different languages, such as: Greek γῆ, Latin *terra*, Ethiopic *medr*, and so on.[14] Various ancient translations of the Bible and their concordances will provide us with a safe basis for such restoration. Moreover, when a relevant passage appears to be quotation from the Bible, we will be assured of the original expression. Similarly, biblical style and idioms used in our sources will indicate the terminology of the original version. Hopefully, our study of surviving Hebrew/Aramaic texts, with which we shall begin, will give us more secure indication of what we're looking for in those texts which survive only in translation.

When we use a reconstructed Hebrew or Aramaic form, we shall add to it an asterisk as the common linguistic indication, either a word, a phrase, or a sentence; for example, *ארץ or *ʾ*ereṣ*, *גבול ישראל or **gebûl yiśrāel*, *ירש את העולם or **yāraš* ʾ*et hā*ʿ*ôlām*, and so on.

1.4. Chapter Arrangement and Periodization

In the next chapter, 2, we shall deal with the Bible. We shall analyse the terms literarily and stylistically, but not chronologically. It is not intended to trace the historical development of their uses within the Bible. Rather we shall treat the Bible as a whole. This paper is dedicated to their usage in the Second Temple period and thereafter, when the Bible was read as a whole; since they did not read the Bible like modern source critics, we need to show what they would see. Accordingly, we ignore the achievements of Old Testament scholars in their source critical studies, and our treatment of secondary literature will be limited. The main purpose of our treatment of the Bible is to discern the semantic field of each term, and to determine

14. According to Hatch and Redpath (1989: I, 240–55) the term γῆ is employed in the LXX as the most usual Greek equivalent for our Hebrew/Aramaic term (*c.* 95%: 2,379 times of 2,504 occurrences in the Bible). χώρα accounts for another 67 occurrences of ʾ*ereṣ* in the Bible (Hatch and Redpath 1989: II, 1481f.). The rest spread over other 27 Greek terms (III, 223).

its stylistic idiomatic uses, which will be the bases for our survey in the following main chapters. In concluding remarks we shall summarize our analyses of the terms, focus on their essential roles in the Creation theology and the Land theology, and consider the significance of the term *ʾereṣ* in these two central biblical theologies, a significance which will reveal an aspect of the biblical worldview. This chapter is supplemented by an appendix, which deals briefly with non-biblical Jewish uses of our terms in the Palestinian inscriptions and in the Elephantine papyri.

Chapter 3 surveys the uses of our terms in ancient non-Jewish circumstances. The materials are taken from Phoenician, New Punic, and Moabite and Aramaic inscriptions, and Aramaic papyri from Egypt and Nabataean papyri from Naḥal Ḥever, which are collected in *KAI*, *HAE*, *TAD* and *TJD*. The purpose of this treatment is to show a cultural background of uses of the terms. We shall categorize them stylistically and idiomatically, then try to discern ideologies implied in them concerning, in particular, Creation theology and Land theology, on the one hand, and to see ordinary usage in daily life, on the other.

Chapters 4–8 constitute the main part of this paper, which focuses upon the post-biblical Palestinian literature. These chapters are principally arranged according to historical periods which are punctuated by political events: Chapter 4: before the Maccabaean revolt (333–167 BCE), Chapter 5: the Hasmonaean period (167–63 BCE), Chapter 7: the early Roman period (63 BCE–70 CE), and Chapter 8: after the destruction of the Second Temple (70–132 CE). An exception is Chapter 6 which deals separately with the Qumran sectarian corpus, because it extends over two (or more) periods but the documents were produced by an identifiable group. The periodization is standard and legitimate, since these political events undoubtedly influenced the Palestinian Jews from the period whether cleric or lay, patriotic or sectarian.

In Chapter 9, the concluding chapter, we shall summarize our findings, and trace the shift of usages of the terms. In this relation we shall also give an overview of the transformation of Jewish worldviews over time.

Chapter 2

THE BIBLICAL BACKGROUND OF THE TERMS

The Hebrew term ארץ (*ʾereṣ*) and its Aramaic equivalents ארע (*ʾaraʿ*) and ארק (*ʾaraq*) appear in the Bible 2,526 times.[1] A basic meaning of it is a tangible dry solid part of the earth, which holds productivity of plants. While maintaining this essential connotation, its uses can be largely divided into two, reference to the earth as a whole and to a land as a specific territory.

ʾereṣ as the earth, contrasted to heaven, is understood in cosmological perspectives. Since human beings are living on the earth, the term can represent the human-earthly world. *ʾereṣ* can be perceived as a land in its territorial dimensions, as well. Among the many occurrences of this meaning, its uses referring to the Land play a significant role in the Bible, though the phrase *ʾereṣ yiśrāēl* appears much less. In this chapter we shall first examine uses of our term, and then such related terms as אדמה, תבל and גבול.

2.1. ʾereṣ *as Tangible Earth*

2.1.1. ʾereṣ *as* terra firma

ʾereṣ refers tangibly to *terra firma*, a dry solid part of the earth contrasted to the sea.[2] The border of *ʾereṣ* against the sea is fixed in the Creation.[3] *ʾereṣ* is also contrasted to the sky.[4] The part of air can be expressed by the phrase 'between the sky and the earth'.[5] On several occasions *ʾereṣ* refers to a part of *terra firma*: 'plain land' contrasted to mountains;[6] and 'continent' compared with islands.[7]

ʾereṣ is used to express living creatures of *terra firma*:

1. *ʾereṣ* 2,504 times, *ʾaraʿ* 21 times, and *ʾaraq* once, see Even-Shoshan (ed.) 1990: 111–19.
2. Gen. 1.9-10; Ps. 136.6; cf. Gen. 1.22; Ezek. 27.29; Hab. 3.9.
3. Ps. 104.9; cf. Ps. 74.17.
4. Gen. 1.20; Amos 3.5; Ezek. 1.15, 19, 21; 10.16, 19.
5. 2 Sam. 18.9; Ezek. 8.3; Zech. 5.9; 1 Chron. 21.16.
6. Isa. 49.13; Ezek. 32.6; Nah. 1.5; Hab. 3.6, 9-10; Pss. 18.8-10; 46.3; 90.2; 104.32; Job 26.7; cf. LXX Job 18.4.
7. Ps. 97.1; Est. 10.1.

חית הארץ 'wild animals of the earth' (opp. cattle)[8] and 'land-animals' (opp. birds),[9]
בהמה אשר בארץ 'land-animals' (opp. birds, creeping things and fish),[10]
בהמת הארץ 'wild beasts' which eat corpses, employed with 'birds of sky',[11]
הרמש על הארץ 'creeping things upon the earth',[12] and 'moving things on the earth', i.e., 'all land-animals' (opp. birds and fish),[13]
השרץ השרץ על הארץ 'swarming creature that swarms upon the earth'.[14]

2.1.2. ʾereṣ *as Ground, the Surface of the Earth*

ʾereṣ can be used in reference to its surface, 'the ground': frost covers upon *ʾereṣ* (Exod. 16.14), the height of things can be measured from *ʾereṣ*,[15] and so on.[16] References are made to *ʾereṣ* 'the ground' in relation to human acts. A man bows down to *ʾereṣ* before God or a king. In this usage the verb השתחוה 'to bow down' is frequently employed.[17] In several passages this verb follows ויקד (*waw* + impf. of קדד) 'to bow down',[18] and some have נפל 'to fall' instead.[19] The phrase נפל ארצה is employed to express 'bowing down to the ground'.[20] This expression, literally 'falling to the ground',[21] can be applied in metaphors, as well.[22]

ʾereṣ is used with a verb שפך 'to pour out' concerning the blood of sacrifices[23] and of men.[24] Pouring out of one's bowels on the ground can express death (2 Sam. 20.10) and heavy sorrow (Lam. 2.11; Job 16.13). It is stated that human beings are like water spilled to the ground which cannot be gathered up (2 Sam. 14.14; cf. Amos 5.8).

Onan spilled and wasted his semen to the ground (Gen. 38.9). Wasting to the ground can mean defeat in war, too (Judg. 20.21, 25). Similarly, striking or throwing

8. Gen. 1.24-25; 9.10; Ezek. 34.28; Job 5.22.
9. Ezek. 29.5; 32.4; Ps. 79.2; cf. Gen. 1.30; 9.2.
10. Deut. 4.17-18; Lev. 11.2-47.
11. Deut. 28.26; Jer. 7.33; 15.3; 16.4; 19.7; 34.20; cf. Isa. 18.6; Job 35.11; cf. also Mic. 5.7; 1 Sam. 17.44.
12. Gen. 1.26, 30; 7.14; 8.17; Lev. 11.44; Mic. 7.17.
13. Gen. 1.28; 7.21; 8.19.
14. Gen. 7.21; Lev. 11.29, 41, 42; cf. Lev. 11.46.
15. Num. 11.31; Ezek. 41.16; 43.14; cf. Ezek. 41.20; 42.6.
16. Deut. 22.6 (cf. Job 39.14); Josh. 7.21; Judg. 6.36-40; Job 18.10; 39.24.
17. Gen. 18.2; 19.1; 24.52; 33.3; 37.10; 42.6; 43.26; 48.12; 1 Sam. 25.41; 2 Sam. 14.33; 18.28; 24.20; 1 Kgs 1.23; 2 Kgs 2.15; 1 Chron. 21.21; Isa. 49.23.
18. Exod. 34.8; 1 Sam. 24.9; 28.14; Neh. 8.6; 1 Kgs 1.31.
19. Josh. 5.14; 1 Sam. 20.41; 25.23; 2 Sam. 1.2; 14.4, 22; 2 Kgs 4.37; Job 1.20; Ruth 2.10. In 2 Chron. 20.18 these three verbs are used together.
20. Gen. 44.14; Josh. 7.6; Judg. 13.20; 1 Sam. 5.3, 4; 17.49; 28.20; with other verbs: 1 Kgs 18.42; Jer. 14.2; 2 Chron. 7.3; Lam. 2.10.
21. Judg. 3.25; 2 Chron. 20.24; Ezek. 38.20; Amos 3.14.
22. 1 Sam. 3.19; 14.45; 26.20; 2 Sam. 14.11; 1 Kgs 1.52; 2 Kgs 10.10; Amos 9.9.
23. Deut. 12.16, 24; 15.23.
24. Isa. 63.6; Ezek. 21.37; 24.7; 32.6; 33.25; 36.18; 1 Chron. 22.8.

to the ground in the sense of destruction can be expressed with various verbs.[25] ʾ*ereṣ* as the ground is once employed in a metaphor of Jerusalem on which enemies walk (Isa. 51.23).

Other human acts related to the ground are: sitting on;[26] lying or laying on;[27] arising or raising from;[28] letting down to;[29] and others.[30] Likewise, pinning to ʾ*ereṣ* is expressed by various phrases.[31]

On the ground there is 'dust'. The phrase עפר הארץ 'the dust of the earth' expresses metaphorically innumerableness,[32] along with its physical sense.[33] It is applied in a metaphor suggestive of beating something into a fine powder, as well.[34] In Isa. 25.12 and 26.5 ʾ*ereṣ* stands in parallelism with dust.[35] Ecclesiastes 12.7 presupposes the idea that man created of dust is to return to ʾ*ereṣ* without wordplay between ʾ*ādām* and ʾ*adāmâ* (cf. Genesis 2–3).

2.1.3. ʾereṣ *as Soil with Productivity of Plants*

According to the Creation narrative, God ordered ʾ*ereṣ* to put forth grass, herb and fruit tree, and the ʾ*ereṣ* responded to the command (Gen. 1.11-12). These are food given by God to human beings and animals.[36] In Eccl. 1.3-4 the permanence of ʾ*ereṣ* as productive soil is compared with the mortality of human beings who toil under the sun. Fertility of ʾ*ereṣ* is presupposed, and the phrase עשב הארץ 'the grass of the earth' is used as a metaphor for numerousness of people.[37] However, when eating 'the grass of the earth' up, locusts cause famine, though their attack is regarded not just as a natural disaster, but as a part of God's plan.[38]

The Bible, of course, knows that ʾ*ereṣ* needs rain to bring forth its products.[39] Rain as well is God's gift for beings on the earth.[40] Thus in Isa. 45.8 fruits sprung

25. Pss. 7.6; 17.11; 74.7; 89.40, 45; 143.3; 147.6; 2 Sam. 2.22; 18.11; Isa. 21.9; 28.2; Ezek. 13.14; 19.12; 26.11; 28.17 (cf. Exod. 4.3); 32.4; Amos 5.7; Obad. 3; Lam. 2.2, 9.

26. Isa. 3.26; 47.1; Ezek. 26.16; Job 2.13; Lam. 2.10.

27. 2 Sam. 8.2; 12.16; 13.31; Lam. 2.21.

28. 1 Sam. 28.23; 2 Sam. 12.17; 20.

29. Gen. 44.11.

30. Deut. 28.56; Lev. 11.21; Jer. 51.27; Eccl. 10.7.

31. Judg. 4.21; 1 Sam. 26.7, 8; cf. 2 Kgs 13.18.

32. Gen. 13.16; 28.14; 2 Chron. 1.9.

33. Exod. 8.12, 13; Isa. 40.12; Amos 2.7; Job 14.19.

34. 2 Sam. 22.43; cf. Ezek. 28.18.

35. Cf. Ps. 44.26.

36. Gen. 1.29; 27.28, 39; Ps. 67.7; 104.14; Job 28.5; cf. Song 2.12; Mk 4.28.

37. Ps. 72.16; Job 5.25; cf. Isa. 40.24; 61.11.

38. Amos 7.1-3; Exod. 10.1-20. Amos 7.2 refers to 'the grass of the Land', and in Exod. 10.12, 15 ʾ*ereṣ* refers to the land of Egypt. Thus ʾ*ereṣ* keeps its nature as productive soil when referring to a specific territory as well as when it signifies the whole earth; see also Ps. 105.35; 2 Kgs 2.19.

39. Hos. 6.3; Ps. 72.6; 2 Sam. 23.4; cf. Gen. 2.6.

40. Gen. 2.5; 27.28; Isa. 55.10; Pss. 65.10; 147.8; Job 5.10; 14.8f.

up by cooperation of rain of heaven and productivity of *ʾereṣ* are compared with salvation and righteousness in relation to God's Creation.

While the productivity of *ʾereṣ* is presupposed, it is seldom connected with agriculture. It is never employed with the verb עבד 'to till', which is used with another term, *ʾadāmâ*.[41] An exception is its use with the verb זרע 'to sow' (Gen. 26.12; Exod. 23.10), though sowing can be done not only by human beings but also by nature (winds, insects, etc.). We can say, therefore, that *ʾereṣ* with productivity indifferent to human labour is regarded in the Bible as a kind of Mother Earth; its productivity, however, is dependent on God's will.

2.2. ʾereṣ *as Cosmological Earth*

ʾereṣ is perceived cosmologically in contrast to שמים (*šāmayim*) as is common in ancient Near Eastern literature.[42] The latter term can refer to 'the firmament' on which sun, moon and stars move, 'the sky' the air space, and 'the heaven' in which God abides. Although the denotation of *ʾereṣ*, too, ranges according to its counterpart, the term keeps its cosmological connotation.

2.2.1. šāmayim *and* ʾereṣ *as God's Creation*

The Bible begins with God's Creation of *šāmayim* and *ʾereṣ*. The notion that God created them is stated throughout the Bible with such various verbs as: ברא 'to create',[43] עשה 'to make',[44] קנה 'to get',[45] נטה 'to stretch out',[46] יצר 'to form',[47] and so on.[48] The creation of *ʾereṣ*, in particular, is sometimes narrated with the verb יסד 'to found',[49] and its 'foundations' are referred to.[50] The completion of the Creation of *ʾereṣ* is sometimes expressed by referring to its 'ends'.[51]

In Gen. 1.2 the proto-universe is called *ʾereṣ*, from which *šāmayim* and *ʾereṣ* were created.[52] Despite Gen. 1.9-10, in which *ʾereṣ* is unambiguously contrasted

41. See § 2.5.1 below.

42. See Bergman and Ottosson 1977: 388–93.

43. Gen. 1.1; 2.4a; Isa. 42.5; 45.18; cf. Isa. 65.17.

44. Gen. 2.4b; Exod. 31.17; 2 Kgs 19.15; Pss. 115.15; 121.2; 124.8; 134.3; Prov. 8.26; 2 Chron. 2.11; Isa. 37.16; 44.24; 45.12; Jer. 10.12; 27.5; 32.17; 51.15; Jer. 10.11 (Aramaic); cf. Isa. 66.22.

45. Gen. 14.19, 22; cf. Prov. 8.22; *KAI* 26, 129 (Chapter 3 below).

46. Isa. 42.5; 44.24; 45.12; Jer. 10.12; 51.15.

47. Isa. 45.18.

48. Gen. 2.1; Pss. 90.2; 119.90; Isa. 45.18; Jer. 33.25; for the uses of these verbs, see Stadelmann 1970: 4–7.

49. Isa. 48.13; 51.13, 16; Jer. 31.37; Zech. 12.1; Pss. 102.26; 104.5; Prov. 3.19; Job 38.4; cf. Ps. 78.69.

50. Isa. 24.18; 40.21; Mic. 6.2; Ps. 82.5; Prov. 8.29; cf. 1 Sam. 2.8; Ps. 75.4.

51. Isa. 40.28; Prov. 30.4; Job 28.24; 37.3; 38.13, 18.

52. Gen. 1.6-8, 14-18; cf. Prov. 8.23.

with 'the sea', the tripartite division of universe into heaven, earth and sea appears relatively rarely in the Bible.[53] Rather usual is the use in which *šāmayim* refers to the firmament, and *ʾereṣ* signifies another half of the universe. Thus what God created, first of all, is the spatio-physical universe, 'the receptacle', in which animate things would be created. For example, in Gen. 2.1 the terms *šāmayim* and *ʾereṣ* refer to the firmament, the earth (including the sea) and the space between them (i.e., the sky), while the phrase כל צבאם 'all their host' designates that which was created in them.[54] In the same manner the idea that the 'whole Creation is God's' is expressed with *šāmayim*, *ʾereṣ* and other terms which signify all living forms in them.[55]

This receptacle has its own laws established by God (Jer. 33.25; Job 38.33). The sun in *šāmayim* provides light on *ʾereṣ*.[56] The rain, the water on *šāmayim*, is given to *ʾereṣ*.[57] The cooperation of *šāmayim* and *ʾereṣ* brings forth food for living things.[58] All natural phenomena are considered to be in accord with God's will. Nature sometimes swerves from these laws according to God's will, which is a response to human acts.[59] More importantly, unusual natural phenomena are expected in eschatological visions: *ʾereṣ* returns to chaos and there is no sun in *šāmayim*;[60] *ʾereṣ* quakes, *šāmayim* trembles, the sun and the moon are darkened, and the stars withdraw their shining.[61] In some instances quaking of *ʾereṣ* (and *šāmayim*), in particular, is caused directly by God.[62] Furthermore, *ʾereṣ* of itself quakes in reaction to God's will or acts,[63] and in a few instances to human deeds.[64]

The idea that *šāmayim* and *ʾereṣ* can react to God's will or human acts may have something to do with their personification: *ʾereṣ* mourns and *šāmayim* grows dark (Jer. 4.28); and *šāmayim* shall be glad and *ʾereṣ* rejoices (1 Chron. 16.31).[65] Since *šāmayim* and *ʾereṣ* are the most stable among things created, they can be witnesses par-excellence; Moses calls them to witness against the people of Israel;[66]

53. Exod. 20.4, 11; Deut. 4.17-18; 5.8; Pss. 69.35; 96.11; 104.19-30; 146.6; Neh. 9.6; Job 12.7-8; cf. Hag. 2.6; Ps. 135.6; Job 11.8-9; for the bipartite division into the earth and the sea, see nn. 2–3 above.

54. Cf. Gen. 2.4b-5; Isa. 42.5; 44.24; 45.12, 18; 51.6; Jer. 10.12; 27.5; 33.25; 51.15, 48; Prov. 8.22, 26.

55. Deut. 10.14; Ps. 89.12; 1 Chron. 29.11; cf. Ps. 24.1; 1 Sam. 2.8 without reference to *šāmayim*. In Exod. 9.29 *ʾereṣ* means not only the earth, but implies also the firmament, as shown by 'hail' and 'thunder', hence 'the receptacle'.

56. Gen. 1.15, 17; 19.23.

57. Amos 9.6; Jer. 10.13; Eccl. 11.3; Job 12.15; 37.6-13; cf. Job 37.17; 38.24.

58. Cf. nn. 39–40 above.

59. E.g., on disaster: Exod. 9.13-33; Deut. 28.23; on favourite reply: Hos. 2.23f.

60. Jer. 4.23; cf. Gen. 1.2.

61. Joel 2.10; cf. Joel 3.3f.; 4.15f.; Amos 8.9.

62. Isa. 2.19, 21; Hag. 2.6, 21; Job 9.6.

63. Judg. 5.4; 2 Sam. 22.8; Isa. 13.13; 24.18, 19, 20; Jer. 10.10; 49.21; 50.46; 51.29; Amos 9.5; Joel 4.16; Pss. 18.8; 46.7; 68.9; 77.19; 97.4; 99.1; 104.32.

64. Ps. 82.5; Prov. 30.21-23.

65. Cf. Jer. 51.48; Pss. 69.35; 96.11; 148.1-12.

66. Deut. 4.26; 30.19; 31.28.

and they are called to listen as witnesses.[67] Their stability is expressed in such an expression as 'like the days of heavens upon the earth'.[68] This expression, however, itself implies their end in the future (cf. Isa. 51.6).

In other occurrences the terms *šāmayim* and *ʾereṣ* denote creatures together with their receptacle. In Gen. 2.4a, a summary statement of the Creation, the two terms represent the whole Creation.[69] Accordingly, there are several expressions for the Creator: 'God in *šāmayim* above and on *ʾereṣ* beneath' (Deut. 4.39; Josh. 2.11);[70] 'there is no God like You in *šāmayim* above or on *ʾereṣ* beneath' (1 Kgs 8.23// 2 Chron. 6.14).[71] God's glory is upon *šāmayim* and *ʾereṣ*, on the whole Creation.[72] *šāmayim* is God's throne and *ʾereṣ* is his footstool, hence God is the King of the whole universe.[73] In these occurrences *šāmayim* is not assigned to the dwelling place of God (cf. 1 Kgs 8.27//2 Chron. 6.18).[74]

However, there is in the Bible the idea that *šāmayim* is God's abode[75] in contrast to *ʾereṣ* where human beings are living.[76] In *šāmayim* God's angels abide, as well.[77] The conception that *šāmayim* is not merely the firmament but represent 'the divine-heavenly world' is in parallelism with its counterpart, *ʾereṣ* as 'the human-earthly world'. That human beings represent all animate things on *ʾereṣ* is described in God's command to the first man and woman (Gen. 1.28).[78] It is stated, therefore, that the history of this world began from the day of man's creation on *ʾereṣ* (Deut. 4.32; cf. Job 20.4). The humbleness of human life on the earthly world is expressed in Job 7.1 (cf. Eccl. 8.14-16).

This use of *ʾereṣ* as human world, of course, does not lose its tangible connotations, since human beings can live, at any rate, only on *ʾereṣ*. A distinct example of this is found in the narrative of 'Noah and the Flood'; God saw the great wickedness of humankind on *ʾereṣ*, and determined to destroy them along with other creatures and *ʾereṣ* as such by flood (Gen. 6.5–9.17; cf. Isa. 54.9). *ʾereṣ* here means *terra firma* which can be destroyed by flood; it also connotes the earthly-world which is represented by human beings and which itself is said to have been corrupted.

67. Deut. 32.1; Isa. 1.2; Mic. 1.2; 6.1f.; cf. Ps. 50.1, 4; Job 20.27; Jer. 2.12; see Delcor 1966.

68. Deut. 11.21; cf. Gen. 8.22; Job 8.9; 1 Chron. 29.15.

69. Cf. concerning the Creation: Gen. 1.1; 14.19, 22; Exod. 31.17; 2 Kgs 19.15; 2 Chron. 2.11; Isa. 37.16; 65.17; 66.22; Jer. 10.11; 32.17; Pss. 121.2; 124.8; 134.3; in other contexts: Hab. 3.3; Pss. 50.4; 113.6; 148.13; 1 Kgs 8.23; 2 Chron. 6.14.

70. Cf. Gen. 24.3; Ezra 5.11; Deut. 3.24.

71. Cf. Exod. 9.14; 2 Kgs 5.15; Jer. 10.11.

72. Ps. 148.13; Hab. 3.3; cf. Num. 14.21; Isa. 6.3; Pss. 8.2-10; 33.5; 72.19; 119.64.

73. Isa. 66.1; cf. Pss. 99.5; 110.1; 132.7; 1 Chron. 28.2; cf. Lam. 2.1.

74. Cf. Ps. 113.4-6.

75. E.g., 1 Kgs 8.30, 32, 39, 43, 45, 49; Isa. 6.1f.; Ezekiel 1.

76. Pss. 33.13f.; 57.6//57.12//108.6; 73.9, 25; 76.9; 102.20; 104.13; 115.16; Eccl. 5.1; Isa. 40.22.

77. Gen. 28.12; Isa. 24.21; cf. Zech. 1.10, 11; 4.9; 6.7; Job 1.7f.//2.2f.

78. Cf. Gen. 1.26; 8.16f.; 9.1, 7.

The human-earthly world can be expressed by the phrase ארץ (ה)חיים 'the world of the living', as well.[79] This expression has its counterpart, ארץ תחתי(ו)ת[80] or תחתיות (ה)ארץ[81] which means underworld, i.e., 'the netherworld'.[82] The existence of netherworld under *ʾereṣ* is assumed in such descriptions as: 'the earth opened its mouth and swallowed them up'.[83] Similarly, an expression תכס הארץ 'the earth covers' is used in relation to burial (Num. 16.33; Job 16.18).

Accordingly, there is in the Bible a tripartite division of the world into *šāmayim*, *ʾereṣ* (*ḥayîm*) and *ʾereṣ taḥtyt* (= Sheol), in which the terms signify the divine-heavenly world, the human-earthly world, and the netherworld, respectively.[84]

Hitherto we have confirmed types of division of the cosmos in the Bible. They can be categorized, according to different cosmological dimensions, into: (i) a bipartite division of the universe into firmament and earth (including sea); (ii) a bipartite division of the world into divine-heavenly and human-earthly; and (iii) a tripartite division of the world into heavenly, earthly and nether.

The type (i) sees the universe as Creation, hence God is transcendent, not living either in heaven or on the earth. Here a single self-completed world is assumed, and, though it is sometimes intervened in by God, imagination of God is rigorously avoided. In the type (ii), in contrast, God's abode is imagined in comparison with the human world. This twofold world is understood in somewhat spatial imagination. In the third type the netherworld, too, is supposed. The threefold world, heavenly, earthly and nether, tends to be imagined, not only spatially but chronologically, since death is imminent for all living beings. This conception of the world allowed for various images of afterlife, resurrection, and eschatological world to come in later periods.

2.2.2. ʾereṣ *as Human World*

Since human beings are living on *ʾereṣ*, there are in the Bible many occurrences of the term in the sense of human-earthly world, or simply 'human world'.[85] Attention is paid specifically to the human world in God's epithets with the phrase כל הארץ

79. Isa. 38.11; 53.8; Jer. 11.19; Ezek. 26.20; 32.23, 24, 25, 26, 27, 32; Pss. 27.13; 52.7; 142.6; Job 28.13; cf. Ps. 116.9 (plural).

80. Ezek. 26.20; 31.14, 16, 18; 32.18, 24.

81. Isa. 44.23; Pss. 63.10; 139.15.

82. For other expressions of the netherworld with the term *ʾereṣ*, cf. Pss. 22.30; 71.20; 88.13; 95.4; Job 10.21, 22; Eccl. 3.21; 1 Sam. 28.13; Isa. 9.1; 29.4; 45.19; Jer. 17.13; Jon. 2.7. For שאול 'Sheol', see Even-Shoshan (ed.) 1990: 1098; for בור 'pit': Isa. 14.15, 19; 38.18; Ezek. 26.20; 31.14, 16; 32.18, 24, 25, 29, 30; Pss. 28.1; 30.4; 88.5; 143.7; Prov. 1.12; for other expressions: Isa. 38.11; Pss. 88.7, 12; 115.17.

83. Num. 16.32; 26.10; Deut. 11.6; Ps. 106.17; cf. Exod. 15.12; Num. 16.34.

84. Pss. 115.16f.; Isa. 14.3-23; Job 11.8f.; see Stadelmann 1970: 9f.

85. By saying 'human world' I imply 'human experiential world', along with its literal meaning. Thus, for example, the phrase 'small things of *ʾereṣ*' of Prov. 30.24-28, in which human beings are not referred to, can be included in this category.

'all the earth': 'the Lord of all the earth',[86] 'the Most High of all the earth',[87] 'the God of all the earth',[88] 'the King of all the earth',[89] 'the Judge of (all) the earth',[90] and 'all the earth is YHWH's'.[91] It is said that God's glory fills all the earth;[92] God's eyes range throughout all the earth (2 Chron. 16.9). Twice the earth is called 'His earth' (Prov. 8.31; Job 37.13). In a saying of Naaman, however, the special status of the Land of Israel in the human world is stressed: 'there is no God in all the earth but in (the Land of) Israel' (2 Kgs 5.15).[93]

That the term refers to the human world rather than a definite land is discernible when it is used with other terms which contain worldwide scope. In Ps. 33.8, for instance, כל הארץ is in parallelism with כל ישבי תבל 'all the inhabitants of the world'. While the term *ʾereṣ*, when employed with *tēbēl*, can denote the whole world in relation to the Creation, it can represent the human world except Israel, namely, Gentiles.[94] Our term, therefore, can be employed with terms which designate foreign nations: גוים 'nations',[95] ממלכות 'kingdoms',[96] מלכים 'kings',[97] לאמים 'peoples',[98] עמים 'peoples'.[99] These words can be used in construct form with our term.[100] In almost all of these instances *ʾereṣ* represents Gentiles.[101]

Our term can be used in construct form with other terms which denote persons of sort (e.g., 'rulers of the earth' [Isa. 40.23; Ps. 2.10]), though it is dependent on

86. Mic. 4.13; Zech. 4.14; 6.5; Josh. 3.11, 13; Ps. 97.5.

87. Pss. 83.19; 97.9.

88. Isa. 54.5.

89. Zech. 14.9; Ps. 47.3, 8; for Ps. 47, see Bergman and Ottosson 1977: 395.

90. Gen. 18.25; cf. Isa. 26.9; 42.4; Pss. 58.12; 82.8; 94.2; 96.13; 105.7; 1 Chron. 16.14, 33.

91. Exod. 19.5, cf. Exod. 9.29 (see n. 55 above); Ps. 24.1; 1 Sam. 2.8.

92. Num. 14.21; Isa. 6.3; Pss. 33.5; 72.19; 119.64, cf. Ps. 148.13; Hab. 3.3.

93. Cf. 2 Sam. 7.23//1 Chron. 17.21; see Harvey 1996: 181.

94. For *ʾereṣ* in parallelism with *tēbēl*, and in relation to Creation: Pss. 19.5; 24.1; 90.2; 97.4; Job 34.13; 37.12; Prov. 8.31; cf. Ps. 33.14 with v. 13; designating Gentiles: Pss. 33.8; 96.13; 98.9; Isa. 13.5b (cf. v. 11), 9 (cf. v. 11); 18.3; 26.9; 34.1; Lam. 4.12; 1 Chron. 16.30; with other connotation: Isa. 14.21. In Isa. 26.18 *ʾereṣ* in parallelism with *tēbēl* seems to connote the whole human world including Israel.

95. Exod. 34.10; Isa. 14.26; 34.1; Jer. 25.30 (cf. v. 31); 46.12; 51.27; Hab. 3.12; Pss. 46.7, 11; 67.3; 82.8; cf. Isa. 14.9.

96. Isa. 14.16; Zeph. 3.8; Ps. 46.7.

97. Ps. 48.3 (cf. v. 5).

98. Isa. 34.1; 60.2.

99. Isa. 12.4f.

100. With *gôyim*: Gen. 18.18; 22.18; 26.4; Deut. 28.1; Jer. 26.6; 33.9; 44.8; Zech. 12.3; with preposition: Gen. 10.32 (cf. Ps. 67.5); with *mamlākôt*: Deut. 28.25; 2 Kgs 19.15, 19; Isa. 23.17; 37.16, 20; Jer. 15.4; 24.9; 25.26; 29.18; 34.1, 17; Ps. 68.33; 2 Chron. 36.23//Ezra 1.2; with *melākîm*: 1 Kgs 5.14; 10.23; 2 Chron. 9.22, 23; Pss. 2.2; 76.13; 89.28; 102.16; 138.4; 148.11; Ezek. 27.33; Lam. 4.12; with *ʿamîm*: Deut. 28.10; Josh. 4.24; Ezek. 31.12; Zeph. 3.20; 1 Kgs 8.43, 53, 60; 2 Chron. 6.33; 32.19; Est. 8.17. Cf. with *mišpāḥâ*: Zech. 14.17, cf. Gen. 12.3; Amos 3.2.

101. Exceptions: Gen. 10.32; Isa. 14.16; Jer. 46.12; 51.27; Ezek. 31.12; Ps. 48.3; Ezra 1.2// 2 Chron. 36.23.

the context if it signifies the human world or a specific land.[102] In most of these instances, too, *ʾereṣ* 'the earth' represents Gentiles.[103]

The term *ʾereṣ* in the sense of human world can be used as the subject of the sentence, especially in construct form of כל הארץ.[104] The phrase can represent the whole population of the world.[105] There are again occasions in which the phrase represents nations other than Israel.[106] When *ʾereṣ* in the sense of human world is used as an object of sentence, the subject is usually God,[107] but occasionally human rulers of the world.[108]

ʾereṣ as human world can be used with prepositions. Expressions בארץ,[109] בכל הארץ,[110] and בקרב הארץ,[111] as a rule, indicate the existence of certain things 'in (the midst of) this world'. The phrase מן הארץ follows verbs which signify the disappearance of certain things 'from the world'.[112] The whole earthly-world can be expressed by such a phrase as על פני כל הארץ 'on the face of all the earth'.[113] Even among these simple uses with prepositions, there are occasions that the term *ʾereṣ* connotes nations other than Israel.[114]

Besides, our term can connote 'human society' in cases where order or morality is the matter of concern (Prov. 30.21-23; Ps. 75.4; Job 9.24). There are idiomatic uses of דרך כל הארץ 'the way of (all) human society', concerning marriage (Gen. 19.31) and death (Josh. 23.14; 1 Kgs 2.2). Mention is made of משוש הארץ 'the exultation of human society' (Isa. 24.11).

ʾereṣ can constitute construct form with terms denoting 'end(s)' such as: קצה, אפס, כנף. As noted above, the ends of the earth are sometimes understood

102. See Isa. 23.8-9; 24.6, 17; 26.21; Jer. 50.23; 51.41, 49; Ezek. 7.21; 39.18; Pss. 47.10; 75.9; 76.10; 148.11; Job 3.14.

103. Exceptions: Isa. 24.6, 17; 26.21 (Job 3.14?). In Jeremiah *kol hāʿāreṣ* is contrasted to Babylon (50.23; 51.41, 49).

104. In Gen. 10.25//1 Chron. 1.19 *hāʿāreṣ* (without *kol*) is used as the subject in the context of the division of the earth into lands of nations.

105. See Gen. 9.19; 11.1, 9; 41.57; Isa. 14.7; Hab. 2.20; Pss. 96.1; 100.1; 1 Chron. 16.23 (cf. Pss. 66.1-4; 98.4); Ps. 96.9; 1 Chron. 16.30 (cf. Ps. 114.7).

106. See 1 Sam. 17.46 (cf. Deut. 28.10; Josh. 4.24; 6.27; Isa. 11.9; Hab. 2.14; Ps. 59.14); 1 Kgs 10.24; Zeph. 3.8; Ps 33.8. In Zeph. 1.11 *kol hāʿāreṣ* refers to the world other than Judah; cf. v. 12 (cf. also Zeph. 6.1-8, esp. v. 7).

107. Isa. 24.1; Jer. 45.4; Hab. 3.12; Zech. 4.10; Pss. 96.13; 98.9; Job 34.13. Exception: Isa. 24.6.

108. Isa. 10.14; 14.16; Jer. 51.7, 25.

109. Gen. 4.12, 14; 6.4, 5, 6; 10.8//1 Chron. 1.10; 2 Sam. 7.9//1 Chron. 17.8; 2 Sam. 7.23//1 Chron. 17.21; 2 Sam. 14.20; Isa. 62.7; Pss. 46.9, 11; 58.3; 67.3; Prov. 11.31; Eccl. 7.20; cf. Prov. 10.30.

110. Gen. 41.57; 47.13; Exod. 9.14, 16; 34.10; 2 Kgs 5.15; Zeph. 3.19; Pss. 19.5; 45.17; Job 42.15.

111. Isa. 19.24; 24.13.

112. Exod. 9.15; Josh. 7.9; 2 Sam. 4.11; Isa. 25.8; Nah. 2.14; Pss. 21.11; 34.17; 104.35; 109.15; Job 18.17.

113. Gen. 7.3; 8.9; 11.4, 8, 9; *ʿal kol penê hāʾāreṣ*: Gen. 41.56; Ezek. 34.6; cf. Job 37.12; see § 2.5.1 (p. 36) and nn. 350f. below. The phrase *ʿal kol hāʾāreṣ* in Isa. 14.26 means 'concerning'.

114. Exod. 9.14, 16; 34.10; 2 Sam. 7.23//1 Chron. 17.21; 2 Kgs 5.15; Ezek. 34.6; Zeph. 3.19; Pss. 45.17; 46.9, 11; 67.3; Isa. 24.13.

in relation to its Creation.[115] Specifically, the 'end' can be imagined as the place from which the mist rises.[116] Occasionally the end signifies the origins of a powerful nation.[117] In other occurrences the expressions seem to mean 'throughout the world'.[118] This is apparent in the phrase מקצה הארץ ועד קצה הארץ[119] and in phrases with plural 'ends'.[120] In particular, the phrase כל אפסי ארץ is applied idiomatically to represent the whole population of the world.[121] In these uses of 'end(s) of *ʾereṣ*' an emphasis is laid on the contrast between Israel and foreign nation(s).[122] The nations are described as enemies of Israel, on the one hand, but their recognition of the God of Israel is expected, on the other. It should be noted, in particular, that the Promised Land can be extended to the whole human world (Pss. 2.8; 72.8).[123] Accordingly, the uses of 'end(s) of *ʾereṣ*' should be understood as attempts to locate the people and religion of Israel among the nations.

The plural ארצות, literally 'lands', can represent the human world, as well (Ps. 107.3). It is the case especially in the phrase כל הארצות.[124] The term can constitute a construct form with words which denote 'peoples'.[125] Foreign gods, too, are indicated by the term כל אלהי הארצות[126] and the like.[127] There appears an expression ארצות החיים 'the lands of the living' (Ps. 116.9), which might suggest an Israelite experience in foreign lands.[128] In the uses of plural form, Israel is usually not included in *ʾarāṣôt*, but rather contrasted.[129] It is, therefore, an expression of special status of Israel among nations (see Ezek. 20.6, 15).

The term *ʾereṣ* in the sense of human world is used mainly in two dimensions: (i) human world as contrasted with God, its Creator, and (ii) human world as other nations, contrasted with Israel. In the former, *ʾereṣ* is apprehended cosmologically in relation to God, while in the latter, it is understood internationally in contrast to foreign nations. These two dimensions correspond with each other; as in the latter the term illuminates the uniqueness of Israel contrasted with other nations, so in the

115. Isa. 40.28; Prov. 30.4; Job 28.24; 37.3; 38.13, 18.

116. Jer. 10.13; 51.16; Ps. 135.7.

117. Deut. 28.49; Ps. 61.3; Isa. 5.26; Jer. 6.22; 25.32; 31.8; 50.41.

118. Isa. 24.16; 42.10; 43.6.

119. Deut. 13.8; 28.64; Jer. 25.33; and Isa. 48.20; 49.6; Jer. 25.31; Ps. 46.10; and also Isa. 62.11.

120. Deut. 33.17; 1 Sam. 2.10; Isa. 8.9; 11.12; 41.5, 9; Jer. 16.19; Mic. 5.3; Hab. 1.6; Pss. 48.11; 59.14; 65.6; 72.8; 110.6; cf. Geyer 1970.

121. Isa. 45.22; 52.10; Pss. 22.28; 67.8; 98.3.

122. In Prov. 17.24 'the end of the earth' denotes 'nations' (= idolatry), in contrast to 'wisdom' (= the Torah).

123. Cf. Pss. 72.8-11, 15-17; 111.6; Zech. 9.9-10; 1 Kgs 8.41-43; Mic. 7.11f.; see Habel 1995: 17–32; see § 2.3.2 below.

124. Gen. 41.54; 2 Kgs 19.11; Isa. 37.11, 18; Jer. 40.11; Ezek. 20.6, 15; 22.4; 36.24; 1 Chron. 14.17; 22.5; 2 Chron. 9.28.

125. Ezek. 20.32; 1 Chron. 29.30; 2 Chron. 12.8; 15.5; 20.29; 32.13.

126. 2 Kgs 18.35; Isa. 36.20; cf. Zeph. 2.11.

127. 2 Chron. 32.13, 17.

128. Cf. n. 79 above.

129. Exceptions: Gen. 41.54; Ps. 116.9.

former, it does not tell of the whole human world as a main theme in its own right, but special concern for the fate of Israel in it is maintained, since the Creator is the God of Israel.[130] The uniqueness of Israel is not only related to the people, but also to the Land, as shown by Naaman's saying (2 Kgs 5.15). Now let us turn to another usage of our term, a usage in which it refers to a land territorially defined.

2.3. ʾereṣ *as Land*

2.3.1. ʾereṣ *as a Land*

ʾereṣ can denote a circumscribed territory, 'land', which can be defined in various manners. First, it can be defined by a name of region in construct form. The most frequent use of this is ארץ מצרים 'the land of Egypt'.[131] Egypt is also called ארץ חם (Pss. 105.23, 27; 106.22), since Egypt is a son of Ham (Gen. 10.6). Correspondingly, a toponym has its eponym in many instances: ארץ כנען[132] etc.[133] Some smaller regions have an eponym, as well.[134] Accordingly, the lands distributed to Israel can be called by the tribal names.[135] There appears the plural form כל ארצות ישראל in 1 Chron. 13.2,[136] though singular ארץ ישראל is more common to express 'the Land of Israel'.[137] The two kingdoms of Israel can be denoted by ארץ יהודה[138] and ארץ ישראל.[139] For the latter phrase, we can discern it from the whole Land of Israel according to the context alone.

The fact that many toponyms in the Bible have their own eponym reveals an ideology that a land was assigned to an ancestor, and his descendants have inherited it from generation to generation.[140] Thereupon a land can be designated after the name of people living in it: 'the land of Canaanites'[141] etc.[142] The Land can be called

130. See von Rad 1936: 142.

131. It appears 219 times in the whole Bible, see Even-Shoshan (ed.) 1990: 700–3.

132. Canaan is a son of Ham (Gen. 9.18; 10.6). In Ezek. 16.29; 17.4 *ʾereṣ kenaʿan* designates 'a land of merchants', see BDB, 488.

133. E.g., Assyria (Asshur): Isa. 7.18; 27.13; Hos. 11.11; Mic. 5.5; cf. Gen. 10.8-12, 22; Moab: Deut. 1.5; 28.69; 32.49; 34.5, 6; Judg. 11.15, 18; Jer. 48.24, 33; cf. Gen. 19.37.

134. Zuph: 1 Sam. 9.5; cf. 1 Sam. 1.1; Shual: 1 Sam. 13.17; cf. 1 Chron. 7.36 (see Edelman 1988); Hepher: 1 Kgs 4.10; cf. Num. 26.32, 33; 27.1-11.

135. Naphtali: 1 Kgs 15.20; 2 Kgs 15.29; Isa. 8.23; Zebulun: Judg. 12.12; Isa. 8.23; Ephraim: Judg. 12.15; Ephraim and Manasseh: Deut. 34.2; Gad: 1 Sam. 13.7; Benjamin: Judg. 21.21; 1 Sam. 9.16; 2 Sam. 21.14; Jer. 1.1; 17.26; 32.8, 44; 33.13; 37.12; cf. 1 Sam. 9.4; Judah: 1 Sam. 22.5; 30.16; Ruth 1.7; 1 Chron. 6.40; 2 Chron. 9.11.

136. Compare 2 Chron. 11.23; 34.33 with 2 Chron. 15.8.

137. 1 Sam. 13.19; Ezek. 40.2; 47.18; 1 Chron. 22.2; 2 Chron. 2.16; 34.7.

138. Deut. 34.2; 2 Kgs 23.24; 25.22; Isa. 26.1; Jer. 31.23; 37.1; 39.10; 40.12; 43.4, 5; 44.9, 14, 28; Amos. 7.12; Zech. 2.4; 2 Chron. 17.2; Neh. 5.14.

139. 2 Kgs 5.2, 4; 6.23; Ezek. 27.17; 2 Chron. 30.25.

140. Cf. Gen. 10.25//1 Chron. 1.19; Deut. 32.8.

141. Exod. 13.11; Deut. 1.7; 11.30; Josh. 13.4; Ezek. 16.3; cf. Gen. 50.11; Neh. 9.24.

142. *Passim*; e.g., peoples of the Land: Exod. 3.17; 13.5; Neh. 9.8 (cf. Exod. 3.8); Amorites: Num. 21.31; Amos. 2.10; Josh. 24.8; Judg. 10.8; 11.21.

'the land of Hebrews' (Gen. 40.15) and 'the land of the sons of Israel' (Josh. 11.22). A land represented by the people living in it is understood in the ethnico-political perspectives. A land, therefore, can be called by the name of the king governing it: e.g., 'the land of (King) Sihon' (Deut. 4.46).[143] From an administrative view, a land can be denoted by the name of a city: e.g., 'the land of Rameses' (Gen. 47.11).[144]

ʾ*ereṣ* can be used also with the name of a mountain: 'the land of Moriah' (Gen. 22.2); 'the land of Ararat' (2 Kgs 19.37//Isa. 37.38). Once it is used with the name of the River Jordan (Ps. 42.7).

ʾ*ereṣ* can be defined also by terms which indicate direction such as 'a north land',[145] etc.[146] The expression ארץ (ה)נגב 'a (the) south land' becomes a name specifically for the region south of Judah, Negev.[147] Similarly, ארץ פתרום 'a southern land' always appears in relation to Egypt, hence refers to south or Upper Egypt.[148]

Besides, a land can be defined by its geographical features: e.g., 'the land of basin' (Gen. 19.28), 'the garden land' (Jer. 2.7), and 'a desert land' (Prov. 21.19).[149] A desert land can be expressed by various phrases: e.g., 'a terrible land' (Isa. 21.1), 'a land of drought' (Isa. 41.18; Ps. 107.35), etc.[150] The desert where Israelites wandered 40 years can be expressed differently: 'a desert land' (Deut. 32.10), 'a land of drought' (Hos. 13.5) and 'a land not sown' (Jer. 2.2).[151] Images of desert can be employed in various metaphors: 'a land of drought' for an unfavourable man (Isa. 53.2), 'a weary land' for a kingdom (Isa. 32.2) and for a soul (Ps. 143.6), and so forth.[152] In Jer. 51.43 the fate of Babylon is proclaimed in images of desert. Similar images can be applied to Israel and Jerusalem, too (Jer. 6.8; Hos. 2.5).

A geographical feature sometimes becomes the name of a land: 'Havilah, the sand land' (Gen. 2.11), 'Galilee, the land of circle' (1 Kgs 9.11), 'Seir, a hairy = well-wooded land' (Gen. 32.4; 36.30), 'Bashan, the fertile land' (1 Chron. 5.11, cf. Josh. 13.11), and 'Mizpah, the land of outlook' (Josh. 11.3). An Israelite station 'Jotbatha', literally 'pleasantness', is said to be 'a land with flowing streams' (Deut. 10.7).

Some lands are given their name in a narrative, in which its origins are explained: 'Babel' (Gen. 11.9),[153] and 'Gilead' (Gen. 31.47f.).[154] We can find wordplays in

143. See Deut. 4.47; 1 Kgs 4.19; Neh. 9.22.

144. Mizpah: Josh. 11.3; Hamath: 2 Kgs 23.33; 25.21; Jer. 39.5; 52.9, 27; Tob: Judg. 11.3, 5; cf. 2 Sam. 10.6, 8; Tappuah: Josh. 17.8.

145. Jer. 3.18; 6.22; 10.22; 16.15; 31.8; 46.10; 50.9; Zech. 2.10; 6.6, 8.

146. Gen. 25.6 (cf. Gen. 29.1); Jer. 23.8; Zech. 6.6; 8.7.

147. Gen. 20.1; 24.62; Num. 13.29; Josh. 15.19; Judg. 1.15; cf. Dan. 11.5, 6, 9, 11, 14, 25, 40.

148. Jer. 44.1; Ezek. 29.14; see BDB, 837.

149. See further Deut. 4.43; Jer. 48.21; Ps. 143.10; Josh. 17.16.

150. Lev. 16.22; Joel 2.20; Prov. 30.16; Job 38.26. See also Isa. 22.18; 30.6; cf. Gen. 34.21; Judg. 18.10; 1 Chron. 4.40.

151. See Jer. 2.6.

152. Ps. 63.2; Jer. 2.31; 17.6 (cf. Ps. 107.34); Ezek. 19.13.

153. Cf. Jer. 50.28; 51.29b.

154. Cf. Num. 32.1, 29; Josh. 17.5, 6; 22.9b, 13, 15, 32a; Judg. 10.4; 20.1; 1 Sam. 13.7; 2 Sam. 17.26; 1 Kgs 4.19; 2 Kgs 10.33; 1 Chron. 2.22; 5.9; Zech. 10.10.

the following instances: ‘Nod, a land of wandering’ (Gen. 4.16); ‘Cabul, a land as good as nothing’ (1 Kgs 9.10-13); and ‘Merathaim, a land of double rebellion’ (Jer. 50.21).

A land can be defined by a phrase that places it in connection with a person or a group: ‘an inhabited land’;[155] ‘the land of (one’s) nativity’;[156] ‘the land of (one’s) fathers’;[157] ‘the land of (one’s) origin’;[158] ‘a foreign land’;[159] ‘a distant land’;[160] ‘a land of distance’;[161] ‘the land of (one’s) sojourning’.[162] From Israelites’ point of view the land of their enemies and the land of exile are articulated by distinct expressions: ‘a/the land(s) of (your) enemy/enemies’;[163] ‘a land not theirs/yours’;[164] ‘another land’;[165] ‘a distant land’;[166] ‘(the) land of (one’s) captivity’;[167] etc.[168] In the book of Jeremiah, in particular, the land of exile is verbalized with ‘not knowing’.[169] In Isa. 26.10 the Land is called ‘a land of rectitude’, in which the wicked (i.e., Gentiles) act wrongfully.

A land is defined by pronominal suffixes. The referent must be determined according to the context.[170] The same can be said of the use of *ʾereṣ* with an article *he*.[171] Occasionally *hāʾāreṣ* is defined by additional determinatives: הארץ ההיא/ההִוא;[172] הארץ הזאת.[173] It can be also defined by a clause led by a relative pronoun אשר.[174] Above all, the Land-promise is expressed by various relative clauses (see the following section). The phrase על פני כל הארץ, which usually designates the whole earthly-world, as noted above,[175] refers to a specific region in three instances.[176] A similar expression עין (כל) הארץ always designates

155. Exod. 16.35; Josh. 5.11.
156. Gen. 11.28; 24.7; 31.13; Jer. 22.10; 46.16; Ezek. 23.15; Ruth 2.11.
157. Gen. 31.3; 48.21.
158. Ezek. 21.35; 29.14.
159. Exod. 2.22; 18.3.
160. Josh. 9.6, 9; 2 Kgs 20.14; 1 Kgs 8.41//2 Chron. 6.32.
161. Isa. 13.5a; 46.11; Jer. 6.20; Prov. 25.25; cf. Isa. 33.17; Jer. 8.19.
162. Gen. 17.8; 28.4; 36.7; 37.1; Exod. 6.4; Ezek. 20.38.
163. Lev. 26.34, 36, 38, 39, 41, 44; 1 Kgs 8.46, 48; Jer. 31.16.
164. Gen. 15.13; Jer. 5.19.
165. Deut. 29.27; Jer. 22.26.
166. Deut. 29.21; Isa. 39.3; 2 Chron. 6.36.
167. Jer. 30.10; 46.27; 1 Kgs 8.47b; 2 Chron. 6.37b, 38; cf. Neh. 3.36.
168. See Gen. 41.52; 1 Kgs 8.47a; 2 Chron. 6.37a; Jer. 4.16; 50.38.
169. Jer. 14.18; 15.14; 16.13; 17.4; 22.28; cf. Num. 14.31; Ezek. 32.9.
170. *Passim*; e.g., Egypt: Exod. 6.1, 11; 7.2; 11.10; Deut. 11.3; 23.8; 29.1; 34.11; 2 Kgs 24.7; Jer. 37.7; Ezek. 32.8; Pss. 105.30, 32, 35, 36; Neh. 9.10. For the Land, see nn. 202, 241 below.
171. *Passim*; e.g., Egypt: Gen. 45.7; Exod. 1.7, 10; 8.10, 20, 21; 9.5; 10.5, 12, 13, 15ab; 12.33; Ezek. 30.11, 12; 31.12.
172. Gen. 2.12; 10.11; 26.12; 35.22; Exod. 3.8; Judg. 11.21; Ezek. 14.17, 19.
173. Gen. 31.13; 50.24; Deut. 4.22; Josh. 17.12; Judg. 1.27; Jer. 16.6; for the Land, see n. 284 below.
174. E.g., Gen. 21.23; 24.5; Deut. 3.8; 9.28; 1 Sam. 27.8.
175. See n. 113 above.
176. 1 Sam. 30.16 (near Besor River); 2 Sam. 18.8 (forest of Ephraim); Zech. 5.3 (the Land); cf. Ezek. 39.14.

a given land.[177] Although ʾ*ereṣ* without any definitive article generally means an indefinite land or a country,[178] it can refer to a specific land.[179]

There are idiomatic uses of our term: כברת הארץ 'length of way'.[180] Another idiom used more frequently is עם הארץ 'the people of the land'. It is irrelevant here to discuss its historical nature, which is debatable among Old Testament scholars.[181] It is enough for us to point out the fact that the idiom can be understood in its literal sense, and the context gives us its referent. In Patriarchal narratives it refers to aborigines of the land of Canaan (Gen. 23.7, 12, 13; Num. 14.9). This use is comparable with the phrase 'the daughters of the land (of Canaan)' (Gen. 27.46; 34.1). Twice the idiom signifies the people of Egypt (Gen. 42.6; Exod. 5.5). Once it signifies 'the people of the world' (Job 12.24).[182] In all other occurrences it refers to 'the people of the Land' i.e., 'Israelites'.[183] The plural עמי הארץ, however, usually means 'the peoples of the world' as we saw above.[184]

In addition to the uses we saw in the previous section, the plural ʾ*arāṣôt* signifies certain lands.[185] This usage is concentrated in the books of Ezekiel, Jeremiah and Chronicles. It is noteworthy that Ezekiel prefers employing it with verbs rooted from פוץ[186] and זרה,[187] and Jeremiah with a verb הדיח,[188] verbs which express the Exile. In addition, it should be noted that the phrase עמי הארצות in the books of Ezra and Nehemiah designates 'the peoples of the lands (within the Land)'.[189] This use is different from that of 2 Chronicles, in which it means 'the peoples of the lands (on the earth)' and can be equated with ʿ*ammê hāʾāreṣ* 'the peoples of the world'.[190]

In addition, ʾ*ereṣ* can mean an estate or a farmstead possessed by individuals (Gen. 23.15; 1 Kgs 11.18). In a few occurrences the land property of individual

177. Exod. 10.5, 15 (Egypt); Num. 22.5, 11 (Moab).

178. Gen. 36.6; 2 Kgs 18.32; Isa. 36.17; 66.8; Ezek. 21.24; 22.24; 38.8; Prov. 28.2; 29.4; 30.14; Eccl. 5.8; 10.16, 17. In parables of Ezek. 14.12-20 and 33.1-6 '*a* land' alludes to Jerusalem and Israel, respectively.

179. Jer. 46.8 (Egypt); 47.2 (the land of Philistines); Ezek. 25.9 (Moab); 30.12; 32.15 (Egypt); Job 24.4 (Uz); Jer. 8.16b; Ps. 35.20; and *passim* (the Land).

180. Gen. 35.16; 48.7; 2 Kgs 5.19.

181. See Healey 1992.

182. For Isa. 24.4, see *BHS* (cf. Isa. 24.21).

183. Lev. 4.27; 20.2, 4; 2 Kgs 11.14, 18, 19, 20; 15.5; 16.15; 21.24; 23.30, 35; 24.14; 25.3, 19; Jer. 1.18; 34.19; 37.2; 44.21; 52.6, 25; Ezek. 7.27; 12.19; 22.29; 39.13; 45.16, 22; 46.9; Hag. 2.4; Zech. 7.5; 2 Chron. 23.13, 20, 21; 26.21; Dan. 9.6. Here I do not differentiate its exact referent in each biblical author's mind; e.g., Haggai refers specifically to 'the people of the land of Judah'.

184. See n. 100 above.

185. Jer. 27.6; 28.8; Ezek. 5.5, 6; 25.7; 29.12; 30.7; 32.9; 35.10; 39.27; Ezra 9.7; 2 Chron. 17.10; Dan. 11.40, 42; with pronominal suffix: Gen. 10.5, 20, 31.

186. Ezek. 11.16, 17; 20.34, 41.

187. Ezek. 6.8; 12.15; 20.23; 22.15; 29.12; 30.23, 26; 36.19; cf. Ps. 106.27.

188. Jer. 16.15; 23.3, 8; 32.37; cf. Dan. 9.7.

189. Ezra 3.3; 9.1, 2, 11; Neh. 9.30; 10.29; in Ezra 4.4 ʿ*am hāʾāreṣ* signifies 'foreigners' in contrast to 'the people of Judah'; see Japhet 1983: 116.

190. 2 Chron. 13.9; 32.13; see Japhet 1983: 112–18; Gunneweg 1983.

Israelites in the Land can be expressed simply by *hāʾāreṣ* or *ʾereṣ* with pronominal suffix (Exod. 23.10; Lev. 25.24b; Num. 35.32), while usually it is expressed by the phrase ארץ האחזה, 'the land of possession' (Lev. 14.34; 25.24; Num. 35.28; Josh. 22.4, 9, 19).[191] In Lev. 27.24 there appears a phrase אחזת הארץ, 'the possession of the land (property)', which in the year of jubilee shall return to the one from whom it was bought.

In Ezek. 48.8-14 an offering of the land for the priests is mentioned as תרומת הארץ 'the offering of the Land' (v. 12) and ראשית הארץ 'the first of the Land' (v. 14), which is holy to the Lord.

2.3.2. ʾereṣ *as the Land*

Among others, uses of *ʾereṣ* referring to the Land bear special theological significance in the Bible. The Land-promise, of which the term 'promise' is manifested in Heb. 11.9,[192] is stated with various terms in the Hebrew Bible. The concept of promise can be expressed by the verb נשבע 'to swear'.[193] Likewise, verbs דבר 'to speak' and אמר 'to say' can denote the promise.[194] To swear can be expressed by the phrase נשא את יד 'to lift (one's) hand'.[195]

Contents of the Land-promise are first of all stated with the verb נתן 'to give'.[196] The Land God gives is diversely defined. In addition to meaning 'swear' as we've just seen, it can be defined by such verbs as שכב 'to lie' (Gen. 28.13) and ראה 'to see' (Gen. 13.15). The latter is frequently employed in relation to the promise[197] and bears significance, since the Land is the one that God 'shows' (hi.: הראה).[198] Furthermore, verbs התהלך 'to walk through, traverse'[199] and דרך 'to tread'[200] are used, as well. The hiphil form of the former verb lays emphasis on God's act.[201]

191. Cf. Gen. 36.43 (of Edomites).

192. Cf. Heb. 11.8-16; see also *Jub.* 19.9.

193. Gen. 24.7; 50.24; Exod. 13.5, 11; 32.13; 33.1; Num. 14.16; Deut. 1.8, 35; 6.10, 18, 23; 8.1; 10.11; 26.3; 31.7, 21, 23; 34.4; Josh. 1.6; 5.6; 21.43; Judg. 2.1; Jer. 32.22; different uses: Deut. 4.21; 11.9; 19.8; cf. שבועה: Gen. 26.3; Jer. 11.5.

194. Gen. 12.7; 15.18; 24.7; Exod. 12.25; 32.13; 33.1; Lev. 20.24; Deut. 6.3; 9.28; 19.8; 27.3; Josh. 11.23; 23.5; Neh. 9.15, 23; noun: Deut. 9.5.

195. Exod. 6.8; Num. 14.30; Ezek. 20.6, 15, 28, 42; 47.14; Neh. 9.15.

196. Gen. 35.12; Exod. 6.8; 12.25; 32.13; 33.1; Lev. 23.10; 25.2; Num. 15.2; 20.12, 24; 27.12; 32.7, 9; Deut. 1.8, 25, 35; 2.12, 29; 3.20; 4.1; 5.31; 6.10, 23; 8.10; 9.23; 10.11; 11.17, 31; 12.1; 15.7; 16.20; 17.14; 18.9; 19.2, 8, 14; 26.2, 3; 27.2; 28.8, 52; 31.7; 32.52; 34.4; Josh. 1.2, 6, 11, 15; 5.6; 18.3; 23.16; 1 Kgs 8.48//2 Chron. 6.38; Jer. 7.7; 30.3; Ezek. 20.28, 42; 36.28; 37.25; Job 15.19; Neh. 9.35, 36; see Orlinsky 1986: 31f.; cf. Appendix 1 below.

197. Num. 13.18; 14.23; 32.8, 9; Deut. 3.25, 28; 32.49, 52; Josh. 2.1; cf. Jer. 22.12; Ezek. 12.6, 12; cf. also Isa. 5.30; 8.22.

198. Gen. 12.1; Deut. 34.1, 4; Josh. 5.6; cf. Isa. 33.17.

199. Gen. 13.17; Josh. 18.4, 8.

200. Deut. 1.36; 11.24, 25; Josh. 14.9.

201. Josh. 24.3; Amos 2.10. For qal form, see Gen. 24.5; Josh. 2.1; 18.9; cf. also 2 Sam. 24.8.

The Land is also defined as: 'a land on which you had not labored' (Josh. 24.13). The same notion can be expressed by the pronominal suffix of the third person plural: '*their* (nations') land'.[202] In the settlement narrative, therefore, the phrase ישבי הארץ 'the inhabitants of the land' refers to non-Israelites, whereas in the Prophets it signifies Israelites.[203]

The Land-promise is related also to the verb נחל 'to possess (a land) as one's allotment or entitlement'. This term can be applied to the hereditary lands allotted to families and tribes in the Land.[204] This usage is close to that of חלק 'to apportion (a land)'.[205] On the other hand, *nāḥal* can be employed in connection to the Land as a whole.[206] The possession of the Land as Israel's allotment is stated as God's act by hiphil הנחיל.[207] The same can be expressed by the phrase נתן (לך) נחלה.[208] In Deut. 32.8-9 it is stated that Israel is the Lord's allotment (נחלתו).[209] In this respect it should be noted that mention is made of נחלת יהוה referring to the Land.[210] The same idea can be expressed by ארץ יהוה. This phrase is used overall in the circumstance of the Exile.[211] Since God is the ultimate owner of the Land, the status of Israel in it is defined as 'aliens and tenants' with God (Lev. 25.23; cf. Pss. 101.6-8; 119.19).[212] The ideology that the Land is God's includes an idea that God is dwelling in it.[213] The Land, therefore, is also called ארץ אחזת יהוה (Josh. 22.19). The term אחזה 'possession', which designates the land-possession of families in

202. Deut. 4.38; 9.5; 12.29; 19.1; Josh. 12.1; 23.5; 24.8, 15; Judg. 6.9, 10; Pss. 105.44; 135.12; 136.21. In Deuteronomy, however, there is an expression '*your* land that the Lord of your God gave you' (Deut. 15.7; 19.2, 3, 10; 26.2; 28.52; cf. n. 241 below).

203. Exod. 23.31; 34.12, 15; Num. 13.28; 14.14; 33.52; Josh. 2.9, 24; 7.9; 9.24; 24.18; Judg. 1.32, 33; 2.2; 1 Chron. 22.18; Neh. 9.24; cf. Lev. 18.27; Ezra 6.21; Josh. 12.1, 7; Deut. 31.16 (cf. Jer. 5.19); for non-Israelite inhabitants after the Settlement, cf. 1 Kgs 9.21//2 Chron. 8.8; 1 Chron. 22.2; 2 Chron. 2.16; for the uses in the Prophets, see n. 243 below.

204. Num. 18.20; 33.54; 34.13, 17, 18, 29; Deut. 3.28; 19.14; 31.7; Josh. 1.6; 19.49a; Ezek. 47.13; for the same uses of the noun *naḥalâ*, see Num. 16.14; 36.2; Josh. 11.23; 14.9 (cf. Deut. 1.36); 19.49b; Isa. 49.8; Ezek. 45.1; 47.14; 48.29; cf. von Rad 1943: 192f.; Habel 1995: 33–5.

205. Num. 26.53, 55; Josh. 13.7; 14.5; 18.10; 19.51; Ezek. 47.21; noun: Num. 18.20; Deut. 10.9; 12.12; 14.27; 18.1; Josh. 14.4; 15.13; 18.5, 6, 7, 9; 19.9.

206. Exod. 23.30; 32.13; Isa. 57.13; 1 Chron. 28.8.

207. Deut. 12.10; 19.3; Jer. 3.18.

208. Deut. 4.21, 38; 15.4; 19.10; 24.4; 25.19; 26.1; 1 Kgs 8.36; Jer. 3.19; Pss. 105.11; 135.12; 136.21-22; 1 Chron. 16.18; 2 Chron. 6.27; cf. Pss. 47.5; 78.55; Num. 34.2. For *naḥalâ* as Israel's allotment, see Judg. 20.6; Isa. 54.17; 58.14; Jer. 17.4; Lam. 5.2; Ezek. 35.15.

209. For Deut 32.8, cf. Ps. 111.6; Jer. 3.19. For textual problems of v. 9, see Tov 1997: 135.

210. 1 Sam. 26.19; 2 Sam. 14.16; 20.19; 21.3; Jer. 2.7; 12.7, 8, 9; 16.18; Pss. 68.10; 79.1; reference to the people: Deut. 9.26, 29; 1 Sam. 10.1; 1 Kgs 8.51; Isa. 63.17; Jer. 10.16; 51.19; Joel 4.2; Mic. 7.18; Pss. 74.2; 78.71; 94.5, 14; 106.5, 40; 127.3; to both the Land and the people: Isa. 19.25; 47.6; Jer. 50.11; Joel 2.17; Mic. 7.14; Ps. 28.9.

211. Isa. 14.25; Jer. 2.7; 16.18; Ezek. 36.5; (LXX 37.22); 38.16; Hos. 9.3; Joel 1.6; 2.18; 4.2; Pss. 10.16; 85.2; for the Land-promise, cf. 2 Sam. 7.23; 1 Kgs 8.36//2 Chron. 6.27; see אלהי הארץ 'the God of the Land' in 2 Kgs 17.26, 27.

212. In the phrase ליהוה הארץ elsewhere in the Bible *ʾereṣ* means 'the world'; cf. nn. 55, 86–92 above; for the notion that the Land is God's, see von Rad 1943: 196–204; W. D. Davies 1974: 24–35; Habel 1995.

213. Lev. 26.11; Num. 35.34; Jer. 14.8; Ezek. 37.27; cf. Exod. 15.13; Ps. 83.13.

many occurrences,[214] can be applied also to the possession of the Land as a whole in the context of promise.[215] Once the possession is expressed by the preposition ל (Num. 34.12).[216]

Before entering the Land, Moses sent men to search it out. To 'search' can be expressed by some verbs. The most frequent use is תור, in particular, in Numbers.[217] Others are חפר,[218] רגל,[219] and חקר.[220] In Ezek. 20.6, it is stated, God searched out the Land for the people. The searchers, except for Joshua and Caleb, however, 'brought a bad report about the Land' (Num. 13.32; 14.36f.).

The fulfilment of promise begins with בא אל הארץ 'coming into the Land'. This phrase is used mainly in an introductory statement to ordinances which must be observed in the Land: 'when you come into the Land'.[221] Another characteristic use of the verb בוא, especially in Deuteronomy, is an association with the verb ירש 'to take possession of': בא וירש and בא לרשת.[222] According to Deut. 26.3 the people shall say that 'I have come into the Land'. Thus 'coming into the Land' is a step of the fulfilment of promise.[223] It is understood as God's act, expressed by hiphil הביא.[224] Closer uses can be found in those of עלה 'to go up'[225] and its hiphil העלה.[226]

When they came into the Land, the Israelites must have dispossessed its original inhabitants. There are many occurrences of the phrase ירש את הארץ 'take possession of the Land' in the context of promise.[227] That this expression connotes

214. Gen. 23.4, 9, 20; 47.11; 49.30; 50.13; Lev. 25.10, 13, 25, 27, 28, 33, 41; 27.16, 21, 22, 24, 28; Num. 27.4, 7; 35.28; Josh. 21.12; Ezek. 45.8; 46.16, 18; Neh. 11.3; 1 Chron. 9.2; 2 Chron. 31.1; cf. of Levites: Lev. 25.32, 33, 34; Num. 35.2; Ezek. 44.28; 45.5; 48.22; 2 Chron. 11.14; of tribes in the Transjordan: Num. 32.5, 22, 29, 32; Josh. 22.4, 9, 19a; of Ephraim: 1 Chron. 7.28; of Edom: Gen. 36.43; of Jerusalem: Ezek. 45.6, 7; 48.20, 21, 22; of slaves: Lev. 25.45-46.

215. Gen. 17.8; 48.4; Lev. 14.34; 25.24; Deut. 32.49; see אחזת בני ישראל: Num. 35.8; Josh. 21.41. In Ps. 2.8 the promise of *naḥalâ* and *ʾaḥuzâ* of Israel extends to 'the ends of the earth'; see n. 123 above.

216. Cf. Num. 32.22; Josh. 14.9.

217. Num. 13.16, 21, 25, 32ab; 14.6, 7, 34, 36, 38; Ezek. 20.6.

218. Deut. 1.22; Josh. 2.2, 3.

219. Josh. 6.22; 7.2; 14.7; Judg. 18.2.

220. Judg. 18.2ab.

221. Exod. 12.25; 34.12; Lev. 14.34; 19.23; 23.10; 25.2; Num. 15.2, 18; 34.2; Deut. 17.14; 18.9; 26.1; cf. Deut. 12.1; 19.1; 21.1.

222. Deut. 1.8; 4.1, 5; 6.18; 8.1; 9.5; 10.11; 11.8, 10, 31; 17.14; 23.21; 26.1; 30.16; Josh. 1.11; 18.3; Ezra 9.11; Neh. 9.15, 24.

223. Cf. Num. 13.27; 14.24, 30; 20.24; 32.9; Deut. 4.21; 32.52.

224. Exod. 6.8; 13.5, 11; Lev. 18.3; 20.22; Num. 14.3, 8, 16, 24, 31; 16.14; Deut. 4.38; 6.10; 7.1; 8.7; 9.4, 28; 11.29; 26.9; 30.5; 31.21, 23; Josh. 24.8; Judg. 2.1; Ezek. 20.15, 28, 42; Neh. 9.23; cf. Num. 20.12; Deut. 31.7; Jer. 25.9, 13; Ezek. 40.2.

225. Exod. 33.1; Num. 13.21; Deut. 1.21; 9.23; Josh. 7.2; Judg. 1.2; cf. Isa. 36.10.

226. Gen. 50.24; Exod. 3.17; cf. Num. 16.13 on Moses; cf. also Exod. 33.3.

227. Gen. 15.7; 28.4; Lev. 20.24; Num. 33.53; Deut. 1.8, 21; 3.20; 4.1, 5, 14, 22, 26; 5.31, 33; 6.1, 18; 7.1; 8.1; 9.4, 5, 6, 23; 10.11; 11.8, 10, 11, 29, 31; 12.1; 15.4; 16.20; 17.14; 19.2, 14; 23.21; 25.19; 26.1; 30.5, 16; Josh. 1.11, 15; 12.1; 13.1; 18.3; 21.43; 24.8; Judg. 2.6; 11.21; Isa. 60.21; Ezek. 33.24, 25, 26; Amos 2.10; Pss. 25.13; 37.9, 11, 22, 29, 34; 44.4; 1 Chron. 28.8; Ezra 9.11; Neh. 9.15, 22, 23, 24; cf. Isa. 57.13; 61.7; cf. מורש: Exod. 6.8; Ezek. 11.15; 33.24; 36.5; יְרֻשָּׁה: Deut. 2.12; Josh. 12.7.

'dispossessing the indigenous peoples of the land' is suggested by uses of its hiphil form taking יֹשבי הארץ as an object.[228] In some instances the dispossession is described as God's act.[229] To drive out the indigenous people can be expressed by phrases גרש מפניך and נתן בידכם, as well.[230] Taking possession of the Land, therefore, can be stated with such expressions as: לקח את הארץ[231] and נכבשה הארץ.[232]

After coming into and taking possession of the Land, they could dwell in it. To dwell in the Land, which constitutes a part of the promise, is expressed by verbs ישב and שכן.[233] The latter verb can be used for residing of God in the Land.[234] Its piel form articulates God's act for Israel (Num. 14.30; Jer. 7.7). In the Land they can live בטח 'securely'.[235] Also references are made to שלום 'peace' which is given to the Land.[236] In Deuteronomy the term הניח 'to give rest to' is preferred in this context.[237] In the books of Joshua and Judges there appears another term שקט 'be quiet'.[238] In 2 Samuel it is twice stated that ויעתר אלהים/יהוה לארץ 'and God/the Lord granted entreaty for the Land' (21.14; 24.25). It is expected to live securely, in peace, and in quiet in the Land. There God will make Israel prosperous, and they will multiply and increase.[239] In the Land God will bless Israel.[240]

The Land is no more '*their* (nations') land', but becomes '*our* land' and '*your* land'.[241] An Israelite living in the Land can be called אזרח הארץ 'a native of the Land' in contrast to גר 'an alien'.[242] Correspondingly, the phrase ישבי הארץ is to refer to Israelites.[243]

228. Num. 33.52, 55; Judg. 1.32, 33; cf. Deut. 19.1; Ps. 105.44; see also Num. 14.24; Ezra 9.12 (cf. Num. 33.53); cf. n. 203 above and n. 243 below. Cf. also Mesha inscription, lines 7f. (see § 3.3 below).

229. Exod. 23.29, 31; Josh. 24.8; cf. 1 Chron. 22.18.

230. Deut. 4.38; 9.5; Josh. 23.5; 2 Chron. 20.7.

231. Josh. 11.16, 23.

232. Num. 32.22, 29; Josh. 18.1; 1 Chron. 22.18.

233. ישב: Lev. 20.22; 25.18; 26.5; Num. 33.53, 55; 35.34; Deut. 11.31; 12.10, 29; 17.14; (19.1); 26.1; Josh. 1.14; 21.43; 24.15; Judg. 6.10; Ezek. 36.28; 37.25; Ps. 140.12-14; cf. Exod. 23.33; Jer. 40.9; 42.10, 13; שכן: Gen. 26.2; Deut. 33.28; Ps. 37.3; Prov. 2.21f.; 10.30; cf. שכב: Gen. 28.13; Lev. 26.6.

234. See n. 213 above.

235. Lev. 25.18; 26.5; Deut. 12.10; 33.28; Jer. 12.5; Ezek. 34.27.

236. Lev. 26.6; Ezek. 34.25; Jer. 12.5.

237. Deut. 3.20 (//Josh. 1.15); 12.10; 25.19; cf. Josh. 1.13; 22.4; cf. הרגיע 'to rest' in Jer. 50.34.

238. Josh. 11.23; 14.15; Judg. 3.11, 30; 5.31; 8.28.

239. Jer. 3.16; cf. Deut. 30.5; 6.3; Gen. 26.22-24; Ps. 41.3; see also von Rad 1943: 191.

240. Deut. 15.4; 28.8; 30.16; cf. Isa. 65.16; for the blessing of peoples, see Gen. 12.3; 18.18; 22.18; 26.4; 28.14; cf. Isa. 19.24.

241. Exod. 23.26, 33; 34.24; Lev. 19.9, 33; 22.24; 23.22; 25.7, 9, 45; 26.1, 5; Deut. 15.11; 24.14; 28.12, 24; Ps. 85.10; Isa. 8.8; 60.18; 62.4; Jer. 4.7; 5.19; Mic. 5.4, 5; cf. n. 202 above.

242. Exod. 12.19, 48; Num. 9.14.

243. Jer. 1.14; 6.12; 10.18; 13.13; 24.8; 25.9, 29; Ezek. 7.7; 12.19; Joel 1.2, 14; 2.1; cf. Jer. 26.17 (cf. Prov. 31.23); 40.6, 7; 52.16; Ezek. 17.13; 20.40; 39.14; Lam. 3.34; Ps. 10.18; 1 Sam. 21.12; 2 Sam. 15.4; Isa. 16.1; cf. n. 203 above.

The blessed life in the Land is fulfilment of the promise. The promise is God's gift for Israel, but in return they must keep God's commandments.[244] The commandments can be summarized as: 'you shall not defile the Land' (Num. 35.34; cf. Deut. 21.23; Josh. 22.19). Proscription against defiling the Land is indicated with various terms.[245] The Land must be kept clean, since it is ארץ יהוה.[246] If the Land is defiled, the Land vomits out its inhabitants (Lev. 18.25-28). Thus it is commanded that the people shall be holy to God (Lev. 20.22-26).[247] Since God is holy, the Land which is God's must be holy,[248] and the people living in it too must be holy by observing the commandments. Non-observance of the law causes defilement of the Land, which means blasphemy;[249] however, Israel did defile the Land.

The prophets transmit God's wrath against Israel by using the same and similar terms, such as 'to defile', 'to profane', 'to pollute', and 'abomination', 'fornication', and 'idols'.[250] Warning against customs of peoples in the Land is repeated again and again in the Bible.[251] The Land reacts to the evil deeds of its inhabitants (Isa. 33.9; Jer. 12.4; 23.10). Furthermore, it can be personified as a witness of the fate of its people (Jer. 22.29; cf. Jer. 6.19).[252]

The result of Israel's defilement of the Land was exile. God himself brought enemies of Israel to the Land to destroy and strike it.[253] The Land was covered with darkness and distress.[254] The 'blow' to the Land[255] was so hard that one is amazed at the severity 'why the Lord did thus to this Land'.[256] Then the people of Israel were brought to the land of captivity (Jer. 16.13).[257] Thus a prediction already stated in Deuteronomy came true (Deut. 4.26, which is, of course, a *vaticinium ex eventu*).[258]

244. Exod. 12.25; 13.5, 10, 11; 34.11; Lev. 14.34-57; 20.22; 22.24, 31; 23.42; 25.2, 18; 26.3-39; Num. 15.2, 18f., 33.51; 35.10; Deut. 4.5, 14, 21f., 40; 6.1-3, 23-25; 7.1f.; 12.1, 9f.; 19.1, 14; 21.1; 26.1. Cf. Deut. 4.1; 6.17-19; 7.12f.; 8.1; 10.13; 11.1, 8 (cf. Ezra 9.12); 16.20; 19.8f.; 30.16, 20; 32.46f.; see von Rad 1943: 201f.; Diepold 1972: 90–6.

245. Lev. 19.29; Num. 35.33; Deut. 24.4; cf. Exod. 23.33.

246. See n. 211 above.

247. Exod. 19.6; Lev. 19.2; Deut. 7.6; 14.2, 21; 26.19; 28.9; Isa. 62.12; 63.18; Dan. 7.27; 8.24; 12.7.

248. Cf. Wilken 1992: 1–19.

249. See W. D. Davies 1974: 24–35, esp. pp. 30–5.

250. Jer. 2.7; 3.1, 2, 9; 9.2; 16.18; 23.10, 15; Ezek. 7.23; 8.17; 9.9; 12.19; 22.24; 23.48; 33.26; 36.17, 18; Zech. 3.9; Isa. 2.7, 8; Ps. 106.38; Ezra 6.21; 9.11; 2 Chron. 34.33.

251. E.g., Exod. 23.33; 34.12, 15; Lev. 18.24-30; Num. 33.52; Deut. 4.25; 7.1-5; 18.9-14; 31.16; Judg. 2.1-3; Jer. 5.19.

252. *ʾereṣ* can also represent the whole population of the Land, see Judg. 18.30; 1 Sam. 14.25, 29; 2 Sam. 15.23; Zech. 12.12.

253. Isa. 28.22; 36.10; Jer. 1.14-18; 8.16; 16.6; 25.9, 13, 29; 26.20; 32.17-35; 35.11; 36.29; 37.19; 1 Kgs 8.37//2 Chron. 6.28; Ps. 60.4.

254. Isa. 5.30; 8.22; cf. Ps. 74.20.

255. Deut. 29.21; cf. Mal. 3.24; Deut. 29.26.

256. Deut. 29.23; 1 Kgs 9.8; 2 Chron. 7.21; cf. Ezek. 36.20.

257. For various expressions of the land of exile, see nn. 163–9 above.

258. Cf. Deut. 11.17; Josh. 23.16; cf. also Jer. 9.11.

In the exile, however, God had 'compassion' on Israel[259] and decided to bring them back to the Land.[260] God promised to restore the fortunes of the Land (Jer. 33.11), since He remembered the Land (Lev. 26.42), and He was pleased with His Land (Ps. 85.2; cf. Isa. 62.4). In 2 Chronicles it is formulated that if 'they return to the Lord', Israel can 'return to the Land' (30.9),[261] and the Lord 'heals their Land' (7.14; cf. Ps. 60.4).

In the Land restored there shall no more be oppressors, destroyers, or marauders.[262] Rather 'God will create a new thing in the Land' (Jer. 31.22f.); a Davidic ruler shall be established who seeks justice and is swift to do righteousness.[263] According to Ezekiel's vision the Land is cleansed (39.12, 14, 16),[264] and shines with God's glory (43.2). In his plan the Land will be redistributed among the twelve tribes, and the portion of the priests will be 'the first of the Land' (Ezek. 48.14). Third Isaiah states that 'one who blesses himself in the Land shall bless himself by the God of truth, and one who swears in the Land shall swear by the God of truth' (Isa. 65.16).

The Land is endowed with various blessings in relation to its fertility. The most frequent and famous expression is 'a land flowing with milk and honey'.[265] Others include: 'a good land',[266] 'a land of desire',[267] and so on.[268] The Land is compared to the Garden of Eden (Joel 2.3). In Deuteronomy there are more embellishments (8.7-10; 11.10-12; 33.28). God's care for the Land is manifested by the rain which God gives (Deut. 11.14).[269] Israel has its own heavens (שמיו) which supply the Land with rain (Deut. 33.28).[270] Most of these endowments are related to the high productivity of the Land. When referring to the Land as a defined territory, the term *ʾereṣ* does not lose its basic meaning as 'soil'.[271]

259. Cf. e.g., Deut. 30.3; Isa. 14.1; 30.18; 49.13; 54.8, 10; 55.7; 60.10; Jer. 12.15; 30.18; 31.20; 33.26; Ezek. 39.25; Mic. 7.19; Zech. 10.6.

260. Jer. 12.15; 24.6; 30.3; 32.15, 37-44; cf. Gen. 48.21.

261. Cf. Gen. 31.3, 13.

262. Isa. 16.4; 60.18; 62.4.

263. Isa. 9.5f.; 16.5; Jer. 23.5; 33.15; cf. Jer. 9.23; Ezek. 37.21-25; Ps. 85.12.

264. Cf. Zech. 13.1f.; 2 Chron. 34.8.

265. Exod. 3.8, 17; 13.5; 33.3; Lev. 20.24; Num. 14.8; 16.13, 14; Deut. 6.3; 11.9; 26.9, 15; 27.3; Josh. 5.6; Jer. 11.5; 32.22; Ezek. 20.6, 15.

266. Num. 13.19; 14.7; Deut. 1.25, 35; 3.25; 4.21, 22; 6.18; 8.7; 9.6; 11.17; Josh. 23.16; 1 Chron. 28.8.

267. Jer. 3.19; Zech. 7.14; Ps. 106.24.

268. See Exod. 3.8; Jer. 2.7; 3.19; 12.5; Ezek. 20.6, 15; Mal. 3.12; Dan. 11.16, 41; Ps. 107.34; Neh. 9.35 (cf. Num. 13.20).

269. Cf. Deut. 28.12, 24; 1 Kgs 8.36//2 Chron. 6.27; Ezek. 34.26; Zech. 8.12; cf. also Gen. 27.28, 39.

270. Cf. Lev. 26.19; Deut. 28.23.

271. Cf. Hos. 2.23f.; for *ʾereṣ* as soil, see § 2.1.3 above.

There are several expressions for 'the products of the Land': טוב הארץ,[272] פרי הארץ,[273] עבור הארץ,[274] יבול הארץ,[275] תבואת הארץ,[276] לחם הארץ,[277] and קציר ארצכה.[278]

In Leviticus 25 the law of the sabbatical year, the rest of the Land, is ordained (vv. 2-5; cf. Exod. 23.10f.). The rest of the Land is a rest for the Lord; this legislation implies that God is the true owner of the Land, and hence He takes special care of it for six years. In the seventh year He needs a rest; so work during this year by Israelites, God's tenants in the Land, shall not be productive. The same idea is found in the Manna story; in that narrative, the heavenly food was not found on the Sabbath (Exod. 16.1-36). The anxiety of the people about what to eat in the seventh year (Lev. 25.20) is answered threefold: if they keep God's commandments, they can live securely in the Land (v. 18); since the Land is fertile enough for them (v. 19); and in the sixth year God commands His blessing for them to yield a crop for three years (v. 21).[279]

The Land, which is a gift for Israel, is blessed with exceptional fertility, as far as they observe God's commandments. Their disobedience, however, causes 'famine'.[280] The fertile Land is to be changed to desert.[281] Rain does not fall on the Land.[282] The Land no more yields its produce.[283] A fire of God's wrath 'devours the Land and its produce' (Deut. 32.22). Thus it is stated: 'and I will make your sky like iron and your Land like copper' (Lev. 26.19; cf. Hag. 1.10).

The Land of promise can be defined by a demonstrative adjective הזאת.[284] But the territory meant by this definition is sometimes vague. It can be defined more precisely by the regional name. The most frequent use is 'the land of Canaan'.[285] It is called 'the land of sojourning' of the Patriarchs, as well.[286] Names of the inhabitants are also employed.[287] There are lists of peoples who were inhabitants of the Land.[288]

272. Isa. 1.19; cf. Ezra 9.12; Deut. 32.22.

273. Num. 13.26; Deut. 1.25; Isa. 4.2; Lev. 25.19.

274. Josh. 5.11, 12.

275. Lev. 26.4; Judg. 6.4; Ezek. 34.27; Zech. 8.12; Ps. 85.13.

276. Lev. 23.39; cf. Josh. 5.12.

277. Num. 15.19.

278. Lev. 19.9; 23.22; cf. Lev. 27.30; Num. 18.13; Ps. 72.16; Song 2.12.

279. See Habel 1995: 97–114.

280. 2 Sam. 24.13//1 Chron. 21.12; 1 Kgs 8.37//2 Chron. 6.28; cf. Jer. 14.15; Ezek. 1.11; cf. also Gen. 12.10; 26.1; Ruth 1.1.

281. Lev. 26.32, 33; Isa. 1.7; 49.19; Jer. 2.15; 4.7, 20, 27; 5.30; 7.34; 9.18; 12.11; 18.16; 25.9, 11, 38; 32.43; 44.22; Ezek. 6.14; 12.19, 20; 15.8; 19.7; 33.28, 29; 36.34, 35; Joel 2.3; Zech. 7.14; Hag. 1.11; cf. Lev. 26.34, 43; Exod. 23.29; Isa. 62.4.

282. Deut. 11.17; Jer. 14.4; Ezek. 22.24; 2 Chron. 7.13; cf. 1 Kgs 17.7.

283. Lev. 26.20; Deut. 29.22; Ps. 107.34; Isa. 7.24; 9.18; Jer. 9.11.

284. Gen. 12.7; 24.7; cf. Gen. 15.7, 18; 48.4; Exod. 32.13; Num. 14.3, 8; Deut. 4.22; 9.4, 6; 26.9; Josh. 1.13; 13.7; plural in Gen. 26.3, 4; for references to other lands, see n. 173 above.

285. Gen. 17.8; Exod. 6.4; Lev. 14.34; 25.38; Num. 13.2; Deut. 32.49; Josh. 14.1; Ps. 105.11; 1 Chron. 16.18; cf. Lev. 18.3; Num. 33.51//35.10; 34.2, 29; Josh. 24.3.

286. Gen. 17.8; 28.4; Exod. 6.4.

287. Canaanites: Exod. 13.11; Deut. 11.30; Philistines: Zeph. 2.5; cf. 1 Kgs 5.1; 2 Chron. 9.26; Amorites: Amos 2.10; cf. references to the east side of Jordan: Num. 21.31; Josh. 24.8; Judg. 10.8; 11.21.

288. Cf. Gen. 10.15-20.

The list used most frequently is 'the Canaanites, the Hittites, the Amorites, the Perizzites, the Hivites, and the Jebusites'.[289] Although the exact boundaries are unknown, these lists are related to the territory of Israel.

There are chiefly three types of territory of the Land in the Bible.[290] The first is the land of Canaan. Detailed accounts of its boundaries can be found in Num. 34.2-12 and Ezek. 47.15-20.[291] According to these passages, the northern borders are Lebo-Hamath, Zedad and Hazar-Enan; the southern are the end of the Dead Sea and the brook (or Wadi) of Egypt;[292] the western is the Great Sea or the Mediterranean; the eastern is the River Jordan. It is deliberate that the territory east of the Jordan (or that occupied by the Gadites, the Reubenites and the half-tribe of Manasseh) is not included in God's promise.[293] It is distinctly stated that the land beyond the Jordan (to the west) is the Land that *God* gave, while the land east of it is that which *Moses* gave.[294] Compared with the east, which is regarded as 'unclean', the land beyond the Jordan is called ארץ אחזת יהוה (Josh. 22.19). Thus עבר את הירדן 'to cross the Jordan' and its noun expression, עבר הירדן,[295] play a significant role in the settlement narrative.[296]

The north-south boundaries, from Lebo-Hamath to the Dead Sea (or the Sea of the Arabah), seem to have been a traditional locution of the territory of the Land,[297] though the northernmost region of the Land is counted as a part of 'the land remaining'.[298] A phrase more frequent, and somewhat historical and realistic in a sense, is 'from Dan to Beer-Sheba', which is used with a term designating the entire Israel such as *kol yiśrāēl*.[299] These references to the north-south borders represent the whole Land including the east side of the Jordan,[300] contrary to the ideology of

289. Exod. 3.8, 17; 23.23; 33.2; 34.11; Deut. 20.17; Josh. 9.1; 12.8; Judg. 3.5; other lists: Gen. 15.19-21; Exod. 13.5; 23.28; Num. 13.29; Deut. 7.1; Josh. 3.10; 11.3; 24.11; 2 Chron. 8.7; Neh. 9.8.

290. For boundaries of the Land, see Kallai (1975, 1997) with further literature.

291. Cf. Aharoni *et al.* 2002, maps 51 and 165 (pp. 47, 126).

292. For 'the brook of Egypt', cf. esp. Josh. 15.2-4, though its exact location and identification are disputed.

293. According to Ezek. 47.15-20, therefore, all the twelve tribes of Israel will have their portion in the west of Jordan.

294. Num. 32.7, 33; Deut. 3.20; Josh. 1.14, 15; 9.24; 13.8; 14.3; 22.4; Neh. 9.22-24; cf. LXX Josh. 13.7.

295. This phrase can refer both to the east and west side of the Jordan according to the context; to the east: Gen. 50.10, 11; Num. 32.19; Deut. 1.1, 5; 3.8; 4.41, 46, 47, 49; Josh. 1.14, 15; 2.10; 7.7; 9.10; 12.1; 13.8, 27; 22.4; 24.8; Judg. 5.17; 10.8; 1 Sam. 31.7; Isa. 8.23; to the west: Deut. 3.20, 25; 11.30; Josh. 5.1; 9.1; 12.7; 22.7.

296. Cf. Num. 13.32; 14.7; 32.7; Deut. 2.29; 3.25, 28; 4.14, 21, 22, 26; 6.1; 11.8, 11, 30, 31; 12.10; 27.2, 3; 34.4; Josh. 1.2, 11; 12.7.

297. See 2 Kgs 14.25; Amos 6.14; cf. 1 Kgs 8.65//2 Chron. 7.8; 1 Chron. 13.5 (compare MT and LXX on Shihor; cf. Josh. 13.3; see Bar-Deroma 1960).

298. Josh. 13.1-6; Judg. 3.1-3; cf. Aharoni *et al.* 2002, map 69 (p. 59); Smend 1983.

299. Judg. 20.1; 1 Sam. 3.20; 2 Sam. 3.10; 17.11; 24.2, 15; 1 Kgs 5.5; 1 Chron. 21.2; 2 Chron. 30.5; cf. Amos 8.14; 2 Chron. 19.4.

300. Except Judg. 20.1.

the settlement narrative.[301] This is a second type of territory of the Land, according to our argument.

A last type extends the eastern border to the River Euphrates: 'to the Sea, to the River (Euphrates)' (Ps. 80.9-12).[302] Another account extends the southern border, too: 'from the River of Egypt to the Great River, the River Euphrates' (Gen. 15.18).[303] There is another expression of the southern border, the Red Sea (Exod. 23.31). These two expressions represent the southern vis à vis Egypt. The definition of the Land of this type accords by and large with the territory over which Solomon reigned (1 Kgs 5.1; 2 Chron. 9.26). It is once called 'all the land of his dominion' (1 Kgs 9.19//2 Chron. 8.6; cf. Jer. 51.28). The term *ʾereṣ* in the phrase פחות הארץ 'the governors of the land' refers to this kingdom of Solomon (1 Kgs 10.15// 2 Chron. 9.14).

The three definitions of the territory have different borders in three directions, north-south-east. The eastern border, in particular, bears some theological significance according to the ideology of biblical narrators.[304] The other three regions – the west side of the Jordan, the Transjordan, and the region to the Euphrates – do not, however, bear the same weight. The significance is graded radiately down to the east.

The three types of territory of the Land can be designated, respectively, as (1) the Land of the Lord, (2) the Land of the twelve tribes of Israel, and (3) the Greater Israel. All of these can be 'the promised Land' or 'the Land of Israel', and be called *hāʾāreṣ* in the Bible.[305] The Land-promise in each of the three understandings is already fulfilled within the Bible; the first is partially fulfilled in the age of Joshua with exception of 'the land remaining', but completely in the days of Solomon and Jeroboam II; the second is a constant situation of Israel from the settlement to Assyrian conquest of the kingdom of Northern Israel, and the third is fulfilled under Solomon. Later Bible readers, however, continued to expect the fulfilment of promise in *their* age according to their interpretation of *hāʾāreṣ*, since its possession is promised to be 'forever'.[306]

In this respect we must remember another type of expectation for the promise, which extends the territory of the Land to 'the ends of the earth'.[307] This suggests that

301. Cf. Deut. 34.1-3; 2 Kgs 10.32f.; see Weinfeld 1983.

302. Cf. Deut. 1.7; 11.24; Josh. 1.4.

303. 'The River of Egypt', i.e., the Nile, occurs once here alone in the Bible. Its emendation to 'the brook of Egypt' is suggested by *BHS*, but see 1 Chron. 13.5 (see n. 292 above). In later Jewish tradition it is identified with the Gihon River = the Nile; see *Jub.* 14.18 with 8.15; 10.29; *Apocr. Gen.* 21.11 with 21.15; cf. Sir. 24.27; *Ant.* 1.39; LXX Jer. 2.18; see Fitzmyer 1971: 148, 152f.

304. See W. D. Davies 1974: 17 n. 3.

305. There is no clear distinction between the uses of *ʾereṣ* and *hāʾāreṣ* in the Bible, but it might not be far from the truth if we suggest a tendency that the latter is used in prose, while the former is preferred in poetic diction.

306. Gen. 13.15; 17.7, 8, 13, 19; 48.4; Exod. 32.13; Jer. 7.7; 25.5; 32.40f.; Ezek. 37.25-26; Ps. 105.8-11//1 Chron. 16.15-18; Ezra 9.12; 1 Chron. 28.8; 2 Chron. 20.7.

307. See n. 123 above.

the term *ʾereṣ* can connote the Land virtually equated with the world (henceforth, we call it 'the maximal Israel' in distinction from the other three types mentioned above).

2.4. Passages in which the Referent of ʾereṣ *is Uncertain*

The semantic field of the term *ʾereṣ*/*ʾaraʿ* includes *terra firma*, the ground, soil, the earth, the world, a land, and the Land. This fact causes us difficulty in determining its precise referent in particular passages. Above all, in not a few passages, we cannot decide with any certainty whether it signifies the world or the Land. If it is so difficult, we must ask why some biblical writers left this important term ambiguous.[308] At the end of the previous section we have already suggested the possibility that the term can apply to the whole world in an expectation for the promise. In other words, it can bear a double meaning, the earth and the Land: connoting both simultaneously. In addition, there may be another double meaning; when contrasted with God in heaven, a land can represent the earth on which it lies, even though lacking global, worldwide or international perspectives. Furthermore, a land can be identified by its inhabitants with the world, since it is virtually 'their world' when their concern is focused on the fate of the people in it. Still, in these cases, too, the term does not lose its tangible senses. It can represent multiple meanings at a time. Because of its many applications, the biblical writers might have chosen the term intentionally to express Israel's relationships to God and to the world.

2.4.1. Some Psalms

In Psalm 119 *ʾereṣ* appears five times (vv. 19, 64, 87, 90, 119). RSV translates our term in v. 19 as 'earth', whereas NRSV and JPSV read 'the land'. The latter translation is preferable, since the verse presupposes the ideology expressed in Lev. 25.23. In contrast, in v. 64 *ʾereṣ* should rather be translated as 'the earth' because of its parallel passage in Ps. 33.5, in which our term certainly signifies 'the earth' according to the context.[309] It is, however, possible that the term in v. 64 connotes simultaneously 'the Land', since God's mercy here virtually means God's laws which were given, first of all, to Israel. The phrase *bāʾāreṣ* in v. 87 is translated as 'on earth' by RSV and NRSV (and LBDJ), whereas ZB reads 'im Lande'. Neither translation makes clear why the phrase *bāʾāreṣ* is attached. It seems to me that the term literally refers here to the pitfalls dug by the persecutors of the psalmist (v. 85). It means, therefore, 'in the ground'. *ʾereṣ* in v. 90 designates 'the earth', for it

308. The use of plural *ʾarāṣôt* referring to the world by later biblical writers might be an attempt to clarify the context.

309. Cf. Num. 14.21; Isa. 6.3; Pss. 72.19; 148.13; Hab. 3.3.

is contrasted with ‘heaven’ (v. 89), and *hakōl* (v. 91) suggests all created things.[310] כל רשעי ארץ in v. 119 may connote ‘all the wicked of the earth’ as NRSV translates, but the phrase כל שוגים מחקיך (v. 118) suggests that the wicked are intended as Israelites who can ‘go astray’ from God’s laws. So the translation ‘all the wicked in the Land’ is favoured, as ZB has it.

In Ps. 12.7 the interpretation of בעליל לארץ is uncertain.[311] RSV and NRSV translate the phrase ‘in a furnace on the ground’ and ZB reads it ‘im Tiegel zu Boden’. These translations are questionable, since it is not understandable how silver refined in a furnace on the ground could be likened to the pure sayings of the Lord. Yet the meaning ‘furnace’ for עליל is utterly dubious.[312] It is more probable that the noun is derived from Aramaic עלל meaning ‘enter’. The preposition ל ‘to, into’ accords well with its usual use. Then the phrase בעליל לארץ can be translated ‘in the entrance to *ʾereṣ*’. It is silver that has been already refined before coming into *ʾereṣ*, that is, when human beings find it. God’s sayings were pure before being sent to *ʾereṣ*, namely, before the people of Israel receive them.[313] If this interpretation is right, the term *ʾereṣ* signifies doubly ‘the ground’ under which silver is found, and ‘the earth’ to which God’s sayings are sent. Still, it may connote ‘the Land’, too. In this Psalm the people of Israel (‘us’ in v. 8) are troubled by בני אדם (v. 2) and ask help from God. Accordingly, בני אדם are not mere human beings, but enemies of Israel. Their words are empty, with flattering lips and a double heart (vv. 3-5). In contrast, God’s sayings are the promise of Israel’s salvation (vv. 6-8). Indeed, the phrase אִמֲרוֹת יהוה throughout the Bible designates ‘commandments and promises of the Lord’, a synonym for Torah.[314] It is God’s gift for Israel.[315] *ʾereṣ* in Ps. 12.7, therefore, is equated with Israel, hence it signifies ‘the Land’.

In Psalm 147 God’s ‘saying’ (v. 15) sent to *ʾereṣ* is connected to natural phenomena (vv. 15-18), and so *ʾereṣ* here seems at first glance to mean ‘the earthly world’.[316] God’s ‘words’ (v. 18), however, are understood as a gift restricted explicitly to Israel (vv. 19f.). Moreover, the context tells of joy for the reconstruction of Jerusalem and the return of the people from the exile (vv. 1-14). The natural phenomena described in vv. 16-18, therefore, allude to the salvation history of Israel and the Land. Consequently, our term in v. 15 connotes ‘the Land’. This interpretation is supported by the wording גבולך in v. 14, which undoubtedly

310. The verb כונן and its hiphil form הכין are used with our term in the context of Creation; cf. Isa. 45.18; Pss. 8.4; 24.2; Prov. 3.19; Jer. 10.12; 51.15; however in Ps. 68.10 it is used with *naḥalâ*, God’s allotment, i.e., the Land.

311. Cf. 2 Sam. 22.31//Ps. 18.31; Ps. 119.140; Prov. 30.5.

312. Cf. BDB, 760.

313. Thus LBDJ, *ad loc.* n. f.

314. Deut. 33.9; Isa. 5.24; Pss. 105.19; 119.11, 38, 41, 50, 58, 67, 76, 82, 103, 116, 123, 133, 140, 148, 154, 158, 162, 170, 172; 138.2; 147.15; 2 Sam. 22.31//Ps. 18.31; Prov. 30.5; Lam. 2.17.

315. Only in Psalm 138 is acceptance by foreign kings expected (v. 4).

316. Thus RSV, NRSV, ZB and LBDJ.

refers to the Land. It is also possible to construe v. 8 as '[the Lord] prepares rain for the Land'.[317]

2.4.2. Some Prophets

In Ezekiel 35 God states judgement against Edom, saying: 'as *kol hā'āreṣ* rejoices, I will make you desolate' (v. 14). The rejoicing is contrasted with Edom rejoicing over Israel (v. 15), hence *kol hā'āreṣ* here must mean 'the whole Land', as LBDJ translates. It may, however, also connote 'the whole world' in a somewhat exaggerated manner.

In Hab. 2.6-20 *'ereṣ* appears twice in the same sentence (vv. 8, 17). Since the worldwide scope of the passage is apparent from the use of *gôyim*, *'amîm* and *'ādām*, it is natural to assume that the term *'ereṣ* here refers to 'the world'.[318] On the other hand, the combination of *'ereṣ* and 'city and all who are living in it' suggests that the narrator sees the vision through an actual experience in his land and city.[319] In other words, the world is seen from an extended perspective of the Land. The term here, therefore, contains a double meaning.

It is uncertain whether the phrase כל ענוי הארץ in Zeph. 2.3 means 'all the humble of the world' or 'of the Land'. Zephaniah contains oracles against the whole world (1.2-3; 2.4-15; 3.6-8) and against Judah and Jerusalem (1.4-13; 3.1-5). The phrase, therefore, designates 'the people of Israel' from a worldwide scope, and 'some among Israel' from a domestic point of view. The two perspectives are connected with each other in 3.12f.; they are 'the humble people' who are 'the remnant of Israel'. It is sound, therefore, to assume that our term in Zeph. 2.3 implies a double meaning. The same can be said of its use in Zeph. 1.18 (twice).[320]

Within Isa. 11.1-10 there is a prophecy of a Davidic messiah, who shall 'decide with equity for ענוי ארץ, and strike *'ereṣ* with the rod of his mouth' (v. 4). According to the present context, he shall rule over peoples and nations, i.e., the world (v. 10). The *'ereṣ* that the messiah shall strike, therefore, is the present world, and ענוי ארץ are 'the afflicted of the world', namely, Israel. Yet it is said that under his rule, wild beasts will live in peace (vv. 6-8; cf. Isa. 65.25a). This means that creation of a new earth is expected. At the same time, the centrality of Jerusalem is presupposed (v. 9a; cf. Isa. 65.25b). These factors suggest that the new earth is identical with the Land extended to the world in this messianic expectation (cf. Isa. 65.17). In this sense it is stated that '*hā'āreṣ* will be full of the knowledge of the Lord' (v. 9b).

317. *'ereṣ* here, of course, connotes simultaneously 'soil' as its nature, cf. Deut. 11.14; 33.28 (see § 2.1.3 above).

318. RSV, NRSV, ZB: 'the earth/Erde'.

319. LBDJ: 'pays'; cf. 1QpHab 12.9f. in which our text is interpreted as '(the cities of) Judah' (see § 6.5.3 below).

320. Cf. Zeph. 3.8, and also Deut. 32.22.

In Isa. 24.1-6 there appears a vision of eschatological judgement, in which the term *ʾereṣ* is used seven times. In the present context the term *ʾereṣ* means 'the earth', because of its apparent parallelism with *tēbēl* (v. 4). If, however, we ignore v. 4, the situation told in this pericope appears to be of the Land at the time of the Exile (esp. vv. 2, 5). This means that the author transfers the experience of Exile into an eschatological judgement of the world which is represented by Israel. The double meaning of *ʾereṣ*, the Land and the world, therefore, overlaps in this pericope too.[321]

Micah 7.13 seems to have been an independent statement, and *ʾereṣ* in it might have been originally intended as a threat against the land of Judah. In the present context, however, it refers to the Land whose borders are extended to the world (vv. 11f.).[322]

2.4.3. בקרב הארץ

It is not always certain if the phrase בקרב הארץ signifies 'in the midst of/ throughout the world' or 'the land'.[323] In Gen. 45.6 Joseph tells of a famine *beqereb hāʾāreṣ*. Although major modern translations of the Bible interpret the phrase as 'in the land (of Egypt)' (RSV, NRSV, LBDJ, JPSV and ZB), it must include the land of Canaan, the then dwelling place of Jacob, who, because of the famine, will have been called to Egypt (vv. 9-13). Also that the famine spread throughout the world is prescribed in Gen. 41.54-57. Consequently, the phrase here designates 'throughout the world'.

God's statement in Exod. 8.18 can be interpreted grammatically in two ways: 'I YHWH am *beqereb hāʾāreṣ*', or 'I am YHWH *beqereb hāʾareṣ*'. According to the Hebrew Bible, the latter is unlikely, since Pharaoh does not know of YHWH (Exod. 5.2), hence God's name bears no significance for him, yet. Rather, in order to let him know who YHWH is, miracles are shown. That YHWH is *beqereb hāʾāreṣ* ought to teach him that *hāʾāreṣ*, the world, is YHWH's (Exod. 9.29; 19.5). The passage, therefore, is to be interpreted that 'I YHWH am in the world'. Still, the term *beqereb* is not limited to 'in, within, in the midst of', but also 'throughout, wherever in' connoting a range which influence of power covers.[324] Consequently, the passage signifies YHWH's omnipresence in the world and his sovereignty over the whole world. That YHWH is in the world (יהוה בקרב הארץ) virtually means that YHWH is the Lord of the world (יְהוָה כל הארץ). This understanding makes the other interpretation possible, too. In Jewish tradition the Tetragrammaton was not pronounced outside of worship,

321. Cf. Johnson 1988: 25f.

322. Cf. LBDJ, *ad loc*. n. h.

323. Clear instances referring to the world: Isa. 19.24; 24.13; to the Land: Deut. 4.5; (15.11); 19.10; (31.16); Isa. 5.8; 6.12; 7.22.

324. It can be said that the phrase *beqereb hāʾāreṣ* is close to such phrases as בכל הארץ and מקצה הארץ ועד קצה הארץ.

and the term *ʾadōnāy* was substituted. Then the Tetragrammaton, the name of God, was to express the substance of God, 'the Lord'. The assertion of the Lord's identity can bear significance for Pharaoh, even though the name is unknown to him.[325] Thus our passage can be interpreted as 'I am the Lord in (of) the world', as already read by LXX: 'I am the Lord, the Lord (or God) of all the earth.'[326]

In Gen. 48.16 Jacob blesses Manasseh and Ephraim, saying: 'let them grow into a multitude *beqereb hāʾāreṣ*'. The phrase here apparently means 'throughout the world', since it is said that Manasseh's seed shall become 'a multitude of nations' (v. 19). It is interesting to observe the fact that the promises of Land and progeny have no relationships dependent on each other, even when they appear together (v. 4).[327] This is understandable since the promise of progeny is a blessing for the people spreading throughout the world, whereas the promise of Land is a blessing for their life in a definite territory. The two promises are not readily compatible with each other. The contradiction can be solved in two ways: to extend the borders of promised Land to the world in which the people shall multiply, or to limit the promise of progeny to the Land. We have a few instances of the latter solution,[328] while there is no explicit expression of the former.[329] The lack of evidence for the former might be caused by the experience of Exile, which in fact made the people of Israel multiply in the world, but was never a blessing for them.[330]

In Isa. 10.23 it is prophesied that 'a decisive destruction will the Lord God of hosts bring *beqereb kol hāʾāreṣ*'. According to the narrower context (vv. 20-23), the phrase may mean 'in the whole Land', since the verses focus on the remnant of Israel. This interpretation can be supported by the use of 'a decisive destruction' in Isa. 28.22, in which the destruction of the Land is announced. The broader context, however, requires another interpretation of the phrase as 'in all the world'. Beginning with לכן 'therefore', v. 24 connects the prophecy on the destruction in v. 23 with pity on Zion and her salvation from Assyria (vv. 24-27).

In Ps. 74.12 God is called 'my King of old, doing salvation *beqereb hāʾāreṣ*'. This verse is followed by a brief list of God's acts in the mythical age and of the Creation (vv. 13-17). It seems, therefore, that the phrase *beqereb hāʾāreṣ* here denotes 'in the midst of the earth'. This psalm as a whole, however, tells of a plea for help at the time of national calamity in the Land (vv. 1-8, 18-23).[331] God's retreat is lamented (vv. 9-11). Then, vv. 12-17 are an expression of the psalmist's conviction of salvation, despite God's silence. That is to say, the wording of v. 12 connotes God's act of salvation 'in the Land', based on the past deeds of God 'in the earth'. Thus the term *ʾereṣ* here conveys a double meaning.

325. Therefore LXX Exod. 5.2 translates 'who is *he*?' instead of 'who is the Lord?'.

326. The addition of 'all' is a paraphrase of *beqereb*, see n. 324 above.

327. Gen. 12.1-3, 7; 13.14-17; 15.5, 7, 18; 17.4-8; 26.3f.; 28.3f., 13-15; 35.11f.; Exod. 32.13.

328. See n. 239 above.

329. But see Isa. 26.15.

330. Cf. Philo (*Flacc.* 45) who connects the dispersion of Jews to their populousness; cf. also *Leg. Gai.* 245; 281f.; see Gafni 1997: 19–40.

331. In vv. 8 and 20 *ʾereṣ* apparently refers to 'the Land'.

2.4.4. במתי ארץ

There is in the Bible another expression with our term, במתי ארץ, denoting 'high places of *ʾereṣ*'. In Amos 4.13 the prophet instructs the idolatrous people who their God is, by referring to his creative activities. Then the clause ודרך על במתי ארץ follows. 'To tread upon the heights' symbolizes a dominion over the whole area around them, since taking high places is strategically decisive in a battle scene.[332] Amos, indeed, immediately continues, 'the Lord, the God of *hosts*, is His name', the term צבאות which provides a military image.[333] Thus, the clause 'to tread on the heights of the earth' symbolizes sovereignty over the whole earth by the Creator, who is the God of Israel.[334] The same clause appears also in Mic. 1.3, in which it symbolizes a theophany to judge all the peoples.

In Deut. 32.13 and Isa. 58.14 the expression *bāmotē ʾereṣ* is employed with another verb הרכיב על 'to make someone ride upon'. In Deut. 32.10-14 Israel's history from the Exodus to their settlement in the Land is accounted. Accordingly, *bāmotē ʾereṣ* upon which God made the people ride and fed them with produce must be identical with the Promised Land (not with the mountainous regions within the Land). Similarly, in Isa. 58.14 the expression *bāmotē ʾereṣ* refers to the Land, since it is in parallelism with Jacob's *naḥalâ*. The implication of these two passages is clear: God (will) put the Land in the possession of Israel. However, the exact connotation of *ʾereṣ* in this phrase is uncertain whether it should be rendered as 'the heights of the Land' or 'the heights of the earth'.[335] The former is possible, for riding upon high places can signify a dominion over the whole Land, as the clause in Amos 4.13 and Mic. 1.3 implies God's sovereignty over the whole earth.[336] The latter is also possible, since the Land contains mountain ranges and it can be called high places of the earth. If this is the case, the phrase can imply that the Land is *bāmôt* (i.e., places of worship)[337] of the world, the Holy Land.[338] In Ezek. 36.2, in fact, we have an expression במות עולם referring to 'the mountains of Israel' (v. 1), which are identical with the Land (v. 5: 'My Land'). The two interpretations need not be mutually exclusive; the former puts a stress on the people's possession of the Land, and the latter on the status of the Land. Both can coexist in a double connotation of the term *bāmâ*, 'height' which symbolizes both a military superiority and a religious holiness, on the one hand, in a double meaning of the term *ʾereṣ*, which can signify both the Promised Land, and the earth/world on/in which the Land is located, on the other. The location of the Land in the world is expressed in Ezek. 38.12 as 'the navel of the earth'.[339] It signifies, according to BDB (371), 'the mountainous country of Israel, central and prominent in the earth'.

332. Cf. Ps. 18.34; Hab. 3.29.

333. See Fowler 1982: 207–9.

334. Cf. God's 'footstool' symbolizing God's lordship: Isa. 66.1; Pss. 99.5; 110.1; 132.7; 1 Chron. 28.2; Lam. 2.1.

335. LBDJ has 'terre' in Deut. 32.13, whereas 'pays' in Isa. 58.14.

336. LXX Deut. 32.13 reads the verse in military context.

337. See BDB, 119.

338. Cf. LXX Isa. 58.14; see Brongers 1975: 214–16.

339. Cf. Judg. 9.37.

2.4.5. Ends of ʾereṣ

The phrases expressing 'the end(s) of *ʾereṣ*' frequently designate 'the end(s) of the world', as we saw above, but they can occasionally refer to 'the end(s) of the Land'. In Jer. 12.12 the phrase מקצה ארץ ועד קצה הארץ is identified with *naḥalâ* in vv. 7-9, i.e., 'the Land'. In Ezek. 7.2, too, the expression 'the four corners of *hāʾāreṣ*' refers to 'the Land of Israel' of the same verse.[340]

2.5. Related Terms

2.5.1. ʾadāmâ

The etymology of the term אדמה can be explained in two ways: derived from the root *ʾadm* 'to be red', hence meaning 'reddish soil'; or as cognate with Arabic *ʾadama* 'he has joined/added', hence meaning 'a covering layer'.[341] Whatever the correct etymology is, the term, as we shall see, includes both as its essential connotation.

ʾadāmâ is understood as a material, from which men and animals are formed and to which they return.[342] From *ʾadāmâ* an altar for the Lord shall be made (Exod. 20.24). *ʾadāmâ* is sprinkled on the head as a sign of mourning, as well.[343] This use of *ʾadāmâ* as a material is not found in that of *ʾereṣ*.[344]

ʾadāmâ covers over the surface of the earth, so that it can signify 'the ground': upon *ʾadāmâ* creep creeping things;[345] on *ʾadāmâ* falls the dew;[346] from *ʾadāmâ* a snare springs up.[347] Under *ʾadāmâ* the netherworld is assumed (Gen. 4.10; Num. 16.30f.).[348] There is an idiomatic expression for dishonour that a corpse not buried shall be דמן על פני האדמה 'dung on the surface of the ground' (Jer. 8.2; 16.4; 25.33; cf. Ps. 83.11). Noah sent out a dove to see if the waters of flood had subsided from the surface of *ʾadāmâ* (Gen. 8.8), and it was drying (Gen. 8.13). These uses of *ʾadāmâ* are very close to one of those of *ʾereṣ* we saw above (§ 2.1.2). A difference between them seems to be that *ʾereṣ* essentially means *terra firma* which includes the ground as its surface, while *ʾadāmâ* refers to the surface as such. Furthermore, as Rost insists, the former is, in many occurrences, used with the movement towards

340. See also Isa. 26.15.
341. Plöger 1977: 88.
342. Gen. 2.7, 19; 3.19; Isa. 45.9; Ps. 146.4; Dan. 12.2; cf. Isa. 64.7; Ps. 103.14; Job 4.19; 10.9. Cf. Eccl. 12.7: *ʾereṣ*.
343. 1 Sam. 4.12; 2 Sam. 1.2; 15.32; Neh. 9.1.
344. Cf. the end of § 2.1.2 (p. 8) above.
345. Gen. 1.25; 6.20; 7.8; 9.2; Lev. 20.25; Deut. 4.18; Ezek. 38.20; Hos. 2.20, cf. n. 12 above.
346. 2 Sam. 17.12; cf. Judg. 6.36-40 with *ʾereṣ*.
347. Amos 3.5 (see n. 355 below).
348. Cf. n. 83 above.

beneath, which implies contrast to its counterpart, the heaven, whereas the latter never is.[349]

Since human beings live on the surface of the ground, *ʾadāmâ* can mean 'the earth' as a whole. The phrase על פני האדמה, in particular, expresses the existence of men, animals, people(s) and kingdoms on the earth.[350] In contrast, the phrase מעל פני האדמה denotes their disappearance from this world.[351] Once the phrase פני אדמה represents all living things on the earth (Ps. 104.30). There are uses of על פני כל הארץ,[352] but there is no occurrence of מעל פני הארץ.

A difference between the uses of *ʾadāmâ* and *ʾereṣ* in the sense of 'whole earth' is found in their idiomatic form. Above all, the term *ʾadāmâ* is never employed with *kol*,[353] compared with *kol hāʾāreṣ* which frequently occurs. In addition, *ʾadāmâ* does not constitute construct form with nouns referring to nations (e.g., *ʿamîm*, *gôyim*, and *mamlākôt*). We have only an idiomatic use of כל משפחות האדמה (Gen. 12.3; 28.14; Amos 3.2) and the phrase מלכי האדמה (Isa. 24.21). Still, there is a more important difference between uses of the two terms: *ʾadāmâ* is not used in contrast to *šāmayim*, with which *ʾereṣ* consists of bipartite division of the universe in many instances. A single exception is found in Isa. 24.21, in which *ʾadāmâ* is contrasted to מרום 'height'.[354] This fact indicates that *ʾadāmâ* is less imagined in cosmological dimensions.[355] Rather, it seems, *ʾadāmâ* as the whole earth is an extension of its basic use for the ground, as suggested by its combination with פנים. *ʾadāmâ* is the place where living things dwell, while *ʾereṣ* designates cosmologically the 'human world' compared with heavenly-world. This is evidenced by an expression 'all the kingdoms of *hāʾāreṣ* (which is) on the face of *hāʾadāmâ*' (Isa. 23.17; Jer. 25.26).

An essential meaning of *ʾadāmâ* is 'the soil', which is developed in relation to agriculture. According to Genesis 2, *ʾadāmâ* was watered by a stream before the formation of Adam (v. 6). It was arable from the outset, and waited for man who tilled it in order to bring forth produce (v. 5). The cooperation between Adam and *ʾadāmâ* bears fruits. Adam, the first man, therefore, tilled the soil even in the Garden of Eden (v. 15). To till the soil is expressed by עבד את האדמה (v. 5).[356] This understanding of *ʾadāmâ* is utterly different from that of *ʾereṣ*, a difference which is apparent in Genesis 1–2: *ʾereṣ* brings its produce by itself according to God's command (1.11f.),[357] whereas *ʾadāmâ* needs Adam, its tiller (2.5, 15); Adam

349. Rost 1965: 81f.

350. Gen. 6.1; 7.23; Exod. 33.16; Num. 12.3; Deut. 7.6; 14.2; 2 Sam. 14.7; Isa. 23.17; Jer. 25.26; cf. Exod. 10.6; 1 Sam. 20.31; cf. Isa. 24.21.

351. Gen. 6.7; 7.4; Exod. 32.12; Deut. 6.15; 1 Sam. 20.15; Jer. 28.16; Amos 9.8; Zeph. 1.2f.

352. See n. 113 above.

353. Except Gen. 47.20 (see below).

354. Cf. Gen. 4.10.

355. In Amos 3.5 a bird falls upon *ʾereṣ* (implying from the sky), whereas a snare springs up from *ʾadāmâ*; thus *ʾadāmâ* is not understood in contrast to the sky. There is no use of *ʾadāmâ* employed with the sea, either.

356. Cf. Gen. 3.23; 4.2, 12; 2 Sam. 9.10; Prov. 12.11; 28.19; 1 Chron. 27.26.

357. Cf. Ps. 67.7; Job 28.5.

subdues *ʾereṣ* (1.28), while he is the worker of *ʾadāmâ* (2.5). The distinctions between the two terms are caused by different viewpoints on the soil. Compared with *ʾereṣ*, *ʾadāmâ* is not understood in cosmological dimensions, but is seen from the eyes of those who feel familiarity to it. The lack of cosmological extension of uses of *ʾadāmâ* can be shown by the fact that it is seldom stated that rain falls upon *ʾadāmâ*.[358] Rather frequent is the comment that rain falls upon *ʾereṣ*,[359] so that *ʾadāmâ* is watered (Gen. 2.5; 7.4; Jer. 14.4). The term *ʾadāmâ* is not put in contrast to heaven.

Engaging in agriculture (עֲבֹדַת הָאדמה [1 Chron. 27.26]) is regarded as an ideal life (Gen. 2.15). Cain, originally a tiller of the soil (עֹבֵד אדמה [Gen. 4.2]), must have become a fugitive and a wanderer of *ʾereṣ* when cursed from *ʾadāmâ* and from which he was driven away (Gen. 4.11-14). From these passages it is apparent that *ʾadāmâ* is a rural part of *ʾereṣ*. The reference to Cain's building of a city (Gen. 4.17) may suggest that rural life on the soil is considered better than city life. In contrast, according to Gen. 3.23 tilling the soil is a result of the sin of Adam, because of which *ʾadāmâ* was cursed (Gen. 3.17; 5.29), so that עֲבֹדַת האדמה was to involve toil and sweat (Gen. 3.17-19). The curse on the soil was relieved by Noah (Gen. 8.21),[360] who was called איש האדמה 'a man of the soil' (Gen. 9.20).[361] These uses of the term *ʾadāmâ* show a striking difference from *ʾereṣ*. There is no instance of *ʾereṣ* employed with עבד, and it is seldom connected with 'agriculture', human labour on the soil.[362]

ʾadāmâ can be sold and bought, so that it means landed property of individuals (Gen. 47.18f.). It, therefore, can be defined by a pronominal suffix.[363] It can be defined by the name of a group in construct form, as well: אדמת כהנים 'the land of priests' (Gen. 47.22, 26). A reference is made to (כל) אדמת מצרים (Gen. 47.20, 26), which does not designate 'the land of Egypt' as a territory, but 'all the landed property of every Egyptians'; the land as a whole is called *hāʾāreṣ* in v. 20. In Exod. 8.17, in which it is put in pair with בתי מצרים, *ʾadāmâ* refers to 'the farm-land on which they are (cultivating)'.

ʾadāmâ is not defined by a name of nation, except the use of אדמת ישראל employed only in the book of Ezekiel,[364] and אדמת יהודה once in Isa. 19.17, beside אדמת מצרים mentioned immediately above. In cases in which the term is defined by a pronominal suffix, a determinative, or a relative clause, the referent is almost always restricted to 'the Land'.[365]

358. Only in 1 Kgs 17.14; 18.1; cf. Isa. 30.23.

359. Gen. 6.17; 7.4, 6, 10, 12, 17, 27.39; 1 Kgs 17.7; Jer. 14.4; Eccl. 11.3; see nn. 39–40 above.

360. Cf. Job 5.6.

361. Cf. Zech. 13.5; Isa. 30.24.

362. Cf. § 2.1.3 above. An exception is the use of *ʾereṣ* with a verb 'to sow' in Gen. 26.12; Exod. 23.10; cf. Isa. 30.23 with *ʾadāmâ*.

363. Gen. 47.18, 19, 22, 23; Isa. 28.24; Ps. 49.12 (plural); Job 31.38; Prov. 12.11; 28.19.

364. Ezek. 7.2; 11.17; 12.19, 22; 18.2; 20.38, 42; 21.7, 8; 25.3, 6; 33.24; 36.6; 37.12; 38.18, 19.

365. Except: Lev. 20.24; Amos 7.17b; Ps. 137.4; Dan. 11.9 (and n. 363 above); cf. 2 Kgs 25.21; Jer. 52.27; and 1 Kgs 17.14; 18.1; 2 Kgs 17.23.

ʾadāmâ referring to the Land can be used in contexts of the Land-promise. It can be employed with such terms as: נשבע,[366] נתן,[367] בא/הביא,[368] ירש,[369] עבר את הירדן,[370] ישב,[371] לבטח,[372] טמא,[373] נשמה/בשממה,[374] השיב/שוב,[375] and so on. Characteristic uses of *ʾadāmâ* are found in such expressions as: 'to place upon the Land';[376] 'to plant (Israel) upon the Land' (Amos 9.15); 'to gather (Israel) upon the Land' (Ezek. 39.28); 'to atone for the Land of His people' (Deut. 32.43);[377] and 'living upon (the surface of) the Land'.[378] Remarkable are frequent uses of the phrase האריך ימים על האדמה 'to prolong days upon the Land' by the Deuteronomist.[379] It is also noteworthy that Ezekiel sometimes prophesies directly, addressing the Land.[380] The destruction of the Land and the Exile can be described with various wordings, as well.[381]

There are references to the fruits of *ʾadāmâ* 'the Land'.[382] The Land is called אדמה שמנה 'a fat land' (Neh. 9.25) and האדמה הטובה הזאת 'this good land' (Josh. 23.13, 15; 1 Kgs 14.15). In Isa. 1.7 the term *ʾadāmâ* by itself denotes 'the fruits of the Land'. The productivity of *ʾadāmâ* assumes the labour of its inhabitants (Isa. 30.23; Jer. 27.11). *ʾadāmâ* responds to God's will (Deut. 11.17; Isa. 32.13; Jer. 14.4; Hag. 1.11). It can be personified (Joel 1.10; cf. 2.21).

The Land is called אדמת יהוה (Isa. 14.2; cf. Zech. 9.16; 2 Chron. 7.20). A reference is made also to אדמת הקדש (Zech. 2.16).[383] The wording of *ʾadāmâ* here rather than *ʾereṣ* might imply that it is the soil of the Land that is holy. This notion is apparent in the act of Naaman who took two mule-loads of *ʾadāmâ* of the Land to worship the God of Israel outside (2 Kgs 5.17). The commandment

366. Num. 11.13; 32.11; Deut. 7.13; 11.9, 21; 26.15; 28.11; 30.20; 31.20.

367. Exod. 20.12; Lev. 20.24; Deut. 4.40; 5.16; 7.13; 11.9, 21; 21.1, 23; 25.15; 26.15; 30.20; Josh. 23.13, 15; 1 Kgs 8.34, 40; 9.7; 14.15; 2 Kgs 21.8; Jer. 16.15; 24.10; 25.5; 35.15; Ezek. 11.17; 28.25; Amos 9.15; 2 Chron. 7.20; in 2 Chron. 33.8 'to assign' is used instead (cf. 2 Kgs 21.8).

368. בא: Deut. 28.21, 63; 30.18; cf. Ezek. 13.9; 20.38; הביא: Ezek. 20.42; 34.13; 36.24; 37.12, 21.

369. Lev. 20.24; Deut. 21.1; 28.21, 63; 30.18; 31.13; 32.47.

370. Deut. 30.18; 31.13; 32.47.

371. Deut. 30.20; Jer. 23.8; 25.5; 27.11; Ezek. 28.25; 36.17; 39.26. The verb ישב takes the preposition על for *ʾadāmâ* except in Jer. 27.11 which has ב, whereas for *ʾereṣ* usually taking ב save in Ezek. 37.25 with על; cf. n. 233 above.

372. Ezek. 34.27; 39.26.

373. Deut. 21.23; Ezek. 36.17.

374. Isa. 6.11; Ezek. 25.3.

375. השיב: Gen. 28.15; 1 Kgs 8.34; Jer. 16.15; 42.12; 2 Chron. 6.25; שוב: Jer. 35.15.

376. Isa. 14.1; Jer. 27.11; Ezek. 37.14.

377. The text is according to 4QDeuteronomy; cf. Num. 35.33.

378. Deut. 4.10; 12.1; 31.13; 1 Kgs 8.40; Jer. 35.7; 2 Chron. 6.31.

379. Exod. 20.12; Deut. 4.40; 11.9; 25.15; 30.18, 20; 32.47; cf. Deut. 11.21; Jer. 35.7.

380. Ezek. 7.2; 12.19; 21.7, 8; 25.3; 36.6.

381. Deut. 28.21, 63; 29.27; Josh. 23.13, 15; 1 Kgs 9.7; 13.34; 14.15; Jer. 12.14; 24.10; 27.10; Amos 5.2; 7.11, 17; 2 Chron. 7.20; 33.8.

382. Exod. 23.19; 34.26; Deut. 7.13; 26.2, 10; 28.4, 11, 18, 33, 42, 51; 30.9; Isa. 30.23; Jer. 7.20; Mal. 3.11; Ps. 105.35; Neh. 10.36, 38.

383. Cf. Ps. 78.54. For Exod. 3.5, see Wilken 1992: 26f. n. 42.

not to defile 'your ᵓ*ădāmâ*' (Deut. 21.23) must be related to the concept of the holy Land. On a foreign ᵓ*ădāmâ* the people of Israel cannot sing a song for God (Ps. 137.4), since it is 'an unclean ᵓ*ădāmâ*' (Amos 7.17; cf. Josh. 22.19a; Hos. 9.3; Ezek. 4.13).

This suggests that the term ᵓ*ădāmâ* is not used in territorial dimensions, compared with uses of ᵓ*ereṣ*. This is also shown by the fact that ᵓ*ereṣ* is used in many instances with the preposition ב which itself already assumes particular limits, while ᵓ*ădāmâ* usually follows על which conveys attachment to the thing. ᵓ*ădāmâ* never connotes 'a state', a territory governed by a nation. It is a non-political term.[384] Accordingly, its uses in the context of Land-promise do not imply the establishment of the state of Israel; rather it expresses an attachment to the soil of the Land, namely, to an agricultural life.

The term ᵓ*ădāmâ* is close to ᵓ*ereṣ* in its referent; it can refer to the ground, the earth, a landed property, and the Land. It is, however, different from the latter; it is used neither in the cosmological dimensions nor in territorial. It is rather a material, the ground covering the surface of the earth, and an agricultural concept, signifying 'the soil cultivated by farmers'.

2.5.2. tēbēl

The term תבל, 'world', appears thirty-six times in the Bible, of which fifteen times in Psalms and nine times in the book of Isaiah. It never employs the determinative article *he*, nor *kol*, compared with *kol hā*ᵓ*āreṣ*. It is used in parallelism with ᵓ*ereṣ* twenty-two times,[385] with *kol hā*ᵓ*āreṣ* four times[386] and with מים/ים 'sea/water' three times.[387] It appears almost always in poetry. These facts indicate that the term can be a poetic synonym for ᵓ*ereṣ*.[388]

tēbēl is referred to in statements of the Creation.[389] Its foundations are referred to, as well.[390] It is also used in relation to the judgement.[391] *tēbēl* is frequently referred to with its inhabitants: ישבי תבל;[392] תבל וישבי בה;[393] תבל ומלאה/כל צאצאיה.[394] Mention is made of פני תבל (Isa. 14.21; 27.6; Job 37.12) and even עפרות תבל (Prov. 8.26). Once קצה תבל is put in parallelism with *kol hā*ᵓ*āreṣ* (Ps. 19.5).

384. Thus Rost 1965.

385. 1 Sam. 2.8; Isa. 14.17, 21; 18.3; 24.4; 26.9, 18; 34.1; Jer. 10.12; 51.15; Nah. 1.5; Pss. 24.1; 77.19; 89.12; 90.2; 96.13; 97.4; 98.9; Prov. 8.26; Job 18.17-18; 34.13; Lam. 4.12.

386. Pss. 19.5; 33.8; 96.9-10; 1 Chron. 16.30.

387. 2 Sam. 22.16//Ps. 18.16; Ps. 98.7.

388. Thus BDB, 385; see also Stadelmann 1970: 129f.

389. 1 Sam. 2.8; Jer. 10.12; 51.15; Pss. 83.1; 89.12; 90.2; 96.10; Job 34.13; 1 Chron. 16.30.

390. 2 Sam. 22.16//Ps. 18.16; cf. Ps. 89.12; cf. n. 50 above.

391. Pss. 9.9; 96.13; 98.9; Isa 13.11; 26.9.

392. Isa. 18.3; 26.9, 18; Ps. 33.8; Lam. 4.12.

393. Pss. 24.1; 98.7; Nah. 1.5.

394. Pss. 50.12; 89.12; Isa. 34.1.

tēbēl is never contrasted directly to the heaven, so that its connotation is limited to the earthly habitable world. It is manifested in the phrase תבל ארצה/ו 'the/His world of earth' (Job 37.12; Prov. 8.31).[395] The uses of *tēbēl* can be virtually substituted by *ʾereṣ*, as already shown by their parallelisms. In the LXX *tēbēl* is usually translated as ἡ οἰκουμένη.[396]

2.5.3. gebûl

The term גבול appears 240 times in the Bible. It means 'border, boundary', a line marking limits of an area: the border of the earth against the sea;[397] the boundary of individual property.[398] In the book of Ezekiel the term is used for a partition in the Temple (40.12), and for the rim of the altar (43.17, 20). It can express a border of a city (Num. 35.26) and of a land.[399] The borders of the Land are described with this term in Numbers 34 and Ezekiel 47–48, and in Joshua 12–19 with detailed accounts of its distribution to the twelve tribes. These are the term's unique uses that the term *ʾereṣ* does not convey.

gebûl can denote 'territory' enclosed within borders. References are made to: 'the territory of Egypt' (Gen. 47.21; Exod. 10.14, 19); 'the Canaanite territory' (Gen. 10.19), etc.[400] Edom is called 'a territory of wickedness' (Mal. 1.4). Smaller regions can be expressed by the term, as well.[401] Each name of the twelve tribes of Israel can be attached to the term.[402] In Ezek. 48.12-13 'the territory of the priests' is referred to.[403]

The Land can be expressed by the phrase גבול ישראל.[404] Defined by a pronominal suffix, too, the term can refer to the Land.[405] The Land is called 'My (God's) territory' (1 Chron. 4.10) and 'the territory of His holiness' (Ps. 78.54).[406]

Although the term *gebûl* referring to a territory is very close to *ʾereṣ* in its usage, the former mostly connotes its essential meaning 'boundary' whereas the latter can refer to a land without any particular attention to its borders.

The semantic field of the term *ʾereṣ* is adjacent to that of *ʾadāmâ*, *tēbēl* and *gebûl*. In other words, *ʾereṣ* connotes the other three terms simultaneously, so that

395. Cf. BDB, 385; Stadelmann 1970: 130 n. 691 on Job 37.12.
396. 25 times; other translations: γῆ (4 times); ἡ ὑπ' οὐρανός (once); ἡ σύμπασα (once).
397. Jer. 5.22; Ps. 104.9.
398. Deut. 19.14; 27.17; Hos. 5.10; Prov. 15.25; 22.28; 23.10.
399. Num. 20.23; 21.13, 24; 22.36; Deut. 2.18; 3.14, 16; Josh. 12.4; Judg. 11.18; 1 Kgs 5.1// 2 Chron. 9.26; 1 Sam. 6.12; Ezek. 29.10; Obad. 7.
400. See Judg. 1.36; 11.22; Isa. 15.8.
401. Josh. 13.11; 16.2, 3.
402. Josh. 16.5; 17.7; 19.47.
403. Cf. Gen. 47.22, 26.
404. Judg. 19.29; 1 Sam. 7.13; 11.3, 7; 27.1; 2 Sam. 21.5; 1 Kgs 1.3; 2 Kgs 10.32; 14.25; 1 Chron. 21.12; Mal. 1.5.
405. Exod. 13.7; 23.31; 34.24; Deut. 12.20; 16.4; 19.8; Isa. 60.18; Jer. 15.13; 17.3; 31.17; Joel 4.6; Mic. 5.5; Ps. 147.4; 1 Chron. 4.10
406. Cf. § 2.5.1 (pp. 38f.) above.

it is distinct from them. It signifies, not merely the earth as the habitable world, but the earth contrasted to the heaven in the cosmological perspectives. It designates, not merely the soil nor a territory, but a productive land in territorial dimensions.

2.6. Conclusion

The term *ʾereṣ* can represent the earth, a half part of universe. It can also designate the human world consisting of nations other than Israel. In the former, *ʾereṣ* is apprehended cosmologically in relation to God's Creation activities, while in the latter, it represents foreign nations in contrast to Israel in international dimensions. The two dimensions correspond with each other; as in the latter, the term illuminates the uniqueness of Israel contrasted to other nations, so in the former, it does not tell of the whole human world as a main theme in its own right, but special concerns for the fate of Israel in it are maintained, since the Creator is the God of Israel.

The uses of *ʾereṣ* concerning the Land-promise presuppose the two ideas that Israel is the Lord's people and that the Land is the Lord's (ארץ יהוה). The Lord's Land is holy, and so it shall not be polluted cultically or ethically. In other words, Israel is the Lord's people, who shall take possession of the Lord's Land, as far as they observe the Law. Thus the special relationships between the Lord and the people are expressed by means of the Promised Land and the Law, that is, the covenant. The two concepts, Israel and the Land, are ideologically an inseparable pair, forming a central biblical theology.

Since the borders of the Promised Land are variously defined in the Bible, the term *ʾereṣ* can be employed in an eschatological vision in which a messianic king of Israel will rule over the whole world. In this vision the term is seen neither as universalistic concerns generalizing all the nations, nor in apocalyptic perspectives regarding the world to come, but in territorial dimensions as the Land extending to the ends of the world.

The *ʾereṣ* in cosmological dimensions, portraying the greatness of the God of Israel, the Creator, illustrates the uniqueness of the people of Israel among nations. The *ʾereṣ* in territorial dimensions, depicting the special relationships between God and Israel, illuminates the distinctive status of Israel among nations. Thus the term *ʾereṣ*, while designating different referents, the earth and the Land, expresses Israel-centrically the relationships between the God of Israel and the world, and between the people of Israel and nations of the world (God-Israel-nations relationships). In other words, the term plays a role in placing Israel in the world in relation to God. In this sense the uses of *ʾereṣ* bespeak a kind of nationalism of Israel. This implication of *ʾereṣ* can be found throughout the Bible (except for a part of the Writings such as Job, Esther, Ruth, and Song of Solomon).

The Bible is the holy scriptures of the national religion of Israel, and so it is naturally illuminated by various nationalistic ideologies. Even when a biblical passage seems to depict a universalistic soteriology, it is actually an expression of nationalistic hope of Israel's dominion over the world, a universalism which is based on nationalism. One of the terms expressing such ideologies is *ʾereṣ*, which plays a role in placing the national history within the world history. Its multiple connotations, however, allow later readers to interpret it in various manners.

2.7. Appendix 1: Non-Biblical Jewish Uses of the Terms ʾereṣ *and* ʾaraʿ/ʾaraq *from the Biblical Period*

In this appendix we shall survey the non-biblical Jewish uses of our terms in the eighth–seventh centuries BCE Hebrew inscriptions from Palestine (*HAE*) and the fifth century BCE Aramaic papyri from Elephantine (*TAD*).[407]

2.7.1. ʾereṣ *in Jewish Inscriptions from Palestine*

In *HAE* there are two inscriptions in which the term *ʾereṣ* appears. An inscription from Khirbet Beth Lay of the first half of the seventh century BCE reads: 'YHWH is the God of all the earth; the mountains of Judah belong to the God of Jerusalem' (BLay [7].1).[408] The same expression אלהי כל הארץ appears in Isa. 54.5, and similar phrases are employed throughout the Bible.[409] A comparable expression can be found in a non-Jewish Aramaic inscription, as well (*KAI* 202B.25f.).[410]

An ostracon from Jerusalem of the late eighth or early seventh century BCE contains the following letters: [..]-קן ארץ (Jer[8].30, line 3).[411] P. D. Miller Jr reconstructs the text as אל קן ארץ 'El, the Creator of earth', by referring to ancient inscriptions bearing this epithet.[412] There is, however, a difficulty in his proposal. As Miller himself acknowledges, 'Hebrew orthography of that period clearly requires a final *he*' (i.e., קנה).[413] Further, the form may be a part of another word which ends with קן, or קן ארץ might mean 'possessor of the land' (i.e., an estate).[414] Since the lines 1-2 provide personal names, it is natural to assume that the line 3 might have any designation of the persons, or their deeds.[415] It is difficult to determine which the better reading is, and consequently we cannot learn much from this ostracon.

407. There is no occurrence of our terms in *CII* and *CPI*.
408. *HAE* I, 245f.
409. See nn. 55, 86–91 above.
410. See Chapter 3 below.
411. *HAE* I, 197f.
412. Miller 1980.
413. Miller 1980: 45; cf. Lipinski 2004.
414. Thus, *HAE* I, 198 n. c.
415. But see Miller 1980: 43.

2.7.2. ʾaraʿ/ʾaraq *in the Elephantine Papyri*

The term *ʾaraʿ* in the Elephantine papyri can mean 'the ground', the surface of the earth. 'They came to the fortress of Elephantine with their weapons, broke into that Temple, demolished it to the ground (נדשוהי עד ארעא)' (*TAD* A4.7.8f.// A4.8.7f.).[416] This use of *ʾaraʿ*, which expresses the movement of a thing down to the ground, is very common in the Bible.[417] The term *ʾaraʿ* as the ground can be the base of a building (*TAD* B2.1.5): 'That wall shall adjoin the side of my house from the ground upwards (מן ארעא ועד עלא)'.[418]

The term *ʾaraʿ* is once used in the sense of 'the earth': על אנפי ארעא כלה (*TAD* B2.6.17-20). This Aramaic expression is equivalent to the biblical על פני כל הארץ.[419]

In other papyri our term is employed to express an 'estate', individual property. In a document, which deals with renunciation of a claim to the land property by another neighbour, the term is always used with qualifications (*TAD* B2.2): ארקא זילי 'the land of mine' (l. 5), ארקא זך 'that land' (ll. 6-7, 7, 12, 13, 14, 15), ארעא זך 'that land' (l. 16), and ארק לדרגמן 'the land of Dargamana' (l. 7). As evident, the terms *ʾaraq* and *ʾaraʿ* are interchangeable. It is notable that the land possession is legitimated by the expression 'to swear by YHW' (ll. 4, 6, 11; cf. ll. 7-8).

In another document, which deals with a bequest of a Jew to his daughter (*TAD* B2.3), the verb יהב 'to give' is repetitiously employed (ll. 8, 10, 13, 19), and the rights over the land are not limited to the daughter, but extend to her children, 'and your sons after you', even עד עלם 'forever' (ll. 9, 11). The use of these terms and expressions concerning the possession of one's estate is very similar to those in the biblical Land-theology; similarity which suggests that the terminology of the biblical Land-promise might follow after a contract of this kind.[420]

2.7.3. Summary

The inscription from Khirbet Beth Lay attests to the use of the expression יהוה אלהי כל הארץ outside the Bible in the seventh century BCE. From Elephantine papyri we can learn that a claim of an individual to his own estate might lie behind the terminology in the biblical Land theology, such as 'to swear', 'to give' and 'forever'. The two biblical theologies concerning *ʾereṣ*, the Creation theology and the Land theology, might reflect these ordinary Jewish lives.

416. *TAD*'s translation.
417. Cf. § 2.1.2 above.
418. Cf. Ezek. 41.20.
419. See n. 113 above, and cf. *KAI* 27.13-15 (Chapter 3 below).
420. Our term is used in the sense of 'estate' also in *TAD* B2.4 lines 3, 5, 8, 14; B3.4 line 5 (see Kutscher 1954); D2.10 line 9. Although the term appears also in *TAD* D3.19 line 3, the meaning is unclear because of lacunae.

Chapter 3

NON-JEWISH USAGE OF THE TERMS

The terms *ʾereṣ* and *ʾaraʿ*/*ʾaraq* were current in ancient non-Jewish contexts, as well. A brief survey of the uses of our terms in the surrounding areas may be appropriate as a general background of their biblical and post-biblical Jewish usage. In the inscriptions collected in *KAI*, our term is testified in Phoenician, New Punic, and Moabite inscriptions, and in Aramaic inscriptions from Syria and Egypt. We shall treat the materials according to *KAI*, and then supplement the Aramaic papyri from Egypt collected in *TAD* and Nabataean papyri from Naḥal Ḥever in *TJD*.

3.1. Phoenician Inscriptions

Among the sixty Phoenician inscriptions collected in *KAI*, the term *ʾrṣ* appears in seven inscriptions dated between the eighth and third centuries BCE.[1]

In the Phoenician inscriptions, the term *ʾrṣ* can signify 'the earth' in contrast to heavens. In an inscription from Karatepe, a reference is made to gods as follows: 'the Baʿal of heavens, and El who has created the earth (אל קן ארץ), and the Sun (god) of eternity' (*KAI* 26A+B, III.18f.). The expression אל קן ארץ is very similar to the biblical locution אל עליון קנה שמים וארץ (Gen. 14.19, 22; cf. Prov. 8.22).[2] In an inscription from Arslan Tas, we find 'by the oaths of heavens and earth [for]ever, by the oaths of the Baʿal of the surface of the earth (פן ארץ)' (*KAI* 27.13-15).[3] A similar form to swearing by heavens and earth appears in the Bible, as well.[4] The expression פן ארץ is also equivalent to the biblical פני הארץ.[5]

In Phoenician, the term *ʾrṣ* can designate a territorial 'land', as well. This is manifested in the expression גבל ארץ 'the border of the land' (*KAI* 14.20). It can be attached to the name of a place: ארץ עמק אדן 'the land of Adana plain' (*KAI* 26A, I.4f.; II.15f.). A land can be defined by a topographic characteristic, as well;

1. *KAI* 26 (Karatepe, *c*. 720 BCE); *KAI* 27 (Arslan Tas, seventh century BCE); *KAI* 14 (Sidon, beginning of fifth century BCE); *KAI* 15 (Sidon, fifth century BCE); *KAI* 10 (Byblos, *c*. fifth–fourth century BCE); *KAI* 43 (Lapethos, 275 BCE?); *KAI* 19 (Maʿsûb, 222 BCE).

2. Cf. a New Punic inscription from Leptis Magna (*KAI* 129.1; see below) and an Aramaic inscription from Hatra (*KAI* 244; see below); for this expression, see *KAI* II, 42f.; Miller 1980: 43f.

3. See *KAI* II, 45; cf. Gibson 1971–82: III, 78–88.

4. See Chapter 2 n. 66 above.

5. See Chapter 2 n. 113 above; cf. a Jewish papyrus from Elephantine (*TAD* B2.6.17-20; § 2.7.2 above).

צדן ארץ ים 'Sidon the land of sea' (*KAI* 14.16, 18; cf. *KAI* 15: 'Sidon of the sea'). In *KAI* 15 another epithet is given to Sidon: ארץ רשפם. Although it is unclear if the term רשפם means 'Reshef', an underworld god, 'lightening flashes', or 'the Warriors', its function to qualify Sidon as a good land is apparent.[6] This epithet is an expression of the Sidonians' pride of and love for their own homeland.

Since *ʾrṣ* can mean '*the* land' for its inhabitants, it can be used without any qualification, as *hāʾāreṣ* in many biblical passages. The expression בארץ can mean the existence of a certain thing in the land where the king (= the speaker) reigned: 'as they built all the other [temple]s in the land' (*KAI* 19.9f.); 'and I broke the scoffers and annihilated all the evils which were in the land' (*KAI* 26A, I.8f.). Similarly, mention is made of רב ארץ 'the great one of the land (of Lapethos)' (*KAI* 43.6),[7] and עם ארץ 'the people of the land (of Byblos)' (*KAI* 10.10 [twice]), which is an equivalent to the biblical *ʿam hāʾāreṣ*.[8]

The term *ʾrṣ* as a territorial land can be used in the plural, as well: ארצת עזת 'strong lands' (*KAI* 26A, I.18); ארצת דגן האדרת 'the glorious lands of grain' (*KAI* 14.19). The last two examples show that the term *ʾrṣ* can represent a land as a political unity which is qualified by such an adjective as 'strong', on the one hand, it can express a land as productive soil which is qualified by such a product as 'grain', on the other (cf. Deut. 33.28).[9]

In the inscription last mentioned (*KAI* 14) the meritorious deeds of Eshmunazar, the king of Sidonians, are enumerated. One of them is depicted as follows: 'And furthermore the Lord of the kings gave us Dor and Jaffa, the glorious lands of grain in the plain of Sharon, for the mighty deeds which I did. And we added them to the borders of the land to belong (them) to the Sidonians for eve[r]' (lines 18-20). In these lines the king lays claim to the legitimate possession of Dor and Jaffa as a gift of 'the lord of the kings' (= the king of Persia) and to their eternal possession by Sidonians. This claim is expressed in a manner similar to the biblical Land theology, in which, too, the terms 'to give' and 'forever' play a significant role.[10]

The inscription from Karatepe (*KAI* 26) also shows that to expand the territory is a strong concern of the governor. It is stated: 'I enlarged (ירחב) the land of Adana plain from the exit of the sun to its entrance' (I.4f.); 'And I subjected strong lands in the entrance of the sun, which all the kings who were before me had not subjected' (I.18f.). The governor emphasizes that the land he subjects has become better because of his deeds: 'and I broke the scoffers and annihilated all the evils which were in the land' (I.8f.); 'in my days the land of Adana plain was satisfied and pleasant' (II.15f.). By calling himself 'the servant of Baʿal' at the beginning of this inscription (I.1f.), the governor claims the divine legitimization of the expansion of his territory.

6. See Fulco 1976: 47, 69; cf. *KAI* II, 24; for a similar expression ארקרשף (*KAI* 214.11), see Fulco 1976: 44–6.

7. See *KAI* II, 60f.

8. Cf. Chapter 2 n. 183 above.

9. Cf. Chapter 2 nn. 265–8 above.

10. Cf. Chapter 2 nn. 196, 306 above.

The Phoenician inscriptions reveal that the term *ʾrṣ* was used in two dimensions, cosmological and territorial. In the cosmological dimensions, it is perceived in contrast to heavens in relation to the Creation. From the territorial perspectives, the possession of a land and the expansion of its territory are divinely legitimated. The usage of our term in Phoenician shows apparent parallelism with its biblical uses.

3.2. New Punic Inscriptions

Among fifty-seven New Punic inscriptions, our term occurs in five inscriptions dated from the beginning of the first to the second centuries CE.[11]

In the inscription from Leptis Magna (*KAI* 129), there appears the expression אל קן ארץ (line 1). This wording is the same as the one appearing in the Phoenician inscription from Karatepe (*KAI* 26A+B, III.18).[12] Here the term *ʾrṣ* is perceived in universal dimensions.

That the term can refer to a territorial land is evident from its plural use: 'the ruler of lands, the lord of kings' (*KAI* 161.2).[13] The parallel use of 'lands' and 'kings' shows that the *ʾrṣ* is regarded as a territory reigned by a king.

In two New Punic inscriptions from Leptis Magna, which have a longer Latin version respectively (*KAI* 121; 126), the term *ʾrṣ* is used for the translation of *patria*, 'fatherland': 'Annobal Rufus, the ornamenter of the (father)land' (*KAI* 121.1); '(Tiberius Claudius Quirina Sestius) the lover of the (father)land, the lover of the sons of the people, the ornamenter of the (father)land' (*KAI* 126.4f.). These inscriptions explicitly show that the term *ʾrṣ* can represent, not only a territorial land politically defined, but also *patria*, fatherland, to which people have a sentimental attachment.

3.3. Moabite Inscription

KAI contains one Moabite inscription from Diban, known as Mesha inscription (*KAI* 181; *c*. 850 BCE). It depicts the battles over Moabite territory between Mesha the king of Moab and Omri and his son the kings of Israel.[14]

In this inscription the term *ʾrṣ* is perceived in territorial dimensions, as expected from the topic at hand. It can be defined by the name of a place: 'all the land of Mehadaba' (lines 7f.); 'the land of Ataroth' (line 10). It can be defined by the determinative *he*, as well (ll. 28f., 31). It can also be defined by a pronominal

11. *KAI* 121 (Leptis Magna, 2 CE); *KAI* 126 (Leptis Magna, 92 CE); *KAI* 129 (Leptis Magna, beginning of second century CE); *KAI* 141 (Dschebel Massoudj) and *KAI* 161 (Cherchel) are undated. Our term does not appear in Punic inscriptions.

12. Cf. n. 2 above.

13. Cf. 'lands' in *KAI* 141.1.

14. For the text, see Jackson and Dearman 1989; for the translation, Jackson 1989: 97f.; for historical background, see Dearman 1989; cf. also Gibson 1971–82: I, 71–84.

suffix: 'Omri was the king of Israel, and he afflicted Moab for many days, because Chemosh was angry with his land (i.e., the land of Moab)' (ll. 4-6). The fact that Chemosh's anger is directed to the 'land' shows Moabites' strong concern for the territory. It is interesting to see the use of the verbs ירש and ישב in this inscription: 'and Omri had taken possession of all the land of Mehadaba and dwelled in it during his days and a half of the days of his son, forty years' (ll. 7f.). The term *yrš* can mean 'to inherit' in the Bible, but here it undoubtedly connotes 'to seize' or 'to conquer'. While the terms *yrš* and *yšb* appear in the biblical Land-promise,[15] they are used here from the Moabite eyes as a hostile deed.

3.4. Non-Jewish Aramaic Inscriptions and Papyri

Of seventy-five Aramaic inscriptions collected in *KAI,* nine inscriptions preserve the term *ʾaraʿ/ʾaraq*.[16] *TAD* contains four non-Jewish Aramaic papyri and one inscription in which our term occurs.[17]

The term *ʾaraʿ/ʾaraq* in these Aramaic inscriptions and papyri can denote 'the earth' in contrast to heavens in the designation of gods: 'and the gods of heaven[s and the god]s of earth' (*KAI* 202B.25f.)[18]; '[the gods of] Heaven and Earth and Beelshmayn' (*KAI* 266.1-3 = *TAD* A1.1.1-3). In *KAI* 244 there appears an expression 'Beelshmayn, the Creator of the earth' (line 3; cf. *KAI* 26A+B, III.18f.; *KAI* 129.1).[19] In an inscription from Sefire, the pair of *ʾaraq* and *šemayin* is regarded as the place in which all the creatures exist: '(And) [may Ha]dad [pour (over it)] every sort of evil (which exists) on earth and in heaven and every sort of trouble' (*KAI* 222A.25f.).[20]

ʾaraq as the earth was regarded as consisting of four parts: 'from the exit of the sun to the setting place and [from ...] the four quarters of the earth (רבעתארק)' (*KAI* 215.13f.); 'Tiglatpileser, the Lord of the four quarters of the earth (רבעי ארק)' (*KAI* 216.3f.; 217.1f.).[21]

The term *ʾaraq* can be used as designation of a territorial 'land'. It can be defined by the name of a place: 'the land of *yʾdy*' (*KAI* 215.5, 7).[22] It can be defined by a pronominal suffix, as well (*KAI* 222A.28; 222B.27; 224.6).

15. Cf. Num. 33.53, 55; Deut. 11.31; 12.29; 19.1; 26.1; Josh. 21.43.

16. *KAI* 202 (Afis); *KAI* 214 (Zenjirli, middle eighth century BCE); *KAI* 215 (Zenjirli, second half of eighth century BCE); *KAI* 216 (Zenjirli, second half of eighth century BCE); *KAI* 217 (Zenjirli, between 733/32 and 727 BCE); *KAI* 222 (Sefire, middle eighth century BCE, before 740 BCE); *KAI* 223 (Sefire, middle eighth century BCE, before 740 BCE); *KAI* 224 (Sefire, middle eighth century BCE, before 740 BCE); *KAI* 244 (Hatra, first–second century CE).

17. *TAD* A1.1 = *KAI* 266 (604/3 BCE); *TAD* A6.15 (late fifth century BCE); *TAD* B8.10 (fifth century BCE); *TAD* C1.1 (second half of fifth century BCE); *TAD* D23.1.Va (early fifth century BCE inscription).

18. Cf. Gibson 1971–82: II, 6–17.

19. We have here רעה as substitute for ארעה; see *KAI* II, 298.

20. *KAI* 222 = Fitzmyer 1967: no. I; Fitzmyer's translation (p. 15); cf. Gibson 1971–82: II, 18–56.

21. For this expression, see *KAI* II, 228; *CAD* VIII, 331f.; cf. also Isa. 11.12.

22. For יאדי, see *KAI* II, 214; Gibson 1971–82: II, 70.

Our term can be used in relation to its products: ‘the grain of the lands’ (*TAD* A6.15.6); ‘a land of barley ... [... a l]and of wheat and a land of garlic and a land of [...] they till the land and vineyard’ (*KAI* 214.5-7).[23] In the last line, the term *ʾaraq* is used with the verb עבד, which is never employed with Hebrew *ʾereṣ* in the Bible.[24] A similar use can be seen in an inscription from Sheikh Fadl Cave, which states: ‘and his/the land I shall sow (with salt)’ (*TAD* D23.1.Va. 13).[25] In this case, *ʾaraʿ* means a ‘field-estate’ possessed by an individual.

Once in the Ahiqar story from the Elephantine papyrus, the term refers to ‘the ground’: ‘Beautiful is the king to see like (the) sun (or: Shamash) and precious is his glory to (them that) tread upon the ground (as) *f*[ree]men (or: in tran[*quility*])’ (*TAD* C1.1 line 92).[26]

In a papyrus from Saqqarah, there appears the following statement: ‘not (barren?) land herein since as JOINT HOLDING we hold-(it)-as-heirs [...]’ (*TAD* B8.10).[27] Although the sentence remains unclear, the term *ʾaraʿ* here probably connotes one’s ‘estate’, a piece of land possessed by an individual.[28]

3.5. Nabataean Papyri

In Nabataean papyri there appears twice an expression ארע חררה ‘arid land’ (*TJD* Naḥal Ḥever 2.6; 3.7). The term *ʾaraʿ*, therefore, can refer to an area characterized by its physical features.

In a papyrus dating from 94 CE there appears the phrase על אנפי ארעא ‘on the surface of earth’ in contrast to heavens (*TJD* Naḥal Ḥever 1.33).

In another papyrus from 99 CE mention is made of ארע מר[אנ]א ‘the land of [ou]r lord’, which was a land-estate possessed personally by the Nabataean king (*TJD* Naḥal Ḥever 2.4f.). In another papyrus there appears a phrase ארען ‘land-parcels’ (*TJD* Naḥal Ḥever 1.21). The term *ʾaraʿ*, therefore, can convey the sense of ‘estate’, a piece of land possessed by an individual.

3.6. Conclusion

The terms *ʾrṣ* and *ʾaraʿ*/*ʾaraq* in non-Jewish inscriptions and papyri can signify ‘the earth’ in contrast to heavens, in particular, in the designation of gods (*KAI* 26A+B, III.18; 202B.25f.; 244.3). A god is entitled as the Creator of the earth (*KAI* 26A+B,

23. *TAD*’s translation; cf. Deut. 8.8.

24. Cf. above § 2.5.1 (pp. 36f.) and below § 4.2.1.1 (pp. 53f. and n. 29 there).

25. *TAD*’s translation.

26. *TAD*’s translation, except the rendering of our term. Although the text is found among the Elephantine papyri, we treat it here, since it seems not to be of Jewish origin; see *HJP* III, 232–9.

27. *TAD* B8.10 = J. B. Segal 1983: nos. 3+16; *TAD*’s translation.

28. Cf. our argument at the end of § 2.7.2 above (and n. 420 there).

III.18; 129.1; 244.3). Thus, heavens and earth represent the entire created world (*KAI* 27.13-15; 222A.26; 266.1f.). The idea that the earth (and heavens) is the created world is close to the biblical Creation theology.

Our terms can also represent the entire earthly world, especially in the expression of 'four quarters of the earth' in relation to the Assyrian imperial power (*KAI* 215.14; 216.4; 217.2). This connotation seems to be similar to some biblical uses of 'the ends of the earth', in which it is expected that the king of Israel may rule over the entire world.[29]

The terms can represent a territorial 'land', as well. They can be defined by the name of a place (*KAI* 26A, I.4f.; II.15f.; 181.7f., 10; 215.5, 7), a topographic characteristic (*KAI* 14.16, 18; *TJD* Naḥal Ḥever 2.6; 3.7), and an epithetic noun (*KAI* 15). They can signify *the* land with or without the determinative article (*KAI* 10.10; 14.20; 19.9f.; 26A, I.8f.; 43.6; 181.28f., 31; 214. 5-7). They can be defined by pronominal suffixes, as well (*KAI* 181.4-6; 222A.27f., B.25-28; 224.6). The plural form is also usual (*KAI* 14.19; 26A, I.18; 141.1; 161.2). The terms also can be qualified by their product (*KAI* 14.19; *TAD* A6.15.6). They can also signify an 'estate' possessed by an individual (*TAD* B8.10; *TJD* Naḥal Ḥever 1.21; 2.4f.).

It is interesting to see the territorial concerns of the governors who left these inscriptions. The inscriptions from Karatepe (*KAI* 26) and Sidon (*KAI* 14) reveal that the governors were strongly concerned with the possession and expansion of their territories. Their acquisition of the territory is legitimated either by their good deeds or by a deity. Mesha inscription provides us with a background of the use of the terms *yāraš* and *yāšab* in the biblical Land-theology. The two New Punic inscriptions show the inhabitants' attachment to their land as the 'fatherland' (*KAI* 121; 126).

The biblical theologies regarding *ʾereṣ*, both the Creation theology and the Land theology, and Jewish attachment to the Land of Israel in later periods can be understood within these broader cultural environments.

29. Pss. 2.8; 72.8; cf. Chapter 2 n. 123 above.

Chapter 4

Before the Maccabaean Revolt

In this chapter we shall treat Hebrew/Aramaic Palestinian writings from the period before the Maccabaean revolt (*c.* 333–167 BCE).[1] These are: (1) the Astronomical Book (*1 Enoch* 72–82), (2) the Book of Watchers (*1 Enoch* 1–36), (3) Sirach, and (4) the Epistle of Enoch (*1 Enoch* 91–107). Other small fragmentary writings shall be mentioned only briefly at the end.

*4.1. The Astronomical Book (*1 Enoch *72–82)*

1 Enoch, known as the Ethiopic Book of Enoch, is now recognized as a composite work consisting of at least five independent books, all dating from different periods. We shall deal with them individually in their likely historical settings.[2] Now we are concerned with the third section of *1 Enoch*, the Astronomical Book (chs 72–82), which can be dated in the third century BCE or earlier.[3]

The discovery at Qumran of Aramaic fragments of *1 Enoch* demonstrates that Aramaic was the original language of its major parts.[4] These fragments, as well as general equivalence of the terms, demonstrate the retroversion of Aramaic *ʾaraʿ* from Ethiopic *medr* (and Greek γῆ).[5] In Palestinian Aramaic generally other

1. We do not deal with the following works: *Prayer of Nabonidus*, *Epistle of Jeremiah*, and the book of Tobit, which are of diaspora origins, and Demetrius' *On the Kings in Judaea*, *Artapanus*, *Pseudo-Eupolemus*, and *Fragments of Pseudo-Greek Poets*, which are originally written in Greek.

2. For *1 Enoch* generally, see Charles 1912; Milik 1976; Knibb 1978; Greenfield and Stone 1979a; Stone 1984: 395–406; VanderKam 1984a; Black 1985; *HJP* III, 250–68; Kvanvig 1988; García Martínez and Tigchelaar 1989–90; García Martínez 1992: 45–96; Nickelsburg 2001: 1–125.

3. For a third century BCE date, see Greenfield and Stone 1979a: 93; Beckwith 1981; Nickelsburg 1981a: 47; 2005: 44; VanderKam 1984a: 79–88; *HJP* III, 254f.; García Martínez 1992: 54; for a Persian date of the Astronomical Book, see Milik 1976: 8; Kvanvig 1988: 154–8, 329–34; Neugebauer (in Black 1985: 387); Nickelsburg 1992a: 509; 2001: 25. Chapter 80 of *1 Enoch* is probably a later addition; see VanderKam 1984a: 78; cf. Charles 1912: 147f.; Albani 1994: 33–6, 129–34; García Martínez 1992: 57. The addition may be dated from the first century CE (see Chapter 7 nn. 32, 166 below). For ch. 81, see § 4.4 and n. 105 below.

4. Knibb 1978: II, 6f.

5. See 'Aramaic-Greek-Ethiopic Glossary' of Milik 1976 (pp. 369f., 398, 405). For uses of Ethiopic *ʿālam* in the Astronomical Book, see § 7.2.4 below.

synonymous terms תבל and אדמה are scarcely used,[6] so 'the earth' and 'land' can be expressed virtually only by *ʾaraʿ*.[7]

4.1.1. medr/ʾaraʿ *in the Astronomical Book*

Since the Astronomical Book is 'the book of the revolution of the lights of heaven' (72.1), it is natural that the term *medr/*ʾaraʿ* in it is used in contrast to heaven, the firmament: 'they (all the lights of heaven) might rule on the face of heaven (= 'firmament'),[8] and appear over the earth' (75.3).[9] The firmament is attached to the ends of the earth, where Enoch saw twelve gates open to celestial bodies (75.6)[10] and to all the winds (76.1).[11] The *medr/*ʾaraʿ* contrasted to the firmament implies the earth including the sea. It forms a half part of the universe (cf. § 2.2.2 above).

In 77.3b-8//4QEnastr[b] 23.8-10, however, *medr/ʾaraʿ* is geographically viewed as *terra firma* in contrast to mountains, rivers, seas, and islands.[12] In 82.9-20 Enoch tells 'the signs of the days on earth' of four seasons.[13] The term *medr/*ʾaraʿ* here virtually means the habitable world. Furthermore, in 4QEnastr[d] 1.i.2-3 there is assumed the productivity of *ʾaraʿ* by the cooperation with rain (l. 2), and עשב ארעא 'grass of the earth' is referred to (l. 3). Likewise, there appears in 82.19 a phrase 'the fruits of the earth', equivalent to Hebrew פרי הארץ/האדמה in the Bible, in which, though, the expression usually refers to 'the fruits of the Land'.[14]

According to the sequence of the narrative, Enoch's eyes turn from upper heaven down to the earth, to its geographical features and its natural ability as soil. The *medr/*ʾaraʿ* in the Astronomical Book is conceived empirically as a part of an everlasting cosmos in which creatures circulate between death and rebirth. In 4QEnastr[c] 1.ii.1-2 (*//1 En.* 76.4) it is stated: '[... And from four of them the winds depart which] are for the healing of the earth (לרפיא ארעא)

6. In Sokoloff's dictionary of Palestinian Aramaic, there is no entry of *tēbēl* (Sokoloff 1990; cf. Jastrow 1903: 1644); among the Dead Sea Scrolls the Aramaic *tēbēl* is attested only in the Targum of Job (*DSSC* II, 940; see n. 12 below). For Aramaic *ʾadmâ* Sokoloff refers only to two passages from Targum Neophyti (Sokoloff 1990: 36; cf. Jastrow 1903: 17), and there is no attestation in the Dead Sea Scrolls (see pp. 53f. and n. 29 below). These two Aramaic terms are attested only in targums.

7. Since the reconstruction of Aramaic *ʾaraʿ* from Ethiopic and/or Greek translations is generally certainp., we do not try to explain all occurrences of *medr*/γῆ in *1 Enoch*.

8. For Ethiopic *gaṣṣa samāy*, see Leslau 1989: 213.

9. Translation of Knibb (1978). Cf. 75.4; 4QEnastr[c] 1.ii.17f.; cf. also Gen. 1.15, 17; 19.23.

10. Cf. Jer. 10.13; 51.16; Ps. 135.7; cf. *1 En.* 77.3.

11. Cf. Job 37.17; 38.24.

12. ארעא is attested in 4QEnastr[b] 23.8. Milik (1976: 289) reconstructs על תבלא (line 10) from Ethiopic *westa medr* (77.4), but this is unlikely, since Aramaic use of *tēbēl* is scarcely attested (cf. n. 6 above).

13. Although the Ethiopic version seems to be corrupted, it is suggested by 4QEnastr[d] that the original text might narrate of all the four seasons.

14. Cf. Chapter 2 nn. 273, 382; but see Gen. 4.3: פרי האדמה 'the fruits of the earth'.

and its revitalization.'[15] The latter phrase indicates a cycle of death and rebirth in the empirical earthly world. The universal perspective expressed in this phrase contrasts with a similar biblical phrase רפא את הארץ which signifies the healing of the Land.[16]

4.1.2. Summary

The uses of *medr*/*ʾaraʿ* in the Astronomical Book lack any politico-nationalistic territorial dimensions. This corresponds with its general peaceful tone. It lacks any antagonism towards foreign nations or towards any circle within the Jewish community.[17] It may reflect the milieu of the Astronomical Book, a relatively peaceful age of the Land.

*4.2. The Book of Watchers (*1 Enoch *1–36)*

The Book of Watchers is a collection of traditions, and can be divided into five sections: (1) introduction (chs 1–5), (2) the myth of the Watchers' rebellion (chs 6–11), (3) Enoch's commissioning as a prophet of judgement (chs 12–16), (4) Enoch's first journey (chs 17–19), and (5) Enoch's second journey (chs 20–36).[18] The second section is the oldest, and the third section serves as a commentary to the second. The fourth presumes the third, and the fifth acknowledges the fourth. The first section serves as an introduction to the whole Book of Watchers.[19]

Since the Book of Watchers is a composite work of diverse traditions from different periods, it is convenient to study separately uses of our term in each section, and finally to summarize them.[20]

We have a nearly complete Greek translation of the Book of Watchers and Aramaic fragments from Qumran, along with the Ethiopic version. The comparison of these texts assures the general equivalence of Aramaic *ʾaraʿ* to Greek γῆ and Ethiopic *medr*.

15. *DSSSE*'s translation.

16. 2 Chron. 7.14; Ps. 60.4; cf. *1 En.* 10.7.

17. See VanderKam 1984a: 90f.

18. The division is according to Nickelsburg 1992a: II, 509–11; cf. Nickelsburg 1981a: 48–55; 2001: 7, 25; 2005: 46–52; cf. also Charles 1912: 1f.; VanderKam 1984a: 110.

19. Nickelsburg 1981a: 48–55; 2005: 47.

20. The composition of the Book of Watchers dates from the third century BCE; see Stone 1978: 484; VanderKam 1984a: 111–14. In this section I use Nickelsburg's translation (2001), with modifications.

4.2.1. γῆ/medr/ʾaraʿ *in the Book of Watchers*

4.2.1.1. Chapters 6–11

The term γῆ/*medr*/*ʾaraʿ* in this portion can mean the *terra firma*, the dry solid part of the earth. A reference is made to 'the metals of the earth' (8.1 [Gr. Sync]), which Asael showed men and taught them how to make jewellery and ornaments for the beautification of women. The Watchers taught them 'the signs of the earth' (נחש[י] ארע), as well as the signs of the lightening flashes (*1 En.* 8.3 [Gr. Sync]//4QEn^{b} 1.iii.1-5). The signs probably refer to terrestrial phenomena of prognostication in relation to magical arts.[21]

In chs 6–11 there is a narration of evil deeds of the Watchers coming from heaven down to the earth.[22] Our term, therefore, signifies the earthly world in contrast to the heavenly world. Michael, Sariel, Raphael and Gabriel looked down from heaven 'upon the earth' (9.1). In 4QEn^{b} 1.iii.10a-10 (//*1 En.* 9.8; cf. 10.7; 11.1) preserved is a phrase בני ארעא 'the sons of the earth',[23] which is contrasted to 'the sons of heaven', i.e., angels (6.2). The 'valleys of the earth'[24] is assigned to the prison of Shemihazah and his associates (10.11f.; cf. 10.4f.), and the existence of the netherworld seems to be assumed, as suggested in 9.10.

γῆ/*ʾaraʿ* representing the earthly world is described in chs 6–11 as full of bloodshed and iniquity.[25] It is stated that when Giants turned against men, 'the earth brought accusation against the lawless ones' (7.6). Here the term γῆ/*ʾaraʿ* represents 'men' (8.4) and 'the souls of men' (9.3).[26] Then God decides to renew the earth, saying: 'that the whole earth will perish' and 'a deluge is about to come on the whole earth and destroy everything on the earth' (10.2; cf. Gen. 6.13, 17). The first 'whole earth' again represents all human beings (except Noah and his family), as suggested by its replacement of 'all flesh' in Gen. 6.13.

Then God commands to Raphael to 'heal the earth' and to 'announce the healing of the earth' (10.7), and to Michael to 'destroy all perversity from the face of the earth' (10.16) and to 'cleanse the earth from all iniquity' (10.20); then, 'all the earth will be tilled in righteousness' (10.18) and 'all the earth will be cleansed from all defilement and from all uncleanness' (10.22; see 10.11–11.2). The expression 'from the face of the earth' (10.16) is probably derived from מעל פני האדמה of Gen. 6.7 (cf. Gen. 7.4), though *ʾaraʿ* must be used in Aramaic instead of *ʾadmâ*, since the latter is seldom in use (probably, *מן אנפי ארעא; cf. *Apocr. Gen.* 4.12).[27] The idea 'all the earth will be tilled' (10.18) is probably taken from Gen. 9.20 in which Noah

21. See Nickelsburg 2001: 197–201.

22. For source-critical studies of chs 6–11, see Hanson 1977; Nickelsburg 1977a, 2001: 165–73; cf. Newsom 1980.

23. See Milik 1976: 171; Greek and Ethiopic have 'the earth' instead.

24. Greek reading; Ethiopic: 'beneath the hills of the earth'. Aramaic *ʾarʿaʾ* is legible in 4QEn^{b} 1.iv.11.

25. *1 En.* 8.2, 4 (//4QEn^{a} 1.iv.5//4QEn^{b} 1.iii.5f.); 9.1, 6, 9, 10; 10.8, 20.

26. In 9.2 Ethiopic *medr* represents human beings, though the text is uncertain; see Nickelsburg 2001: 203 n. 2b.

27. See n. 6 above; Milik 1976: 189.

is called איש האדמה.[28] Here, too, the Aramaic must have ʾ*ara*ʿ instead of ʾ*admâ*. In the Bible, as we have seen, the Hebrew ʾ*ereṣ* is never employed with the verb עבד 'to till', which is used with ʾ*adāmâ* (§§ 2.1.3; 2.5.1). In Aramaic, however, ʾ*ara*ʿ is normally used with פלח 'to till' (probably, *תתפלח כול ארעא).[29] The original Aramaic phrase behind 'to heal the earth' in 10.7 must be *רפא לארעא because of a wordplay with the name of the angel רפאל. The same phrase is used in the Astronomical Book (4QEnastr^{c} 1.ii.1-2//*1 En.* 76.4), in which it designates a seasonal shift of the productivity of the earth. In the Bible the clause רפא את הארץ signifies 'to heal the Land'.[30] In contrast, in *1 En.* 10.7 it is the last, decisive and eternal healing of the earth. Similarly, the cleansing of ʾ*ereṣ* is known from the Bible, in which, though, it means the cleansing of the Land.[31] Here (*1 En.* 10.20, 22) the cleansing of the earth has universal eschatological dimensions. An eschatological expectation is expressed in these passages, despite the description of the antediluvian world.

The last point is well summarized by Nickelsburg, who comments that the author 'is utilizing an *Urzeit-Endzeit* typology, according to which the judgment and new beginning in Noah's time are a prototype of the final judgment and new age'.[32] The eschatological expectation reveals that the antediluvian evil described in chs 6–11 reflects the author's actual experience of it in the Land.[33] It was the situation of his days that there was 'much bloodshed in the Land', and 'all the Land was filled with the godlessness and violence that had befallen it' (9.1); 'the whole Land is filled with iniquity' (9.9); the groan 'does not cease to come forth from before the iniquities that have come in the Land' (9.10). The 'healing' (10.7) and 'cleansing' (10.22) of the Land were, in fact, a hope of the people. The bitter experience seems to have been caused by foreign powers, as suggested by the reference to 'the peoples' (10.21) and to 'the plant of righteousness' symbolizing Israel (10.16, cf. *1 En.* 93.2, 5, 10).[34] The statements that 'all the earth will be tilled in righteousness' (10.18) and that 'all the sons of men will become righteous, and all the peoples will worship (Me)' (10.21) express the nationalistic hope of Israel's dominion over the whole world. This renewed world will be blessed by abundant fruits (10.19; 11.1f.), and human beings will live long in it (10.17). Thus, the term γῆ/*medr*/*ʾ*ara*ʿ in chs 6–11, which on the surface of the narrative denotes the antediluvian world, also implicitly expresses the reality of the Land of the author's days, on the one hand,

28. See Nickelsburg 2001: 227.

29. *Apocr. Gen.* 12.13, which is a paraphrase of Gen. 9.20. In Targum Onkelos the term *pālaḥ* is normally employed with ʾ*ara*ʿ; in Gen. 9.20 Noah is called גבל פלח בארעא; in Gen. 4.2 the Aramaic פלח בארעא is applied to Hebrew עֹבד אדמה. Cf. *KAI* 214.5-7: יעבדו ארק (§ 3.4 above).

30. 2 Chron. 7.14; Ps. 60.4.

31. Ezek. 39.12, 14, 16; 2 Chron. 34.8.

32. Nickelsburg 1977a: 388; cf. Hanson 1977: 288.

33. Cf. Nickelsburg 1977a: 388f.

34. Nickelsburg (1977a: 390f.) ascribes the experience to the wars of the Diadochi (323–302 BCE).

spelling the postdiluvian world in the narrative context, it intends an eschatological new world equated with the maximal Israel, on the other.

4.2.1.2. Chapters 12–16

Chapters 12–16 presuppose and elaborate upon chs 6–11.[35] In chs 12–16 our term is used in contrast to the heavenly world that the Watchers left. They are called ‘the sons of heaven’ (13.8; 14.3; cf. 6.2) in contrast to ‘the sons of the earth’, i.e., human beings (12.4 [Gr.]; 15.3).[36] This contrast is explicitly recounted in 15.5-7. Since, however, by mingling with earthly women, the Watchers have violated the created order which distinguishes between the heavenly realm and the earthly one (15.3f.), and ‘they wrought great desolation on the earth’ (12.5; cf. 16.3), they are not permitted to ‘ascend into heaven’ and are to be bound ‘in the earth’ (14.5).[37] Furthermore, an explanation is given that the giants are the origins of evil spirits on the earth (15.8-10). The five occurrences of the term γῆ/**ʾaraʿ* in these three verses reflect the author’s actual concerns for the world where he was living. In the following verse the activities of the evil spirits are described as follows: ‘And the spirits of the giants <lead astray>, do violence, make desolate, and attack and wrestle and hurl upon the earth and <cause illness>’ (15.11).[38] Despite such terminology as ‘attack and wrestle and hurl’, there is no mention of ‘bloodshedding’, which is a major problem in chs 6–11. It seems that the problems in chs 12–16 are spiritual rather than physical violence. Naming the giants ‘evil spirits’ suggests a shift of historical situation of chs 12–16 from that of chs 6–11. In the latter, as we have seen above, the opponents of the author are foreign powers, whereas in the former, the narrator seems to face domestic problems.[39]

4.2.1.3. Chapters 17–19

A detailed construction of the earth is described in chs 17–18: mention is made of ‘the mouth of all the rivers of the earth and the mouth of the abyss’ at the north-western end of the earth (17.8), ‘the foundations of the earth’ (18.1; cf. 18.12; 21.2), and ‘the cornerstone of the earth’ (18.2; cf. Job 38.6); the earth and the firmament are supported by four winds (18.2f.), which are ‘the pillars of heaven’ (18.3; cf. Job 26.11); the winds bear the clouds upon the earth (18.5a). The earth can be called ἡ μεγάλη γῆ, at whose edge the heavens come to an end (18.10). The firmament of heaven is attached to ‘the ends of the earth’ (18.5b), as in the Astronomical Book (75.6; 76.1-14). Here γῆ/**ʾaraʿ* forms a half part of the universe, God’s creation.

Enoch also saw at the end of heaven and earth a place assigned to ‘a prison for the stars of heaven and the host of heaven’ (18.12-14). They are imprisoned

35. Nickelsburg (2001: 230) dates these chapters between 300 and 250 BCE.

36. Cf. 4QEn^{b} 1.iii.10a-10 [//*1En.* 9.8]; *1 En.* 10.7; 11.1; cf. 4QEn^{g} 1.iv.20 [//*1 En.* 91.14]; *1 En.* 100.6; 102.3; 105.1.

37. See Nickelsburg 2001: 269–72.

38. For textual problems, see Knibb 1978: II, 101f.; Nickelsburg 2001: 268, 273f.

39. Cf. Nickelsburg 1981b: 586; 2001: 230f.

there since they 'transgressed the command of the Lord' (18.15). These stars are employed, of course, as a metaphor of the author's opponents, who go 'astray to sacrifice to demons as to gods' (19.1). They must be idolatrous Jews who transgress God's law. Here, too, the author faces domestic problems, as the narrator of chs 12–16 does.

4.2.1.4. Chapters 20–36

In chs 20–36 our term is used in relation to the cosmography. Enoch journeys to 'the ends of the earth' (23.1; 33.1, 2; 34.1; 35.1; 36.1): towards the western ends Enoch saw a chaotic place which has 'neither heaven above nor firmly founded earth', where is the place of punishment for the disobedient stars (21.2; cf. 18.12); at the ends of four directions he saw the gates of heaven, from which winds blow (33.2; 34.2; 35.1; 36.1f.; cf. 75.6; 76.1-14). It is assumed that Mt Zion is at 'the center of the earth' (26.1; cf. Ezek. 38.12), and it is called a 'blessed land' (27.1).

γῆ/*'*ara*ʿ as *terra firma* is assigned as the burial place (22.10), and perishing 'from the face of the earth' means death (22.7).

Our term also represents the earthly world in contrast to heaven. God will 'visit the earth' to carry out the final judgement (25.3). While the idea of eschatological God's 'visitation' is known from the Bible,[40] the expression 'God will visit the earth' appears here for the first time, an expression which became traditional in later Palestinian Jewish writings.[41] 'Then', it is stated, 'they (the chosen) will live a long life upon the earth, such as your fathers lived also in their days' (25.6b; cf. 10.17). The earth here connotes this earthly world compared with the netherworld prepared for the souls of dead (ch. 22). This eschatology does not include such hopes as the resurrection of the dead or the eternal life,[42] but is restricted to a happy long life in this world and worship of God in Jerusalem.

In chs 20–36 no reference is made to the fallen Watchers, the giants or the evil spirits narrated in chs 6–19. Rather, there appears a contrast between the righteous and the sinners. These sinners, who must be the opponents of our author, are 'all the cursed, who utter with their mouth an improper word against the Lord and speak hard things against His glory' (27.2). They seem to be Jews who, in our author's view, are blasphemous (cf. 1.9; 5.4).

4.2.1.5. Chapters 1–5

Our term represents God's creative work, and its stability is assumed in 2.2–4.1 (//4QEn[c] 1.i.20-27//4QEn[a] 1.ii.1-9).[43] γῆ/*medr*/*'ara*ʿ is in its firm stability understood as a model of the best observant of God's law in contrast to human disobedience (2.1–5.3).[44] Nevertheless, the earth from an eschatological point of view swerves from its stability on 'the day of tribulation' (1.1); in the face of the theophany,

40. E.g., Isa. 10.3; 24.22; 29.6; Jer. 6.15; 8.12; 10.15; Hos. 9.7; Mic. 7.4; cf. Sir. 18.20.
41. See Chapter 8 n. 33 below.
42. But cf. Nickelsburg 2001: 315.
43. Cf. Gen. 8.22, see also Chapter 2 nn. 66–8 above.
44. Cf. Nickelsburg 2001: 152–5.

'the earth will be wholly rent asunder, and everything on the earth will perish, and there will be judgment on all' (1.7; cf. Mic. 1.4; Isa. 24.19f.). In 1.5 mention is made of 'all the ends of the earth' twice. Milik reconstructs its original Aramaic as *כל קצות ארעה (4QEn^{a} 1.i.6-7),[45] and translates it as 'all the creatures (?) of the earth', since he considers that the expression 'is to be understood as "the totality of the creatures, especially men, living on earth"'.[46] The expression '(all) the ends of the earth' can represent the human world and the whole population of the world, as the biblical phrase כל אפסי ארץ does.[47] If Milik's reconstruction of the text is by and large correct, or the original text intends the judgement of all humanity as suggested by 'all' (1.7) and 'all flesh' (1.9), the phrase is to represent the whole of humanity in the world.[48]

In 5.7 there appears an expression well known in the biblical Land theology: 'and they (the chosen) will take possession of *ʾ*araʿ*'.[49] Although the part including this verse is missing from the Aramaic fragments at Qumran, the Greek/Ethiopic phrase κληρονομέω τὴν γῆν/*warasa lamedr* must reflect the Aramaic *ירת לארעא, an expression equivalent to the biblical ירש את הארץ referring technically to 'the Land possession' in the context of promise.[50] The γῆ/*medr*/*ʾ*araʿ* here, however, must intend, not 'the Land', but 'the earth', since it will be possessed by the chosen after 'the day of distress' (1.1) when 'there will be judgment upon all' (1.7), and the worldwide scope of the narrative is apparent from the use of 'all the ends of the earth' (1.5). Accordingly, an eschatological 'earth' is the γῆ/*medr*/*ʾ*araʿ* that will be possessed by the chosen.

The narrator of chs 1–5 reinterprets the biblical Land-theology in a universal eschatological perspective. This does not mean that he was a universalist. The term 'chosen' as his self-designation and the reference to 'you' (5.4-7) as his opponents, show that the narrator is governed by *intra*-national interests. The mention of 'all flesh' (1.9) without international perspectives suggests that foreign nations are out of his scope. The worldview revealed in the uses of γῆ/*medr*/*ʾ*araʿ* in these chapters is narrower than the biblical *ʾereṣ*. As we summarized above (§ 2.6), the term *ʾereṣ* in the Bible is applied to express the relationships between God-Israel-nations. Here the term γῆ/*medr*/*ʾ*araʿ* expresses the relationships between God-the chosen (within Jews)-sinners (within Jews). This domestic scope can be an indication of the historical milieu of the narrator and his group.

45. Milik 1976: 142; see Sokoloff (1979: 199, 205), who suggests the reading *קצוי instead of *קצות. There is no attestation from the Dead Sea Scrolls of קצות ארעא, while we have קצוי ארעא in 4Q541 9.i.4 and 11Q10 13.5; see *DSSC* 918.

46. Milik 1976: 145; cf. Sokoloff 1979: 205.

47. See Chapter 2 n. 121 above.

48. Nickelsburg (2001: 142, 146) reconstructs the text differently, but not so convincing; cf. VanderKam 1973: 139–44; Knibb 1978: II, 59.

49. A Greek manuscript repeats this phrase in 5.6, 8.

50. See Chapter 2 n. 227 above.

4.2.2. Summary

The uses of the term γῆ/*medr*/*ʾ*ara*ʿ in the Book of Watchers are close to those of ʾ*ereṣ* in the Bible. It signifies the earth as a half part of the created universe and the earthly world in contrast to the heavenly one and the netherworld, and represents the human world. There is, however, no explicit reference to the Land.

Chapters 6–11, the oldest portion, pursue two main topics: the origins of evil and an eschatological vision. The first reveals the hard situation of the Land, oppressed by foreign powers who are compared to the giants. The author's hope expressed in the second is the destruction of the oppressors and the triumph of maximal Israel over the whole world. Here the term γῆ/*medr*/*ʾ*ara*ʿ expresses relationships between God-Israel-nations, as ʾ*ereṣ* in the Bible. The author was an apocalyptic nationalist in the sense that he tried to overcome a national crisis in terms of eschatological hope.

This first subject is further pursued by the following two sections. The narrator of chs 12–16 interprets the 'giants' as 'evil spirits'. By so doing, he opens a way to identify them with his opponents within Jews. The editor of chs 17–19 sees the evil spirits as idolatrous Jews. The final judgement against them is expected. The second theme is treated in the last and the first sections. In chs 20–36, which are governed by geographical interests of the earth, there are expected a blessed long life of the righteous and their worship of God in Jerusalem at the *eschaton*. The author of chs 1–5 reinterprets a well known biblical phrase ירש את הארץ from a universal perspective.

These four sections express the authors' concerns regarding the structure of the whole universe and the final judgement of 'all flesh'. Their universal inclination seems to be apparent. Nevertheless, they lack international perspectives, since their opponents are the sinners among Jews (although there were influences of foreign politics and culture behind them). The universal appearances without international concerns can be a result of their attempts to cope with the domestic problems by developing the universal soteriology known from chs 6–11. Consequently, their intra-national issues were expressed by universal wordings. One of such terms is ʾ*ara*ʿ, which now expresses the relationships between God-the chosen (within Jews)-the sinners (within Jews). The authors of these four sections were neither nationalists who represented national interests, nor universalists who were concerned for all human beings indifferent to nationality. They were sectarians who complained about the then national authority who, in their eyes, disturbed the orders of this created cosmos.[51]

51. The Book of Watchers attests to the emergence of sectarian movements in Palestine of the third century BCE; see Stone 1978.

4.3. Sirach

The original language of Sirach was Hebrew. This is shown by discoveries of Hebrew fragments of Sirach from Cairo Geniza, Qumran and Masada,[52] along with explicit attestation in the Prologue to the Greek translation by Ben Sira's grandson (vv. 21-22). The Hebrew documents unearthed up to now cover approximately two thirds of the original. The complete text of Sirach is transmitted to us through Greek and Syriac, both of which were translated from Hebrew. The text used in our arguments must be eclectic, and textual problems will be noted where necessary.

4.3.1. γῆ/ʾereṣ *in Sirach*

In chs 1 and 24, praising the greatness of creation, Ben Sira assumes a tripartite division of the created universe into οὐρανός/*שמים 'heaven', γῆ/*ʾ*ereṣ* 'earth', and ἄβυσσος/*תהום 'abyss'.[53] The heaven and the earth represent God's creation. They form the 'receptacle' in which living things would be created (16.29f.). Created in an eternal order, the receptacle is regarded as the best observer of God's words (16.26-28; cf. 42.15–43.26).[54] Unusual natural phenomena are considered manifestations of God's might on the earth (16.18f.; 43.15, 17a, 16a).

Distinguishing the term (מרום(ים 'heavenly height(s)' from שמים, and שאול 'Hades' from תהום, our author shows his knowledge of a threefold world consisting of *mārôm/merômîm*, ʾ*ereṣ* and *šeʾôl*. The term *mārôm/merômîm* is used mostly in reference to the abode of God and Wisdom,[55] and *šeʾôl* to the mortality of living beings.[56] However, Ben Sira does not elaborate on these concepts. The contrast between *mārôm* and ʾ*ereṣ* in 40.11 (Heb.) demonstrates human mortality compared with the eternity of Wisdom.[57] The two terms are once employed to praise Solomon (47.15). ʾ*ereṣ*, one-third of the universe, therefore, can denote the human-earthly world (48.15; 49.14). As in the Bible, the phrase כל אפסי ארץ can represent the whole human populace (36.22).[58]

ʾ*ereṣ* is once employed to express the underground, from which Samuel lifted up his voice in prophecy (46.20; cf. 1 Sam. 28.3-19). It of course can mean the tangible ground, as well (47.22 [Heb.]; 50.17).[59] Ben Sira assumes the productivity of plants

52. See *HJP* III, 208f.; cf. also Talmon and Yadin 1999: 233–52.

53. Sir. (1.3 [cf. Job 38.5-18]); 16.18; (24.3-6); the brackets indicate verses without Hebrew attestation (henceforth the same in this section). See also nn. 55–6 below.

54. Cf. Jer. 33.25; Job 38.33.

55. To *mārôm/merômîm* three Greek words are applied; ὑψηλός: (24.4); ὕψος: 16.17; (17.32; 27.25); 43.1, 8; ὕψιστος: 26.16; 43.9; *šāmayim* is always translated into οὐρανός; see M. Z. Segal 1958; Academy 1973.

56. ᾅδης/*šeʾôl*: (9.12); 14.12, 16; (17.27; 21.10; 28.21); 41.4; 48.5; 51:6; ἄβυσσος/*tehôm*: (1.3); 16.18; (24.5, 29); 42.18; 43.23. But cf. 51.5: ᾅδης/[*teh*]*ôm*.

57. See 10.9; 16.30–17.1; 17.32; 33(Gr. 36).10.

58. See Chapter 2 n. 121 above.

59. Both in the form ארצה; cf. § 2.1.2 above.

of *ʾereṣ*, as well. Above all, he refers to medicines, which God brings forth from the earth (38.4; cf. *1 En*. 7.1; 8.3).

Along with tangible and cosmological uses of *ʾereṣ*, Ben Sira knows of territorial ones. Reviewing Israelite history, he uses a well known biblical phrase: 'a land flowing with milk and honey' (46.8).[60] Once he calls the Land במתי ארץ 'high places of the earth' (46.9). Mention is made of עם הארץ in 50.19, in which it refers to ordinary Jews as distinct from the priests and Levites.[61]

4.3.2. Passages in which the Referent of ʾereṣ *is Uncertain*[62]

4.3.2.1. Sirach 10.14-17

Sirach 10.6-18 warns readers against pride, referring to the proud king who shall be punished by God. There are close relationships between v. 8 and v. 14, which speak of 'sovereignty' and 'pride', and 'throne' and 'the proud', respectively. The reference to nations' uprootedness in v. 15 is induced by a wordplay between גאים and גוים. What is said in these passages is that nations (גוים) are proud (גאים), and so their sovereignty passes; ultimately it will be given to 'the afflicted' (v. 15) who are 'humble' (v. 14). The afflicted/humble are, of course, Israel, as in the Bible.[63] Warning generally against pride, Ben Sira expresses a nationalistic hope (cf. 35 [Gr. 32].23; 33 [Gr. 36].1-12; 39.23; 44.21).[64]

In this context we can understand vv. 16-17. Ben Sira hopes that 'the traces of nations God sweeps away, and their root to *ʾereṣ* He pulls up' (v. 16). The *ʾereṣ* here means the 'soil' with which the 'root' is pulled up in a metaphorical image of a tree. At the same time, however, it signifies their 'land'. God uproots the nations to their lands, so that 'He scours them from the world (*ʾereṣ*) and plucks them up and exterminates their memory from the world (*ʾereṣ*)' (v. 17).

4.3.2.2. Sirach 44.3a

This passage is included in the prologue to the 'Praise of the Fathers' (chs 44–50). Y. Yadin translates רודי ארץ במלכותם that '(men) who wielded dominion over the earth in their royalty'.[65] However, it seems implausible that the dominion over 'the earth' is intended here. The term רודים probably refers to kings of Israel.[66]

60. Cf. Chapter 2 n. 265. See also 48.15 (cf. Deut. 28.63f.; Prov. 2.22). In 45.22 we have a reference to the Land, but the text is uncertain (cf. Num. 18.20); see Segal 1958: 315 n. 39; Yadin 1965: 35f. (= Talmon and Yadin 1999: 193f.).

61. Cf. Segal 1958: 346.

62. English translation in this section is mine, otherwise noted.

63. עני(ם): 2 Sam. 22.28; Isa. 14.32; 26.6; 49.13; Pss. 9.19; 10.2, 9; 12.6; 14.6; 18.28; 22.25; 68.11; 69.30; 74.19, 21; Zeph. 3.12; ענוי(ם): Isa. 29.19; 61.1; Pss. 9.13; 10.12, 17; 69.33; 76.10; 147.6; 149.4; Zeph. 2.3.

64. Cf. Isa. 61.5-6; Psalms 9; 10; 22.28-30; 47; 72; 149.

65. Yadin 1965: 49 (= Talmon and Yadin 1999: 225).

66. See Segal 1958: 304.

Those who are enumerated in the Praise are David, Solomon, Rehoboam, Jeroboam, Hezekiah, and Josiah (47.1–49.4). They had dominion over 'the Land', and their royalty sometimes extended over, or was limited to part of, it. According to biblical narratives, there never were kings in the history of Israel who could wield the dominion over the earth. Such a king belongs to a nationalistic eschatological hope of Judaism.

It is certain that Ben Sira too shares a similar nationalistic hope. Quoting deliberately from various biblical passages, he refers to God's promise to Abraham in 44.21:

a. Thereupon in swear He established to him	b. to bless in his seed nations
c. [to multiple his seed like sands of the sea	d. and to set his seed high above all nations][67]
e. to allot them from sea to sea	f. and from the River to the ends of the earth.

The contents of the promise are slightly different from the biblical narrative in the book of Genesis. After enumerating in the promise the blessing of nations through Israel (21b//Gen. 22.18; cf. Gen. 18.18; 26.4) and progeny (21c//Gen. 22.17), our author quotes Deut. 26.19 (21d) which originally is not a promise to Abraham, but to Israel. This sudden quotation reveals that Ben Sira finds in the promise the primacy of Israel above the nations. Then, our author mentions the promise of the Land (21e-f). Notable is the quotation of 21e-f from Ps. 72.8//Zech. 9.10 (except the verb).[68] Ben Sira understands that the Land promised to Abraham is not limited to the land of Canaan (Gen. 17.8), nor to the land from the river of Egypt to the River Euphrates (Gen. 15.18), but extends to 'the ends of the earth'.[69] This ideology accords well with 21b-d, the primacy of Israel; God sets Israel highest above all the nations, and so He allots Israel the whole world. Ben Sira sees in the promise to Abraham God's election of Israel among nations (cf. Sir. 17.17; 24.6-12). He, therefore, chooses as his source Gen. 22.17-18 (21b-c) including the term גוים which distinguishes Israel from the other nations, rather than Gen. 12.2-3 holding instead a phrase 'all the families of the earth' which generalizes all the nations. The supremacy of Israel above the nations (21d) assures the possession of the world as its allotment (21e-f). This possession is understood politico-religiously, as evident from the reference to 'the nations' (cf. 10.14-17 we've just seen). Referring to the well-known promise to Abraham, Ben Sira expresses an eschatological nationalistic hope, which is explicitly described in the prayer of 36.1-22 (Gr. 33.1-13a+36.16b-22). In his eschatological description, however, Ben Sira does not assume that Israelites will live everywhere in the world. Rather he expects that the twelve tribes will be gathered together and take possession of their allotment 'as ancient days' (36.13 [Gr. 33.13a+36.16b]; cf. 44.22c-23). That is to say, Israel shall

67. Hebrew ms. B skips 21c-d. The text is restored according to Syriac which retains reading better than Greek; see Segal 1958: 306, 309; Reiterer 1980: 20f., 100–8.

68. Cf. Pss. 2.8; 72.8-11, 15-17; 111.6; Zech. 9.9-10; 1 Kgs 8.41-43; Mic. 7.11f.

69. This may suggest that Ben Sira interprets the biblical *ʾereṣ* of the promise (Gen. 12.7; 13.17; 15.18) in the sense of 'world'.

rule over the whole world, on the one hand, the twelve tribes of Israel shall live together in the Pentateuchal Land, on the other. Thus, two concepts of the promised Land coexist in Sirach: Israel will rule the world while living in the Land.

In his eschatological descriptions, however, Ben Sira does not give any role to a messianic king. It is probably because he prefers priestly leadership to royal (cf. 45.25). Why, then, does he praise רודי ארץ? It seems that here Ben Sira is nostalgic for the good old days, especially under David and Solomon, in comparison with his own days when foreign overlords rule Israel and Gentiles inhabit the Land (cf. 50.25f.).

4.3.2.3. Sirach 50.22-24

After the praise of Simon the High Priest, Ben Sira requires 'you' (pl. [v. 23]) to bless God 'who does wonder *bāʾāreṣ*' (v. 22a).[70] Verses 23-24 are connected with 45.25c-26, in which, too, 'you' (pl.) are mentioned in relation to Phinehas. In 45.24, in correspondence with 50.24, stated are 'a covenant of peace' established for Phinehas and 'the eternal High Priesthood' for his offspring. The 'you' in 45.25c-26 are undoubtedly the high priests, i.e., Simon and his seed. The 'you' of 50.23, to whom wisdom of heart is given as in 45.26, must be identical with them. The requirement 'bless' of v. 22a is, accordingly, to be addressed to them.[71] Then, God's 'wonder *bāʾāreṣ*' includes glorious Simon and his seed, the covenant of Phinehas with them, and their high priesthood enduring like the days of heaven. The location of the wonders is none other than 'the Land'. Nevertheless, it seems that Ben Sira intends here 'the earth'. This is evident from the general term *ʾādām* (22b), along with the reference to heaven (24d). Moreover, God's Creation is mentioned everywhere in the whole Sirach. This means that Ben Sira sees the wonders among Israel in relation to God's Creation.

4.3.2.4. Sirach 23.27

A reconstruction of 23.27 provided by Segal includes the phrase 'all the inhabitants of *ʾereṣ*'.[72] This passage forms a conclusion to the first part of the book.[73] Ben Sira concludes as he began; what is good is to fear the Lord and to observe His commandments (1.11-20; 2.7-9, 15-18; cf. 50.29, the ending of the second part). To whom is this advice addressed? The Syriac translator apparently understands it to be addressed to all human beings, for he adds ܒܥܠܡܐ 'in the world'. It is implausible, however, that our author expects all human beings including Gentiles will accept this advice, for he wants Gentiles to be in dread (פחד, not יראה) of the Lord (36[Gr. 33].2), and to know that there is no God but the Lord (36[Gr. 33].5, 22). Gentiles are just required to acknowledge the Lord. In contrast, to follow

70. The Greek translator considerably alters vv. 23-24 and changes the addressee of the requirement to 'us'.

71. Cf. Segal 1958: 348.

72. Segal 1958: 142, 144. Greek skips a part of this verse.

73. See Segal 1958: 15f.

the Lord is required only of Israel (46.10; cf. 23.12). Accordingly, those who are required to fear the Lord must be 'all the inhabitants of the Land'. They are, in fact, the readers; the author, writing in Hebrew in Jerusalem, anticipated them.[74]

4.3.2.5. Sirach 39.4

The meaning of 39.4 is quite clear.[75] The main problem for us is the original Hebrew wording of ἐν γῇ ἀλλοτρίων ἐθνῶν. Segal restores the text as בארץ עמים.[76] It is a likely candidate, but we need further considerations. First, there is no use of ארץ עמים/גוים (with singular ʾ*ereṣ*) in the Bible, though familiar in rabbinic literature.[77] Second, the context requires the plural ʾ*arāṣôt*,[78] though the singular, too, can make sense in Hebrew as in Greek. Third, the singular γῆ can be a translation of the plural ʾ*arāṣôt*.[79] The plural γαῖ is used very rarely in the LXX.[80] Fourth, in Sirach the Greek ἔθνος is almost always employed for Hebrew גוי,[81] and λαός for עם.[82] In addition, there is no use of plural ʿ*amîm* in Sirach. Fifth, we have in the Bible, though only once in Ps. 105.44, a phrase ארצות הגוים, which is also attested among the Dead Sea Scrolls (1QM 2.7; *Acts of a Greek King* [4Q248] 8; cf. 4Q377 1.i.9 with ʿ*amîm*). *Acts of a Greek King* is considered to have been one of the sources of Daniel.[83] If so, we are to have an attestation of the use of this expression more or less contemporary to Sirach. These considerations with sources available lead us to conclude that the original might be בארצות הגוים. The rabbinic phrase ʾ*ereṣ* ʿ*amîm*, which contrasts unclean foreign lands with the holy Land, seems too early for Sirach of the second century BCE.

4.3.3. Related Terms with Reference to the Greek Equivalent

4.3.3.1. tēbēl

The term *tēbēl* appears five times in the Hebrew manuscripts (10.4; 16.19; 37.3; 39.22; 43.3).

10.4: ממשלת תבל. This phrase never appears in the Bible (cf. Ps. 145.13; Sir. 17.17; 24.6), so this wording is Ben Sira's (but see 1QS 3.17f.). It is difficult to know the reason why he chose this expression, rather than *kol hā*ʾ*āreṣ*, which makes a better parallelism with the following passage. The Greek translator

74. See Mendels 1987: 9–17, esp. 11.
75. Cf. Sir. 34(Gr. 31).9-13.
76. Segal 1958: 252, 259.
77. E.g., *m. Naz.* 7.3; *m. Ohol.* 2.3; 18.6; *m. Toh.* 4.5; 5.1.
78. Syriac: מדינתא (pl.); cf. Syr. 48.15.
79. The plural ʾ*arāṣôt* appears 76 times in the Bible, for which the singular γῆ is applied 32 times (*c.* 42%) in the LXX; the plural χῶραι is employed 29 times (*c.* 38%).
80. Only six times.
81. 10.8, 16; 16.6, 9; 36.2; 44.19, 21; 49.5; 50.25a; twice for ʿ*am* (36.3; 50.25b).
82. 9.17; 10.1, 2; 16.17; 31.9 (Gr. 34.9); 33.27 (Gr. 30.27); 35.25 (Gr. 32.25); 36.17, 22; 37.23; 41.18; 42.11; 45.9, 15, 23; 46.13; 47.5, 23; 48.15; 50.4, 19; twice for *gôy* (44.4; 50.26).
83. See Broshi 2000.

applies γῆ to *tēbēl*, not ἡ οἰκουμένη, a usual equivalent in the LXX.[84] It might be noteworthy that he never employs the latter term in his whole work.

In 16.19 the phrase יסודי תבל is in parallelism with *ʾereṣ* in the preceding passage.[85] The Greek translator again takes γῆ. He does not feel it necessary to discern the two Hebrew terms.

37.3: The phrase פני תבל employed with the verb מלא is known from the Bible (Isa. 14.21; 27.6).[86] The Greek translator finds it necessary to distinguish here between *ʾereṣ* and *tēbēl*, and chooses the term ἡ ξηρά for the latter. The distinction might be made between ξηρά covered with deceit and γῆ covered with wisdom (24.3).

In 39.22 the Greek translator continues to distinguish the term *tēbēl* from *ʾereṣ*, and employs ξηρά to make a contrast with river and flood.

In 43.3 the term *tēbēl* is translated into Greek χώρα, which is never applied to the term elsewhere in the LXX.[87] The choice of this Greek term can be explained as follows: the translator interprets the verb ירתיח in the sense of יחריב with the help of חרב, for probably he doesn't know of this Hebrew verb;[88] then, however, he hesitates to use ξηρά for *tēbēl* because of the Greek verb he has chosen, ἀναξηραίνειν, which already includes the sense of ξηρά; so that he has to look for another term apart from γῆ to maintain the distinction between *ʾereṣ* and *tēbēl*, and finds the term χώρα which can mean 'the land' (opp. sea).[89]

The uses of *tēbēl* in Sirach are not different from those in the Bible. It is a synonym of *ʾereṣ*, and can be replaced by the latter. The Greek translator's attitude towards it is inconsistent, however. He chooses three Greek words, one understandable (γῆ), and two uncommon (ξηρά, χώρα).[90] The inconsistency must be a result of his avoidance of ἡ οἰκουμένη, a rather usual equivalent to *tēbēl*. His hesitation in applying it might be based on its connotation in his day of 'the Hellenistic world' in contrast to barbarians.[91] For him, the dominion of God over *tēbēl* is beyond the Hellenistic οἰκουμένη.

4.3.3.2. ʾadāmâ

The term *ʾadāmâ* appears in the Hebrew manuscripts only once, in 47.24, in which it signifies the Land. The wording להדיחם מאדמתם, which never appears in the

84. For Greek terms employed for *tēbēl* in the LXX, see Chapter 2 n. 396 above.

85. Cf. Ps. 104.32; Jon. 2.7; cf. also Chapter 2 nn. 385f. above. There is no use of יסודי תבל in the Bible, but מוסדות תבל (2 Sam. 22.16//Ps. 18.16).

86. For textual problems, see Segal 1958: 235 n. 3.

87. The Greek χώρα is almost always applied in the LXX to *ʾereṣ* (*c.* 58%) and *medînâ* (*c.* 30%); cf. Hatch and Redpath 1989: II, 1481f.

88. The root רתח appears only three times in the Bible (Ezek. 24.5; Job 30.27; 41.23).

89. See Bauer 2000: 1093. Cf. χῶραι (plural) in the sense of 'lands' (10.16; 47.17).

90. The last two terms indeed have variant readings in all their occurrences, see Ziegler's apparatus (1965, *ad loc.*).

91. See Michel 1978.

Bible as it is (cf. Jer. 27.10), seems deliberate, inspired by 2 Kgs 17.21-23 (cf. Sir. 48.15).

In Sir. 17.1 the term *ʾ*adāmâ* could be employed, since its wordplay with *ʾādām* of Genesis 2–3 must have been well known to Ben Sira (Gen. 2.7; 3.19).[92] Likewise, Segal's retroversion of ὁ ἐργαζόμενος γῆν (Sir. 20.28) into *עובד אדמה is credible (cf. Prov. 12.11).[93]

These uses of *ʾadāmâ* in Sirach are biblical. The Greek translation γῆ is also usual, as in the LXX.[94]

4.3.3.3. ʿāpār

In Sirach the Greek γῆ is employed for *ʿāpār*, three times in the phrase γῆ καὶ σποδός corresponding to עפר ואפר (10.9; [17.32]; 40.3). *ʿāpār* is a material from which living beings are made, and symbolizes their mortality (33.10 [Gr. 36.10]).

4.3.3.4. nāḥal/naḥalâ

In Sirach there appear verbal and nounal forms of נחל, which are relatively frequently used. They express close relationships to the possession of the promised Land (36.13 [Gr. 33.13a+36.16b]; 44.21-23).[95] In accordance with the biblical narratives, mention is made of the *naḥalâ* of Aaron and his seed (45.20-25; cf. Num. 18.20-32; Deut. 18.1; Josh. 13.14), and that of Israel and of Caleb (46.1-10).[96]

There are also unique uses. In 23.12 there appears a phrase κληρονομία Ιακωβ/*נחלת יעקב. The same phrase is used in Isa. 58.14, too, in which it refers to the Land.[97] In our passage, however, it means not the Land but the people of Israel.[98] Similarly, in 24.7-12 the term κληρονομία/**naḥalâ* is used in the sense of people.[99] Although the dwelling place of Wisdom is connected to Zion and Jerusalem (vv. 10-11), verse 12 explicitly indicates that κληρονομία/**naḥalâ* here refers primarily to the people of Israel, not to the Land (cf. Deut. 32.9). This does not mean that Wisdom can be found everywhere the people exists, e.g., in the Diaspora.[100] Rather, the Land is presupposed as the dwelling place of the people,

92. See Segal's retroversion (1958: 102).

93. Segal 1958: 123; cf. § 2.5.1 above

94. About 96%.

95. 36.13: יתנחלו/κατακληρονόμησον αὐτούς; 44.21: הנחילם/κατακληρονομέω αὐτούς; 44.23: יתן לו נחלתו/ἔδωκεν αὐτῷ ἐν κληρονομίᾳ. See § 4.3.2.2 above.

96. There are also generic uses; verb: 10.11; (19.3; 20.25; 22.4); noun: 9.6; (22.23; 33.24 [Gr. 30.32]); 42.3; 44.11.

97. Cf. Judg. 20.6; Isa. 54.17; Ezek. 35.15.

98. Cf. Segal 1958: 140.

99. *naḥalâ* is translated in LXX 170 times, of which κληρονομία is applied 143 times, and κληρονομεῖν 7 times (*c.* 88%; κληρονομία appears as a translation 167 times, i.e., *c.* 85.6% for *naḥalâ* [143/167]). General equivalence of κληρονομία to *naḥalâ*, is assured by these data, as well as the Hebrew attestations of Sirach (9.6; 42.3; 44.11, 23; 45.20, 22, 25ab; 46.8, 9).

100. Cf. Mendels 1987: 14f.

hence of Wisdom, for Ben Sira himself is a dweller of the Land. Because of this presupposition, however, the emphasis seems to be laid on the people.[101]

In 24.19-20 Wisdom states 'the memory of me is sweeter than honey, and the allotment of me (ἡ κρηλονομία μου/*naḥalātî) sweeter than honeycomb' (cf. Ps. 19.11, in which what is sweeter than honey is the Torah). Sirach identifies Wisdom with the Torah, so he applies the term *naḥalâ, a biblical expression of the Land-possession, to the Torah-possession. In Sir. 24.23 the Torah is regarded as 'a possession for the congregation of Jacob' quoting from Deut. 33.4 (מורשה instead of *naḥalâ*).

While employing biblical uses of the term, Ben Sira sometimes interprets it in somewhat spiritualized manner.

4.3.4. Summary

Since Ben Sira relates Wisdom to God's Creation, the term *ʾereṣ* primarily represents the earthly world forming a part of the tripartite division of the universe, which observes the laws ordained by God. This earthly world also forms a part of the threefold world, though he avoids further inquiry of the heavenly world and the netherworld, which is developed in the Book of Watchers. He concentrates on man's way of life in this world, and events after death are beyond his concern (cf. Sir. 17.27-28; 41.4).

When turning his eyes from the cosmological universe to this human world, Ben Sira repeats traditional uses of *ʾereṣ* designating foreign nations in contrast to Israel. Yet the term in the sense of the Land appears relatively rarely, though he employs some biblical expressions.

Despite a general peaceful tone of Sirach as a whole, a nationalistic Israel-centric tendency is apparent. Ben Sira's antagonism towards foreigners must have been caused by his experience of the change of overlords between Ptolemies and Seleucids. Nevertheless, his nationalism was not expressed in terms of the real Land (*ʾereṣ*) where he lived. Rather, the emphasis was laid on Israel, the chosen people who were set high above all nations. This is probably because Ben Sira intended to cope mainly with a crisis of Jewish religion caused by the people's estrangement from the traditional way of life under influence of foreign culture. He made efforts to bring them back to Judaism by recommendation and instruction, but showed no real programme to establish a political independence from foreign powers. The emancipation of the people was expected only as an eschatological hope, in which restoration of the twelve tribes in the Land and realization of biblical promise of the maximal Israel were imagined. Although he shared an eschatological hope hostile to foreign powers, Ben Sira did not become an apocalyptist. Although he faced intra-national problems, he did not become a sectarian. He intended to be a

101. In the Bible *naḥalâ* can refer both to the Land and the people; see Chapter 2 n. 210 above.

nationalistic spiritual leader of the people, remaining faithful to the traditional way of life.

4.4. *The Epistle of Enoch (*1 Enoch *91–107)*

The Epistle of Enoch can be divided into several units: (1) an introductory statement with a short apocalypse (91.1-10, 18-19), (2) an introduction to the Epistle (92), (3) the Apocalypse of Weeks (93.1-10+91.11-17), (4) a nature poem (93.11-14), (5) the Epistle consisting of paraeneses (94–105), and (6) Noah's birth (106–107). The Apocalypse of Weeks was a work originally independent from the rest of Epistle of Enoch, and a later editor was responsible for their combination.[102] The last section (chs 106–107) appears to be a later addition derived from a Noachic text.[103] *1 Enoch* 106.13–107.1, according to VanderKam, constitute with ch. 91 'a kind of *inclusio* around the core of the Epistle'.[104] Thus, the original Epistle consisted of chs 92 and 94–105; a redactor composed the Epistle of Enoch by connecting the Apocalypse of Weeks, the nature poem, and the Epistle, adding the editorial chapters 91 and 106–107. He also connected the Book of Watchers and the Epistle of Enoch by adding 81.1–82.4.[105] In this section we shall separately treat the Apocalypse of Weeks, the Epistle, and the editorial portions.[106]

The Epistle of Enoch known in Ethiopic is partially available in Greek and Aramaic.[107] These texts assure the retroversion of Aramaic *ʾaraʿ* from Greek γῆ and Ethiopic *medr*, as in the case of the Astronomical Book and the Book of Watchers.

4.4.1. γῆ/medr/ʾaraʿ *in the Apocalypse of Weeks*

The Apocalypse of Weeks divides world history from antediluvian ages to the *eschaton* into ten weeks; the first seven weeks are *vaticinia ex eventu* up to the author's time and the last three narrate eschatological events.[108] The eschatological judgement will be carried out in three stages: first against the wicked within Jews (91.12), second against כול בני ארעא כלה 'all the sons of the whole earth', i.e., the Gentiles (91.14//4QEn^{g} 1.iv.19-22),[109] and third against the wicked or fallen

102. See Milik 1976: 255f.; VanderKam 1984a: 145; García Martínez 1992: 80–4.

103. See García Martínez 1992: 27.

104. VanderKam 1984b: 515; see also Nickelsburg 2001: 422, 545f.

105. See Nickelsburg 1981a: 150f.; 1992a; 511; 2001: 22–6; 335–8; 2005: 114f.; cf. also Charles 1912: 173 n.; Black 1985: 18f., 252, 411.

106. For a pre-Maccabaean date (*c.* 175–167 BCE) of the entire Epistle of Enoch, see VanderKam 1984a: 142–9; 1984b. In this section I use Nickelburg's translation (2001) with modifications.

107. See Black 1970: 7f.; Milik 1976: 47f.

108. See VanderKam 1984a: 145–9; 1984b: 518–23.

109. Eth.: *lakwellu ʿālam* 'to all the world'; see § 7.2.4 (p. 151, n. 58) below.

angels (91.15).[110] The perspectives extend from Jews through the whole earth to the heaven.

The phrases כול בני ארעא כלה and כול ארעא in 91.14//4QEn^{g} 1.iv.19-22 represent the human-earthly world. In both, a worldwide scope is emphasized by כול and כלה. This perspective, however, seems not to reflect the author's direct international concerns. The author sees sins in apostasy so that he designates his age as 'a perverse generation' (93.9). He primarily faces a religious crisis within Jews, a crisis which has happened under the influence of foreign culture brought on earth by the rebel angels. Accordingly, the two expressions do not show his universalistic concerns, but his cosmological prospect. The Apocalypse of Weeks' eschatology, which is viewed in parallelism with the Deluge (93.4: 'the *first* end'), reflects the author's inquiry into the causes of his contemporary Jews' perversity and his hope of vanishing them from the world, on the one hand; it betrays his sectarian mind which regards his community as chosen and righteous and his opponents as perverse and wicked.

4.4.2. γῆ / medr/ʾaraʿ *in the Epistle*

The term γῆ / *medr*/*ʾ*araʿ in the Epistle can refer to the *terra firma*, the dry solid part of the earth, in contrast to the sea (101.7, 8b).[111] A reference is made to an earthquake, along with trembling of heavenly luminaries, symbolizing eschatological disturbances (102.2; cf. *1 En.* 1.6f.).[112]

In 93.13f. (//4QEn^{g} 1.v.21-23) 'the length and breadth of ארעא כולה' are in parallelism with the extent and heights of heaven. The *ʾaraʿ* here forms a half part of the universe created. God's Creation of heaven and earth is mentioned in 101.8a, too. It is noteworthy that the Epistle no longer develops (pseudo-) scientific concerns about this created universe, a main topic of the Astronomical Book and the Book of Watchers, but, on the contrary, praises God's Creation as it is by showing human inability to know of it (93.11-14//4QEn^{g} 1.v.15-23).[113]

Mention is made of the heavenly world where God and angels abide (98.6, 7; 104.1). In this respect, an interesting passage can be found in 98.4: 'lawlessness was not sent upon the earth, but men created it by themselves'. It explicitly contradicts the assumption of the origins of sin in the Book of Watchers, according to which sin was brought to the earth by fallen angels.[114] There also appears a biblical expression 'be swallowed up in the earth' (99.2 [Gr.]),[115] which symbolizes the sinners' fate of

110. See Black 1985: 293f.

111. Gr. 101.8b omits 'on the earth'; see Black 1985: 310; Nickelsburg 2001: 505.

112. Cf. Chapter 2 nn. 61–4 above.

113. In this nature poem the phrases 'the sons of men' and 'man' (4QEn^{g} 1.v.17, 22: כול אנוש) are used to express the limitation of human ability, i.e., humanity, expressions which are different from 'the sons of the earth' (91.14//4QEn^{g} 1.iv.20; 100.6; 102.3; 105.1); see below.

114. Cf. Milik 1976: 53f.

115. Eth.: 'be trodden down upon the earth'; see Nickelsburg 2001: 483.

eternal damnation in Sheol (103.7f.).[116] The netherworld is the subject matter of chs 102–103 (cf. *1 Enoch* 22). Thus the threefold world is assumed in the Epistle, and γῆ/ *medr*/*ʾ*araʿ* represents the earthly world.[117] On the earth human beings dwell (92.1b), and on the earth God abundantly provides all the good things, from which, however, the sinners eat, drink, and are satisfied (98.11); then, the wise will see many wicked deeds of the sinners on the earth (98.1-3),[118] and the author throws 'woe' to the sinners 'who lay the foundations of sin and deceit, and cause bitterness on the earth' (99.12). The author comforts the righteous dead in 102.5. A contrast is clearly made here between 'the earth' on which the fleshly life of the righteous has been unrewarded and 'Sheol' where their souls will rejoice and be glad (103.4).[119]

In the Epistle there appears the phrase οἱ υἱοὶ τῆς γῆς/*בני ארעא 'the sons of the earth' (100.6; 102.3; 105.1//4QEn^{c} 5.i.21). In the Book of Watchers this phrase represents all human beings on the earth in contrast to angels, 'the sons of heaven'.[120] In the Apocalypse of Weeks (91.14) it signifies literally all human beings, but implies specifically the Gentiles according to the context. In the Epistle, however, it connotes something else. It is apparent that 'the sons of the earth' in 100.6 are identified with rich sinners (99.11-16; 100.7-13)[121] in contrast to 'the wise',[122] as indicated by 'their wealth' and 'iniquity'. The passage means that at the time of final judgement (100.4f.) even the rich sinners will at last understand the correctness of the teachings in this Epistle and recognize the inability of their wealth to save them and their fate of damnation. The same can be said of 'the sinners' and 'the sons of the earth' in 102.1-3. This passage follows the previous discourse in which the sinners are condemned by the author because they do not fear God upon the earth (101.1, 7, 9).[123] At the final judgement, continues the author, the sinners will have to fear God and to be shaken and frightened, for they won't be able to flee or be saved (102.1). In a similar manner, 'the sons of the earth' will seek to hide themselves from God, be shaken and tremble (v. 3a). Thus, they are identical with 'you sinners' in 101 and 102.1, 3b.

The same phrase in 105.1//4QEn^{c} 5.i.21, however, seems to have somewhat different connotations. In this concluding passage the author requires his community members to carry out the missionary work to 'the sons of the earth'. It corresponds to the introduction to the Epistle (92.1). Despite the universal appearances of this phrase, however, the author seems not to have in his mind the Gentile mission, which Nickelsburg tries to find in this expression.[124] 'The sons of the earth' in 100.6 and 102.3, as we've just seen, are actually identical with the Jews around the

116. Cf. Num. 16.32; Exod. 15.4.

117. *1 En.* 92.1ab; 98.1, 4, 11; 99.12; 100.10; 102.5 [Gr.]; 105.1.

118. For the interpretation of 'many (things)' in 98.1, see Nickelsburg 2001: 475f.

119. Ethiopic *medr* appears in 92.1 and 105.1b, but there are textual problems; see Nickelsburg 2001: 430f., 535.

120. Cf. *1 En.* 9.8//4QEn^{b} 1.iii.10a-10; 12.4 [Gr.]; 15.3; cf. also 6.2; 13.8; 14.3.

121. Cf. Charles 1912: 250.

122. Cf. 98.1; 104.12.

123. The 'sons of men' in 101.1 (Gr.) is also identified with 'the sinners' (v. 7).

124. Nickelsburg 2001: 535, and 86f., 413, 449f., 502; cf. his earlier article 1982: 343–5.

author's community; foreign nations are referred to only in one verse with a negative implication (98.4 [twice]). Throughout the Epistle, indeed, the problems the author faces are idolatry and social injustice, problems which are primarily domestic, concerning the Jewish community of Palestine (although there are influences of foreign politics and culture behind them).[125] The universal terminology of the Epistle does not reflect the author's international concerns such as the Gentile mission, but his cosmological perspectives. In this respect Charles offers an interesting proposal; according to him the phrase 'the sons of the earth' is a counterpart to the 'sons of heaven' of 101.1 (Eth.) designating 'the righteous'.[126] This proposal cannot be supported as it stands, since the Greek text of 101.1 reads 'sons of men' instead, and it does not designate the righteous, but the sinners.[127] Nevertheless, our observation that the phrase 'the sons of the earth' in the Epistle signifies 'the sinners' suggests that the self-designation of the author's community as 'the righteous' at least implicitly connotes 'the sons of heaven'.[128] The author, indeed, once calls the righteous 'companions of the host of heavens' (104.6). The expression 'the sons of the earth' reflects the author's cosmological eschatological scope contrasting heaven and earth, not international. Then 'the sons of the earth' are to be the sinners, on the one hand (100.6; 102.3), and to be the targets of the mission, on the other (105.1).[129] This does not include any contradiction. In the author's dualistic perspective, all human beings are to be divided into the righteous and sinners (although the Gentiles are out of his scope). 'The sons of the earth', therefore, can be both the sinners, who neither join the community nor behave in a manner the author considers appropriate, and the missionary targets, who are candidates of the community, 'companions of the host of heavens'.

In addition, it is noteworthy that there once appears the term κληρονομία, referring to the Mosaic Law (99.14; cf. 99.2). This is a reinterpretation of the famous biblical term *naḥulâ* expressing the promised Land (cf. Sir. 24.20, 23).

4.4.3. γῆ/ medr/ʾaraʿ *in the Editorial Portions*

At the beginning of the editorial narrative it is related that Enoch was set 'on the earth' before the door of his house (81.5). The term *medr/*ʾaraʿ* here explicitly represents the earthly world in vertical contrast to the heavenly one. After his one-year period of instruction (81.6), he was brought to 'the ends of the earth' (106.8). The expression 'the ends of the earth' here keeps its literal sense, and this place,

125. See Nickelsburg 1977b, 1978–9.

126. Charles 1912: 250f.

127. See n. 123 above.

128. For the idea of Israel being sons of God, cf. Exod. 4.22; Deut. 14.1; Hos. 11.1; 4Q504 1-2.iii.5-7; Sir. 36.17; *Jub.* 1.24; 2.20; *Ps. Sol.* 17.27; *1 En.* 62.11; *m. Abot* 3.14; for individual Israelites, cf. *T. Lev.* 4.2; Wis. 2.13, 18.

129. Cf. Charles 1912: 250f., 262.

where Enoch dwells with the angels (106.7), is probably the garden of Eden (cf. *1 Enoch* 32; *Jub.* 4.23).[130]

In 91.5-10 and 106.13–107.3 Enoch gives instruction concerning the occurrence of two judgements upon the earth. There is an apparent parallel pattern in 91.5-10 and 106.13–107.3, a pattern which schematizes the history into 'sin – flood – *greater* sin – judgment';[131] upon the earth there will be violence (91.5a), sins and iniquities (106.18), and then there will be upon the earth a great scourge (91.5b) and great wrath (106.15); and 'again' or 'after this' iniquity will be consummated upon the earth (91.6; 106.19), and then from the earth idols and temples will be removed (91.9) and violence will cease (107.1); finally the earth will rest (4QEn^{g} ii.16 [//91.10?]) and good things will come upon the earth (107.1). In 91.5-10 the author/editor shortens the world history described in the Apocalypse of Weeks, focusing on the two judgements. Chapters 106–107 provide a clear explanation that the first judgement refers to the Deluge, an explanation which is absent in the rest of Enochic corpus.

While the term *medr*/**ʾaraʿ* in these passages undoubtedly signifies 'the earth' or 'the world', its uses must reflect the situation of the Land in the editor's own days. He regarded the increasing iniquity in the Land as an analogy to the situation of Noah's day, and expected the final judgement similar to the Deluge. Despite his intra-national concerns, he used the universal term, 'earth', because his eschatology replicated the Deluge.

4.4.4. Summary

The author of the Apocalypse of Weeks applies the term *ʾaraʿ* to express the cosmic scale of the final judgement. He sees perversity in his contemporary Jews under the influence of foreign culture which originated in the fallen angels. He expects the judgements in this order; first on apostate Jews, then on 'all the sons of the whole earth', and finally on the wicked angels of heaven. Thus, the cosmological eschatology is a result of Jewish cultural crisis.

The author of the Epistle denies the heavenly origin of sin, and ascribes it to human responsibility. He is woeful about the injustice of his rich, Jewish contemporaries. Despite these intra-national concerns, he sometimes designates them as 'the sons of the earth'. This wording does not reflect his global missionary prospect, but his party's self-consciousness as 'companions of the host of heavens'.

The editor of the Epistle of Enoch, following the Apocalypse of Weeks, clarifies that there are two judgements on the earth, the one Noachic Deluge and the other eschatological.

In the entire Epistle of Enoch the term γῆ/ *medr*/**ʾaraʿ* is always employed in universal dimensions, and there is no use of it referring to a territorial land. Even

130. See Nickelsburg 2001: 544f.
131. See VanderKam 1984b: 515.

the biblical term *naḥalâ* is reinterpreted as the Law in the Epistle. The expression 'the sons of the earth' is also used with a cosmological connotation in contrast to angels, but it does not show the Epistle of Enoch's universalistic concern which generalizes all mankind indifferent to nationality. The Epistle of Enoch lacks any concerns for Gentiles, and focuses on intra-national issues. The authors/editors oppose unjust Jews who, in their eyes, are no longer worthy of salvation. They individualize the Jewish people and dualistically divide them into the righteous and sinners. The phrase 'the sons of the earth', therefore, is applied to the latter to deprive the privileged nationality of sinful Jews. The dualistic intra-national discrimination characterizes the Epistle of Enoch as a sectarian work.

4.5. Other Writings

4.5.1. Aramaic Levi Document

In the text available, the term *ʾaraʿ* appears five times in Aramaic Cairo Geniza manuscripts and γῆ six times in Greek Mount Athos manuscript.[132]

Aramaic: 'the land of Egypt' (18.73, 76, 80//Cambridge d.2, 12, 22); 'the land of Canaan' (18.78//Cambridge d.16); 'the first fruits of (whole) *ʾarʿāʾ*' (18.4//Bodleian a.1).[133]

Greek: 'surface of the earth' in parallelism with 'under heaven' (2.3, supp. 13); 'earth' with which the blood of flesh shall be covered (18.56); 'world' in which the seed of Levi shall be blessed (18.59, 61). Naming his son Gershom, Levi said, 'My seed shall be sojourners in the land in which I was born' (i.e., Babylonia), and continues, 'we are sojourners like him in the land which is considered ours' (18.63; cf. *T. Levi* 11.2; Gen. 46.11; Exod. 2.22).[134]

4.5.2. The Song of the Three Jews (Greek Daniel 3.51-90)

In the Song of the Three Jews[135] the term γῆ appears twice or three times: 'the earth' in contrast to the heaven (v. 74; cf. v. 58); 'the earth' as soil with productivity of plants (v. 76). In v. 81 of LXX, though lacking in Theodotian, our term is used in reference to 'cattle and wild animals of the earth' (cf. Gen. 1.24f.; Ps. 148.10).

132. See Kugler 1996; cf. also Charles 1908: xi, liii–liv, 245–6; Milik 1955; 1976: 23f., 252f.; Hollander and de Jonge 1985; Greenfield and Stone 1979b; 1993; DJD XXII, 1–24; *DSSSE* 49–59, 446–55.

133. The referent of *ʾaraʿ* is uncertain because of lacunae.

134. For the text and translation, see Kugler 1996: 111–13.

135. For its Hebrew original and a third century BCE date, see Nickelsburg 1984: 151; Kottsieper 1998: 223.

4.6. *Conclusion*

In this chapter we have treated mainly three books of *1 Enoch* and Sirach. In the former, there is no explicit reference to the Land. This might be, in a sense, evident from the outset, since this literature chooses as its hero Enoch, who, according to the Bible, lived in the antediluvian world before the division of the earth among the nations. This choice itself reveals concerns of those who chose him. A legend of his miraculous end must have inspired various interests of Jews. Some Jews, who had (pseudo-) scientific and calendrical concerns about the cosmic order, assigned Enoch as the seer who would witness astronomical movements completed in a 364-day calendar. The Astronomical Book is the oldest remains of their writings. That is to say, the author of the Astronomical Book chose Enoch as a hero in order to express his cultic concerns in terms of cosmic order. It is natural, therefore, that the term γῆ/*medr*/*ʾaraʿ* of the books of *1 Enoch* is primarily utilized in cosmological dimensions.

Apart from Enochic traditions, a universal eschatology developed in the fourth century BCE. The myth of the Watchers' rebellion (*1 Enoch* 6–11) is a piece of such development. It expresses animosity against foreign overlords who overran the Land and its eschatological vision contains the realization of the maximal Israel. In the third century BCE this material was taken into Enochic traditions by some Jews who opposed their Hellenism-oriented compatriots in order to express their final salvation (the Book of Watchers). Then, the cosmology, which had originated in (pseudo-) scientific calendrical concerns, was combined with the universal eschatology. The seer of cosmic order became the seer of world history from its creation to the *eschaton*. The writing and redactorial activities were continued and accelerated in the time of Hellenistic reform, and an Enochic corpus was composed (the Book of Watchers and the Epistle of Enoch). Reflecting this process, the Enochic corpus is full of cosmological eschatological descriptions. The term γῆ/*medr*/*ʾaraʿ* is employed in the sense of 'the earth' or 'the earthly world' to express its creation and destruction.

The cosmological eschatology of the Enochic corpus does not demonstrate its universalistic concerns. It pays little attention to the Gentiles (except chs 6–11). It rather reveals its sectarian character, which separates the righteous Jews from the sinful Jews. The distinction is based on the idea that to be worthy of salvation is not dependent on one's nationality as a descendant of Israel, but is determined by one's way of life. Thus, the biblical ideology of election of Israel, which makes an *inter*-national discrimination, is now transformed into *intra*-national discrimination; though the validity of the former is not denied and the priority of Jewish nationality is assumed. The Enochic corpus, therefore, can be characterized by a Jewish sectarianism. The coexistence of intra-national concerns and contrastive cosmological soteriology is not surprising. It is a result of an attempt to cope with the domestic problems by a cosmic scale eschatology, which itself is nothing new. The Bible contains a type of universal soteriology based on nationalism. Israel's superiority to nations is a biblical ideology, its eschatological dominion over nations is a biblical vision, too. Jewish sectarianism diverges from the biblical assumption in one point; it individualizes the nation itself and dualistically divides it into insiders and outsiders. The pair of universalism and individualism, both of which are predicated upon nationalism, represents an aspect of Second Temple sectarianism (or particularism). The term γῆ/*medr*/ʾ*ara*ʿ plays an interesting role in this worldview; it reflects a condition of 'the Land' in reality, which is projected on 'the earth' in soteriology.

Sirach saw the foundations of the cosmic order in Wisdom. Accordingly, his uses of the term γῆ/ʾ*ereṣ* tend to be cosmological. At the same time, he was a nationalist with antagonism towards foreign nations. His eschatological hope, therefore, was a nationalistic universalism, namely, Israel's dominion over the whole world. It is interesting to see the fact that Ben Sira shared such an eschatological hope with the apocalyptic portion of *1 Enoch* 6–11. Sirach, however, still remembered the special significance of the Land and expected the restoration of the twelve tribes in the Pentateuchal Land. Thus, two Land theologies coexist in Sirach, the maximal Israel and the Lord's Land as Israel's allotment.

In these writings from the period before the Maccabaean revolt, a common characteristic is cosmological perspectives. The constitution of the universe was intensely surveyed. The world was observed in relation to its Creation and *eschaton*. The biblical Land theology was reinterpreted as a promise of the maximal Israel: the biblical expression ירש את הארץ was applied to the promise of the earth possession to the righteous (*1 En.* 5.7), and the Land promised to Abraham was extended to the ends of the earth (Sir. 44.21). Another term expressing biblical Land theology, *naḥalâ*, was applied to a metaphor of the Torah (Sir. 24.20, 23; *1 En.* 99.14; but Sir. 36.13 [Gr. 33.13a+36.16b]; cf. Sir. 44.22c-23). Whether nationalist or sectarian, they were concerned with the universe and desired to take possession of it physically or intellectually. This seems to be due to Hellenistic worldviews: philosophical inquiry of cosmos, on the one hand, and imperialism, on the other. Under these Hellenistic influences, the conception of the Land as a defined territory had lost its traditional significance.

Chapter 5

Hasmonaean Period

In this chapter we discuss works from the period between 167–63 BCE. They are: (1) Daniel, (2) the Book of Dreams (*1 Enoch* 83–90), (3) Baruch, (4) *Temple Scroll*, (5) Judith, (6) 1 Maccabees, (7) *Jubilees*, and (8) *Genesis Apocryphon*. While Qumran sectarian literature will be independently discussed in the next chapter, we shall supplement in the Appendix our treatments with some Dead Sea Scrolls which can be ascribed to pre- or non-Qumranic.[1]

5.1. Daniel

The book of Daniel was composed in the midst of the Maccabaean uprising (*c.* 167–164 BCE).[2] Chapters 1–6 contain a large earlier collection, which was utilized by the final editor to serve his didactic purposes. We shall first see uses of our term in chs 1–6, and then discuss those in chs 7–12.

5.1.1. ʾereṣ/ʾaraʿ *in Daniel 1–6*

In Dan. 6.28 *ʾaraʿ* is contrasted to *šemayyāʾ*. The *ʾaraʿ* here means the 'earthly world', since God's deliverance of Daniel is reckoned as a sign and wonder on the earth. The *šemayyāʾ*, however, seems not to refer to the heavenly world, for in chs 1–6 no imaginations of it appear. A main subject matter of these chapters is God's ultimate sovereignty over the human world. Accordingly, the *šemayyāʾ* means the 'firmament',[3] and the two terms *šemayyāʾ* and *ʾaraʿ* represent this world created by God; hence the sovereignty over it is to be in the hands of its Creator. The same can be seen in the use of these two terms in Dan. 4.32, in which phrases 'the host of heaven' and 'the inhabitants of the earth' represent creation. The dominion over the world, which is a matter of concern, can be expressed with the term *ʾaraʿ*, especially with *kol* 'all' and/or *sôf* 'end' (2.35, 39b; 3.31; 4.8, 17, 19; 6.26).

1. We do not treat *Testaments of the Twelve Patriarchs*, since its present form contains considerable interpolations by Christians (and Jews); see Collins 1984: 331–44.
2. See Nickelsburg 2005: 17; *HJP* III, 247.
3. Except for phrases 'the God of heaven' (2.18, 19, 28, 37, 44), 'the King of heaven' (4.34), and *šemayyāʾ* for God (4.23, 28).

In another usage, it denotes the tangible *terra firma* (4.7, 12ab, 20). Once *ʾereṣ* refers to 'a land' (1.2). There is a rare use in which ארעא means 'earthward, downward', i.e., 'lower, inferior' (2.39a).[4]

5.1.2. ʾereṣ/ʾaraʿ *in Daniel 7–12*

In Dan. 8.9-12 Daniel sees a vision of a small horn. The term *ʾereṣ* in v. 10 denotes 'the earth' in contrast to the heaven on the surface of the narrative. Since, however, the small horn is employed as an allegory of Antiochus IV Epiphanes, 'some of the host' and 'some of the stars' being thrown down must reflect real experience of Jews, particularly of the priests, who were persecuted and 'thrown down to the ground'.[5] One such experience is that 'it (the horn) cast truth to the ground' (8.12). Similarly, our term is relatively frequently employed to express 'down to the ground' (8.7, 18; 10.9, 15; all in the form ארצה).[6]

Alexander the Great's quick conquest of nations is depicted by a goat 'coming across the face of the whole *ʾereṣ* without touching *ʾereṣ*' (8.5). The latter *ʾereṣ* refers to the surface of the earth, while the former means the earthly world. The term's use in the sense of 'earthly world' appears three times in ch. 7 (vv. 17, 23ab), in which the events on the heavenly world (vv. 9-14) correspond with those on the earthly one; hence a cosmological twofold world is assumed.

The most frequent usage of our term is reference to 'a land' (11 times).[7] The plural *ʾarāṣôt* is used three times (9.7; 11.40, 42a). Notable is reference to the Land as ארץ הצבי 'the Land of beauty' (11.16, 41).[8] Mention is once made of כל עם הארץ designating ordinary Jews of the Land (9.6).

Compared with chs 1–6 and ch. 7, in which our term is predominately seen from cosmological perspectives, in chs 8–12 it is understood in territorial dimensions. Our term, however, is not utilized in descriptions of eschatological hopes.

A reference is made to the eternal 'kingdom' of Israel in 7.26f. Although the hope of Jewish sovereignty over the world is closer to the ideology of the maximal Israel, it is expressed with a political term, מלכות (cf. Dan. 2.44). While ch. 8 laments the persecution of Epiphanes against the Land, the Temple, and the holy people, eschatological expectation is very limited. Only the restoration of the sanctuary and the destruction of the king are described (vv. 14, 25). Similarly, regarding the persecution as a result of Israel's sin, ch. 9 asks God only for the restoration of Jerusalem and the end of the desolator (vv. 17-20, 27). After narrating anguish at the end of time, which includes bitter experience of the 'Land of beauty', the author of chs 10–12 continues the description of the time of salvation. He lists

4. See BDB, 1083.
5. See Lacocque 1979: 162; Goldingay 1989: 209–11; Collins 1993: 333.
6. Cf. 7.4: מן ארעא.
7. 9.6, 7, 15; 11.16, 19, 28ab, 40, 41, 42ab.
8. Cf. Dan. 8.9; 11.45; cf. also Ezek. 20.6, 15; Jer. 3.19.

the emancipation of the people, resurrection of the dead, and designation of eternal life or eternal shame (12.1-3).

5.1.3. Summary

Compared with the pre-Maccabaean writings (including Daniel 1–6), the term *ʾereṣ* in Daniel 8–12 is less seen in cosmological perspectives, than territorial. The shift of uses is certainly caused by the change of situation of the days. The crisis in the Land awoke Jews to its traditional significance. Yet, despite the fact that the visions of Daniel 7–12 were inspired by hard experience in the Land, the eschatological hopes expressed in these chapters do not repeat any of God's traditional promises of the Land. Rather, prominent is the hope of resurrection and eternal life. The biblical promise of salvation, which shall have been realized in the real world, was now forced to be asked in a different realm of the world in the face of an actual death penalty executed by the persecutor.

*5.2. The Book of Dreams (*1 Enoch *83–90)*

The Book of Dreams, the fourth section of *1 Enoch*, consists of two dream visions of Enoch. The first concerns the Deluge (chs 83–84), and the second, commonly called the Animal Apocalypse, narrates a zoomorphic history from the creation of the first man through the author's own age to the future messianic time (chs 85–90). While the two dream visions could be taken from different traditions, in the present text the two are incorporated and utilized to compose a single work (cf. 83.2; 90.42). The composition can be dated during the Maccabaean revolt.[9]

The Book of Dreams is preserved in Ethiopic, but partially available in a Greek translation and in Aramaic fragments from Qumran. The retroversion of Aramaic *ʾaraʿ* from Ethiopic *medr* can be demonstrated by Aramaic attestations and general equivalence of the terms.[10]

5.2.1. medr/*ʾaraʿ *in the First Dream (chs 83–84)*

In 83.3-4 the tripartite division of the universe into heaven, earth, and abyss is assumed, and the earth (*medr*/*ʾ*araʿ*) is comprised of mountains and hills and plains on which trees grow.[11] The heaven here is the firmament upon which celestial

9. Milik 1976: 44; Nickelsburg 1981a: 92 f.; 2005: 86; VanderKam 1984a: 161–3; *HJP* III, 255.

10. See Chapter 4 nn. 6–7 above. In this section I use Nickelsburg's English translation (2001), otherwise noted.

11. Cf. Exod. 15.12; *1 En.* 1.6-7.

bodies move on fixed paths (83.11).[12] In this vision the cosmos is seen materially, but its upheaval symbolizes the destruction of the human world in it.

When he saw the vision, Enoch cried out, 'the earth has been destroyed' (83.5). Despite the description of the vision and Enoch's cry, the earth itself is expected to remain. The earth is the space for living beings, on which a remnant may remain (83.8a; 84.5a) or from which the flesh which has aroused God's wrath shall be removed (84.6). If all the flesh of men is removed, it will be devastated (84.5b). What shall be destroyed is the human world on the earth (83.8b, 9ab). Mahalalel explained that what Enoch saw was concerning 'the secrets of all the sin of the earth' (83.7), that is, the sin of human beings on the earth.

Once our term is used in a paraphrase of Isa. 66.1 (84.2b). This passage expresses God's sovereignty over the whole created universe, and the emphasis of its eternity contrasts with the vision Enoch saw.[13]

5.2.2. medr/ʾaraʿ *in the Animal Apocalypse (chs 85–90)*

The second vision begins with the creation of the first man Adam, who is metaphorically expressed as a white bull which 'came forth from *medr*/**ʾaraʿ*' (85.3). The *medr*/**ʾaraʿ* here refers to the *terra firma* from which animals were created (cf. Gen. 1.24). A reference is made to 'all the animals upon the earth', which, employed with 'all the birds of heaven', alludes to Gentiles in contrast to Israel, 'the sheep' (90.30). In the dream of Noah's Deluge (89.1-8) the term *medr*/*ʾaraʿ* is employed to express the *terra firma*, as is *ʾereṣ* in Genesis 6–8 (89.2, 3, 4, 8).[14] Mention is made of 'an abyss of the earth' (88.3) and 'an abyss ... in the middle of the earth, which was full of fire' (90.26; cf. *1 En*. 26.1). Similarly, there is an expression that 'the earth was split' (90.18). These are expressions for punishment, using our term in the sense of *terra firma*.[15]

A reference is made to a shaking of the earth (88.2). This earthquake was caused by the 'elephants and camels and asses', which were given a sword and struck one another. The three kinds of animal allude to the giants in *1 Enoch* 6–11,[16] and the description is taken from *1 En*. 10.9-10, in which, however, no earthquake is assumed. The earthquake of 88.2 seems to symbolize the evil deeds of the giants and the disturbances caused by them spread over the human world (cf. *1 En*. 7.1–9.1). The term *medr*/**ʾaraʿ* here, therefore, connotes a double meaning: the *terra firma* shaken and the human world disturbed. Similarly, the cry of the earth mentioned in 87.1 represents the complaint and cry of men (cf. *1 En*. 7.6; 8.4; 9.2-11). There is a vision of a black bullock and a red one, which is an allusion to the

12. Cf. *1 En*. 2.1; 36.2f.; 72–74.
13. See Nickelsburg 2001: 352; cf. Chapter 2 n. 73 above.
14. Aramaic *ʾaraʿ* is attested in 4QEn^e 5.i.17-18 (= 89.3); 5.ii.4 (= 89.8); see Knibb 1978: II, 199–201.
15. Cf. Num. 16.31f.; 26.10; Deut. 11.6.; Ps. 106.17; *1 En*. 18.11-16; 21.1-10; 26.4–27.2.
16. Cf. Gr. Sync. *ad loc.*; *Jub*. 7.22.

biblical story of Cain and Abel (85.3-7). The black one, it is stated, pursued the red one 'over the earth' (v. 4), of which the term *medr/*ʾaraʿ* seems to connote 'the human world'.[17]

When he raised his eyes to heaven and saw in a vision beings like white men, Enoch was lifted to a high place and was shown 'a tower high above the earth' (87.3). The tower may be a symbol of a heavenly sanctuary,[18] hence the *medr/*ʾaraʿ* here is contrasted to the heaven. There appears the phrase 'the sons of the earth' (86.6), which occurs relatively frequently in *1 Enoch* as a whole.[19] According to the sequence of the narrative, there is no referent of this phrase, since all the characters mentioned in this chapter are animals. The author apparently 'here forgets his rôle, and uses non-symbolical language'.[20] The sons of the earth here are contrasted to the star in 86.1 fallen from heaven, which is one of 'the sons of the heaven' according to the Book of Watchers (*1 En.* 6.2-8; cf. 13.8; 14.3) on which our chapter relies.

The term is once used in the sense of 'the ground', upon which the bones of the sheep (= Israelites) fell (90.4). To 'fall upon *medr/*ʾaraʿ*' here means ruination.

In the description of Israel's history, the author alludes to the Pentateuchal settlement narrative, in which mention is made of 'a pleasant and glorious Land (*medr/*ʾaraʿ*)' and 'the pleasant Land (*medr/*ʾaraʿ*)' (89.40). While this is just a brief reproduction of the fulfilment of the biblical promise of the Land, the very reference to the Land itself is significant, since the Land is almost ignored in other Enochic writings (only in *1 En.* 56.6f.). The designation of 'the pleasant Land' here, as well as the reference to 'the Land of beauty' in Dan. 11.16, 41, suggests that the people remembered the significance of the Land under the Antiochian persecution.

After a long description of Israel's history up to the author's days, an eschatological vision is narrated (90.17-38). The messianic age shall begin with God's enthronement in the Land; after striking the earth by the staff of His anger (v. 18), it is stated: 'a throne was constructed in the pleasant land (*medr/*ʾaraʿ*) and the Lord of the sheep sat upon it' (v. 20).[21] It is significant that the Land plays an eschatological role together with Jerusalem which is 'in the middle of the earth' (90.26). Now the Land belongs not merely to a biblical past, but to an expectation for the future. The reference to the Land as the place of the final judgement is our author's innovation in the entire Enochic corpus. An earthly setting for the judgement is found also in *1 En.* 1.4 and 25.3, in which, though, the location is assigned to Mt Sinai and Jerusalem, respectively.[22] Our author is the first in the post-biblical period who employed the territorial Land in an apocalyptic eschatology.

17. Nickelsburg (2001: 371) proposes a text emendation.
18. See Black 1985: 261; Nickelsburg 2001: 374.
19. Cf. 12.4 (Gr.); 15.3; 91.14 //4QEn^{g} 1.iv.20; 100.6; 102.3; 105.1//4QEn^{c} 5.i.21.
20. Charles 1912: 188.
21. For God's visitation to the Land, cf. CD 7.9 (see § 6.3.1 below).
22. Cf. Nickelsburg 2001: 403.

5.2.3. Summary

In these two dream visions the term *medr*/*ʾaraʿ* represents the tangible earth and the human world. It is, however, not seen from a cosmological concern in its own right. Although the author assumes the existence of angels,[23] there is no speculation on the heavenly world, nor on the netherworld. His concern is concentrated on the history of this real world, its thorough destruction and the survival of a remnant.

The real world with which our author is concerned is, in effect, the Land which was oppressed by Gentiles in his days. Our term in the sense of the Land appears three times, all in the form 'the pleasant Land'. The Land is differentiated from other lands, and is understood in territorial dimensions. It is significant that the author not only remembered the special status of the territorial Land, but also utilized it in his eschatological vision. Thus, it seems that the distinct land gained new theological significance under national crisis.

5.3. Baruch

We can assume that the book of Baruch, known to us in Greek and other translations, was originally composed in Hebrew in Palestine of 163–162 BCE.[24] Since it utilizes biblical passages, we can fairly well reconstruct Hebrew expressions from the Greek text, at least, concerning our term.[25]

*5.3.1. γῆ/*ʾereṣ in Baruch*

The term γῆ/**ʾereṣ* is used in the sense of *terra firma* in contrast to the heaven and the sea (3.16, 20, 23, 38; cf. 3.29f.; Job 28.1-13), and to mountain and valley (5.7). The earth created is called 'the earth for all time' (3.32).[26] The endurance of the earth is expressed by a biblical phrase: 'like the days of heaven upon the earth' (1.11; see Deut. 11.21; cf. Gen. 8.22; Job 8.9; 1 Chron. 29.15).[27] In 2.15 the phrase πᾶσα ἡ γῆ/**kol hāʾāreṣ* 'all the earth' represents the whole human population except Israel.[28]

23. 84.4; 86.1, 3; 87.2f.; 88.1-3; 89.59-65, 68-72, 74-77; 90.1, 5, 13f., 17, 21-25.

24. For the date, see Moore 1974; 1992a; Tov 1976: 111–33; Goldstein 1979–80; Burke 1982: 17ff.; *HJP* III, 733–41; Mendels 1992a; Nickelsburg, 1981a: 109–14; 1984: 145f.; 2005: 97; Steck 1993: 294–303; 1998: 22f.; see also § 5.3.2 below; for the unity of the whole book of Baruch, see Steck 1993: 253–65; 1998: 18–20.

25. For attempts to reconstruct Hebrew original, see Tov 1975; Burke 1982; Kahana 1969b.

26. The Hebrew term for *terra firma* must be *ʾereṣ*; see Hebrew reconstruction by the studies in the previous note.

27. See Tov 1975: 14f.

28. For the Hebrew reconstruction, see Tov 1975: 21; cf. 1 Sam. 17.46; 1 Kgs 8.43, 60; 2 Kgs 19.19//Isa. 37.20; 2 Chron. 6.33; Sir. 36.22; Dan. 9.18f.

Our term can signify a distinct territory, as well: 'the land of Judah' (1.8) and 'the land of Egypt' (1.19, 20; 2.11).[29] Mention is made of the land of exile: 'the land of their captivity' (*ארץ שבים [2.30, 32]);[30] 'a land of an enemy' (*ארץ אויב [3.10a]);[31] and 'a foreign land' (*ארץ נכריה [3.10b]).[32]

The Land, too, is mentioned six times, of which five occurrences appear in the prayer (1.20; 2.21, 23, 34, 35). This prayer is an expansion with deuteronomic and Jeremianic materials of a prayer of confession, which is preserved in Dan. 9.4-19.[33] In the prayer of Daniel 9, however, there is no single mention of the Land. This means that the five passages of Baruch, in which the Land is referred to, are the intentional expansion of our author.

(1) 1.20: This is an expansion of Dan. 9.11 with partial quotations from Jer. 11.4-5. By so doing he denotes God's purpose of the Exodus, employing a famous biblical phrase 'a land flowing with milk and honey'.

(2) 2.21: This verse is a mixed citation of Jer. 27.11-12 with some modifications. Jer. 27.11 is spoken to 'any nation' (cf. v. 3) whereas 27.12 to King Zedekiah. Our author applies the two verses to Israel ('you') and connects a land promise to 'any nation' with the biblical Land-promise to Israel's forefathers (here the original Hebrew can be *ʾ*adāmâ*, as in Jer. 27.11).[34]

(3) 2.23: This verse, a mixed citation from Jer. 7.34 and 48.9, includes the clause: 'and the whole Land shall be a desolation without inhabitants'. The reference to the Land (taken from Jer. 7.34: *hāʾāreṣ*) contrasts with Dan. 9 in which only the desolation of Jerusalem is mentioned.

(4)–(5) 2.34, 35: These verses include biblical passages referring to the promised Land (v. 34//Jer. 30.3 [ʾ*ereṣ*] and v. 35//1 Kgs 14.15 [ʾ*adāmâ*]). Compared with Dan. 9.18, which focuses upon the fate of Jerusalem, the author's concern for the biblical Land of promise is explicitly reflected in Bar. 2.19-35.[35]

Another reference to the Land appears in a famous biblical phrase 'the people of the land' (*ʿ*am hāʾāreṣ* [1.9]). The verse quotes Jer. 24.1, in which, though,

29. Hebrew term for a territorial land must be ʾ*ereṣ*; see § 2.3.1 above.

30. See Tov 1975: 24f.; cf. Jer. 30.10; 46.27; 1 Kgs 8.47; 2 Chron. 6.37, 38.

31. See Burke 1982: 65, 79–81; cf. Lev. 26.34, 36, 38, 39, 41, 44; 1 Kgs 8.46, 48; Jer. 31.16.

32. See Burke 1982: 65, 79–81; cf. Exod. 2.22; 18.3.

33. Moore 1974; 1977: 291–3; 1992a: 699; Nickelsburg 1984: 143f.; Steck 1993: 88–92.

34. Tov (1975: 23) reconstructs Hebrew ושבו על הארץ (Gr.: καὶ καθίσατε ἐπὶ τὴν γῆν). In the context of Land-promise of the Bible, however, the verb *yāšab* and the noun ʾ*ereṣ* are in most cases connected by the preposition ב. Contrastively, ʾ*adāmâ* is mostly connected with *yāšab* by על (see Chapter 2 n. 371 above). Only once in Jer. 27.11 there appears ישב בה referring to ʾ*adāmâ*, but it is preceded by הניח על האדמה. Considering these data, the original Hebrew should be reconstructed as *ושבו על האדמה; cf. Kahana 1969b: 357; cf. also Deut. 30.20; Jer. 25.5; Ezek. 28.25.

35. Of these five occurrences, two passages might have *ʾ*adāmâ* instead of *ʾ*ereṣ* (2.21, 35). The terminology does not suggest the author's conscious choice, but he merely follows biblical passages on which he relies.

the phrase is not included. It seems to mean 'the ordinary people', as its uses in Jeremiah and Second Kings.[36]

5.3.2. Summary

The book of Baruch shows its intimacy with the Hebrew Bible, and so its uses of the terms γῆ/*ʾ*ereṣ* (and *ʾ*ădāmâ*) are also biblical. Using our term in the sense of the earth, the author sees it from two points of view: the earth as God's creation (3.32), and the earth as the human world except Israel (2.15). These uses express the special status of Israel among nations on the earth. On the other hand, when he uses the term in territorial dimensions, notable is the contrast between 'the land of captivity' and 'the Land of promise', both of which are expressed with biblical phrases. The superficial theme of exile and return reveals the author's actual concerns for the people in the Land. By repeating confession of the people's sins and the biblical promise of the Land, the author emphasizes that return to the Lord will bring them a peaceful life in the Land (cf. 2 Chron. 30.9).

As the fictional setting of Exile suggests, the problem of the author's time was primarily caused by Gentile rulers (i.e., the Seleucids). Our author, however, understood this international problem as an *intra*-national one. His attitude towards Gentile rulers was ambivalent, therefore (compare 1.11f.; 2.21-23 with 4.25, 31-35). This intra-national perspective is different from that of Daniel (except ch. 9), which expresses antagonism towards foreign rulers from international perspectives. The difference might be the result of the different situations under which they were written. Daniel was written at the beginning of the Maccabaean revolt when the persecution with the death penalty by Antiochus IV was harsh. Daniel, therefore, concerns the destruction of foreign empires and salvation of victims' afterlife. Baruch was written when hopes arose for a good relationship with a new ruler. The author of Baruch recommended Jews to make peace with this foreign ruler rather than to continue battles, since the recent disaster was, in his opinion, caused ultimately by the people's sins against God. A final restoration of Jerusalem and destruction of foreign enemies would be brought by God Himself (4.5–5.7). Until then, the author requires, Jews should submit to foreign rulers so as to live in peace in the Land. While sharing eschatological hopes with his contemporary Jews, the author tried to cope with the problem in a realistic politico-religious way. In order to persuade the readers, he applied biblical passages to his age: 'Thus says the Lord: Bow your shoulders and serve the king of Babylon, and you will dwell upon the Soil (γῆ/*ʾ*ădāmâ*) that I gave to your fathers' (2.21). The author saw the situation of his age as similar to the Exile. By creating a fictional setting of Exile, he revived the Land-promise, a central message of the Hebrew Bible.

36. Cf. Jer. 1.18; 34.19; 37.2; 44.21; 52.6 (//2 Kgs 25.3), 25ab (//2 Kgs 25.19ab); 2 Kgs 11.14, 18, 19, 20; 15.5; 16.15; 21.24; 23.30, 35; 24.14; Dan. 9.6; see also Moore 1977: 272.

5.4. Temple Scroll

Temple Scroll, written in Hebrew, is known from two manuscripts of Qumran Cave 11 (11QT^{a-b} = 11Q19-20) and one Cave 4 manuscript (4QT = 4Q524). While *Temple Scroll* is known only from the Qumran caves, we treat it here since its less polemical character suggests that the work originates before the Qumran sect was distinctively established.[37] We can date it towards the middle of the second century BCE.[38]

5.4.1. ʾereṣ *in* Temple Scroll

The term *ʾereṣ* in *Temple Scroll* can connote tangibly the *terra firma* (32.12-15; 48.4f.; 50.20) and the 'ground' (32.9f.; 52.11f.; 53.5f.). It is probably once used in reference to the 'human world' with a familiar biblical expression מקצי הארץ ועד קצי הארץ 'from one end of the earth to the other end of the earth' in 11QT^{a} 55.02 (= 11QT^{b} 16.3-5; cf. Deut. 13.8).[39] It should be noted that no reference is made to our term in relation to the Creation in entire *Temple Scroll*. The term *šāmayim* 'heaven' appears only once (50.18//Deut. 17.3), and no mention is made of *tēbēl* 'world'. *Temple Scroll* lacks any Creation theology and cosmology.[40]

In contrast, the term is frequently employed in reference to a territorial 'land', and to the Land, in particular. This usage occurs predominantly in the last third of *Temple Scroll* (cols 48–67) which deals with matters outside the Temple and the Temple City. Mention is made of 'the land of Egypt' twice in relation to the Exodus (11QT^{a} 54.16//Deut. 13.6; 11QT^{a} 61.14//Deut. 20.1). The plural 'lands' is used twice in the King's Law (59.2, 5f.). While these passages are primarily based on Deuteronomy 28, the expressions ארצות רבות 'many lands' and ארצות אויביהמה 'the lands of their enemies' are deliberately taken from other biblical passages (Jer. 28.8, and Lev. 26.36, 39; Ezek. 39.27, respectively).

In other occurrences our term refers to 'the Land'. The beginning of col. 2, which is based primarily on Exod. 34.10-16, certainly contains, though in lacunae, the phrase 'the inhabitant(s) of the Land' (2.4, 12//Exod. 34.12, 15). Seven nations might be listed as in 62.14f. (cf. Samaritan Pentateuch Exod. 34.11; MT Deut. 7.1).[41] The quotations of these biblical lists may suggest the existence of foreign nations within the Land in the author/redactor's day, on the one hand;[42] the fact that

37. For non- or pre-Qumranic provenance, see Levine 1978; Schiffman 1980, 1988; McCready 1982–4; Swanson 1994; García Martínez 2000; cf. Wentling 1989–90.

38. Wise 1990: 26–31, 110–27, 198–200; García Martínez 2000.

39. Cf. Chapter 2 n. 119 above.

40. An eschatological expectation in 29.9f. contains only a new creation of the Temple; no cosmology is developed in *Temple Scroll*.

41. See Yadin 1983: II, 2; cf. Deut. 7.1; Josh. 3.10; 24.11; see also Chapter 2 n. 289 above.

42. Thus Stegemann 1983: 158.

he began his work with the prohibition of idolatry may mean his deliberate warning against the Hellenizers of his days, on the other.[43]

The introductory statement of col. 2 is immediately followed by laws concerning the Temple and the Temple city (cols 3–47). Columns 48–67 are concerning lives of the people outside the Temple city. In col. 48 the people is characterized as 'a holy people' and 'the sons of the Lord' (ll. 7-10).[44] This characterization of the people is contiguously connected to their Land: 'And you shall not defile your Land' (48.10f.; cf. Num. 35.34).[45] By inserting this statement the author/redactor deliberately shifts the subjects of the scroll from the sanctity of the Temple and the Temple city (cols 3–47) to the holiness of the people and the Land (cols 48–67), so that the holiness of the Temple radiates to the people and the Land.

The passage last cited (48.10f.) is followed by the law concerning places of burial (48.11-13; cf. 51.19–52.3). The commands about impurity are concluded by the statements that the people must avoid any abominations, for they are a holy people among whom God dwells (51.6-10). Accordingly, the Land, too, must be holy, for it is the place for them to observe the laws God gave.[46]

While the holiness of the Land is presupposed, higher sanctity is assigned to the Temple and its city.[47] The term *ʾereṣ*, therefore, can be used in contrast to the Temple (47.13f.). Mention is made of 'the new oil of the Land' which should be atoned for before God, i.e., in the Temple city (22.15f.).[48] Thus, the holiness is radiately graded from the Temple through the Temple city down to the Land.[49] *Temple Scroll* is the oldest attestation of the concept of the Holy Land in post-biblical literature, though the term ארץ הקודש does not appear.[50]

The biblical idea that the Land is given by God is presupposed in *Temple Scroll*; hence the promise is never mentioned. The formula 'the Land that I give you' is used as an introduction to laws or as a condition to be in it.[51]

In the King's Law there appears once the expression *ʾereṣ yiśrāēl* (58.6f.), which is very rare in use in the whole Dead Sea Scrolls and other post-biblical literature (prior to rabbinic literature).[52] Since this statement is found in laws of war, here the territory of the Land must be meant. In the next law, indeed, the term *gebûl*,

43. Thus Schiffman 1994: 112–14, but cf. VanderKam 1994c: 130–2; see also Mink 1987: 35–8; Weinfeld 1991–2: 178f.

44. See Deut. 14.1-2, 21; Lev. 19.28; cf. Exod. 19.6; Lev. 19.2; 20.26; Deut. 7.6; 26.19; 28.9; Isa. 62.12; 63.18; Dan. 12.7.

45. Cf. 11QT[a] 64.12f.//Deut. 21.23.

46. For impurity of the dead in *Temple Scroll* applying to the whole Land, see Schiffman 1990.

47. See Crawford 2001.

48. See Yadin 1983: I, 111–14, 118.

49. Cf. Shemesh 1999–2000.

50. Cf. 2 Macc. 1.7.

51. *TS* 51.15f.//Deut. 16.20; *TS* 56.12//Deut. 17.14; *TS* 60.16f.//Deut. 18.9; cf. Deut. 4.1; 6.18; 12.1.

52. See 4QMMT B 63; cf. 1 Sam. 13.19; Ezek. 40.2; 47.18; 1 Chron. 22.2; 2 Chron. 2.16; 34.7; *LAB* 25.1.

'border', appears in relation to the Land (58.7-9). The reference to *gebûl* implies that the territory of the Land is to be fixed to a degree. Although no mention is made of concrete borders, several references to the twelve tribes suggest that a traditional biblical Land is in the author/redactor's mind. In addition, this passage presupposes a situation that enemies come from abroad.

In accordance with its base text, *Temple Scroll* knows a distinction between the nations outside and inside the Land (62.11-16//Deut. 20.15-18). Here seven nations are enumerated as the beginning of *Temple Scroll* (2.2-4), and in both passages their annihilation from the Land is mentioned in relation to their temptation of the people into idolatry.[53] Furthermore, according to Yadin's restoration *Temple Scroll* includes the quotation of Deut. 12.20, in which a promise of the enlargement of the territory is referred to (53.07).[54] Although these passages are just quotations from the Bible, their inclusion in this work suggests that the author/redactor regards the annihilation of the foreign nations of the Land and the enlargement of its territory as an ideal, if not a real policy. In *Temple Scroll*, we can say, the restoration of biblical Land of Israel as the holy territory is in prospect.[55]

The closing column of the King's Law contains God's curse to the people (59.1-13). At the end of the curse (59.9-13) the author/redactor probably alludes to the return to Zion from the Exile, but the recent redemption from the Seleucids may be also in his mind. His hopes include the multiplication of the people in ארץ אבותיהמה 'the Land of their fathers' (59.12), which will be accomplished by their return to God (59.9f.; cf. 2 Chron. 30.9). The phrase ארץ אבות appears rarely in ancient Jewish literature. Besides Gen. 31.3; 48.21, it is employed only in 1 Maccabees, a younger contemporary to *Temple Scroll*. In 1 Maccabees, however, it can refer to a foreign land (10.55, 67; 15.10).[56] Instead other expressions נחלת אבותינו* 'the allotment of our fathers' (1 Macc. 15.33f.) and גבול ישראל* 'the territory of Israel' (2.46; 9.23) are employed in reference to the Land.[57] In Judith, too, the terms *naḥalâ* (8.22) and *gebûl yiśrāēl* (14.4; 15.4; 16.4) are employed to express the Land (see below). The deliberate employment in *Temple Scroll* of the phrase 'the Land of fathers' which is contrasted with 'lands of enemies' (59.5), on the one hand, and the uses of 'the allotment of fathers' and 'the territory of Israel' in 1 Maccabees and Judith, on the other, express a sentimental attachment to the Land among Jews, a sentiment which emerged anew in the mid-second century BCE.

5.4.2. Summary

It is impressive that there is no cosmological use of the term *ʾereṣ* in *Temple Scroll*. In contrast, it is mostly used in the territorial dimensions, especially in reference to

53. Cf. הגואים/הגויים = 'the nations (in the Land)': *TS* 60.17//Deut. 18.9; *TS* 60.21–61.01//Deut. 18.14.
54. Yadin 1983: II, 236f.
55. See *TS* 21.2; 23.7; 24.10–25.01; 39.11-13; 44.4–45.2. Cf. Mendels 1987: 123.
56. In 1 Macc. 10.72 it refers to the Land; see below.
57. *naḥalâ* = the Land: *TS* 62.13//Deut. 20.16; *TS* 64.13//Deut. 21.23.

the Land. Following mainly biblical expressions, the Land is signified as the holy place where the people of Israel should observe God's commandments. Although *Temple Scroll* lacks any words which bless the Land (cf. Deut. 8.7-10) and Land theologies in it are solely biblical, its emphasis on the holiness of the Land in relation to the sacredness of the Temple and the people is significant. It is the location of the sacred Temple and the holy people, among whom God dwells.

The Land is once called *ʾereṣ yiśrāēl* which the king should defend from foreign enemies. It is a territory defined by borders, and the foreign nations are to be expelled from it. Its enlargement is expected. Although any real programme or legitimization to reclaim the territory from the nations of the Land is not posed, the restoration of *ʾereṣ yiśrāēl* in territorial dimensions revives in *Temple Scroll*, at least, as an ideal.

Thus, the Land in *Temple Scroll* is esteemed as a holy place on the one hand, as a defined territory on the other.[58] Jews of the mid-second century BCE, who overcame the severe experience of persecution, attached anew a theological significance to ארץ אבות, and the Land regained its status as the holy territory in post-biblical Judaism.

5.5. *Judith*

The book of Judith is available in the LXX and secondary translations. Hebraisms and posited misunderstandings reflected in the LXX indicate its Hebrew original.[59] The LXX's literal rendering of Hebrew idioms assures the reconstruction of our Hebrew terms from Greek.[60] This work can be dated in the reign of John Hyrcanus I.[61]

5.5.1. γῆ/*ʾereṣ *in Judith*

In Judith the term γῆ/**ʾereṣ*, employed with οὐρανοί/**šāmayim*, is applied to praise God as the Creator (13.18b). God, therefore, is called 'the Lord of heavens and earth' (9.12).[62] The heavens and earth, God's creation, can be called to witness because of their stability (7.28).[63] In Judith there is no inquiry into the heavenly world or the netherworld, the heavens and earth (and sea) consistently represent

58. Cf. Mink 1987: 46.

59. Grintz 1986: 56–63; *HJP* III, 219; Moore 1985: 66f.

60. Attempts to reconstruct the Hebrew original have been made by Grintz (1986) and Simon (1969), both of which we shall constantly consult. The English translation of Judith is mine, otherwise noted.

61. Avi-Yonah 1984: 44; Aharoni *et al.* 2002: 157; Moore 1992b: 1123.

62. In the Bible there is no instance of the phrase *אדון שמים וארץ; a similar phrase can be found in Ezra 5.11; cf. Gen. 24.3; Deut. 3.24; 4.39; Josh. 2.11; see also Acts 4.24.

63. Cf. Chapter 2 nn. 66f. above.

a single self-completed universe (cf. 14.2). In these uses **šāmayim* and *ʾ*ereṣ* express God's lordship over the whole created world.[64]

Nebuchadnezzar calls himself 'the great king, the lord of all the earth' (2.5).[65] Similar titles are also applied to him: 'the lord of all the earth' (6.4),[66] 'the king of all the earth' (11.1, 7).[67] Nebuchadnezzar's ambition is stated as 'to annihilate all the gods of the earth,[68] so that all nations should worship Nebuchadnezzar alone, and that all their tongues and tribes should call him god' (3.8). His claim to be the one and only god is described as a challenge to the Creator, the true one and only God, a challenge which is embodied in his attack on God's people.[69] The designations of Nebuchadnezzar, 'the lord/king of all the earth' (i.e., 'of the human world'), are in contrast to that of the Creator, 'the Lord of heavens and earth' (i.e., 'of the universe'). The difference of designation expresses the superiority of the God of Israel over Nebuchadnezzar.

The reaction to this 'lord of all the earth' is ironically described that 'all the inhabitants of all the earth scorned the words of Nebuchadnezzar', for 'before them he was just one man' (1.11). His vengeance turns towards 'all the earth' (1.12; 2.1, 2, 6, 7, 11, 19).[70] Thus, the story setting gives Nebuchadnezzar a comical role of 'the lord of all the earth' who takes vengeance on 'all the earth'.

There are other uses of γῆ/*ʾ*ereṣ* in the sense of the human world; Judith was honoured 'throughout the whole world' (16.21),[71] and so on.[72] The phrase 'ends of the earth' represents the human world, as well (2.9; 11.21).[73]

64. See 'the God of heavens': 5.8; 6.19.

65. Cf. Grintz 1986: 84.

66. Cf. Chapter 2 n. 86 above.

67. Cf. Chapter 2 n. 89 above.

68. Considering Nebuchadnezzar's designations, our term must be translated as 'all the gods of the earth', not 'the land' (NRSV, LBDJ).

69. Craven (1983: 68f. and n. 11) insists that in Judith Nebuchadnezzar does not claim the title 'god', and that the verse 3.8 is Holofernes' ironical transgression of his lord's command stated in 2.5-13. The verse, however, not only describes Holofernes' acts, but also the narrator's own explanation of the reason for his acts. The verse, therefore, explains Nebuchadnezzar's 'secret plan' (2.2) to be a god. His self-designation, 'the lord', already implies his claim to divinity; cf. 1.11 (see next paragraph).

70. The translations of our term in these verses by NRSV, LBDJ and Löhr (1994) are utterly inconsistent. These uses of πᾶσα ἡ γῆ/**kol hāʾāreṣ* must be understood in parallelism with the self-designation of Nebuchadnezzar, hence it should be translated as 'all the earth', though, according to the context, the phrase seems to mention a larger western region listed in 1.7-10; see Grintz 1986: 80 on 1.11f.; Craven 1983: 70f. The term γῆ/*ʾ*ereṣ* in 7.4, 18 also signifies, in an exaggerated manner, the face of 'the earth', not of the Land.

71. γῆ/*ʾ*ereṣ* of 16.21 must mean 'earth' (= world), not 'land', since her honour in this verse is an ironical fulfilment of Holofernes' prediction in 11.23, and the peace of Israelites in 16.25 owes to her reputation 'throughout the whole world' (cf. 16.10).

72. 5.21; 10.19; 11.8, 16, 23; 13.18a; all in the form πᾶσα ἡ γῆ/**kol hāʾāreṣ*.

73. The Greek term γῆ in the sense of 'earth' in Judith hitherto we've seen must be the translation of Hebrew *ʾereṣ*, since it is contrasted to heaven and/or is used with **kol*; these are lacking in the uses of *ʾadāmâ* and *tēbēl*; see §§ 2.5.1; 2.5.2 above.

There are uses of γῆ/*ʾ*ereṣ* referring to a particular region. Individual territories can be mentioned with our term; the land of Goshen (1.9), etc.[74] Mesopotamia is called 'the land of their (Patriarchs') sojourning' in relation to the history of Israel (5.9).[75] In 5.18 the land of exile is called 'a land not theirs' (cf. Jer. 5.19). There once appears a term διασπορά, which might be a translation of *ארצות אשר נפוצו בהן, as Grintz reconstructs (5.19).[76]

Mention is made of 'the captivity of the Land and the desolation of our allotment' (8.22). The Hebrew original of the expression τὴν αἰχμαλωσίαν τῆς γῆς might be *גלות הארץ or *שבי/שבות הארץ.[78] The γῆ/*ʾ*ereṣ* here represents the people in the Land who may be taken into exile, whereas the Land itself which may be desolated is expressed by the term 'allotment' (ἡ κληρονομία ἡμῶν/*נחלתנו or *ירֻשתנו).[79]

Once a famous biblical phrase *כעפר הארץ 'like the dust of the earth' is used in a metaphor of innumerableness (2.20).[80] In addition, there are probably two instances of the term *ʾ*adāmâ* in Judith. The phrase 'earth and water' in 2.7 can be retranslated into *אדמה ומים.[81] Here *ʾ*adāmâ* means a clod of earth to be brought before the king (cf. 2 Kgs 5.17). A reference is made to 'from the face of the earth' (6.2). It must be taken from Hebrew *מעל פני האדמה, since it is a familiar biblical phrase while there is no attestation of מעל פני הארץ in the Bible.[82]

We have twelve uses of ὅριον/**gebûl* 'territory' in Judith.[83] Of these, three occurrences refer to *גבול ישראל (14.4; 15.4; 16.4).[84] Its exact borders are unclear, but considering a reference to the men of Gilead and Galilee who pursued Assyrians to Damascus (15.5), *gebûl yiśrāēl* in the author's mind is the Hexateuchal one including these two regions.

74. See 1.12; 5.7, 9, 10, 12, 15. Referring to a land with toponym is a characteristic use of the term ʾ*ereṣ*; see § 2.3.1 above.

75. For this expression, see Grintz 1986: 112.

76. Grintz 1986: 114; cf. Ezek. 11.17; 20.34, 41; Simon (1969) translates: הגולה אשר נפֹצו שם.

77. Grintz 1986: 136. There is no use of this expression in the Bible, but cf. Isa. 20.4; Jer. 24.5; 28.4; 29.22; 40.1.

78. שבות הארץ: Jer. 33.11; cf. also Jer. 33.7; 48.47; 49.39; Ezek. 16.53; 29.14; Joel 4.1; שבי with a place name: Isa. 20.4; 52.2; Ezra 3.8.

79. For the reconstruction **naḥalātēnû*, cf. Ps. 78.62; Isa. 49.8; Simon 1969: 366; for **yerušātēnû*, cf. 2 Chron. 20.11; Grintz 1986: 136. In 9.12 God is called Israel's κληρονομία/**naḥalâ*. In 16.21 it signifies tribal allotments.

80. Cf. Chapter 2 n. 32 above.

81. So Grintz (1986: 85); but Simon (1969: 356): עפר ומים.

82. See § 2.5.1 and n. 351 there. The latter expression is not attested in the Dead Sea Scrolls, either.

83. 1.5, 10, 12ab; 2.10, 25ab; 4.4; 14.4; 15.4, 5; 16.4; except the one in 3.8 which might be a textual corruption; see Grintz 1986: 96. Hebrew *gebûl* is translated in the LXX 223 times, of which ὅριον is employed 209 times (*c.* 93.7%); the equivalence of these terms is certain.

84. Cf. Chapter 2 n. 404 above.

5.5.2. Summary

A prominent use of the term γῆ/* ʾ*ereṣ* in Judith is the author's conscious application to 'all the earth'. This phrase expresses Nebuchadnezzar's ambition to be the one and only god in the whole human world. Throughout the entire story the author instructs his readers that the true God of the world is the Lord of heavens and earth, the Creator; hence Jews are able to maintain hopes for salvation unless they sin against Him. This reveals the background of the story, which is a conflict between foreign overlordship and Judaism. Learning from the success of the Maccabaean revolt, the author recommends Jews to keep their traditional way of life by narrating a victory of a faithful Jewess over an ambitious foreign ruler.

The author has Achior tell the biblical history of Israel from the origins of the Patriarchs to the people's return from the Exile (5.5-21). In this narrative, the Land which the Israelites possessed after the Exodus is smaller than the one assigned in the Bible: 'all the mountainous region' (5.15). This is the same mountainous region where Judaeans had settled when returning from the Exile (5.19), and where Jews were living at the main event of Judith (5.5). The region can be identified virtually with Judaea.[85] This means that the author claims Jewish rights only to the Judaea of his age, despite his reference to biblical *gebûl yiśrāēl* extending, at least, to Gilead and Galilee. Indeed, while assuming the existence of nations other than Israel living in the Palestine of his days (1.8, 12, 2.28; 5.2; 7.8), the author shows no concern about their territory. He even admits the proselytism of Achior, an Ammonite (14.10; cf. Deut. 23.3). Accordingly, our author was not an expansionist in relation to the Jewish political territory. His international perspectives, which can be seen from his uses of 'all the earth', reveal his antagonism towards foreign imperialism, but do not connote a hope of Israel's rule over the world. This reflects the peaceful atmosphere of his days when Jewish independence was established after bitter wars (cf. 16.25). Enjoying freedom from foreign rule, the author now seeks to teach the people that the God of Israel is the one and only Lord, whose voice no one can resist (16.14).

5.6. 1 Maccabees

It is widely held that 1 Maccabees, now available in Greek and other translations, was originally written in Hebrew. The Greek version shows literal translation as its character, and the original Hebrew can be presumed to be biblical.[86] The retroversion of Hebrew terms and phrases from the Greek version is assured by comparison with biblical passages.[87]

85. Cf. 'Judaea': 3.9; 4.1, 7; 11.19; 'all Judaea': 1.12; 4.13; 8.21; 'all the people of Judaea': 4.3.

86. Goldstein 1976: 14.

87. We shall constantly consult with a Hebrew reconstruction of Kahana (1969c). We can date 1 Maccabees in the reign of Hyrcanus I; see Bar-Kochva 1989: 151–70. The English translation of 1 Maccabees is mine, otherwise noted.

5.6.1. γῆ/*ʾereṣ *in 1 Maccabees*

The term γῆ/*ʾ*ereṣ* in 1 Maccabees can denote the *terra firma* in contrast to the sea (15.14).[88] Mention is made of 'the land of plain' (3.40).[89] A poetic expression 'the earth was shaken' appears in reaction to a human act (9.13).[90] Employed with the verb πίπτω/*נפל, the term γῆ/*ʾ*ereṣ* means 'the ground' (4.40; 6.46).[91] The pair of οὐρανός/**šāmayim* and γῆ/*ʾ*ereṣ* represents the most stable creation, which can testify for those Jews who were killed unjustly on the Sabbath (2.37).[92]

The term γῆ/*ʾ*ereṣ* is used in the sense of 'the human world', especially in the introduction. Alexander the Great killed 'the kings of the earth' (1.2),[93] advanced 'to the ends of the earth' (1.3a), and 'the earth became quiet before him' (1.3b); after his death, his officers and their descendants put on crowns, 'and evils increased in the earth' (1.9). It is stated that Romans subdued the kings coming against them 'from the end of the earth' (8.4). In the letter of Antiochus VII Sidetes it is written that 'your honor will become manifest in the whole earth' (15.9). Once our term represents 'this world' or 'the world of the living' in contrast to the netherworld (2.40).[94]

The human world can be expressed by 'all the lands' (15.23). This expression, however, connotes territorial dimensions, as evident from the plural form itself. In other occurrences, therefore, the plural χῶραι/*ארצות simply signifies certain 'lands' or 'regions' (1.4; 3.31, 37; 6.1; 8.8; 15.15, 19).[95]

There is frequent use of γῆ/χώρα/*ʾ*ereṣ* referring to a particular land: 'the land of Philistines' (3.24, 41; 4.22; 5.6, 68),[96] 'the land of Negev (or south)' (5.65),[97] etc.[98] The expression 'a foreign land' is also used (6.13; 15.33). γῆ/χώρα/*ʾ*ereṣ* in the sense of a land can be defined by a personal pronominal suffix, as well.[99] There are uses of ἡ γῆ/ἡ χώρα/**hāʾāreṣ* referring to a certain land.[100]

It can be defined by another qualification, 'fathers' referring to a foreigner's land (10.55, 67; 15.10). These uses are somewhat unique, since the phrase ארץ אבות appears rarely in the Bible and refers to the Land (Gen. 31.3; 48.21; cf. *TS* 59.12).

88. Cf. Chapter 2 n. 2.
89. Cf. Deut. 4.43; Jer. 48.21; Ps. 143.10.
90. Cf. Chapter 2 n. 64 above.
91. Cf. Chapter 2 nn. 20f. above.
92. Cf. Chapter 2 nn. 66f. above.
93. Cf. Chapter 2 n. 100 above.
94. Cf. Josh. 7.9; Nah. 2.14; Pss. 34.17; 109.15; 4QJub^c 4 (//*Jub*. 2.27).
95. The application of χῶραι for *ʾarāṣôt* instead of γαῖ is usual in the LXX; see Chapter 4 nn. 79f. above.
96. 3.24 has γῆ Φυλιστείμ, and the rest have γῆ ἀλλοφύλων which is a usual translation for ארץ פלשתים in the LXX.
97. The Greek expression ἐν τῇ γῇ τῇ πρὸς νότον seems to be taken from LXX Num. 13.29 (30); the original Hebrew could be *ארץ הנגב; cf. Chapter 2 n. 147.
98. See 1.1, 16, 19ab; 5.55; 8.3, 8; 12.25.
99. 1.24; 5.48; 8.16; 9.69, 72; 10.13, 52; 13.24; 15.4.
100. Other than the Land: 3.41; 8.10; 12.32; 15.4, 29. For references to the Land, see below.

Behind this usage there seems to be an ideology that a land was assigned to an ancestor, and his descendants have inherited it from generation to generation, an ideology that legitimates also Jewish possession of the Land (15.33f.).

In 1 Maccabees the Land is never called 'the land of Israel', but 'the land of Judah' in many instances.[101] The term referring to the Land can be modified by a personal pronominal suffix: 'our Land' (5.48; 7.6; 15.35), 'their land' (3.36; 10.72; 14.31, 36; 15.19, 21), etc.[102]

There are many occurrences of simple ἡ γῆ/ ἡ χώρα/**hāʾāreṣ* referring to the Land. It can react to its inhabitants as the *terra firma* (1.28). The Land keeps its nature as the soil (14.8).[103] In 6.49 the sabbatical year is expressed by the clause σάββατον ἦν τῇ γῇ/*שבת היתה לארץ.[104] The decree of Antiochus Epiphanes is expressed with our term: he sent letters 'to go after customs strange to the Land' (1.44). In response to this decree many of the people 'did evil in the Land' (1.52). A biblical phrase 'a great blow' is used several times, twice in relation to the Land (13.32; 15.35).[105] When describing the cessation of wars, 1 Maccabees prefers to employ a biblical clause '(and) the Land was quiet' (7.50; 9.57; 11.38, 52; 14.4; cf. 1.3).[106] Of Simon it is said that 'he made peace in the Land' (14.11). In these uses **hāʾāreṣ* is virtually identical with the land of Judaea, not with a biblical *ʾereṣ yiśrāʾēl* including regions beyond it.

The terms referring to Judaea can be employed with verbs expressing movements: 'go to' and/or 'come to',[107] and 'return to'.[108] Invasion of enemies into the Land is described by ἐμβατεύω εἰς, though the Hebrew original(s) is uncertain (12.25; 13.20; 14.31; 15.40).[109] The 'seizure' of the Land can be expressed by (κατα) κρατέω/*החזיק.[110]

101. 3.39; 5.45, 53, 68; 6.5; 7.10, 22, 50; 9.1, 57, 72; 10.30, 33, 37; 12.4, 46, 52; 13.1, 12; cf. ὅρια Ισραηλ/**gebûl yiśrāʾēl*: 2.46; 9.23.

102. 12.25; 15.6; see also 7.7.

103. Cf. Lev. 26.4; Ezek. 34.27; Zech. 8.12. See § 5.6.2.2 below.

104. For Hebrew reconstruction, see Kahana 1969c: 129.

105. 15.35 has 'our Land' instead of 'the Land'. Cf. 1 Macc. 1.30; 5.3, 34; 7.22; 8.4; 14.36; 15.29; see also Num. 11.33; Judg. 11.33; 15.8; 1 Sam. 4.10; 6.19; 19.8; 23.5; 1 Kgs 20.21; 2 Chron. 13.17; 28.5.

106. 7.50 and 9.57 have 'the land of Judah' instead of 'the Land'; for this expression, cf. Josh. 11.23; 14.15; Judg. 3.11, 30; 5.31; 8.28.

107. ἔρχομαι: 3.39; 5.45, 53; 7.10; 9.69; 12.52; 13.1, 12; ἀπέρχομαι: 5.48; 12.46; πορεύομαι: 6.5; εἰσπορεύομαι: 13.49; παραγίνομαι: 4.35; ἄγω: 5.23.

108. ἐπιστρέφω εἰς: 5.68; ἀποστρέφω εἰς: 16.10.

109. For ἐμβατεύω, see LXX Josh. 19.49, 51.

110. 7.22; 14.6; 16.13. From the Greek renderings Kahana (1969c) reconstructs three Hebrew words: תפש, משל, and כבש, respectively. In the LXX, however, κρατέω and κατακρατέω are, in many instances, applied to החזיק; see Hatch and Redpath 1989: II, 734, 783; verbs rooted from חזק suit with other occurrences of these Greek terms; cf. κρατέω: 1.2; 2.10; 10.52; 15.7, 33; κατακρατέω: 6.54; 8.2, 3, 4, 5, 10; 11.1, 49, 56; 15.3, 28, 33. If our argument is sound, 14.6 can be reconstructed as follows: *וירחב את הגבול לעמו ויחזיק בארץ 'and he expanded the territory for his people, and held fast to the Land'.

Mention is made of 'rulers of the Land' (9.25, 53; 14.17). In 14.28 'the elders of the Land'[111] are also mentioned along with 'rulers of the nation' as members of the great assembly.[112]

There are passages in which the referent of our term is uncertain.

(1) 3.29: οἱ φόροι τῆς χώρας mean tax payments from the provinces of the whole kingdom of Antiochus IV, hence the χώρα here virtually refers to his kingdom.[113] Then, the 'dissension and blow', which caused the reduction of tributes, are to have happened, not only in Judaea, but also in some other provinces, hence the phrase ἐν τῇ γῇ/**bāʾāreṣ* means the territory under Seleucid rule.[114] Although we have no historical data referring to 'dissension and blow' caused by Antiochus IV's 'abolishment of the laws' in any lands other than Judaea, this is assumed by the author of 1 Maccabees who applies Antiochus IV's decree of religious restriction to 'his whole kingdom' (1.41f., 51).[115]

(2) 9.24: While it is certain that the term ἡ χώρα/**hāʾāreṣ* here refers to the Land, its connotation is unclear. Josephus interprets the term as 'many' who could not hold out against the afflictions caused by the famine and their enemies (*Ant.* 13.3). Considering the uses of αὐτομολέω in 7.19, 24, in which it refers to 'turncoats' from Judas' side, it seems that **hāʾāreṣ* here too represents the inhabitants of the Land who were gone over to the renegades.[116]

(3) 3.9: The expression ἕως ἐσχάτου γῆς here is usually translated as 'to the end(s) of the earth'.[117] Similar phrases ἕως ἄκρων τῆς γῆς in 1.3 and ἀπ' ἄκρου τῆς γῆς in 8.4 designate undoubtedly 'to/from the end(s) of the earth' (see above). The reference to Judas' gathering in 'those who were perishing', however, probably forecasts his gathering of Jews from Galilee and Gilead described in ch. 5, places which locate at the end of the Land.[118] If so, there was in the author's mind an idea of the traditional biblical *ʾereṣ yiśrāēl*, an ideology which is more explicitly worded by the phrase *נחלת אבותינו in 15.33f. (see § 5.6.2.3 below). This ideology, however, is no more developed in this work, and the use of *ʾereṣ* referring to *ʾereṣ yiśrāēl* beyond Judaea is discernible here in 3.9 alone.

(4) 14.10, 13: The expression ἕως ἄκρου γῆς in 14.10 probably means 'the end of the earth', for a reference is made to 'Rome, and as far as Sparta' in the next paragraph (14.16f.). This international scope can be applied to the use of ἐπὶ τῆς γῆς in 14.13.[119]

111. Cf. Jer. 26.17.

112. Other occurrences of ἡ χώρα/**hāʾāreṣ* (= the land of Judah): 7.20, 24; 9.61, 65; 11.62, 64; 13.34; 14.29, 37, 42, 43, 44; 16.4, 14, 18.

113. Thus Bar-Kochva 1989: 229.

114. Goldstein (1976: 249) deliberately translates the phrase 'in his land'. The distinction between Greek χώρα and γῆ may possibly reflect the difference of the original Hebrew, *medînâ* and *ʾereṣ* (in the LXX *medînâ* is translated into χώρα 35 times [*c.* 76 %]), or the translator might understand the second occurrence of *ʾereṣ* in the sense of 'world' in an exaggerated manner.

115. See *Ant.* 12.294; Grabbe 1992: I, 247–56.

116. Thus Kahana 1969c: 140; Goldstein 1976: 376f.; cf. Chapter 2 n. 252 above.

117. NRSV, LBDJ, *APAT*.

118. Thus, Schwartz 1986: 670f. n. 11; cf. Isa. 26.15; Jer. 12.12; Ezek. 7.2.

119. See Goldstein 1976: 491 (on 14.13) and 351 (on 8.4).

5.6.2. Related Terms

5.6.2.1. γῆ/*ʿāpār

It seems that in 11.71 the term *ʿ*āpār* 'dust' is employed, and it is translated into Greek γῆ (cf. Josh. 7.6).

5.6.2.2. γῆ/*ʾadāmâ

The term *ʾ*adāmâ* is used at least once, in 14.8a. In the Bible 'tilling' is accompanied by *ʾ*adāmâ*, but never by *ʾereṣ*.[120]

There appears in 11.34 an expression 'crops of the land'; but it cannot be determined if the original Hebrew was *תבואת הארץ or *תבואת האדמה (cf. Lev. 23.39; Isa. 30.23).[121]

5.6.2.3. κληρονομία/*naḥalâ

The term **naḥalâ*, which is rendered by the Greek κληρονομία,[122] is undoubtedly employed with biblical senses. Mention is made of the land possession of Caleb in 2.56 (cf. Josh. 14.6-15). More importantly, the legitimacy of possession of the Land is expressed by this term in 15.33f.; the expression ἡ κληρονομία τῶν πατέρων ἡμῶν/*נחלת אבתינו is contrasted with γῆ ἀλλοτρία/ *ארץ נכריה. The claim to the Land possession outside Judaea as 'the allotment of our fathers' implicitly connotes an ideology of restoration of the whole *ʾereṣ yiśrāēl* as Jewish territory. This ideology became a real policy of the Hasmonaean dynasty thenceforwards.[123]

5.6.2.4. ὅρια/*gebûl

There appears Greek ὅρια (plural) 21 times, and it must be a translation of Hebrew **gebûl*.[124] It can designate 'border, boundary', a line marking limits of an area (3.32; 11.59). In many instances, however, it means 'territory' enclosed within borders (5.9; 6.25; 14.2).

The term can signify a territory governed by a *polis* (10.31, 89; 15.29). It can also refer to a province (14.34).[125] Once the term is used in the sense of 'the precinct of the Temple' (10.43).

Concerning the Land, a phrase ὅρια Ιουδαία appears several times. It can convey the senses of 'the borders of Judaea' (5.60; 14.33), and of 'the territory of Judaea' (7.24; 11.34; 15.30). Employed with a pronominal suffix, the term can also express the territory of Judaea (3.36, 42; 9.72). In the eulogy of Simon it is stated: 'he extended the territory for his people, and held fast to the Land' (14.6).[126]

120. See § 2.5.1 above.

121. Kahana (1969c: 153): *hāʾadāmâ*; Stern (1972: 106): *hāʾāreṣ*.

122. See n. Chapter 4 n. 99.

123. In 6.24 κληρονομίαι (pl.) means 'property'. For the verb κληρονομέω, cf. 1.32; 2.10, 57.

124. The plural *gebûlôt* is used rarely and always with pronominal suffix in the Bible (only 7 passages of 240 occurrences of the term; see Even-Shoshan 1990: 217f.). See n. 83 above.

125. See Goldstein 1976: 305 on 5.68.

126. See n. 110 above; cf. Exod. 34.24; Deut. 12.20; 19.8; 1 Chron. 4.10.

Our author applies a familiar biblical phrase **gebûl yiśrāēl* in 2.46 and 9.23. In the former, he reports Mattathias' forcible circumcision of all the uncircumcised boys found within **gebûl yiśrāēl*. In the latter, the author explains that after the death of Judas, the renegades emerged **bekol gebûl yiśrāel*. In both instances the territory can be identified with Judaea, not with the biblical *gebûl yiśrāēl* consisting of the territories of the twelve tribes.[127] By employing this phrase, it seems, the author intends to express, not a politically ideal territory, but the one with religious significance as 'God's holy territory' (Ps. 78.54). This connotation is close to his uses of the term 'Israel' for the Jewish people.

5.6.3. Summary

The most frequent usage of the term **ʾereṣ* in 1 Maccabees is reference to the Land. In these occurrences the term is almost applied to Judaea, not a biblical 'Land of Israel' (an exception can be found in 3.9). This reflects a historical situation of our author's days when Jewish dominion was not far beyond Judaea. The author, therefore, imposes the religious significance of *gebûl yiśrāēl* upon Judaea (2.46; 9.23). On the other hand, when emphasizing the legitimacy of Jewish possession of the promised Land, the author chooses another biblical term – κληρονομία/ **naḥalâ* (15.33f.). Our term, in contrast, is never employed in relation to the Land-promise, despite the fact that 1 Maccabees models biblical stories in many instances. That is to say, the term **ʾereṣ* mentioning the Land in 1 Maccabees is used with a real political connotation, while ideologies concerning the Land are expressed by other biblical terms. The uses of these terms reflect a situation in which biblical Land theology made an appearance as a real political theme of the Hasmonaean dynasty, namely, a policy of expansion of the Jewish territory.[128]

5.7. Jubilees

Jubilees is preserved in its entirety in Ethiopic alone, while partially available in Latin and other versions and Hebrew fragments discovered at Qumran, which attest to Hebrew as its original language.[129] Since *Jubilees* is a parabiblical literature, its language must be biblical, too. The comparison with relevant biblical passages and idioms can assure the reconstruction of Hebrew terms from Ethiopic.[130]

127. Cf. Judg. 19.29; 1 Sam. 7.13; 11.3, 7; 27.1; 2 Sam. 21.5; 1 Kgs 1.3; 2 Kgs 10.32; 14.25; 1 Chron. 21.12; Ezek. 11.10, 11; Mal. 1.5.

128. Cf. Mendels 1987: 47–50.

129. 1Q17-18 (1QJub^{a-b}); 2Q19-20; 3Q5; 4Q176ab; 4Q216-224 (4QJub^{a-h}); 11Q12; for versions, see VanderKam 1977: 1–101; 1994a.

130. For the date, see Mendels 1987: 57–88; see also n. 211 below; cf. Charles 1902: li–lxviii; VanderKam 1977: 207–13; 1997: 3–24. The English translation of *Jubilees* is mine, otherwise noted.

5.7.1. medr/*ʾereṣ *in* Jubilees

In *Jubilees* the term *medr*/*ʾ*ereṣ* appears many times, and its uses can be classified in the same way as in the Bible: (1) the tangible earth, (2) the cosmological earth, and (3) a territorial land.[131] In this section we shall analyse the term according to this classification and supplement it with a discussion of *Jubilees*' eschatological expectations concerning our term.

5.7.1.1. medr/*ʾereṣ *as Tangible Earth*

The term *medr*/*ʾ*ereṣ* can refer tangibly to the *terra firma*, a dry solid part of the earth contrasted to the water,[132] to the sky (7.30; 11.19ab),[133] and to mountains (2.7a).[134] References are made to every creeping thing which creeps (or walks) on the earth.[135] There are expressions of things falling down to the 'ground', as well (10.26, 30; 41.5; 43.8//Gen. 38.9).

The term *medr*/*ʾ*ereṣ* connotes 'soil' with productivity of plants as its nature: 'the fruit of the earth' (11.13),[136] 'the fat of the earth' (22.6),[137] and 'the grain of the land' (42.2).[138] The author of *Jubilees* knows of healing by means of 'trees of the earth' (10.12).[139]

The products of *medr*/*ʾ*ereṣ* can be brought forth only by cooperation with rain.[140] God sends down rain and dew upon the earth (12.4). The dew of heaven and the dew of the earth are regarded as a symbol of God's blessing (26.23; cf. Gen. 27.28), and their lack means to be desert (26.33; cf. Gen. 27.39). Famine is caused by the denial of rain to the earth.[141] Human cooperation with the earth, too, is presupposed in the phrases 'sow (in) the soil'.[142]

The author somewhat emphasizes the role of the sun in relation to the products of the earth.[143] The role he gives the sun in this regard must have something to do with his solar calendar (2.9//4QJub[a] 6.7f.).

131. Since these usages are characteristic of Hebrew *ʾereṣ*, as we saw in Chapter 2 above, we shall discuss the matter of Hebrew retroversion only when other possibilities are recognized.

132. 5.26ab (//Gen. 7.17-20), 27 (//Gen. 7.24), 30 (//Gen. 8.5, 13), 31ab (//Gen. 8.14); 6.25ab (//Gen. 8.13); 6.4, 15, 16; 7.21; see also 2.14a; 6.5b.

133. Cf. Chapter 2 n. 4.

134. Cf. Chapter 2 n. 6 above.

135. 2.13 [//Gen. 1.25], 14b; 3.1ab; 5.2, 20; 6.6; 7.24; see 4QJub[a] 7.3 (//2.14); cf. § 2.1.1 above; *1 En.* 7.5.

136. Hebrew original might be *פרי הארץ (Num. 13.26; Deut. 1.25; Isa. 4.2; Lev. 25.19) or *פרי האדמה (Deut. 7.13; 26.2, 10; 28.4, 11, 18, 33, 42, 51; 30.9; Jer. 7.20; Mal. 3.11; Ps. 105.35); see n. 200 below.

137. Cf. Gen. 27.28, 39.

138. Ethiopic reads *zarʾa bamedr*, but the Latin text (*frumentum terrae*) seems better, since in the parallel passages in Gen. 41.35, 49 appears the term בר 'grain'. Here the term *ʾ*ereṣ* connotes not only the soil, but also the land of Egypt, as Eth. ms. 12 (A) has.

139. The original Hebrew is probably *עצי הארץ, not **hāʾadāmâ*, since the trees here are natural ones and not agricultural products (see § 2.1.3 above). Cf. *1 En.* 7.1; Sir. 38.4-8; see also Charles 1895: 37 nn. 20, 22 and Appendix I, 179.

140. Cf. Chapter 2 nn. 39f. above.

141. 42.1; cf. 40.1, 3; 42.2, 13.

142. 11.11, 18, 22; 45.10; cf. Gen. 26.12.

143. 2.10//4QJub[a] 6.9; 2.12//4QJub[a] 6.13f.

5.7.1.2. medr/*ʾereṣ *as Cosmological Earth*

The *medr*/*ʾ*ereṣ is one of the seven things God created on the first day (2.2//Gen. 1.1-5; cf. *Jub.* 2.16).[144] The heaven and earth can represent a space in which all the creatures are made.[145] *samāy*/**šāmayim* is the firmament on which celestial bodies move (2.8). *medr*/**ʾereṣ* forms a half part of the created world, and the creatures are collectively expressed by 'everything (that is/was) on the earth'.[146] *samāy*/**šāmayim* is assigned also to the abode of God and angels, who kept the Sabbath in heaven (2.30; cf. 2.18). Thus, *samāy*/**šāmayim* can represent the heavenly-world (4.15; 5.6 and 27.21) and *medr*/**ʾereṣ* the earthly-world (4.6; 25.20).

The term *medr*/**ʾereṣ* can refer to the place of burial (4.29; 23.31).[147] Mention is made of 'the valleys of the earth', in which the wicked angels should be tied up (5.6, 10).[148] Under the valleys there are 'springs of abyss' (5.29; 6.26). The abyss is related to Sheol, which is assigned to the place of judgement (5.14; 22.22; 24.31). Thus, the threefold world consisting of heaven, earth and Sheol is assumed, though the heavenly world and the netherworld are not elaborated in detail.

medr/**ʾereṣ*, the earthly-world, therefore, can be called *medr ḥeyāwān*/*ארץ (ה)חיים 'the world of the living' (22.22; 36.9).[149] As far as the earth endures, human history goes on. There are several expressions of its endurance: 'all the days of the earth';[150] 'like the days of heaven above the earth';[151] '(all) the (days of the) generations of the earth'.[152] The existence of a certain nation can be expressed in a similar manner: 'in their [Philistines'] days upon the earth' (24.29). These expressions presuppose the long endurance of the earth, but also connote its end. There is in fact an explicit reference to a new creation of the earth (1.29). To the *eschaton*, not all nations can survive; some nations may disappear from the earth, from history. There are frequent references to uprootedness and destruction of a nation from the earth. The children of Israel, for instance, must keep the Sabbath not to 'be uprooted from the earth' (2.27//4QJub^c 4);[153] Jacob praises Judah, saying: 'all who hate you and afflict you and curse you will be uprooted and destroyed from the earth and be cursed' (31.20).[154] Remarkably, references are made to the

144. See VanderKam 1994b.

145. 2.25; 7.36; 36.7; cf. 1.29; 4.21; 19.25; 22.6. In 25.11; 32.18 'heaven and earth' represent whole Creation.

146. 2.12; 3.3; 5.16; 7.35; 12.4. In 2.14c *medr*/**ʾereṣ* represents all the creatures on the earth.

147. Cf. Num. 16.33; Job 16.18.

148. Cf. *1 En.* 88.1-3; 90.25f.

149. Cf. Chapter 2 n. 79 above.

150. 6.4, 12, 16; 22.15; cf. Gen. 8.22; Job 8.9; 1 Chron. 29.15.

151. 19.27; cf. Deut. 11.21.

152. 4.18; 6.10; 12.24; 16.28; 19.20; 21.24//4QJub^d 2.30//4QJub^f 1.8 (כול דורות הארץ); 22.9; 30.8.

153. See 6.12, 14; 15.26, 28, 34; 21.22//4QJub^f 1.4; 30.22; 33.19; 37.6; cf. Josh. 7.9; Nah. 2.14; Pss. 34.17; 109.15.

154. These occurrences of uprootedness should be understood as 'from the earth', rather than 'from the Land', since *medr*/**ʾereṣ* in these expressions is virtually identical with 'the world of the living', and there is no threat of exile in the context, but death penalty; cf. Amaru 1994: 27–30, 43–7, 140–2, 147–9.

uprootedness of foreign nations dwelling in the Land: Canaanites (20.4; 22.20f.; cf. 10.29-34; 7.10-13), Idumaeans (35.14; 36.9), Philistines (24.28-33; cf. Amos 9.2-4), Amorites (29.11),[155] and Moabites and Ammonites (16.9).[156] These passages must reflect the author's antagonism towards the nations of the Land.[157] At any rate, the endurance of the earth means that the earth as a space for animate beings is inevitably involved in human history.

*medr/*ʾereṣ* is specifically connected to existence and deeds of human beings, which make history: in the days of Cain houses were built 'on the earth' (4.9).[158] Allusions are made to the beginning of certain acts on the earth: Enosh 'was the first to call on the Lord's name on the earth' (4.12).[159] In these uses *medr/*ʾereṣ* is virtually equated with the 'human world'.

Among human deeds on the earth, frequent references are made to 'injustice'. It is the cause of the Deluge (5.2-3; 7.23). Similar descriptions can be found in an eschatological vision (23.14, 18). Injustice is connected to evil spirits.[160] Specific sins are also mentioned; the violation of a territory allotted to others (9.15); going astray after the graven images and after impurity (11.16). Fornication on the earth is repeatedly mentioned (16.5-9; 33.2-20).

In connection with injustice, particular attention is paid to bloodshedding on the earth. The expression 'pouring blood out upon the earth' is frequently employed.[161] The repetitious description of blood pouring is connected to a command not to shed or eat blood (cf. 6.7-14; 7.28f.; 21.18-20), a command which can be found in the Noachide covenant (Gen. 9.4-6). Yet, *Jubilees* goes beyond biblical rules: 'No blood shall be seen on you of all the blood' (7.30a; cf. 21.17a). It is ordered to cover blood poured out upon the earth.[162] The reason is explained as follows: 'for the blood which is poured out defiles the earth, and the earth cannot be purified from the blood of man except through the blood of the one who poured it out'.[163] In these passages, *medr/*ʾereṣ* defiled by injustice, by blood in particular, is understood in cosmological dimensions.[164] A reference, therefore, is made to Noah's 'atonement for (all the sins of) the earth' after the Deluge (6.2; cf. 1QapGen 10.13). Furthermore, an eschatological purification of the earth is expected (4.26; 50.5; see below).

155. Here we have a different expression: 'there is for them no length of days on the earth'.

156. See also 5.9; 7.27; 10.3; 22.22.

157. These occurrences of *medr/*ʾereṣ*, too, should be rendered as 'the earth', and not 'the Land' (cf. n. 154 above), though it may connote both, since one of the author's interests is actual restoration of the biblical Land in Jewish hands (see below); cf. Charles 1902: lv–lvi.

158. See also 4.4 (//Gen. 4.11f.), 7, 19; 22.22//4QJub[f] 2.i.1-2.

159. See also 4.17; 16.21.

160. 10.11; cf. 5.1; 10.1-14; 23.29; see Charles 1902: 81 n.

161. 7.24, 25, 27; 11.2; 23.20, 23; see 4QJub[d] 2.18 (//*Jub*. 21.19).

162. 7.30b; cf. 21.17b; Lev. 17.13.

163. 21.19//4QJub[d] 2.18-20; cf. *Jub*. 7.32f.; Num. 35.33.

164. In *Jubilees* 'blood poured out upon the earth' is connected with its impurity and sin. We, therefore, categorize these uses, not in the 'ground', but in the 'earthly-world'. In the Bible, in contrast, the commandments not to defile *ʾereṣ* are related to the Land; cf. Lev. 19.29; Num. 35.33f.; Deut. 24.4.

Conversely, righteousness is celebrated (10.17). Commands to do righteousness are repeated. It is ordered to do justice and truth in the sinful earthly-world, and a promise is given to Israel to be planted in the earth as a plant of truth.[165]

Mention is made of God's blessing on the earth. The multiplication of mankind on the earth is regarded as God's blessing.[166] Special blessings are given to Abraham and his seed (12.23//Gen 12.1-3). God gave him seed 'upon the earth' so that they might take possession of the Land (17.3). Abraham's blessings for his sons and grandsons are repetitiously depicted.[167] In addition, the phrase 'all the nations of the earth' appears several times. Its uses can be divided into two; their blessing in Israel (12.23; 18.16; 24.11; cf. 20.10), and Israel's election from them (19.18; 22.9). In these uses the nations of the earth are distinguished from Israel, as in the Bible.

5.7.1.3. medr/*ʾereṣ *as Land*

The term ***medr/*ʾereṣ*** can refer to 'a land' allotted to nations of the earth. In *Jubilees* 8–9 the division of the earth for Noah's three sons is described in detail in a manner different from that of Genesis 10.[168] At the time when Peleg was born, Noah's sons 'began to divide the earth for themselves' (8.8), though 'in a bad way' (8.9). Then, an authoritative division was made by Noah under supervision of an angel (8.10). Noah 'divided the earth by lots which his three sons would possess (*ʾaḫaza*)' (8.11).[169]

Shem's lot is assigned 'in the middle of the earth' (8.12), and includes sacred places on the earth: the Garden of Eden (cf. 3.12), Mt Sinai, and Mt Zion in the middle of the navel of the earth (8.19; cf. 4.26).[170] Thus, the land of Shem is assigned to the dwelling of the Lord, 'the God of Shem' (8.18). It is 'a blessed and excellent portion',[171] 'a blessed and wide land, and everything that is in it is very good' (8.21). Compared with the land of Ham (8.22-24; cf. Gen. 10.6-20) and the land of Japheth (8.25-29; cf. Gen. 10.2-5), 'the land of Shem is neither hot nor cold, but it is a mixture of cold and heat' (8.30). The world map is schematized as Europe to Japheth, Asia to Shem, and Africa to Ham. This schematization sets the stage for the following narrative of Canaan's usurpation of the Land (10.28-34). This division of the earth is authoritative and eternal (8.12, 24, 29). Noah has his sons swear by oath to curse everyone who seeks to possess the portion which does not come out by his lot (9.14f.).

Ham, Shem and Japheth divided their portion among their sons (ch. 9). Ham and his sons went into 'the land which he was to possess' (10.28). Canaan, however, did not go to 'the land of his allotment' (10.29), but dwelt in 'the land of Lebanon'

165. 7.34; 20.2; 21.24//4QJub[d] 2.29f.//4QJub[f] 1.7f.; 36.3, 4, 6.

166. *Jub.* 6.5, 9//Gen. 9.1, 7; *Jub.* 10.4; cf. *Jub.* 5.1.

167. 19.17-20; 22.24; 20.9f.; 21.25//4QJub[d] 2.33f.; 31.7, 18.

168. For Hellenistic influence on the world map depicted in *Jubilees*, cf. F. Schmidt 1990.

169. For Eth. *ʾaḫaza*, see n. 205 below.

170. For Mt Zion as the Lord's mountain, cf. *Jub.* 18.7, 13; for its eschatological role, cf. *Jub.* 1.27-29; 4.26; for navel of the earth, cf. Ezek. 38.12; *1 En.* 26.1.

171. Ethiopic *makfalt* may be equivalent to Hebrew חלק.

(10.29). Against this act, his father and brothers reminded him of the oath which they had sworn before Noah, saying: 'You have settled in a land which is not yours', 'Do not dwell in the dwelling of Shem' (10.30-32). Since Canaan did not listen to them (10.33), Canaanites are cursed and are destined to be uprooted from the earth (20.4; 22.20f.; cf. 7.10-13). Thus, *Jubilees* explains why the Land was named the land of Canaan (10.34), denounces the illegitimate possession of the Land by Canaanites, and claims the legitimacy of its ownership by later Israel, the descendants of Shem ('until this day' [10.33]). This claim is close to the one made in 1 Macc. 15.33f., though much fuller in its scale. The entire story of division of the earth in chs 8–10 undoubtedly aims to legitimate this claim.

This claim is also consistent in uses of the expression 'the land of Lebanon'.[172] Lebanon in the Bible refers to the wooded mountain-range on the northern border of Israel.[173] In *Jubilees*, however, its borders are defined as 'from Hamath to the entrance of Egypt' (10.33),[174] very close to a traditional definition of the Land (cf. 1 Kgs 8.65//2 Chron. 7.8).[175] Thus, it is equated with the land of Canaan (10.29, 34).[176] The author of *Jubilees* gives the original name of the Land as 'the land of Lebanon', since it is illegitimately named 'the land of Canaan' because of Canaan's usurpation.[177]

The term *medr/*ʾereṣ* as a land can be defined by an eponym or a toponym (Egypt, Shinar, etc.). There are in *Jubilees* such non-biblical uses as 'the land of Eden' (4.24; 8.16, 21), 'the land of Red Sea' (8.21), etc.[178]

A land can also be defined by a phrase or a relative clause that places it in connection with a person or a group. Attention is paid to the place where Adam was created (3.9). After being expelled from the Garden of Eden, Adam and his

172. 8.21; 9.4; 10.29, 33; 12.15.

173. Cf. BDB, 526f.

174. 'Hamath' probably intends Lebo-Hamath, a traditional north border of the Land, see 13.2f. The 'entrance of Egypt' is identified, according to 10.29, with 'the River of Egypt', that is, the Nile. This southern border is taken from Gen. 15.18; cf. Chapter 2 n. 303 above.

175. Although the eastern border of the promised Land in 14.18 extends to 'the River Euphrates' in accordance with Gen. 15.18-21, Canaan seems to live on the west side of the Jordan River according to 10.29. This accords with the list of Shem's portions in 8.21, according to which the land of Lebanon is distinguished from the land of Bashan, i.e., Transjordan. *Jub.* 13.2f. too limits the promise of the Land 'from entrance of Hamath to the tall oak' despite Gen. 12.7 in which no territorial definition is given. This suggests that the author's actual concern is focused on the promise of 'the Lord's Land', despite his knowledge of the promise of 'the Greater Israel'; compare with *Apocr. Gen.* 21.8-19, which we shall see below.

176. According to 12.15, Terah and his sons went out of Ur of the Chaldees 'so that they might come into the land of Lebanon, that is (*wa*), into the land of Canaan'. While Ethiopic *wa* (= Hebrew ו) here is usually translated as 'and', it should be taken as an explicative. Henceforth, therefore, the phrase 'the land of Lebanon' is never used, but 'the land of Canaan'.

177. The toponym 'Lebanon' is chosen probably because it has no eponym in the Bible; cf. Deut. 1.7; 11.24; Josh. 1.4; Zech. 10.10.

178. 'The land of Kabratan' in 32.32 is taken from כברת הארץ ('some distance') of Gen. 35.16, but is understood as a proper name as in the LXX.

wife dwelt in 'the land of Elda',[179] 'the land of their creation' (3.32).[180] When Adam died, his sons buried him 'in the land of his creation' (4.29). Thus *Jubilees* fills up a lacuna of biblical narrative which keeps silent on the place of Adam's life outside the Garden of Eden.[181]

Mention is made of 'the land of (one's) sojourning' in relation to the Patriarchs (15.10; 16.20; 24.9; 27.11; 36.20; 39.1).[182] Some of them appear in the context of the Land-promise (15.10; 24.9; 27.11).[183]

5.7.1.4. medr/*ʾereṣ *of Promise*

The Land-promise to the Patriarchs is presupposed at the beginning of the first speech of the Lord to Moses (1.7//4QJub[a] 2.2-3). While *Jubilees* reproduces biblical expressions of the Land-promise verbatim by and large,[184] there are cases where the author adds his own comments or creates new statements. To the story of Sarah's death and burial (Genesis 23) a comment is added: '(Abraham) did not say a single word concerning the promise of the Land' (19.9).[185] This addition emphasizes the faithful character of Abraham,[186] and explains the reason Abraham paid for the place which ought to be his by its original assignment to Shem and by God's promise. By so doing, the author claims again the legitimacy of Israel's possession of the Land. In the brief report of the feast of the day Isaac was weaned (Gen. 21.8), *Jubilees* sets a situation that Ishmael was attendant at the feast (17.2), and adds a comment: '(Abraham) rejoiced because the Lord had given him seed upon the earth to possess the Land' (17.3). By this addition, the specific role of Isaac (and his line) to possess the Land is emphasized in contrast to the fate of Ishmael, another son (17.4-14). The author creates a testament of Abraham to Jacob (22.10-30), in which his eternal possession of the Land is referred to (v. 27; cf. 13.7; 14.7). Similarly, *Jubilees* has Rebecca make a blessing for Jacob concerning God's giving of 'this pleasant Land' as 'a possession forever' (25.17).[187]

The Land can be ornamented by various qualifications in relation to its fertility.[188] Above all, a special status is assigned to the Land on account of the Temple built

179. Ethiopic *medr ʾēldā* is probably a corruption of *ארץ מולדה/ת; see Charles 1902: 29 n. VanderKam 1989: II, 21 n.

180. *Jubilees* seems to reinterpret Gen. 3.23 to mean 'to till the land (not material, but territorial) from which he was taken'.

181. There are other definitions of *medr/*ʾereṣ* in the sense of 'a land'; direction: 10.28; 13.10; 28.1; 29.12; nature: 18.2 (cf. Gen. 22.2).

182. Cf. Chapter 2 n. 162 above.

183. There are many uses of *medr/*ʾereṣ* in the sense of a land with the definite article or a pronominal suffix. Mention is made of 'the Sabbaths of the Land' in 50.2f., 13.

184. *Jub.* 12.22-24//Gen. 12.1-3; *Jub.* 13.3//Gen. 12.7; *Jub.* 13.19-21//Gen. 13.14-17; *Jub.* 14.7//Gen. 15.7 (cf. Gen. 17.7f.); *Jub.* 14.18//Gen. 15.18-21; *Jub.* 15.10//Gen. 17.8; *Jub.* 24.8-11// Gen. 26.1-5; *Jub.* 27.11//Gen. 28.3f.; *Jub.* 27.22-24//Gen. 28.13-15; *Jub.* 45.14//Gen. 48.22. In these reproductions, the author's special attention to Abraham's descendants ('seed'), who must be his contemporary Jews, is apparent in his additions and modifications of the biblical story.

185. For the translation, see VanderKam 1989: II, 111 n.

186. Cf. Endres 1987: 20.

187. For this expression in 25.17, see n. 205 below.

188. 1.7; 8.21; 13.2, 6; 25.17.

in it (1.10//4QJub[a] 2.9f.; 49.18f.). As apparent from 49.18, the promised Land is identified with the land of Canaan.[189] This is also attested to by the author's repetitious accusation against Canaan.

In these two passages (1.10; 49.18f.) the location of the Temple is not specified, although the author must have known of the existence of the Jerusalem Temple in his own days. The statements that 'they abandoned ... My temple' (1.10) and that 'until the temple of the Lord is built upon the Land' (49.18; cf. *TS* 29.9f.) suggest that the author does not regard as valid enough the Jerusalem Temple cult current in his days. Rather, he gives an eschatological role to Mt Zion. God orders the angel of the presence to 'dictate[190] for Moses from the beginning of creation until My temple is built among them for all eternity. ... Then Zion and Jerusalem will be holy' (1.27f.). At the time of the new creation 'the temple of the Lord will be created in Jerusalem on Mt. Zion' (1.29). Mt Zion bears a special role as the location of the eschatological temple: 'Mt. Zion will be sanctified in the new creation for the sanctification of the earth. On account of this the earth will be sanctified from all its sins and its uncleanness throughout the generations of eternity' (4.26). These passages also assume that the actual Jerusalem Temple of the author's time is not as holy as could be, hence Mt Zion needs to be sanctified in the new creation. On the other hand, a unique relationship between the Land and the earth emerges by this eschatological role of Mt Zion. The Land gains a special status upon the earth on account of Mt Zion, whose eschatological function as the Lord's Temple extends to the entire earth. Thus, interestingly enough, territorial dimensions of the Land can be integrated into cosmological (and eschatological) perspectives of the earth, the Land and the earth, both of which are expressed by the term *medr*/*ʾ*ereṣ*.

There are, indeed, several references to the earth-possession of Israel. In Abraham's prayer for Jacob the eschatological hope of Israel's dominion over all the nations is envisioned (22.11-15). This is evident from the expression 'rule over all the seed of Seth' (v. 12). The sanctification of some of Israel 'throughout all the earth' intends the same goal (v. 11; cf. Gen. 27.29). Israel will rule the world as 'a holy people' (v. 12)[191] and as 'the people of the Lord's allotment' (v. 15),[192] after justification of their 'ways' (v. 12) and their purification from 'injustice of impurity' (v. 14). From this worldwide scope, the biblical expression ירש את הארץ is applied to Israel's possession of 'all the earth' (v. 14).[193]

The dominion of Israel over the entire world is again promised to Jacob directly by God (32.19). The author extends the promise from the Land in Gen. 35.12 maximally to 'all the earth under heaven'.[194] Its possession by Israel will endure

189. Cf. 12.28; 13.1-3; 14.7; 15.10; 46.13; 50.4.

190. For the reading 'dictate', see VanderKam 1981, 1989: II, 6.

191. Cf. Exod. 19.6; Deut. 7.6; 14.2, 21; 26.19; 28.9; Isa. 62.12; 63.18; Dan. 12.7.

192. Cf. Deut. 9.26, 29; 32.8f.; 1 Sam. 10.1; 1 Kgs 8.51; Isa. 63.17; Jer. 10.16; 51.19; Joel 4.2; Mic. 7.18; Pss. 74.2; 78.71; 94.5, 14; 106.5, 40; 127.3.

193. Cf. *1 En.* 5.7; Sir. 36.1-22; 44.21.

194. The expression 'under heaven' undoubtedly indicates that *medr*/*ʾ*ereṣ* here means 'the earth'. Compare VanderKam 1989: II, 213 ('land') and 2001: 72 ('earth').

'forever'. Israel's dominion over the world must be in relation to the repetitious reference to the blessing of 'all the nations of the earth' in Israel (12.23; 18.16; 24.11; cf. 20.10). The power over nations is specifically assigned to Judah (31.18). In the closing chapter (ch. 50) the author has the angel of the presence tell of Israel: 'And jubilees will pass by until Israel is purified from all the sin of fornication, and impurity, and contamination, and sin and error. And they will dwell in confidence in all the earth (*medr*/*ʾ*ereṣ*). And then they will not have any satan or evil one. And the earth (*medr*/*ʾ*ereṣ*) will be purified from that time until all days' (50.5). Translators render the term *medr*/*ʾ*ereṣ* here as 'the land',[195] probably because vv. 2-4 speak of the entrance of Israelites into the Land and its Sabbaths. Our passage, however, does not continue the issue of the Land, but envisions an eschatological ideal.[196] The purification of Israel and of the earth belongs to eschatological visions of *Jubilees* (4.26; 22.12, 15). The disappearance of 'satan and evil one' is also included in the author's eschatological description (23.29). Accordingly, Israel's dwelling 'in all the earth' (50.5) must be related to their eschatological possession of 'all the earth' (22.14; 32.19). This idea is also expressed in the promise of progeny to Jacob by Abraham (19.21) and by Rebecca (25.20).[197] It might be an exegetical application to Jacob of God's blessings for Adam and Noah along with Abraham in the book of Genesis.[198]

5.7.2. Related Terms

5.7.2.1. medr/*ʾadāmâ

Although there is no direct Hebrew attestation of the term *ʾadāmâ* from Qumran finds, we can infer its uses from biblical parallel passages (*Jub.* 3.25//Gen. 3.17-19; *Jub.* 3.35//Gen. 3.23; *Jub.* 4.28//Gen. 5.29). In 11.23f. the term *medr* is used in the sense of 'ground' in relation to a farm implement, so it may be the translation of *ʾ*adāmâ*.[199] Mention is made of 'the fruits of your [Isaac's] land' (20.9), and 'the firstfruits of the land' (22.4), in both of which *medr* can be ascribed to *ʾ*adāmâ*.[200]

195. Littmann (1994); Charles (1902); Wintermute (1985); VanderKam (1989); Amaru (1994: 48).

196. Thus VanderKam 2001: 84.

197. Translators agree to render our term of 19.21 as 'the earth', but do not of 25.20; 'the earth': Littmann (1994), Charles (1902); 'the land': Wintermute (1985), VanderKam (1989: II, 162). The reference to the 'joy of heaven and earth' and to 'the great day of peace' in 25.20 indicates that the progeny is not limited in the Land, but extends to the earth; cf. Amaru 1994: 39, 145f. n. 61; for the eschatological 'great peace', cf. *Jub*. 23.30.

198. Gen. 1.28; 9.1, 7; 13.16; 15.5; cf. *Jub*. 19.24f., 27; 22.13. Cf. the promise of progeny in *Jubilees* to Noah: 6.5, 9; 10.4; to Abraham: 13.20; to Isaac: 24.22; to Jacob: 19.22; 27.23 (all but to Noah contain the phrase 'the sands of the earth'); of these, the promise in 13.20; 24.22; 27.23 does not connote Israel's multiplication on the earth.

199. So Goldman 1969: 48. For a textual problem, see VanderKam 1989: II, 69 n.

200. For *Jub*. 20.9; cf. Deut. 7.13; 28.4, 11, 18, 42, 51; see also n. 136 above. For *Jub*. 22.4; cf. Exod. 23.19; 34.26; Neh. 10.36 (there is no use of בכורי הארץ in the Bible).

*ʾ*adāmâ* can also be used in universal dimensions. In relation to the Deluge story, obliteration of beings from the earth is expressed by *מעל פני האדמה.[201] The blessing of nations in Israel is promised to Jacob with the biblical wording *כל משפחת האדמה (27.23//Gen. 28.14).[202] Compared with *ʾ*ereṣ*, however, such uses of *ʾ*adāmâ*, as far as we can see, are relatively limited.[203]

5.7.2.2. rest/*naḥalâ

The term *rest*/**naḥalâ* 'allotment'[204] is used in the context of land possession, though not idiomatically of Israel, but generally of nations.[205] Instead, there are idiomatic uses of it in relation to the people; Israel is *rest*/**naḥalâ* of the Lord.[206] It is one of such expressions for the special status of the people as: 'a people of treasure',[207] 'a holy people',[208] 'sons of God',[209] etc. Thus, *rest*/**naḥalâ* is an expression for God's election of Israel among nations.

5.7.3. Summary

Beside the tangible senses, the term *medr*/*ʾ*ereṣ* represents the earthly world created for animate beings, mankind in particular. *medr*/*ʾ*ereṣ* as the earth connotes two dimensions in relation to the existence of mankind. It is a space for living but

201. 5.4; 7.25, 27; cf. Gen. 6.7; 7.4; see n. 82 above, § 2.5.1 and n. 351 there.

202. According to Latin; Ethiopic reads 'families of nations'; cf. VanderKam 1989: II, 176 n.

203. In *Jub.* 4.3 it is stated that Abel's blood cried out 'from the earth to heaven'. The original Hebrew of 'earth' here is uncertain whether *ʾadāmâ* or *ʾereṣ*, since, while the biblical base text (Gen. 4.10) uses *ʾadāmâ*, this term is not employed in contrast with heaven in the Bible; see § 2.5.1 above.

204. The Ethiopic *rest* is a nounal form of *warasa*, which is equivalent to Hebrew *yāraš*. In Hebrew, while the verb *yāraš* frequently appears in the context of Land-promise, its noun *yerûšâ* is infrequently employed; the noun *naḥalâ* holds special significance, whereas the use of its verb *nāḥal* is limited. These considerations, as well as general equivalence of the terms, show that the Ethiopic *rest* is a translation of Hebrew *naḥalâ*.

205. See generally 8.10; of Japheth: 8.29; 9.7, 13; of Canaan: 10.29; of Shem: 8.12; of Israel: 49.19. Still, in Ethiopic two verbs are mainly employed to express the land possession, *ʾaḫaza* and *warasa*. The former is used generally, while the latter is applied only to Israel (Abraham and Jacob); for *ʾaḫaza*, see generally: 8.11, 9.14; of Shem: 8.12, 17; of Ham: 8.24, 10.28; of Japheth: 8.29; 9.9; of Abraham: 14.7; of Israel: 49.18; 50.2; for *warasa*, see of Abraham: 14.8; 17.3; 18.15; 22.27; of Jacob: 22.14; 27.11; 32.19. The original Hebrew for these Ethiopic words is not always certain; probable candidates are *ירש, *אחז and *נחל. Goldman (1969) employs various renderings. A nominal use of the expression *אחֻזת עלם seems to be used at least once, in 25.17 in relation to the Land possession of Jacob's seed (cf. Gen. 17.8; 48.4; Lev. 14.34; 25.24).

206. 1.19, 21; 22.9, 10, 29; 33.20; cf. 2.19f.; 15.30-32.

207. 16.18; 19.18; 33.20; cf. Exod. 19.5f.; Deut. 7.6; 14.2; 26.18; cf. Charles 1902: 116 n.; VanderKam 1989: II, 98 n.

208. 16.18; 22.12; 33.20; cf. Exod. 19.6; Lev. 19.2; 20.26; Deut. 7.6; 14.2, 21; 26.19; 28.9; Isa. 62.12; 63.18; Dan. 7.27; 8.24; 12.7.

209. 1.24, 25, 28; cf. 19.29; cf. Exod. 4.22f.; Deut. 14.1; 32.6; Isa. 43.6; 63.16; Jer. 31.9; Hos. 2.1.

mortal beings in synchronic contrast to the heavenly-world and the netherworld, on the one hand, and it is a diachronic representation of human affairs, on the other. Accordingly, as injustice increases upon the earth, the earth itself can sin, be corrupted, and be defiled. It must be purified. The purification needs its new creation. Thus, the author of *Jubilees* bears in mind this cosmological eschatological conception of *ʾereṣ*, namely, the salvation history of the world.

After the Deluge, which is the first destruction of the earth, it is divided into the sons of Noah. Then *medr*/**ʾereṣ* gains another sense 'a land'. The allotment of *medr*/**ʾereṣ* is authoritative, fixed and eternal. The violation of territory is prohibited with an oath of a curse. Canaan, it is depicted, did violate the oath and dwelled in the land of Lebanon, the portion of Shem, which would be the Land of later Israel. By the long detailed description of division of the earth (chs 8–10), the author claims the legitimate possession of the biblical Land of promise by his contemporary Jews, and advocates theologically the Hasmonaean expansion policy. The frequent references to the uprootedness of the nations of the Land from the earth accord with this claim. The author reproduces the biblical Land-promise verbatim by and large, as well.

The cosmological eschatological perspectives of *medr*/**ʾereṣ* and its territorial dimensions do not merely coexist in *Jubilees*. The earth (*medr*/**ʾereṣ*) will be purified at the new creation when Mt Zion of Jerusalem in the Land (*medr*/**ʾereṣ*) is sanctified (1.27-29; cf. 49.18f.). When the people of Israel living in the Land is purified from all sin, they will possess and rule all the earth (22.11-15; 32.19; 50.5), and all the nations of the earth will be blessed in them (12.23; 18.16; 24.11; cf. 20.10). This salvation history is designed by God from the time of Creation; God created Mt Zion as a holy place in the middle of the navel of the earth (8.19); on the seventh day of His Creation, on the first Sabbath, God separated Israel from among all the nations to be His people (2.17-20). The eschatological roles of Mt Zion and the people are in parallelism with each other; the earth will be purified through Mt Zion, and all the nations will be blessed through the chosen people. The eschatological salvation of the world is dependent on the people who have been sanctified. The people, therefore, must fulfil their task of observing the laws to be purified from all sin. The Land, in which Mt Zion will be sanctified, is the place for this task. The Land is Israel's possession in this world, and the earth will be theirs in the world to come. Thus, a main purpose of *Jubilees* to instruct Jews to observe their laws is certainly connected with the double concept of *medr*/**ʾereṣ*, the Land and the earth.

The relationships of this double concept can be explained in a different manner. One may observe that the author's attitude to 'the Land' includes political aspects, in comparison with his highly theological and ideological stance to 'the earth' despite his detailed description of its division to nations. This is evident from his explicit hostility towards the nations of the Land, Idumaeans in particular, in contrast to the almost lack of antagonism towards nations outside the Land, but for Gentile culture. This means that the author is trying to cope with problems emerging within the Land where he lives. The problems must include the existence of nations in the

Land and Hellenization of some of his contemporary Jews. The former is a religio-political issue, while the latter is cultural. The solution our author chose is twofold: on the one hand, he describes the sinful deeds of ancestors of the nations of the Land (Canaan, Esau, and others) in order to claim the legitimate Jewish possession of the whole Land; on the other, he promises his readers the final Jewish dominion over the whole world through their lawful life in the Land, by attributing the election of Israel and observance of laws to the primitive history, in order to instruct the significance of the Jewish way of life separating it from other cultures. The real problems, territorial and cultural, are incorporated into cosmological eschatological appearances. In *Jubilees*, therefore, eschatological tension is almost absent.

The author was neither a sectarian who divided 'the righteous' and 'sinners' within Jews, nor a universalist disregarding the significance of the promised Land as a defined territory. He was a nationalist warning against Hellenization of Jews by emphasizing the supremacy of Israel and the Jewish way of life above Gentile cultures. While supporting the Hasmonaean expansion policy from theological viewpoints, he kept a certain distance from the then temple cult.[210] The double concept of *medr*/* *ʾereṣ* in *Jubilees* reveals that the work is a result of the development of cosmological eschatology of the pre-Maccabaean period and territorialism under Hasmonaean independence. He was the first who clearly distinguished divergent biblical promises of *ʾereṣ* into the promise of 'the Lord's Land' in this world, and the promise of 'maximal Israel' in the world to come.[211]

5.8. Genesis Apocryphon

Genesis Apocryphon, an Aramaic rewritten Bible, is known only from the findings of Qumran. Since it represents no sectarian biases, we treat it here, not in the next chapter which is devoted to the works originating in the Qumran Community.[212]

210. The distance might be caused by the author's special concern about the solar calendar which was probably not current. His calendrical concern, however, does not necessarily make him a sectarian, just as the Astronomical Book (*1 En.* 72–82) is not a sectarian work, although I do not deny the possibility that he was a member of the broader Essene movements.

211. It is worthwhile to compare *Jubilees* with Sirach, since the latter also posits two Land theologies, the maximal Israel and the restoration of the twelve tribes in the Land. Sirach depicts both in his eschatological hopes, and so the restoration of the Land belongs to *eschaton* for him; for *Jubilees* it is already in reality. *Jubilees* shows a development of theologies concerning *ʾereṣ* much more than those in the works hitherto we've seen. This can be a criterion to date *Jubilees* later than them (cf. Mendels 1987: 57–88).

212. For non-sectarian origin, see Fitzmyer 1971: 11–14; Nickelsburg 1981a: 263, 1984: 106 (but cf. 2005: 177); *HJP* III, 323; for a first century BCE date, see Kutscher 1957, 1958: 15, 22; Fitzmyer 1971: 16–19; *HJP* III, 322f.; see also § 5.8.2 below. The English translation of *Genesis Apocryphon* is mine, otherwise noted.

5.8.1. ʾaraʿ *in* Genesis Apocryphon

The term *ʾaraʿ* in *Genesis Apocryphon* can mean the *terra firma* in contrast to waters (11.11; 13.11). In the promise of progeny a famous phrase כעפר ארעא is used (21.13; cf. Gen. 13.16).

It can connote 'the soil' from which plants spring forth (11.12 [cf. Gen. 8.19]; 11.16f. [cf. Gen. 9.3]). The term is employed of agricultural acts: 'to till the earth' (12.13; cf. Gen. 9.20; *Jub.* 7.1). The use of ארעא here instead of אדמתא with the verb פלח is characteristic of Aramaic. In Hebrew *ʾereṣ* is not employed with עבד, while in Aramaic the term *ʾadmâ* is used only rarely.[213]

From a cosmological perspective, God is called 'the Lord of heaven and earth' (22.16, 21; cf. Gen. 14.19, 22).[214] Although the Creation story is missing from the scroll, this expression presupposes the idea that God is the Creator of the universe.

The heaven is specifically assigned to the abode of God and angels. God is called 'the King of heavens' (2.14) and 'the Lord of heavens' (7.7; 12.17). References are made to 'the Watchers' (2.1, 16; 7.2), 'four angels' (15.14), and 'the sons of heaven' (2.5, 16; 6.11) in contrast to 'the sons of the earth' (6.16).[215] Thus the term *šemayyāʾ* can represent the heavenly-world and the term *ʾaraʿ* the earthly-world. After the Deluge, Noah 'atoned for all the earth' (10.13). This is a signification of Noah's act of sacrifice described in Gen. 8.20, in a manner similar to *Jub.* 6.2. After finding all the earth filled with plants, Noah blessed God 'because He had mercy on the earth' (11.13f.). The blessing, which is an addition to the biblical narrative, signifies the Deluge and the survival of Noah and his sons as 'mercy'.[216]

In Abram's prayer for Sarai, which is an addition to the biblical story (Genesis 12), God's supremacy above the human world is twice expressed in comparison with 'the kings of the earth' (20.13, 15f.). This expression is applied here probably because of the context of this prayer that Abram complains to God about the Pharaoh Zoan, the king of Egypt. Yet, the expression itself also suggests an international perspective of *Genesis Apocryphon*.

In cols 16–17 the division of the earth by Noah among his sons and grandsons is narrated, in a way similar to the one described in *Jubilees* 8–9 (cf. Genesis 10). From the legible text, the portion of Japheth includes 'all the land of North' (16.10), and its borders are 'the River Tina' (16.9) and the waters of the Great Sea (16.11; cf. *Jub.* 8.25-29). The apportioning to Japheth is closed by a statement that 'he [Noah] apportioned by lot for Japheth and his sons to possess as an eternal possession (ירותת עלמים)' (16.12; cf. *Jub.* 8.12, 24, 29). As for Shem's portion,

213. See §§ 2.1.3; 2.5.1; 4.2.1.1; Chapter 4 nn. 6, 29.

214. Cf. Fitzmyer 1971: 177.

215. Cf. 'the sons of heaven': *1 En.* 6.2; 13.8; 14.3; 101.1 (Eth.); 'the sons of the earth': *1 En.* 9.2//4QEn[b] 1.iii.10a-10; *1 En.* 12.4 (Gr.); 15.3; 86.6; 91.14; 100.6; 102.3; 105.1//4QEn[c] 5.i.21.

216. Further occurrences of *ʾaraʿ* in the sense of 'the earth' (the precise meaning is unclear because of lacunae): 1.27, 28; 5.11; 7.1; 12.2, 9; 14.17.

two boundaries are legible: 'the River of Tina' (16.15) and 'the Great Salt Sea' (= Mediterranean [16.17; cf. *Jub.* 8.12]).[217] Shem divided his portion between his sons (17.7). The portion of Arpachshad, the ancestor of Abraham, includes 'all the land that the Euphrates irrigates' and 'Amana' (17.12, 14; cf. *Jub.* 9.4). Although the description of Ham's portion is missing from the scroll, 19.13 suggests that his portion is assigned to Africa. Accordingly, the overall scheme of the world map seems close to that of *Jubilees* 8; Europe to Japheth, Asia to Shem, and Africa to Ham. The story of division of the earth in this scheme, as that of *Jubilees* 8, seems to aim at legitimating God's promise of the Land to Abram.

God's promise to Abram remains legible in col. 21. Its base text is Gen. 13.14b-17, in which there are several unclear points. *Genesis Apocryphon* fills up the unclarities by modifying the biblical wordings and adding detailed complements. According to Gen. 13.14-15 the land God promised to Abram is the land that he 'looks upon' from a certain place where (occasionally) he 'is'. *Genesis Apocryphon* specifies Bethel as the place where Abram 'dwelled' (21.7, 9; cf. *Jub.* 13.15, 19), and it has God command him to go up to 'Ramath-Hazor' from which he shall look upon the Land (21.8). Furthermore, *Genesis Apocryphon* modifies God's saying of promise in Gen. 13.15 'all the Land that you look upon' to 'all this Land' (21.9f.). These modifications serve to explain the concept of the Land-promise. The Land is not an unspecified area that one sees from a place where he occasionally is, but a territory already defined by God, hence it is 'this land' (cf. Gen. 15.18).[218] The Land is so vast that one needs go up to a higher place to look at its farthest borders, hence Ramath-Hazor, 'the highest spot in the mountains of Judaea'.[219] It is, however, not suitable for God's appearance, hence Bethel, a holy place in which there is an altar of the Lord (21.8; cf. Gen. 12.8; 13.3f.). Thus, (1) God defined from the outset the exact territory that He would give to Israel, (2) appeared to Abram at a holy place, and (3) directed him to climb the highest spot to look upon the Land. The Land-promise, according to *Genesis Apocryphon*, is not a whim of God, but a well-worked plan.

The Abram of *Genesis Apocryphon* actually obeyed the commands and went up to Ramath-Hazor and looked upon the Land on the following morning (21.10f.). The territory depicted in 21.11f. represents 'the Greater Israel'. It is taken from Gen. 15.18: 'from the River of Egypt to the Great River, the River Euphrates'.[220] The 'River of Egypt' appears only here in the entire Bible, and so its identification is uncertain.[221] Whatever its original referent is, however, *Genesis Apocryphon* undoubtedly identifies it with 'the Gihon River', i.e., the Nile (21.15; cf. Gen. 2.13), which is the southern border.[222] 'Lebanon and Senir' (21.11), the northwestern territory, probably refer to Mount Lebanon and the Anti-Lebanon

217. Cf. 21.16; see Fitzmyer 1971: 153.
218. Cf. Chapter 2 n. 284 above.
219. Fitzmyer 1971: 146.
220. Cf. Exod. 23.31; Deut. 1.7-8; 11.24; Josh. 1.4; Ps. 80.9-12.
221. Cf. Chapter 2 n. 303 above.
222. Fitzmyer 1971: 148, 152f.

range, respectively. The western-eastern borders are the Mediterranean-Euphrates. This territory contains 'Hauran', an eastern area, 'the land of Gebal', a southeastern area,[223] and 'the Great Desert', a far eastern and southeastern area.[224] The vastness of the Land is emphasized by God Himself: 'Rise up, walk and go, and look how great is its length and how great is its width' (21.13f.; 'how great' is added to Gen. 13.17). This Land is promised emphatically to Abram's 'seed', Israel, 'for all ages' (21.9f., 12, 14).

Following God's command, Abram made a trip throughout the Land (21.15-19), a trip which is not mentioned in the Bible. Beginning from the Gihon River, he went to the north along the Mediterranean to the Mt Taurus, which is called Mount Amanus (cf. 17.14), turned to the east till the River Euphrates, went to the southeast along the river to the Red Sea (= the Persian Gulf), went along the sea coast (of the Indian Ocean and the Arabian Sea) till the tongue of the Sea of Reeds (the Gulf of Suez), and returned to the starting point.[225] Thus, Abram traversed along all the borders, only on the borders, of the Land. His journey undoubtedly aims to confirm its exact territory. The Land virtually extends to all Asia southwest of the Euphrates, including the entire Arabian Peninsula and the Sinai Peninsula. This territory is probably equal to the portion of Arpachshad (17.11-15), since the Land of *Genesis Apocryphon* is identical with his portion depicted in *Jub.* 9.4.[226] This is not surprising since, according to Gen. 11.10-26, Abram is Arpachshad's legitimate descendant, who ought to possess the ancestor's possession. The last statement of Abram, regarding his return in peace and finding his household sound (21.19), implies that the journey lasted for a long period because of the vastness of the Land (though less than one year; see 22.27-29).

This detailed description of the Land is remarkable. Even if the author was just governed by a midrashic motif to fill up lacunae of the biblical story, the fact that he took the account of Gen. 13.14b-17 as an opportunity to propose a detailed portrait of the Land of promise is significant. His favourable attitude towards the biblical promise of 'Greater Israel' is distinct from other parabiblical literature. *Jubilees* just reproduces Gen. 13.14b-17 and 15.18-21 without any paraphrase on the territory of the Land (*Jub.* 13.19-21; 14.18). Pseudo-Philo deliberately limits the Land of promise to 'the land of Canaan' (*LAB* 8.2f.). There was an eschatological expectation of 'the maximal Israel' from the fourth or third century BCE onward, but among post-biblical Jewish literature as far as we know *Genesis Apocryphon* is a single instance that exhibited the promise of 'Greater Israel' as an already extant territory.

In this respect, it should be noted that in the description of the Land-promise no attention is paid to 'the land of Canaan', or Palestine, where the author was living. It cannot be accidental due to the loss of some major part of the text. The author uses

223. Gebal = Seir: 21.29; cf. Gen. 14.6; *Ant.* 2.6; 3.40; 9.188; cf. Fitzmyer 1971: 149, 165.
224. Cf. Fitzmyer 1971: 149f.
225. For these places, see Fitzmyer 1971, *ad loc.*
226. Cf. F. Schmidt 1990: 122f., maps I–III.

phrases 'this land' and 'our land' in reference to Palestine. When going to Egypt, the Abram of *Genesis Apocryphon* emphatically states that 'then we [Abram and Sarai] crossed *our land* and we entered the land of the sons of Ham, the land of Egypt' (19.13; cf. Gen. 12.10); *Genesis Apocryphon* adds to Gen. 13.1-4 Abram's blessing to God: 'I gave thanks there before God ... because He had returned me to *this land* in peace' (21.3f.).[227] The 'this land' and 'our land' must have been 'this land' and 'our land' for the author of *Genesis Apocryphon* and his addressee. For them the biblical land of Canaan or Palestine was no longer the *promised Land*, but *their land* already.

We can observe a nuanced connotation of the 'this land' and the promised 'Greater Israel' from the retelling of Genesis 14 in *Apocr. Gen.* 21.23–22.26. At the beginning of the episode *Genesis Apocryphon* modifies the biblical text and adds a brief comment: 'In the fourteenth year the king of Elam led all his allies, and they went up by way of the desert, striking and plundering from the Euphrates River (onward). And they struck Rephaim ...' (21.27f.; cf. Gen. 14.5f.). At the middle of the story where Abram defeated the kings *Genesis Apocryphon* modifies as follows: 'he rescued from them all that they had captured and all that they had plundered and all their own goods' (22.10f.; cf. Gen. 14.16). At the end of this incident *Genesis Apocryphon* again makes an addition: 'And all the captives who were with him [Abram] from this land he released and sent them all away' (22.24f.). In sum, according to *Genesis Apocryphon*, the king of Elam and his allies not only struck the peoples of Transjordan as described in Genesis 14, but all the way from 'the River Euphrates' through 'the desert' they were striking and plundering. Abram 'rescued' all the captives, and finally released and sent them back from 'this land'. These additions clearly show the author's territorial concern. The kings, who crossed the River Euphrates, are invaders of 'the Land' which has been already given to Abram. Hence, Abram had to 'rescue' captives in his territory. The deliberate reference to 'the desert' confirms that it is Abram's possession given by God (21.11: 'all the Great Desert' in the Land-promise). On the other hand, the emphatic use of 'this land', from which the captives were released and sent back to their own homeland, indicates that Abram himself lived in the author's 'this land', that is, Palestine. Thus the author claims that Jewish sovereignty shall extend over the territory till the Euphrates, while assuming Palestine to be already Jewish.

This claim and assumption must betray a situation of Palestine of the author's time. It is the period when Palestine was already Jewish, and a Jewish ruler tried to extend his territory, especially to the east and the southeast (Hauran, the land of Gebal, and the Great Desert). The situation fits well with the later period of Alexander Jannaeus. After wars against Nabataean kings and a civil war of six years,[228] Jannaeus succeeded in the campaigns towards Hellenistic cities in the east of Jordan, as far as Gerasa, a city bordered to the desert (83–80 BCE).[229] On his

227. Cf. also 19.10//Gen. 12.10.

228. The wars against Nabataeans: *War* 1.90, 103; *Ant.* 13.375, 392; the civil war: *War* 1.90-98; *Ant.* 13.376-83; 4QpNah 3–4.i.1-8; see Stern 1981; Kasher 1988: 84–103.

229. *War* 1.104f.; *Ant.* 13.393f.

return to Jerusalem, Jannaeus was welcomed by the people with rejoicing.[230] He further continued campaigns to the east even in illness until his death in the region of Gerasa (76 BCE).[231] It is apparent that Jannaeus' primary concern is to extend the Jewish territory to the east of Jordan, the then Nabataean territory. This must have formed the context of *Genesis Apocryphon*. It was written when Jews had the self-confidence to extend their territory towards the east. We can, therefore, date it to the late Jannaeus' period, approximately 83–76 BCE.

5.8.2. Summary

The uses of the term *ʾaraʿ* in *Genesis Apocryphon* show the author's strong concerns for the people of Israel and their territory. God is the Creator who fills the earth (*ʾaraʿ*) with plants. God intervenes in the history of the earthly world (*ʾaraʿ*) with mercy. The sovereignty of God over the universe is specifically set above human kings on the earth (*ʾaraʿ*). This perception reveals the author's international perspective which contrasts Israel with foreign nations. This perspective is explicit in the story of the division of the earth into nations. The portion of Arpachshad prepares God's promise of the Land (*ʾaraʿ*) to Abraham and his seed, Israel. The Land in *Genesis Apocryphon* represents 'the Greater Israel' extending to the Euphrates. The author expresses the Land-promise, not as an eschatological hope, but as political reality of the Jewish territory.

Genesis Apocryphon is a work emerging from the period when Jews enjoyed the fruit of Hasmonaean expansion policy and felt strong self-confidence in international relationships. Although we do not know of the author's attitude towards the king Jannaeus, with whom the people were in long conflict, we can say at least that *Genesis Apocryphon* theologically supports the king's campaigns to the east. The author, therefore, cannot be characterized as a sectarian, but a nationalist, who expected a realization of the Greater Israel in territorial dimensions.

5.9. Conclusion

In the third century BCE and in the first third of the second century BCE under the Hellenistic imperial rule, as we saw in Chapter 4 above, Jews of the Land learned a cosmic scope, according to which the term *ʾereṣ/ʾaraʿ* was used in cosmological eschatological dimensions, and the biblical Land-promise, too, was mostly reinterpreted as the maximal Israel. The Antiochian crisis, the Maccabaean uprising and its success, and the establishment of Jewish independence under Hasmonaean dynasty brought a shift of Jewish worldviews, and according to the shift also the uses of our term underwent changes.

230. *War* 1.105; *Ant.* 13.394.
231. *Ant.* 13.398; cf. *War* 1.106.

The Antiochian crisis, which threatened the Land, sharpened cosmological soteriology, which was inherited from the fourth century BCE onward. The final author of Daniel expected God's direct intervention in the crisis and the realization of His sovereignty over the whole world. Although he remembered that the land where he lived was 'the Land of beauty', God's gift to their ancestors, the author of Daniel did not utilize its biblical connotation of 'promise' in his eschatological descriptions. The author of the Book of Dreams, who shared with the book of Daniel similar universal hopes, however, recognized the religious significance of the Land and gave it an eschatological role. When Antiochus IV Epiphanes died and the persecution temporarily ceased, the author of Baruch looked back at the cause of the crisis having been the sins of the people against God. He instructed them to return to their God, reminding them of the biblical promise of the Land by employing a fictional setting of the Exile. Since he fully acknowledged the biblical significance of the Land where he lived, the term *ʾereṣ* in Baruch expresses, as in the Bible, unique relationships between God-Israel-nations, namely, the Creator of the earth (*ʾereṣ*) is the God of Israel, who gave them the Land (*ʾereṣ*), and whom all the earth (*kol hāʾāreṣ* = nations) shall know. Thus, we can conclude that as a result of the Antiochian crisis, the Land, and its Hebrew/Aramaic expression *ʾereṣ*/*ʾaraʿ*, regained the traditional significance.

After the Maccabaean revolt came to an end successfully, *Temple Scroll* was compiled. It focuses on the ordinances concerning the Temple and its city, and lives of the people outside the Temple city in the Land (*ʾereṣ*). *Temple Scroll* assumes the Temple's sanctity which extends radiately through the Temple city down to the Land. The concept of the holy Land requires fixed borders (*gebûl*), hence it is to be a holy territory. From the holy Land abominable nations are to be expelled. *Temple Scroll* proposed anew the restoration of biblical 'Land of Israel' as an ideal for the Torah-oriented people.

When Jewish independence was established, the author of Judith instructed the people to obey God, enjoying freedom from the foreign overlordship. Utilizing our term, he contrasted 'the Lord of heavens and earth' with a foreign king who desired to be 'the lord of all the earth'. This use expresses, national-theocentrically, the supremacy of the God of Israel over imperial kings in the world. The author's use of other biblical terms, *gebûl yiśrāēl* and *naḥalâ*, reveals his territorial consciousness of the Land, though he seems not to have been a promoter of expansionism. In 1 Maccabees our term is predominantly used in territorial dimensions. In many occurrences it refers to Judaea, the then Jewish political territory. On the other hand, 1 Maccabees, too, applies the biblical terms *gebûl yiśrāēl* and *naḥalâ* with theological ideological connotations to Jewish claim for the Land possession. The uses of these traditional terms in Judith and 1 Maccabees attest to the beginning of the Hasmonaean expansionism.

Under the reign of Hyrcanus I expansionism was no longer merely a theological ideal, but became a real policy. The author of *Jubilees* supported this policy and theologically legitimated the Jewish possession of the biblical Land of Canaan. At the same time, he retained an ideology of the maximal Israel in his eschatological vision. Thus, two Land theologies coexist in *Jubilees*, the one in real, the other cosmological eschatological, both of which can be expressed by the term *ʾ*ereṣ*. After the restoration of traditional Land of Israel, the king Jannaeus made attempts to expand Jewish territory towards the east. *Genesis Apocryphon* supported this policy and expected the realization of the Greater Israel which, according to its author, had been promised to Abraham by God.

The events from the Antiochian crisis to the establishment of the Hasmonaean kingdom brought gradual changes to uses of the terms *ʾereṣ/ʾaraʿ*, *naḥalâ* and *gebûl*. Their territorial dimensions, which had been virtually lost before the crisis, regained a traditional significance and promoted the Hasmonaean expansionism theologically and ideologically. The expansionism reached its theological climax in *Genesis Apocryphon*. Although the cosmological eschatological connotation of the term was not utterly lost, Jewish consciousness of *ʾereṣ/ʾaraʿ* as a real political territory became more and more explicit over time.

5.10. Appendix 2: Pre- or Non-Qumranic Dead Sea Scrolls

There are Dead Sea Scrolls whose provenance is pre- or non-Qumranic (e.g., *Temple Scroll* and *Genesis Apocryphon*). In this section we shall deal with other such writings, which, though, remain for us in tiny fragmentary forms. Admitting that it is difficult to determine the date and provenance of certain Dead Sea Scrolls, we shall provisionally follow scholarly opinions.[232] Since the texts dealt with here are mostly fragmentary, we must satisfy ourselves with just categorizing uses of the terms with which we are concerned.[233]

5.10.1. ʾereṣ/ʾaraʿ *as the Earth*

In pre- or non-Qumranic Dead Sea Scrolls the term *ʾereṣ* can mean tangibly the *terra firma*,[234] the ground,[235] and the soil.[236] In *Daily Prayers* the term *ʾereṣ* appears in the fixed opening clause of the morning prayer: ‘And when the sun rises to illuminate the earth, they shall bless’.[237] *ʾereṣ/ʾaraʿ* can mean the cosmological

232. Principally I follow Dimant (1995) and Schiffman and VanderKam (2000), as well as DJD series.

233. We do not treat the Targum of Job (11Q10), since our term in it usually follows the Hebrew text and is rendered literally.

234. 1Q22 1.ii.10f. (in lacuna); 4Q422 2.6, 7, (8), (11) (the brackets of line number indicate the term or the clause being in lacuna).

235. 1Q22 1.iv.2; Mas 1039-211 7 (cf. Josh. 23.14; 1 Sam. 3.19; see Talmon and Yadin 1999: 108–10); 4Q391 25.2.

236. 4Q88 9.9; 1Q34bis 2+1.2; 3.i.3f.; 4Q509 131–132.ii.8.

237. 4Q503 1–6.iii.12; 4.(1); 10.1; 24–25.3; 29–32.7, (17); 33–35.i.(12); 33–35.ii.(1), 10; 37–38.(18); 40–41.ii.(4); 48–50.7; 51–55.(12); 64.7; cf. 4Q422 2.10, 12.

earth in contrast to heaven and/or in relation to the Creation.[238] The earth can react to God's action,[239] and *šāmayim* and *ʾereṣ* can be called as witness.[240] It can also represent the human world,[241] especially nations in contrast to Israel.[242] This usage can be seen in another phrase, *kol tēbēl*, as well.[243] Our term is also utilized in universal eschatologies, in which it expresses, not only the universal scale of the events,[244] but also the national hope of the dominion over the world by the people or their messiah.[245] After the end of this world, it is stated in 4QRenewed Earth, '*kol tēbēl* will be like Eden ... [... and] *hāʾāreṣ* will be quiet forever' (4Q475 5f.).[246] In the following line (l. 7) mention is made of 'a beloved son', who may represent collectively the people of Israel.[247] If so, the author's universal eschatology is an expression of nationalism. A nationalistic sentiment is clearly discernible in the description of the election of Israel, God's sons, 'from all the earth'.[248]

5.10.2. ʾereṣ/ʾaraʿ *as a Land*

The international perspective which views the world as consisting of nations is manifested in the plural form of our term, *ʾarāṣôt*, which occurs relatively frequently in the Dead Sea Scrolls.[249] There appear expressions ארצות גוים[250] and ארצות עמים אחרים.[251] *ʾarāṣôt* expresses God's sovereignty over the nations[252] and the special status of the people of Israel[253] and the Land[254] among them. The territorial dimensions of our term are apparent in this plural form.

238. 1Q22 1.i.(5); 4Q372 1.30; 4Q381 1.3; 76–77.16a; 4Q88 10.5; 11Q5 26.14; 11Q11 3.1-3; 4Q504 1–2.vii.7; 5.i.6; 1Q34bis 2+1.3; 3.i.4; 4Q521 2.ii+4.1; 7+5.ii.2; 3Q12 1.3 (Aramaic); 4Q422 1.(6), (9); 4Q377 2.ii.8; 4Q185 1–2.i.10, (13) (cf. 1–2.ii.1-3); 4Q370 1.i.4; 2.(5).

239. 4Q381 24a+b.10//Ps. 18.8; cf. Chapter 2 n. 63 above.

240. 11Q11 3.5-7.

241. 4Q504 8.14.

242. 4Q378 3.i.6; 4Q381 69.1; 76–77.16b.

243. 4Q372 1.22; 4Q475 4, 5; for this expression, see 11Q5 22.11f.// 4Q88 8.7-9; 4Q177 3.7; 4Q298 2.5; 4Q369 1.ii.7; 4Q372 1.11; cf. 1QH^{a} 14.15.

244. 4Q215a 1.ii.4f.; 3.1; 4Q246 1.i.4-7; 1.ii.1-3 (Aramaic).

245. 4Q381 76–77.14-16; 4Q88 9.5–10.7; 4Q475 4-7; 4Q246 1.ii.4-9 (Aramaic); 4Q521 2.ii+4.1f.

246. See 4QEn^{g} 1.ii.16 (*//1 En.* 91.10 [?]); *T. Sim.* 6.4; *T. Levi* 18.4; cf. Elgiven 1999: 585f.

247. Thus Elgiven (1999: 586–8).

248. 4Q504 1–2.iii.2-10; 4.2-4 (cf. 1 Kgs 11.32, 2 Chron. 6.34; 4QMMT B 60-61; *Jub.* 49.18f.); 11Q5 22.11f.//4Q88 8.7-9.

249. 4Q160 3–4.ii.4, 5; 4Q248 5, 8; 4Q372 1.5, 10; 4Q374 2.i.4; 2.ii.5; 4Q377 1.i.9; 4Q381 16.1; 4Q385a 4.9; 4Q387 1.9; 4Q389 8.ii.3; 4Q393 5.2; 4Q504 1–2.v.11f.; vi.12f.; 4Q302 2.ii.4; 3.ii.10; 4Q379 28.2; 4Q463 1.2; 11Q19 59.2, 5; see Chapter 6 n. 66 below.

250. 4Q248 8; cf. Ps. 105.44; 1QM 2.7; Sir. 39.4.

251. 4Q377 1.i.9; cf. Exod. 3.8.

252. 4Q160 3–4.ii.4-6; 4Q302 3.ii.9f.

253. 4Q160 3–4.ii.4-6; 4Q248 5, 8; 4Q504 1–2.v.11f.; vi.12f.

254. 4Q372 1.5, 10; 4Q374 2.ii.5; 4Q377 1.i.9; 4Q385a 4.9; 4Q387 1.9; 4Q389 8.ii.3; 4Q463 1.2.

There are many uses of its singular form referring to a land. Mention is made of 'the land of Egypt',[255] 'the land of Canaan',[256] etc.[257] A territorial land can be called 'this land'[258] and 'their land'.[259] In *Jeremiah Apocryphon* there appears a unique locution 'the land of Jerusalem' (4Q385a 18.ia-b.3), which is, probably, called 'an uninha[bited] land' (4Q383 1.3; cf. Jer. 6.8). The land of exile is expressed by 'the land(s) of [their] captivity',[260] 'the lands of [yo]ur enemies',[261] and 'a land which is not theirs'.[262]

There are many uses of our term referring to the Land.[263] *Joshua Apocryphon* utilizes Deut. 8.7-10 to illustrate the Land promise,[264] and regards the deeds of opponents as profanation of the Land and Jerusalem.[265] Mention is made of the devastation of the Land.[266] In *Words of Moses* there once appears an expression בעד הארץ 'on behalf of the Land' in parallelism with בעד בני ישראל (1Q22 1.iv.1). In *Festival Prayers* the Land is called 'our Land'.[267] In *Words of the Luminaries* the Land seems to be called 'Your (God's) Land' (4Q504 26.6). In *Jeremiah Apocryphon* the term *ʾereṣ* (the Land) is used in parallelism with *ʾaḥûzâ*, a term of the biblical Land theology (4Q390 2.ii.9f.). Another term expressing the Land theology, *naḥalâ*, is also applied to refer to the Land.[268] Besides, the term *ʾadāmâ* is also employed to refer to the Land.[269]

There are further occurrences of the term *ʾereṣ/ʾaraʿ*, but its referent cannot be determined because of lacunae.[270]

255. 1Q22 1.i.(1); 1.ii.6; 4Q158 14.i.4; 4Q365 23.2 (= Lev. 23.43); 4Q379 4.1-(2); 12.4f.; 4Q385a 18.ii.6; 4Q389 1.4, 5; 4Q545 1a–b.ii.16 (//4Q544 1.12); 4Q558 65.3.

256. 4Q379 12.5f.; 4Q543 3.2//4Q545 1a–b.ii.18//4Q546 2.4; 4Q547 9.6, 9.

257. 4Q385a 18.ii.6; 18.ia–b.9; 4Q389 1.2; 4Q504 8.7; 4Q454 3; 4Q368 4.1; 4Q382 1.4.

258. 4Q158 3.2; 4Q543 2a–b.5; 4Q545 1a–b.ii.11; cf. 4Q422 3.10: 'the face of the land' (= Egypt).

259. 4Q504 1–2.iv.11; 4Q422 3.8, 9, 10, 11.

260. 4Q385a 4.9; 18.ia-b.7; 4Q389 8.ii.3; 4Q390 1.5; cf. Jer. 30.10; 46.27; cf. Chapter 2 n. 167 above.

261. 4Q387 1.9; 4Q463 1.2; cf. Samaritan Lev. 26.44; cf. Chapter 2 n. 163 above.

262. 4Q464 3.ii.3; cf. Gen. 15.13; cf. Chapter 2 n. 164 above.

263. 1Q22 1.i.9; 1.iii.1; 1.iv.1; 4Q158 7–8.4; 4Q365 23.4, 6; 4Q374 2.ii.5; 4Q372 1.6, 19; 4Q378 11.4-6; 4Q379 22.ii.14; 4Q387 2.iii.3-5; 4Q388a 7.ii.6; 4Q390 1.8; 2.ii.9; 4Q179 1.i.12; 4Q385 3.6; 4Q386 1.ii.7; 4Q391 2.2; 4Q244 12.3//4Q243 13.(4); 4Q504 1–2.v.3; 26.6; 4Q509 8.4//4Q508 22–23.3; 4Q509 189.2; 4Q481b 1.

264. 4Q378 11.3-7; cf. 4Q509 8.4//4Q508 22–23.3. Cf. 4QDeut[n] (4Q41) and 4QDeut[j] (4Q37), in which Deut. 8.5-10 appears as a separate unit; see White 1990; Weinfeld 1992: 427–9; cf. also 4Q434 2.8 (see § 6.6.3 below).

265. 4Q379 22.ii.11-15; cf. 4Q175 25-29.

266. 4Q387a 1.8; 4Q388a 7.ii.6; 4Q387 2.iii.3-5; 4Q179 1.i.12f.; 4Q243 13.4//4Q244 12.3; cf. 4Q481b 1.

267. 4Q509 8.4//4Q508 22–23.3; 4Q509 62.1; 189.2.

268. 4Q365 23.5; 4Q179 1.i.12f.

269. 1Q22 1.i.6 (cf. Deut. 4.10; 12.1; 31.13); 4Q386 1.ii.2 (*ʾadmat yiśrāēl*).

270. 1Q25 5.2; 1Q41 3.1; 4Q158 14.i.3; 4Q274 3.ii.7; 4Q275 1.5; 4Q368 10.i.7; 4Q381 44.2; 50.4; 69.6; 78.6; 4Q386 1.ii.1; 4Q388 6.5, 6; 4Q389 4.2; 4Q390 4.2; 4Q450 1.3; 2.1; 4Q460 8.2; 9.i.4; 4Q464 5.ii.4; 4Q468a 3; 4Q468c 8; 4Q468f 2, 3; 4Q468cc 3; 4Q483 1.2; 4Q503 15–16.9; 72.5; 4Q508 30.2; 4Q509 81.2; 4Q543 23.2; 4Q545 4.15; 4Q558 10.1; 37.ii.4; 4Q560 1.ii.7; 4Q571 2; 5Q23 1; 6Q13 2; 6Q20 2, 3; 11Q11 4.3, 9.

The uses of the term *ʾereṣ/ʾaraʿ* and such related terms as *tēbēl*, *naḥalâ* and *ʾadāmâ* in these scrolls, in spite of their fragmentary status, reflect general tendencies of the Hasmonaean period when the Land as a distinct territory regained its traditional biblical significance.

Chapter 6

Qumranic Writings

In this chapter we shall deal with the writings originating in the Qumran Community. These are: (1) *Community Rule*, (2) *Hodayot*, (3) *Damascus Document*, (4) *War Scroll*, and (5) *Pesharim*. We shall supplement them with (6) other Qumranic materials, of which tiny fragments alone remain.[1]

6.1. Community Rule

The term *ʾereṣ* appears five times in 1QS (and once in 1QSa and twice in 1QSb). Of these, it appears twice in a phrase לכפר בעד הארץ 'to atone for *hāʾāreṣ*' (1QS 8.6, 10; and 1QSa 1.3), and on two other occasions, too, it has connection with the same verb (1QS 8.3; 9.4). In these occurrences translators do not agree whether to render it as 'the earth' or 'the Land'. The divergence may suggest that the narrower context does not allow us to determine the precise referent. Moreover, 1QS contains relatively frequent occurrences of another term, *tēbēl*, which must be related to the usage of our term. Accordingly, we shall first examine both terms, and then infer the referent of our term in 1QS.

6.1.1. Texts with ʾereṣ *in 1QS*

In the opening paragraph of 1QS the members (or leaders) of the Community are instructed to do righteousness and to keep away from the evil (1.1b-7a). The expression 'to do truth and righteousness and justice *bāʾāreṣ*' (ll. 5f.) seems to be influenced by Jer. 4.2; 9.23; 23.5; 33.15.[2] While probably referring to 'the earth' in Jer. 9.23, the term *ʾereṣ* in Jer. 23.5 and 33.15 may signify 'the Land'. Concerning the term in our passage, translators disagree with one another.[3]

A similar statement is repeated in 1QS 8.1-4a. The clause 'to keep faith *bāʾāreṣ* with a steadfast mind' (l. 3) is taken from Isa. 26.2-3, in which, though, the phrase

1. In this chapter the English translation of the Dead Sea Scrolls is mine, otherwise noted.

2. Cf. Jer. 22.15; Isa. 9.5f.; 16.5.

3. Land: Wernberg-Møller 1957: 22; Lohse 1971: 5; Knibb 1987: 78; Maier 1995: 168; earth: Dupont-Sommer 1959: 88; Leaney 1966: 117; *DSSHAG* I, 7; García Martínez 1994: 3; *DSSSE*, 71; Vermes 1997: 98.

bāʾāreṣ does not occur. While many translators agree to render it as 'the Land'[4] probably because of Isa. 26.1 in which 'the land of Judah' is mentioned,[5] the intention of the author, who added just this phrase to the Isaianic text, is indeed difficult to know, as Licht notes.[6]

In the following paragraph (8.4b-10a), eschatological roles of the Council of the Community are described. That the Community's roles described here extend to the *eschaton* (hence eschatological roles) is evident from its self-designations as 'an eternal plant' (l. 5) and 'witnesses of truth for judgment' (l. 6) and from the references to its role at the final judgement of the wicked (ll. 6f., 10). The Community members are the chosen in order 'to atone for *hāʾāreṣ*' in the end of days (ll. 6, 10; cf. 1QSa 1.1-3). The expression לכפר בעד הארץ does not appear in the Bible. A similar one can be found in Num. 35.33b, in which the term *ʾereṣ* signifies the Land (cf. vv. 33a, 34).[7] The atonement for *medr*/**ʾereṣ*/*ʾaraʿ* is mentioned in *Jub.* 6.2 and *Apocr. Gen.* 10.13, in both of which Noah's atoning for 'the earth' after the Deluge is described. Similarly, cleansing of the earth is depicted in *1 En.* 10.22 and *Jub.* 4.26; 50.5, in all of which an eschatological cleansing of the earth is expected. In addition, the idea that the righteous will be chosen as 'witnesses' at the judgement can be found in *1 En.* 93.10//4QEn^{g} 1.iv.12-14.[8] It should be noted that all these writings (i.e., *1 Enoch*, *Jubilees* and *Genesis Apocryphon*) were known to the Qumran Community. Translators again differ from one another in their rendering of our term.[9]

Concerning the expression לכפר בעד הארץ, M. Knibb states that '"The land" means the land of Israel, but even more the inhabitants.'[10] The *ʾereṣ*, however, whether it means the Land or the earth, hardly represents its inhabitants, since in this section, too, the distinction between the Community members and the wicked, namely dualism, is maintained (8.6f.). The atonement in 1QS is, indeed, limited to the members (3.6-9, 11-12; 5.6), and the outsiders are excluded from it (2.8; 3.4). Rather, the *ʾereṣ* here signifies *ʾereṣ* itself, which is defiled by its inhabitants. Referring to relevant biblical passages, P. Garnet comments on our expression that 'the atonement is to be effected by the punishment of the wicked, so that the land will no longer be polluted with their abominations.'[11] He correctly observes the biblical Land theology, but it remains uncertain whether the author of 1QS follows

4. Among the translators listed in the previous note, only Dupont-Sommer (1959: 106) and García Martínez (1994: 12) read it as 'on the earth'.

5. So Wernberg-Møller 1957: 123.

6. Licht 1996: 178 n. 3.

7. Cf. also Deut. 32.43.

8. Cf. Knibb 1987: 131.

9. Land: Knibb 1987: 128; Lohse 1971: 29, 31; Maier 1995: 187; Vermes 1997: 109; *DSSSE*, 89; earth: Wernberg-Møller 1957: 33; Dupont-Sommer 1959: 106; García Martínez 1994: 12. *DSSHAG* (I, 35) curiously renders the term in 8.6 as 'earth', whereas in 8.10 'land'.

10. Knibb 1987: 131.

11. Garnet 1977: 66.

the biblical implication, or employs ideas from extra-biblical literature, to which Garnet does not refer. Neither of these two interpretations is decisive.

A similar expression can be found in 1QS 9.3-5a. The phrase לרצון לארץ 'to be acceptable for *hā'āreṣ*' (l. 4) must be closely related to the expressions 'the chosen of (God's) will to atone for *hā'āreṣ*' (8.6) and 'they shall be acceptable to atone for *hā'āreṣ*' (8.10). Here, again, the translators do not agree with one another whether to render it as 'the earth' or 'the Land'.[12]

The uses of *'ereṣ* in 1QS are consistent; the Community members must 'do truth and righteousness and justice *bā'āreṣ*' (1.5f.) and 'keep faith *bā'āreṣ*' (8.3) so that they may be chosen and acceptable by God 'in order to atone for *hā'āreṣ*' (8.6, 10). One of the purposes of the Community to do justice is to atone for *hā'āreṣ*, an atonement which shall be carried out by their prayer and right behaviour instead of the offices of the sacrificial cult in the Jerusalem Temple (9.4b-5a).[13] It can be said, therefore, that the term *'ereṣ* in 1QS constantly holds the same referent, either 'the earth' or 'the Land'. The texts cited above, however, do not allow us to determine the referent. We must explore in broader context, asking if the author utilizes the term in universal dimensions or territorial.

6.1.2. tēbēl *in 1QS*

1QS 3.13–4.26 contain a teaching of two spirits, a fundamental idea which is presupposed in the Qumran writings and which must express the Community's view of mankind and of the world. In this section the term *tēbēl* appears four times and plays a significant role.

The section 1QS 3.13-25a includes the idea that God created man to rule *tēbēl* 'the world' (ll. 17f.). It can be taken from Gen. 1.28 and Psalm 8, neither of which, however, uses the term *tēbēl*, but *'ereṣ*.[14] The wording ממשלת תבל is known from Sir. 10.4, which states God's sovereignty over the world.

This section explains the origins of righteous men and unjust men and the situation of the world in which the Community lives, the world which is governed by injustice. The sovereignty of darkness, however, is only temporarily admitted by God, and it shall be shortly destroyed, according to 'the mysteries of God' (3.23). The author's eyes look back to the creation of man and quickly turn to the last days when the Community lives. On the other hand, he dualistically divides mankind, who are oriented by the two opposed heavenly figures. Thus, the author's eschatological time understanding coexists with the universal worldview.

The eschatological events the author expects are described in 4.18b-23a. The eschatological hopes expressed in these lines are concerned with the purification of

12. Land: Leaney 1966: 210; Lohse 1971: 33; Knibb 1987: 138; *DSSHAG* I, 39; Maier 1995: 190; Vermes 1997: 110; earth: Milik 1951: 151; Dupont-Sommer 1959: 108; García Martínez 1994: 13; *DSSSE*, 91; Wernberg-Møller 1957: 35, 133 n. 8.

13. Cf. Lichtenberger 1980.

14. Cf. *2 Bar.* 14.17; Wis. 9.2f.; *4 Ezra* 6.54.

the world and of the chosen ones. The present world governed by injustice is defiled by the wicked behaviour. In the world to come, therefore, it must be cleansed and governed by the truth.[15]

The term *tēbēl* in 1QS is used in relation to the creation of man and the *eschaton*. It represents the author's universal and eschatological perspectives (also in 5.19). Speaking of 'the world', 1QS employs a universalistic word 'man' (or 'men'),[16] instead of 'nations', a term expressing nationalistic sentiment. But this does not show universalistic concerns of 1QS, since it focuses upon inner Jewish issues and lacks concerns for the Gentiles. It is evident that the superiority of Israel as a nation is presupposed, as shown by the expression 'the God of Israel' (3.25). The term 'Israel', however, can be applied not only to the nation as a whole, but also to the Community (2.22) or to its ordinary fellows in contrast to priestly and Levitical members (5.22).[17] The same can be observed in the use of the phrase 'all the people', which refers to lay associates of the Community (2.21; 6.9). The expression 'the men of injustice', from which the members should separate (5.1f., 10-13; 8.13f.), refers primarily to the Community's opponents among Jews (theoretically Gentiles can be included in this expression, but they are out of the author's scope). 'Israel' can signify, therefore, an ideal group consisting of the Community members and future, but predestined, adherents of Jewish origin to its way of life (6.13: 'every volunteer from Israel').[18] In other words, 'Israel' designates nationality distinct from foreign nations, but the nationality alone is not enough to belong to 'Israel'.[19] The author individualizes Israel and dualistically divides them into the Sons of Light and the Sons of Darkness. The choice of the universalistic term 'man' is a result of this individualization, as well as the author's worldwide eschatology. This use of 'man' is an expression of his sectarianism based on dualistic worldview, a sectarianism which presupposes Jewish nationalism as an assumption which does not need to be voiced.[20] For the final solution of intra-national problems he faces, the author expects God's direct intervention into world history, which ought to be expressed in universal soteriology. He employs, therefore, universal terminology, *tēbēl* and 'man'. The worldview of 1QS is close to the sectarianism in the third century BCE, in which *ʾaraʿ* and 'the sons of the earth' are utilized.[21]

6.1.3. ʾereṣ *in 1QS*

The eschatological expectation expressed with the term *tēbēl* must be related to the expression לכפר בעד הארץ. At the end of history, *tēbēl* which is defiled by

15. The phrase אמת תבל (4.19) probably connotes 'the truth in the world' (cf. 4.6); see Licht 1996: 96.

16. אדם: 4.23; אנוש: 3.17; איש: 4.2, 16, 24; בני איש: 3.13; 4.15, 20, 26; גבר: 4.20, 23.

17. Cf. Harvey 1996: 189–91.

18. Cf. 1QS 1.21-24; 8.4, 5, 9, 11, 12f.; 9.6, 11.

19. Cf. Bockmuehl 2001: 389.

20. Cf. Schwartz 1990.

21. Cf. §§ 4.2.2; 4.4.4; 4.6 above.

the wicked shall be cleansed through the purification of the chosen. The concept of purification is very close to that of atonement, as shown by parallel use of the terms 'atone' and 'cleanse' in 3.6-9. Then, the phrase לכפר בעד הארץ, which is an eschatological role of the Community, can be another expression of the cleansing of *tēbēl*. When all the wicked are destroyed from the world, the Community, the chosen ones, shall atone for the earth.[22] This atonement is similar to the one depicted in *Jub.* 6.2 and *Apocr. Gen.* 10.13, according to which Noah atoned for the earth after the Deluge when all injustice was swept away from the earth. It has also close connection to the eschatological cleansing of the earth described in *1 En.* 10.22 and *Jub.* 4.26; 50.5. We can conclude, therefore, that the author of 1QS applied the term *ʾereṣ* along with *tēbēl* to express his universal eschatological expectation, employing the idea, not from the biblical Land theology, but from extra-biblical writings known to him.

For this purpose, the Community members must 'do truth and righteousness and justice on the earth (*bāʾāreṣ*)' (1.5f.) and 'keep faith on the earth (*bāʾāreṣ*)' (8.3). The deliberate reference to *bāʾāreṣ*, which seems to be superfluous at first glance, intends probably to contrast it with the heaven. In the world to come, it is stated, God will 'make the upright ones understand the knowledge of the Most High and to instruct the wisdom of the sons of heavens to the perfect way' (4.22). It is also blessed that God 'has united their assembly to the sons of heavens to be the Council of the Community' (11.8). The author regards the Community as a counterpart to 'the sons of heavens' (cf. *1 En.* 104.6).[23] Thus, the Community's role is assigned to 'the earth' in comparison with 'the sons of heavens'.[24]

6.1.4. Related Terms

6.1.4.1. gebûl

The term *gebûl* occurs twice in 1QS col. 10 (ll. 11, 25). In both passages the term is related to God's teachings, which the Community members should guard by a 'fence' in which they should remain.

6.1.4.2. naḥalâ

The term *naḥalâ* appears twice in the phrase נחלת איש (באמת) 'man's allotment (in truth)' (4.16, 24). God allots to everyone two spirits, whether the spirit of truth or the spirit of injustice. According to this division each man walks in the path of truth or in the path of injustice. Furthermore, the spirit given to him is graded, and the degree of his work is dependent on its quantity whether great or small. The grade is his birthright. The term *naḥalâ* here is man's 'allotment' of graded spirit.[25]

22. Thus Licht 1996: 172f.; cf. 4Q434 2.1-4.
23. See Maier 1960.
24. Cf. 4Q427 7.ii.18; 4Q181 1.ii.2-4 (see below).
25. Cf. CD 13.12; 1QH[a] 6.19; 18.28; 4Q171 4.12; 4Q413 1–2.2; 4Q416 4.3; 4Q418 172.5.

6.1.5. ʾereṣ *in 1QSa*

At the beginning of 1QSa (1.1-3), an introduction to the Rule, the term *ʾereṣ*, though in a lacuna, apparently appears in the expression לכפר בעד הארץ (1.3). The Community regards itself as an eschatological congregation (1.1), which turned aside from 'the people' (1.3); hence the 'wickedness' (1.3) in which they keep their covenant must be found among Jews outside the Community. The atoning for *hāʾāreṣ* then seems to intend the atoning for the Land which is defiled by those Jews. On the other hand, a role assigned to the Congregation is that of the messianic army to prepare the final war (1.6, 21, 23f., 26), which includes 'the war to subdue the nations' (1.21). This reveals the author's international perspective. Then, the eschatological atonement must include the whole earth. The intra-national antagonism and universal dimensions are united in the expression 'to atone for *hāʾāreṣ*', in which the author projects his real experience in the Land on the eschatological earth.

6.1.6. ʾereṣ *in 1QSb*

In 1QSb the term *ʾereṣ* appears twice in the benediction addressing the Prince of the Congregation (5.20-29). The expressions 'to decide with equity for the [hum]ble of *ʾereṣ*' (5.22) and 'with your scepter may you devastate *ʾereṣ*' (5.24) are probably taken from Isa. 11.4, in which the term *ʾereṣ* certainly refers to 'the earth' of a messianic era.[26] In our benediction 'the kingdom of His people forever' (5.21) which shall be ruled by the Prince is in relation to his oppression of the peoples and to the nations' service to him (5.27-28). The 'kingdom' is sovereignty of Israel over the whole world. The *ʾereṣ* which the Prince will devastate with his sceptre, therefore, signifies 'the earth'.[27] The phrase ענוי ארץ, too, refers to 'the humble of the earth'. Whereas, however, the terms ענוים and ענים usually refer to 'the people of Israel' in the Bible,[28] the expression 'the humble of *ʾereṣ*' in this benediction apparently denotes the Community members who are seeking God in the anguish within the Land. In this sense they are 'the humble of the Land', too. The author probably projects his experience in the Land on his worldwide eschatological vision, maintaining traditional biblical nationalism.

6.1.7. Summary

The term *ʾereṣ* in 1QS is used in parallelism with *tēbēl*, and expresses the universal eschatological expectation of atoning for the earth and the Community's roles for

26. Cf. Licht 1996: 287.
27. Cf. 1QSb 3.5, 18, 19.
28. Cf. § 4.3.2.1 above and n. 63 there.

that purpose. This accords with 1QS's universalistic terminology, which is indicated by uses of 'man' in the teaching of dual spirits. It is undoubted, however, that the author opposes his compatriots. The coexistence of the intra-national issues in reality and the universal appearances probably derives from the Community's dualistic worldview. It discriminates between the chosen and sinners within Jews because of their opposition, on the one hand; it expects a new world distinct from the present world, on the other. The Community expects the solution of the domestic problems in terms of worldwide eschatology. The priority of Jewish nationality is an implicit assumption, and the Gentiles are beyond this scope. We can conclude, therefore, that the universal appearances of 1QS do not mean 'universalism' generalizing all mankind, but 'sectarianism' making a dualistic discrimination within its own nation. The self-identity of the Community is in effect the so-called 'true Israel'.

1QSa and 1QSb contain nationalism more explicit than in 1QS. These two works expect the sovereignty of Israel over all the nations, over the whole world. In this case, too, however, the 'Israel' is not the entire Jewish nation, but the 'true Israel', consisting of the chosen Jews, namely, the Community members.

The intra-national concerns of these three Rules suggest that the use of the term *ʾereṣ* in them may reflect the Community members' attitude towards the Land; it is defiled by its inhabitants and should be cleansed. They project their real experience in the Land soteriologically on the earth. In this sense, we can say, the term conveys a double meaning.

6.2. Hodayot

6.2.1. ʾereṣ *in* Hodayot

The term *ʾereṣ* in *Hodayot* can signify the *terra firma*[29] and soil.[30] It can represent the half part of the universe in contrast to the heavens (1QH^a 5.13-16; 8.3, 11; 9.10-14; 4QH^a 7.ii.23). It once represents all mankind in parallelism with *tēbēl* (1QH^a 11.32f.). In these instances *ʾereṣ* is used in relation to its creation and *eschaton* – a usage which reveals the author's universal perspective.

It can be used in territorial dimensions, as well. Mention is made of כול עמי הארצות (1QH^a 12.26f.). The passage expresses twofold antagonism towards the psalmist's Jewish opponents and nations ('Your people' and 'all the peoples of the lands'). This seems to reflect real experiences of the psalmist.[31] In 1QH^a cols 12–13 he looks back to the happenings he encountered. According to this hymn, he was driven from his land (1QH^a 12.8f.), sojourned among a foreign people (1QH^a 13.5), and they afflicted him (1QH^a 13.17). Although what really

29. 1QH^a 16.4//4QH^b 7.11; 1QH^a 26.4//4QH^a 7.ii.10//4QH^e 1.9. The column and line numbering of 1QH^a is of *DSSSE*.

30. 1QH^a 16.22-24; 18.26; cf. 5.15.

31. For the authorship, see Douglas 1999.

happened is unknown, it is probable such experiences caused his harsh antagonism towards both his compatriots and the Gentiles, as depicted in 1QH^{a} 12.26f., though intra-national hostility is much harder (esp. in 1QH^{a} cols 10–12).[32] His sentiment to be expelled is likely related to the self-identification of the Community as the sojourners in 'the land of Damascus', a symbol of its exilic context, where they entered into the new covenant (CD 6.19; 8.21//19.33f.; 20.11f.; see below).

Our term appears also at the beginning of 1QH^{a} col. 23 [bottom] (formerly frag. 2): 'and in Your *ʾereṣ* and among sons of gods and among son[s of ...] ... and to recount all Your glory' (ll. 3-4). According to 1QH^{a} 5.17 and 20.29-30 the expression 'to recount (all) Your glory' is put in a universal context that no creature but the chosen can recount the greatness of God's glory (cf. 1QH^{a} 22.4-6). The expression 'sons of gods' indicates the author's universal perspective, and the elect of the Community members is stated in 1QH^{a} col. 23 (top). Then, it seems that the expression 'Your *ʾereṣ*' in 23.3 is a synonym for 'Your dominion' in 5.17; hence it means, not 'Your Land', but 'Your earth'.[33] Here we are dealing, not with the Land theology that 'the Land is the Lord's', but the Creation theology that 'the earth is God's'.[34]

6.2.2. Related Terms

6.2.2.1. tēbēl

The term *tēbēl* is used in parallelism with *ʾereṣ* (1QH^{a} 11.33). It is also employed in relation to the Creation (1QH^{a} 9.8-16) and to the eschatological events (1QH^{a} 6.5f.; 11.35f.).[35] The eschatological expectation contains the dominion over the world by the Community, which will become like the 'world-plant' (1QH^{a} 14.15-17). Thus, the term *tēbēl* in *Hodayot* appears to be in relation to the Creation of the universe and the eschatological dominion of the sect.

We can read *hātēbēl* in 1QH^{a} 16.38, and there probably appears *kol te*[*bel*] in 1QH^{a} 14.15, expressions which are never used in the Bible.[36] While in the Bible *tēbēl* is used as a proper noun, in *Hodayot* it is regarded as a common noun; hence it is used with *he* and *kol* as precisely a synonym of the term *ʾereṣ*.

6.2.2.2. ʾadāmâ

The term *ʾadāmâ* appears in 1QH^{a} 18.3, which states that mankind (*ʾādām*) is nothing but earth (*ʾadāmâ*). Another occurrence is in 1QH^{a} 25.11f., a text which probably concerns the final judgement on the wicked angels in heaven (*mārôm*) and

32. Cf. זר: 1QH^{a} 14.27; ערל: 1QH^{a} 14.20//4Q429 4.i.9; 1QH^{a} 21.5; cf. 4Q458 2.ii.4.

33. Cf. 'His earth': Prov. 8.31; Job 37.13; 4QpNah 1–2.1f.; *1 En.* 53.2; *4 Ezra* 9.20; *2 Bar.* 14.18; 56.2; 83.2; תבל ארצכה: 4Q369 1.ii.2, 7; 4Q499 48.2.

34. Cf. Chapter 2 n. 55 above.

35. For 1QH^{a} 6.5f., cf. Pss. 9.9; 96.13; 98.9; for 1QH^{a} 11.35f., cf. 2 Sam. 24.8; Job 1.7; 2.2.

36. See Chapter 5 n. 243 above.

on unjust men on the earth (*ʾadāmâ*). It is uncertain why the term *ʾadāmâ* is chosen here instead of usual *ʾereṣ*. Possibly it is employed to form a poetic pair of *mārôm*–*ʾadāmâ*, a synonymous pair of *šāmayim*–*ʾereṣ* (cf. Isa. 24.21).

6.2.2.3. gebûl

The term *gebûl* appears in phrases 'a territory of wickedness' (1QH[a] 10.8; 11.24) and 'a realm of living' (15.14f.). The former is presumably taken from Mal. 1.4. In the present context the phrase expresses the situation in which the author lives. The latter never appears in the Bible. The phrase in the present context indicates the realm for those who obtain the eternal life after the final judgement. Thus, the term *gebûl* expresses the dualistic worldview of the author; this world which is governed by the wicked, and the world to come in which the chosen will have eternal life.

6.2.2.4. naḥalâ

The term *naḥalâ* can mean one's knowledge of God's truth, the Community's teachings (1QH[a] 6.19; 18.27-29).

In 1QH[a] 14.8 it refers to the people of Israel in the phrase 'a remnant within Your allotment'. This phrase expresses a double distinction by the sect; Israel as God's allotment which is distinguished from other nations, and the Community as a remnant which is discerned from the people of Israel.[37]

6.2.3. Summary

Among the thirteen occurrences of the term *ʾereṣ* in *Hodayot*, only two instances have territorial dimensions: the one in which the author's personal experience of expulsion is expressed refers to the Land (of Judah?), and the other, in the plural, denotes all the nations other than Israel. In the other four times the term is used in its tangible sense. In the remaining seven occurrences it connotes the cosmological earth or the earthly world, synonym to the term *tēbēl* which appears, at least, seven times.

This calculation shows the author's universal concern.[38] It is founded on twofold hostility, one intra-national, the other international. It is evident from 1QH[a] 12.26f. in which the superiority of the Community over the people and the nations is expected. Its self-identity as the chosen is also twofold, as indicated by the expression 'a remnant within Your allotment' (1QH[a] 14.8); they are chosen among the people of Israel who have been chosen among nations. The elite congregation of mankind envisions its dominion over *tēbēl*. The universal soteriology and the harsh animosity towards intra- and international outsiders characterize *Hodayot* as a sectarian work. The sectarianism is close to that of 1QS, 1QSa and 1QSb. But it is different from 1QS insofar as the latter lacks international perspectives; and

37. The meaning of *naḥalâ* in 1QH[a] 2.ii.16 is uncertain.

38. Cf. 'the sons of heavens' in 4QH[a] 7.ii.18.

also dissimilar to 1QSa and 1QSb because *Hodayot* alone contains the anti-gentile sentiment caused by the psalmist's personal experience.

Hodayot's frequent use of the universal terms *tēbēl* and 'man'[39] is in common with 1QS. Compared with the latter, however, the term *ʾereṣ* in *Hodayot* does not play a significant role in its eschatology. This is probably because of the psalmist's preference of the term *tēbēl*, a poetic synonym of *ʾereṣ*.

6.3. Damascus Document

6.3.1. ʾereṣ *in* Damascus Document

The term *ʾereṣ* in *Damascus Document* can be employed with the name of a region to express a certain territory. References are made to *ʾereṣ yehûdâ* and *ʾereṣ dameśeq* in the passages which state the establishment of the Community.[40] The Community members identified themselves with the sojourners in the land of Damascus, where they entered into the new covenant (CD 6.19; 8.21//19.33f.; 20.11f.). Once it is called 'the land of north' (CD 7.14f.). While the identification of 'the land of Damascus' is disputed,[41] the wordings 'left' and 'sojourned' indicate their voluntary placing of themselves in an exilic context.[42] 'The land of Damascus' symbolizes their exile setting, which expresses their expectation of salvation in a manner similar to biblical 'return' to Zion. In 4QD^{a} 6.iv.3 'the land of sojourning' is possibly laid in parallelism with אדמ]ת הקודש]. If the restoration is correct, the land of Damascus in which they were sojourning would be regarded as holy. In contrast, 'the land of Judah' probably symbolizes the sinfulness of Jews outside the Community (CD 3.21–4.3). The 'Princes of Judah' are condemned (CD 8.3; 19.15f.) and mention is made of 'evildoers of Judah' (20.26f.).[43] While the term *ʾereṣ* in the phrases *ʾereṣ yehûdâ* and *ʾereṣ dameśeq* clearly denotes a specific 'land' in its literal sense, it does not bear a territorial implication, but, rather, a symbolic one.

The term can express 'the Land', as well. In CD 2.14–3.12a the author provides a brief description of Israel's past from the antediluvian period to the Exile. The lines 3.7-12, in which our term is used twice, are devoted to the history from the desert to the Exile. Similarly, the sin of Israel's past and God's punishment against

39. *ʾādām*: 8 times in 1QH^{a}, 3 times in 4QH^{a-b}; *benê (hā)ʾādām*: 10 times in 1QH^{a}, once in 4QH^{a}; *ʾîš/ʾanāšîm*: 29 times in 1QH^{a}, 3 times in 4QH^{a-b}; *benê ʾîš*: twice in 1QH^{a}, once in 4QH^{a}; *ʾenôš*: 13 times in 1QH^{a}, once in 4QH^{a}; *benê ʾenôš*: once in 1QH^{a} (see *DSSC*, *ad loc.*).

40. CD 6.4f.//4QD^{a} 3.ii.12//4QD^{b} 2.12; cf. CD 4.2f. The expression שבי ישראל in CD 6.5 probably means 'those who return (to God) among Israel', according to CD 1.1-9; cf. Knibb 1983: 105–7.

41. Compare Knibb (1983) and Dimant (1984: 494) with Murphy-O'Connor (1974, 1977, 1985) and P. R. Davies (1983).

42. Cf. Collins 1990: 39.

43. Cf. Harvey 1996: 23–5.

them is repeated in CD 5.15–6.2. In these passages the concept of the biblical Land-promise is presupposed, and the Exile is expressed by the devastation or desolation of the Land. It should be noted that both passages are followed by the description of the election of a remnant for Israel and God's Covenant with them (3.12–4.18; 6.2–7.6). Thus the author sets the Community in the exilic context.

An interesting expression סרך הארץ (אשר היה מקדם) 'the rule of the Land (which was since ancient times)' is once used in relation to the custom of marriage (CD 7.6//19.2-3).[44] The usage seems to be close to the biblical idiom דרך (כל) הארץ 'the way of (all) human society' (Gen. 19.31).[45] The expression seems to presuppose the existence of some of the Community members living among other Jews in the Land.[46]

6.3.2. Passages in which the Referent of ʾereṣ *is Uncertain*

6.3.2.1. CD 1.1-12

This section describes the origins of the sect (cf. 4QD[a] 2.i.3-6a//4QD[c] 1.5-8). The author here provides the context of exile and focuses upon 'Israel' (CD 1.3) or 'the people' (4QD[a] 2.i.3). The Community identifies itself with 'a remnant for Israel' (CD 1.4f.) and 'a root of planting' from Israel and Aaron (CD 1.7). Their role is described as לירוש את ארצו and its soil is called אדמתו (CD 1.7f.). Here *ʾarṣô* seems to mean 'His Land' as the exilic context requires. As we have noted above, however, we should consider its symbolic implication. Despite its apparent reference to the Exile under Nebuchadnezzar, the author does not depict the Israelites' return to Zion, and skips over 390 years from the Exile to the dawn of the Community. The setting of Exile here, depicted as concerning past history, symbolizes eschatological salvation of the Community by God's will, according to which return to possess the Lord's *ʾereṣ* is the role of the Community, not of the past biblical Israel. If the Exile is symbolically employed, *ʾarṣô* too can be so employed. It alludes not only to the territorial Land, but also possibly connotes 'His earth'.[47] This is suggested by the eschatological imagination of the Community 'to fill the face of *tēbēl* with their seed' (CD 2.11f.); an imagination in which 'their seed' may be in relation to 'a root of planting' (CD 1.7).[48] If the 'remnant', the sectarians, fill the face of the world, the *ʾereṣ* they will possess is not only the Land, but also the earth. The eschatological possession of the earth by the righteous and the eschatological fertility of soil were known to the Community from *1 Enoch* (5.7; 10.19).[49] Utilizing the biblical Land theology, the author symbolizes the Community's eschatological possession of the earth. The term *ʾereṣ*, conveying the double meaning, expresses sectarian universalism in the terminology of nationalistic territorialism.

44. Cf. CD 10.4; 12.19, 22; 13.7; 14.3, 12.
45. Cf. Josh. 23.14; 1 Kgs 2.2.
46. Thus Baumgarten 1990: 18–20.
47. Cf. n. 33 above.
48. See CD 20.34.
49. See also *1 En.* 10.16, 18; cf. 1QS 8.5; 11.8; 1QH[a] 14.15; 16.6, 9, 10.

6.3.2.2. CD 2.7-12

The passage 'and (God) hid His face from *hāʾāreṣ*', (2.8) which is immediately followed by 'from Israel', constitutes a parallelism with CD 1.3 (cf. CD 3.12f.); hence our term must refer to the Land.[50] The second clause 'in order to leave a remnant for *hāʾāreṣ*' (2.11) also has close connection with 'He left a remnant for Israel' in 1.4-5, and the term *hāʾāreṣ* here too seems to mean the Land.[51] It is, however, also in parallelism with the term *tēbēl* in the next line, which expresses the eschatological hope of the Community, as we've just seen. If they fill the world, they will be not only the remnant for the Land, but also for the earth. Accordingly, we can observe here too the double meaning of *ʾereṣ*.

6.3.2.3. יושב(י) הארץ/לשבת בארץ

In CD 13.20-21, the term *ʾereṣ* is used with the verb *yāšab* 'to dwell'. This passage is concerning the final reward for the Community members who keep their statutes. Those who keep the statutes until the *eschaton* can succeed in dwelling *bāʾāreṣ*, and those who do not cannot. The reward must be in relation to God's purpose to leave 'a remnant for Israel' in order 'to possess His *ʾereṣ*' (CD 1.4-8). Accordingly, the term *ʾereṣ* in our passage conveys the double meaning, 'the Land' on the surface of the narrative, and 'the earth' in the symbolic implication.[52]

There are also nominal uses of the phrase יושב(י) הארץ in CD 4.14 and 10.9. The former, which is a citation from Isa. 24.17 in which the phrase probably means 'the inhabitants of the earth', is sandwiched by explanations concerning the final years towards the *eschaton* (4.12-17). The Isaianic text is apparently connected to 'Israel' in our passage, hence our phrase must mean 'the inhabitant of the Land'.[53]

CD 10.7-10 refers to 'God's wrath against *yôšbê hāʾāreṣ*' (l. 9). The passage is in close relation to *Jub.* 23.9-11, in which it is told that the human life span was shortened after the Deluge and their knowledge leaves them because of their old age (cf. Gen. 6.3). Since *Damascus Document* knows *Jubilees* (cf. CD 16.3f.), our passage must presuppose the Jubilean text. Then, the 'God's wrath' refers to the Deluge; hence our phrase conveys 'the inhabitants of the earth'.[54]

6.3.2.4. CD 7.9//CD 19.5-6

This passage refers to God's eschatological visit to *hāʾāreṣ*. The author's concern with the judgement is limited to Israel alone, as evident from the following citation from Isa. 7.17 which mentions 'you, your people, and your father's house' (CD 7.11f.), or from Zech. 13.7 which refers to 'My shepherd' (CD 19.7-9), and no

50. 'Land/country': Rabin 1958: 6; Dupont-Sommer 1959: 139; Lohse 1971: 69; P. R. Davies 1983; Knibb 1987: 25; Maier 1995: 10; *DSSHAG* II, 15; García Martínez 1994: 34; *DSSSE* 553; Vermes 1997: 128.

51. So the translators in the previous note, except Dupont-Sommer (139: 'terre').

52. 'Land': Rabin (1958: 66), Dupont-Sommer (1959: 173), Lohse (1971: 95), Maier (1995: 28), *DSSHAG* (II, 55), García Martínez (1994: 44), *DSSSE* (573), Vermes (1997: 142).

53. So translators in n. 50 above, except García Martínez (1994: 35) and *DSSSE* (557) translating 'earth-dweller'.

54. So translators in n. 50 above, except *DSSHAG* II, 45: 'the land'.

reference is made to the judgement against the Gentiles. In CD 8.1-3, too, in which God's visit is told of, the judgement is directed against those who enter His covenant but do not hold fast the statutes. The author focuses upon the people, as we've seen above (CD 1.1-8). In 1.7, in particular, a reference is made to God's visit to the people (cf. also CD 20.25f.). Considering the author's intra-national perspectives, it is acceptable to translate the clause as 'when God visits the Land'.[55] It is, however, also sound to render our term as 'the earth',[56] since God's eschatological visit to the earth is known from *1 En.* 25.3 and also from 1QS 3.14, 18; 4.18f. in which God's visit is related to the term *tēbēl*, and our passage tells of the final judgement of God. Judging from his symbolic uses of our term, the author here too utilizes the double meaning of *ʾereṣ*, applying the universal eschatological vocabulary, פקד את הארץ, to his intra-national condemnation.

6.3.3. Related Terms

6.3.3.1. ʾadāmâ

The term *ʾadāmâ* occurs twice in *Damascus Document*. There seems to appear the phrase *ʾadmat hāqôdeš* in parallelism with 'the land of sojourning', which may refer to the land of Damascus (4QD[a] 6.iv.3). In CD 1.8 the expression *ʾadmatô* is used in parallelism with *ʾarṣô* (see § 6.3.2.1 above).

6.3.3.2. tēbēl

The term *tēbēl* appears twice. It is utilized to express the author's eschatological expectations that the seed of Community members will fill 'the surface of the world' (CD 2.11f.), and they will have victory 'over all the sons of the world' (CD 20.34).

6.3.3.3. gebûl

The term *gebûl* is mostly used in relation to the biblical prohibition to move a neighbour's boundary of the land property allotted to individual Israelites (Deut. 19.14; Prov. 22.28; 23.10). Those who transgress this precept shall be cursed (Deut. 27.17). In *Damascus Document* mention is made of 'those who move the boundary'[57] and 'to remove the boundary'.[58] They are the condemned, the opponents of the Community. What the term symbolizes can be known from its other occurrences in CD 20.25f. (גבול התורה) and 4QD[a] 11.11-14. From these passages it is apparent that the term *gebûl* is neither in relation to an individual land property nor to the Land, but is applied to a symbol of 'the fence of the Torah' (cf. *m. Abot* 1.1).[59]

55. So Lohse 1971: 81; *DSSHAG* II, 25; Vermes 1997: 132. Cf. *1 En.* 90.20.

56. So Rabin 1958: 28; Dupont-Sommer 1959: 148; Knibb 1987: 56; Maier 1995: 18; García Martínez 1994: 37; *DSSSE* 561.

57. CD 5.20//4QD[a] 3.ii.7//4QD[b] 2.4; CD 19.16 (//Hos. 5.10); 4QD[a] 1a–b.4; 4QD[f] 1.2.

58. CD 1.16//4QD[a] 2.i.19.

59. See § 6.1.4.1 above.

6.3.3.4. naḥalâ

The term *naḥalâ* occurs twice. It is once employed with the term *gebûl* (CD 1.14-16). The *naḥalâ* of the forefathers which is bounded by *gebûl* (l. 16) must be the Torah, and the author condemns his opponent as 'the Scoffer' (l. 14) for his removing its boundary.

CD 13.11f. (//4QD^{b} 9.iv.8f.) refer to 'one's allotment (*naḥalâ*) in the lot of Light'. A newcomer in the Congregation is ranked by his attributes which are foreordained according to the '(spirit of) Light' given to him (CD 5.18; cf. 1QS 3.17-20; 1QM 13.9). The attributes are his 'allotment' of Light, and their grade, whether great or small, is his birthright (cf. 1QS 4.16, 24; 1QH^{a} 6.19; 18.28).

6.3.4. Summary

The term *ʾereṣ* in *Damascus Document* mostly refers to the Land.[60] The author, reviewing the past history of Israel and describing the desolation of the Land, sets the Community in an exilic context. According to this setting, he describes the eschatological expectation in the vocabulary of the biblical Land theology. He identifies the Community, which sojourns in the land of Damascus, the symbolic exile, with the remnant for Israel to possess the Lord's *ʾereṣ*. Despite the exilic setting, the author's hostility is not directed towards the Gentiles, but towards his domestic opponents. He repetitiously refers to God's wrath, visit and judgement on Israel, but scarcely on the foreign nations.[61] His intra-national concerns are illustrated by the use of the term 'all flesh' in CD 1.2. While it literally designates all human beings, its implication is not generalization of mankind indifferent to nationality. It is apparent from the following lines that 'those who contemn Him' are past Israelites and the compatriot opponents of the Community. The clause 'He has a dispute with all flesh' (1.2) then means that the nationality of Israel does not exempt a Jew from judgement.[62] The term 'all flesh' does not intend de-nationalism, but intra-national discrimination.[63]

Accordingly, *Damascus Document* can be characterized by the exilic setting and the language of biblical Land theology, on the one hand, and by the intra-national concerns, on the other. The latter reflects the real life of the Community, while the former is a symbolic expression of its soteriology modelled on the biblical past. The possession of 'His *ʾereṣ*', therefore, which is the sect's eschatological role, does not have territorial dimensions. The lack of territorialism is shown also by the uses of other terms *gebûl* and *naḥalâ*, both of which express the Land theology in the Bible; in *Damascus Document*, however, *gebûl* means the boundary of the Torah, and *naḥalâ* signifies either the Torah or one's quality according to which

60. Except CD 10.9.

61. See CD 8.9-11//19.22-24; 20.32-34. For *gôyim*, see CD 9.1//4QD^{e} 6.iii.16; CD 11.15//4QD^{f} 5.i.9; CD 12.6, 9; 14.15; 4QD^{a} 5.ii.5; 13.3; 4QD^{e} 2.ii.13; 4QD^{e} 3.iii.21//4QD^{f} 2.9.

62. Cf. Mt. 3.7-10//Lk. 3.7-9; cf. also § 8.1.2.2 below.

63. Cf. § 6.1.2 above.

he is ranked among the Sons of Light. Instead of territorialism, the eschatological hope contains universal dimensions. This is displayed by somewhat sudden uses of another term, *tēbēl*. Employed with it, the term *ʾereṣ* gains another referent 'the earth'. The expression 'to possess *ʾarṣô*' plays an interesting role; portraying the Community's salvation in the language of the biblical Land theology, it envisions the earth possession of the sectaries. The sectarianism of *Damascus Document* is represented by its soteriology consisting of intra-national particularism with harsh hostility towards outsiders and universalism without concerns for the Gentiles, a sectarianism which is very close to that of *Community Rule*.

6.4. War Scroll

6.4.1. ʾereṣ *in* War Scroll

The term *ʾereṣ* in *War Scroll* can mean 'the ground', the surface of the earth (1QM 12.9//19.2//4QM[b] 1.1f.). It can also refer to the cosmological 'earth' compared with heaven in relation to God's Creation (1QM 10.8f., 12f.).[64] Once the enemies of God are called קמי ארץ 'the revels of the earth' (1QM 12.5), in which *ʾereṣ* signifies the earthly world in comparison with the heavenly world where God and angels abide (1QM 12.1); hence the phrase does not mean 'the rebels against the earth', but 'the rebels on the earth'.[65]

The final battle the Community prepares is מלחמה לכול ארצות הגויים 'the war for all the lands of the nations' (1QM 2.7). It is expected at the end of the war that God will deliver into the hands of the poor [i.e. Israel] the enemies of *kol hāʾarāṣôt* (1QM 11.13). The use of plural *ʾarāṣôt*, which is not rare in the Dead Sea Scrolls,[66] may be an expression of Jewish nationalism. A nationalist sentiment is expressed by God-Israel-nations relationships in 1QM 10.8-16. In these lines, the perception that the God of Israel is the Creator of the universe is directly connected to the elect of the people of Israel, which is a well-known biblical concept. In the biblical passages, however, the election is never mentioned with the term מכול עמי הארצות (10.9).[67] Similarly, there is no biblical usage of נחלת ארצות 'the allotment of lands' (10.15). The use of the plural *ʾarāṣôt* here suggests the author's consciousness that the foreign nations are living in their own lands outside the Land; hence the nationalism contains territorial dimensions.

In accordance with this territorial nationalism, the Land is called 'your [Israelites'] Land' (1QM 10.7//Num. 10.9). It is stated that 'Fill Your (God's) Land with glory and Your allotment with blessing' (1QM 12.12//19.4). A similar statement appears several times in the Bible, in which, however, the term *hāʾāreṣ*

64. Cf. Deut. 3.24; Ps. 113.5f.; 1 Kgs 8.23//2 Chron. 6.14.

65. Cf. Yadin 1962: 315 n.

66. 1QpHab 6.8; 1QM 2.7; 10.9, 15; 11.13; 1QH[a] 12.26; 4Q286 7.i.1; 4Q369 2.2; see Chapter 5 n. 249 above.

67. With *mikol hāʿamîm*: Deut. 7.6; 10.15; 14.2; without any reference: Deut. 4.37; 7.7; 1 Kgs 3.8; Pss. 33.12; 135.4; Isa. 14.1; 41.8f.; 44.1; 49.7; Ezek. 20.5.

always means 'the earth'.[68] In our passage the phrase ארצכה, which is employed with נחלתכה, specifically refers to the Land as the Lord's. In this respect the expression מטהרי הארץ (1QM 7.2), who shall bury the dead after the battle, can be understood, namely, they are 'the cleansers of the Land' (cf. Ezek. 39.12).[69] It is surprising to see the eschatological blessings of the Land, not of the earth, in this very document which describes the eschatological battles against 'all the lands of the nations'.[70]

6.4.2. ʾereṣ *in* Book of War (11QSM//4QSM)

It is relevant here to treat *Book of War* (11QSM [11Q14] and 4QSM [4Q285]), which may provide the missing end section of *War Scroll*.[71]

The term *ʾereṣ* appears in 11QSM 1.ii.7-15 (//4QSM 8.3b-10). These lines depict eschatological blessings over the Israelite congregation. In this brief benediction the term *ʾereṣ* appears five times, of which three times it is connected to the fertility of crops of the Land (ll. 8, 10, 11), and twice to the safe and healthy life in it (ll. 13f., 14).[72] It is again striking that the author focuses not upon the earth but upon the Land in his eschatological vision even after the triumph over the Kittim (4QSM 4.5; cf. 1QM 1.6, 9). *Book of War* does not expect the eschatological possession of the earth by Israel, but their happy life in the Land.

6.4.3. Summary

War Scroll envisions the eschatological war involving angels in heaven and all the nations on the earth. It is expected that when the Kittim, the wicked and the sons of darkness are defeated, 'the sons of justice shall shine to all the ends of *tēbēl*' (1QM 1.8). The author's cosmological universal perspective is clearly discernible. As for foreign nations, it is hoped that their wealth shall be brought in Jerusalem and their kings shall serve her, and Israel shall rule over them forever (1QM 12.13-16//19.5-8; cf. 17.7f.). The eschatological visions, however, contain the expectation of the Land being filled with God's glory and blessing (1QM 12.12//19.4), and of the safe and healthy life in it (11QSM 1.ii.7-15a//4QSM 1.3b-9). Thus, the Land is territorially distinct from other lands as the Lord's Land, even after the establishment of Israel's dominion over the entire world.

68. Num. 14.21; Isa. 6.3; Ps. 72.19; cf. Ps. 148.13; Hab. 3.3.

69. Cf. Yadin 1962: 225; 1983: I, 322.

70. In 1QM and 4QM terms *ʾadāmâ* and *gebûl* do not appear; *naḥalâ* is used twice (1QM 10.15; 12.12//19.4) as we've seen; and *tēbēl* is used in 1QM 1.8 which we shall see below.

71. See Milik 1972: 142f.; Vermes 1997: 187; 1999: 40; Nitzan 1993–4: 89f.; cf. also Abegg 1994; Lyons 1999; Alexander 1999–2000.

72. Cf. Lyons 1996: 144 and n. 38.

The coexistence of the hopes for Israel's dominion over foreign nations and for a happy life in the Land indicates the actual situation when *War Scroll* was written, a situation when the Land was ruled by foreign overlords. They are represented by the term 'Kittim', who must be identified with the Romans.[73] Compared with *1 Enoch* 6–11 which is written in a similar situation at the end of the fourth century BCE but makes no reference to the Land, *War Scroll* is much more conscious of the significance of the Land. Furthermore, it seems that the strong antagonism towards the Roman rulers decreased the sectarian tendency of the Community, a tendency characteristic in *Community Rule*, *Hodayot* and *Damascus Document* in which hostility towards the Jews outside the Community is decisive.

6.5. Pesharim

6.5.1. ʾereṣ *in* Psalms Pesher

The term *ʾereṣ* appears in 4QpPs^a (4Q171). It provides interpretations of Psalm 37, and quotes the biblical passages containing the expression ירשו/לרשת ארץ.[74] Its connotation can be inferred by considering eschatological ideas in the commentary.[75]

Eschatological hopes described in 4QpPs^a can be divided into two; the hopes for the perishing of the wicked (2.7-9, 20; 4.9f., 11) and the hopes for the good rewards to the congregation of the poor (2.9-12; 3.1f., 10f.; 4.3). The wicked in the author's mind are the congregation's Jewish opponents, the 'Man of Lies' (1.26) and 'the wicked of Ephraim and Manasseh' (2.18), who 'will be delivered into the hand of ruthless nations' (2.20; 4.9f.). Nevertheless, he employs a universal expression 'every wicked person' (2.8f.) and a cosmological term 'Belial' (2.11). In the hopes for the congregation's rewards, too, such expressions as 'flesh' (2.12) and כול נחלת אדם 'all the allotment of Adam' (3.1f.) are used.[76] The universal appearances despite the author's domestic concerns seem to be close to those of 1QS and CD. The expression נחלת אמת 'the allotment of truth' (4.12) also shows a close relationship to 1QS (1QS 4.24; cf. 1QH^a 18.28f.).[77]

These relationships between 4QpPs^a and 1QS suggest the similarity in their worldview. These works expect eschatological perishing of the wicked from the world (*ʾereṣ*/*tēbēl*) and its final possession by the congregation, despite their actual concerns on domestic affairs. While mention is made of the foreign nations, the author of 4QpPs^a gives them only the role to destroy his compatriot opponents. The

73. See Yadin 1962: 21–5, 245f.; Duhaime 1995: 84 n. 25; Shatzman 1996; *HJP* III, 402–4; Vermes 1997: 162f.

74. 4QpPs^a 2.4//Ps. 37.9; 4QpPs^a 2.9//Ps. 37.11; 4QpPs^a 3.9//Ps. 37.22; 4QpPs^a 4.2//Ps. 37.29; 4QpPs^a 4.10-11//Ps. 37.34.

75. Cf. Stegemann 1963–4: 257 n. 123.

76. Cf. 1QS 4.16, 24.

77. The end of 3.10 may be restored as נחלת כול ה[תבל]; see Strugnell 1969–71: 214; cf. Stegemann 1963–4: 252f., 265 n. 172; Vermes 1997: 489.

fate of Gentiles seems to be out of his consideration, as in 1QS. In short, 4QpPs[a] shares the same sectarianism with 1QS. We can conclude, therefore, that the author of 4QpPs[a] reinterpreted the biblical expression ירשו ארץ as the eschatological possession of 'the earth' by the Community.[78]

6.5.2. ᵓereṣ *in* Isaiah Pesharim

The term *ᵓereṣ* appears three times in the interpretation, apart from biblical quotations.[79] 4QpIsa[a] (4Q161) 2–4.5-7 provides an interpretation on Isa. 10.22f. Since the wording '[their] plan[ting in the] *ᵓereṣ* in truth' (l. 7) seems to express an idea close to *Jub.* 36.6, it is preferable to render our term as 'the earth'.[80]

In 4QpIsa[a] 8–10.3-4 there appears the phrase ענוי ארץ, though in a lacuna (cf. Isa. 10.33f.; 11.4). The present context which contrasts the Kittim and Israel suggests that the phrase may connote 'the meek of the earth' representing Israel.[81]

4QpIsa[b] (4Q162) 2.1f. contains the expressions 'the condemnation of *hāᵓāreṣ*' and 'the visitation of *hāᵓāreṣ*' (cf. Isa. 5.10).[82] Here *hāᵓāreṣ* seems to mean the Land, since the following lines state God's wrath against his people because of 'the men of scorning' in Jerusalem (ll. 6-8). But considering the worldwide scope of *Isaiah Pesharim*, the double connotation of earth and Land is possible (cf. CD 7.9b-13a//CD 19.5f.).

Generally speaking, it seems, 4QIsaiah Pesher[a] holds international scope, while 4QIsaiah Pesher[b] focuses upon intra-national conflicts.

6.5.3. ᵓereṣ *in* Habakkuk Pesher

1QpHab 12.15–13.4 quotes Hab. 2.19-20 and interprets it. The phrase כול הגוים in the interpretation (13.1) clearly indicates that the interpreter understands the biblical *kol hāᵓāreṣ* (Hab. 2.20) in the sense of the human world consisting of nations other than Israel. The reference to *gôyim* suggests the author's territorial dimensions. This is also evident from the use of ארצות רבות 'many lands' in 1QpHab 6.8.[83]

78. Cf. *1 En.* 5.7; Sir. 36.1-22; 44.21; *Jub.* 22.14; 32.19; *LAB* 32.3; *4 Ezra* 6.59; *2 Bar.* 44.13-15; Mt. 5.5.

79. (3QpIsa 4//Isa. 1.1); (4QpIsa[b] 3.2//Isa. 5.30); 4QpIsa[c] 2–3.3//Isa. 8.8; (4QpIsa[c] 4–6.i.15f. //Isa. 9.18); (4QpIsa[a] 8–10.15//Isa. 11.4); 4QpIsa[c] 8–10.5//Isa. 14.26; 4QpIsa[e] 5.1//Isa. 21.9; (4QpIsa[e] 5.4//Isa. 21.14); 4QpIsa[e] 1–2.4//Isa. 40.12 (the brackets indicate the term or the clause being in lacuna).

80. See *Jub.* 7.34; 21.24; cf. also *1 En.* 10.16; Sir. 10.15.

81. Cf. Kittim and *gôyim* in lines 4, 5, 7, 8, 21.

82. For God's visit to the earth, see *1 En.* 25.3; 1QS 3.14, 18; 4.18f.; to the Land, see *1 En.* 90.20.

83. Cf. Jer. 28.8; 11QT[a] 59.2.

Hab. 2.17 is interpreted in 1QpHab 11.17–12.10, in which the biblical expression '*ʾereṣ*, *qiryâ* and all who dwell in it' is explained.[84] While the exact referent of the terms *ʾereṣ* and *qiryâ* in the book of Habakkuk is uncertain, the interpreter definitely identifies them as 'the cities of Judah' (12.9)[85] and 'Jerusalem' (12.7), respectively, by *interpreting* the condemned as 'the Wicked Priest', despite the biblical context in which the woe is certainly directed to Babylon (Chaldea).

There are lines in which the referent of our term is uncertain.

(1) 1QpHab 2.15–3.2 on Hab. 1.6 (1QpHab 3.9f.; 4.12f.)
Since *Habakkuk Pesher* cols 3–4 focus upon the power of Kittim over 'all the nations' (3.4f.), 'all the peoples' (3.6, 11, 13; 4.14), and 'kings and princes' (4.2f.), it is preferable to render the term *ʾereṣ* here as 'the earth'. In *Habakkuk Pesher*, however, 'the peoples' are not contrasted with Israel but with the Kittim, and Israel, too, is enumerated as one of these peoples. The author seems to expect that the Kittim will attack also the Land (esp. Jerusalem, cf. 9.3-7). Then, the term *ʾereṣ* can connote a double meaning, the earth and the Land.[86] The same can be said of its uses in 3.9f. and 4.12f.

(2) 1QpHab 10.14f. on Hab. 2.14
It is acceptable to render the term *ʾereṣ* in 1QpHab 10.14f. (= Hab. 2.14) as 'the earth', since it is here contrasted with 'the sea', and Hab. 2.14 probably connotes universal concerns.[87] Its interpretation, however, contains the phrase 'when they return' (10.16), which is followed by: 'and afterwards knowledge will be revealed to them in abundance like the waters of the sea' (11.1f.). Although there is a lacuna between 10.16 and 11.1, the 'they/them' referred to in these lines are certainly the 'many' who had been misdirected by 'the Spouter of Lies' (10.9-13).[88] The 'they/them' who, in the author's expectation, will return and to whom the knowledge will be revealed must be his contemporary Jews. Thus, the author's scope here is limited to 'the Land'.[89]

The author's perspectives move from wider international affairs to narrower intra-national ones: from the Kittim conquering all the nations to the Wicked Priest, a Jew in Jerusalem. In his eschatological expectation there is a double concern, the fate of the world, and of the Land: the eschatological destruction of the Gentiles and the wicked from the earth (13.1-4), on the one hand, the fulfilment of God's glory in the Land, on the other.

84. Although 1QpHab 9.8 quotes Hab. 2.8b which includes the same phrase, the interpretation does not show any geographical concerns.

85. Cf. 1QpZeph 1-5 on Zeph. 1.18.

86. Earth: Vermes 1997: 479; Land: Brownlee 1977: 65; Horgan 1979: 13; *DSSSE* 13.

87. All scholars but Brownlee in the previous note read 'the earth'.

88. Cf. Nitzan 1986: 13f., 153, 187f.

89. Thus Brownlee 1979: 175.

6.5.4. ʾereṣ *in* Nahum Pesher

In *Nahum Pesher* (4Q169) the term *ʾereṣ* is legible twice, and it is supposed to appear twice in the lacunae of Bible quotations.[90] 4QpNah 1–2.1f. give an interpretation of Nah. 1.3. Although the context is unclear, it is certain that the phrase ארצו signifies 'earth', as shown by the following verb ברא. The use of the expression ארצו in the sense of 'God's earth' is very rare in the Bible, but it is employed several times in the extra-biblical literature.[91]

In 4QpNah 5.1f. a quotation and an interpretation of Nah. 3.13 are given. Again the context is broken, but the expression *kol gebûl yiśrāēl* certainly suggests that the phrase ארצך of Nah. 3.13 is understood in territorial dimensions.

6.5.5. ʾereṣ *in Other* Pesharim

Zephaniah Pesher (1Q15) contains the quotation of Zeph. 1.18–2.2 and its interpretation, in which the biblical *kol yôšbê hāʾāreṣ* (Zeph. 1.18) is paraphrased as [*kol yôšbe*] *ʾereṣ yehûdâ* (1QpZeph 5). This interpretation is in line with 1QpHab 11.17–12.10 we saw above.

4QpHos[b] (4Q167) 2.6 provides an interpretation of Hos. 5.15. Since the context is clearly concerning the last priest (= the Wicked Priest) who will attack the Ephraim (probably the Pharisees), our term certainly refers to the Land.[92]

6.5.6. *Summary*

Psalms Pesher shares the same sectarianism with *Community Rule* and reinterprets the biblical expression ירש את הארץ in universal dimensions. The author of *4QIsaiah Pesher[a]*, expressing his antagonisms towards foreign enemies ('Kittim') on the one hand, towards his compatriots ('the men of scorning') on the other, depicts the Community's eschatological dominion over the earth in an image similar to *Jub*. 36.6. Similarly, *Habakkuk Pesher* shows its hostilities towards the 'Kittim' and the 'Wicked Priest', but it envisions the fulfilment of God's glory in the Land after their destruction. *Nahum Pesher* also expresses its concerns for the universal earth and the territorial Land.

Except for *Psalms Pesher* and *4QIsaiah Pesher[a]*, the *Pesharim* employ our term both in universal and territorial dimensions. The universal scope is an expression of their hostility towards foreign powers, and in this respect they show their concerns for the Land. This worldview is close to that of *War Scroll*. It must reflect their real life, when Jerusalem was conquered by the 'Kittim', the Romans.

90. 4QpNah 1–2.2; 1–2.10//Nah. 1.5; in lacunae: 4QpNah 3–4.i.9//Nah. 2.14; 4QpNah 5.1// Nah. 3.13. 4QpNah 1–2.4 reads [...] ולכלותם מעל פני, which might be followed by *hāʾadāmâ*.

91. See n. 33 above.

92. Another occurrence of our term: 1QpMic 1–5.3//Mic. 1.3.

6.6. Others

6.6.1. ʾereṣ *in* Instruction

Among *Instruction* scrolls the term *ʾereṣ* appears in 4QInstruction[d] (4Q418) and 4QInstruction[g] (4Q423). In 4QInstruction[d] 81+81a.14 there occurs the following expression: '[...] the world (*hātēbēl*), in it shall walk כול נוחלי ארץ'. While the context is uncertain because of lacunae, the use of the term *tēbēl* suggests the author's universal concerns (cf. l. 4). In *Instruction* there are no territorial dimensions. Furthermore, the terms rooted from *nḥl* are employed relatively frequently in 4QInstruction[d] with such expressions as: נוחלי אמת 'those who possess as allotment truth' (55.6), נחלת כול חי 'the allotment of every living being' (81+81a.20), and נחלת איש באמת 'the allotment of man in truth' (172.5). These expressions have close relationships with *Community Rule* and *Psalms Pesher* which employ similar phrases to express its sectarianism.[93] The phrase כול נוחלי ארץ, therefore, is to be rendered as 'all who possess as allotment the earth'.[94]

In 4QInstruction[g] 3.3 (//1Q26 2.3) the expression אחוזת ארץ is used. Since it appears in relation to its product, the phrase may mean the land property of an individual, as in Lev. 27.24.

6.6.2. ʾereṣ *in* Mysteries

In *Mysteries* (1QMyst [1Q27], 4QMyst[a-c] [4Q299–301]) the term *ʾereṣ* appears seven times, of which three occurrences allow us to determine its referent (4QMyst[a] 6.ii.6; 79.5; 4QMyst[c] 3a–b.6).[95]

4QMyst[a] 6.ii.5f. reads: 'What a father for sons ... [...] except *ʾereṣ*'. Although the context is lost, the parabolic use of father and sons suggests that *ʾereṣ* in this line means 'a land' (property?). ארץ צביו in 4QMyst[a] 79.5, though the context is unclear, is perhaps intended for 'the land of His beauty', i.e., the Land.

4QMyst[c] 3a–b.6 reads: 'And over what is *bāʾāreṣ* He gave him dominion'. While it is unclear to whom God gave the dominion, our term here may signify 'the earth' since frag. 3 praises God in general terms.

In 1QMyst 1.i.6f. another term *tēbēl* is used twice in an eschatological hope.

93. This relationship indicates the Qumranic provenance of *Instruction*, although its pre-Qumranic origins are insisted by Harrington 2000: 826; see Vermes 1997: 402.

94. The term *ʾereṣ* is legible also in 4QInstruction[d] 65.2; 80.1; 176.1, but the context is unclear because of lacunae.

95. Others: 4QMyst[a] 4.3; 9.2; 81.1; 4QMyst[b] 1a.i.3.

6.6.3. ʾereṣ *in* Barkhi Naphshi

Among five *Barkhi Naphshi* scrolls the term *ʾereṣ* appears only in *Barkhi Naphshi*ᵃ (4Q434). Once *ʾereṣ* denotes the *terra firma* in the expression 'the beasts of the earth' contrasted to 'the birds of the heavens' (7b.2f.).[96]

The other relevant passages in this text come in frag. 2 which is identified by M. Weinfeld as an early form of rabbinic Grace after Meals for Mourners.[97] In our text 'mourning' in line 1 is applied to Jerusalem (l. 6).[98] In the following lines *ʾereṣ* is used in the context of new Creation (ll. 2-4). The psalmist's universal perspective is apparent in these lines: the foreign nations and the wicked shall be destroyed, heaven and earth will be renewed[99] and the earth will be filled with God's glory,[100] and the sectaries will rejoice[101] and their guilt will be atoned for.[102]

In line 8, however, there appears the expression 'their desirable land'.[103] It is probably related to the blessing of the Land, since the rabbinic Grace after Meals also contains the blessing of the Land with a similar wording (*b. Ber*. 49a), and the Qumran Community seems to have recited, as the blessing after meals, Deut. 8.5-10 which praises the Land.[104] Thus, two dimensions, universal and territorial, coexist in the eschatological soteriology of *Barkhi Naphshi*ᵃ frag. 2.

6.6.4. ʾereṣ *in* Ages of Creation

In 4Q181 1.ii.2-4 'the sons of heavens and earth' (l. 2) who have been delivered to a wicked community must be the Community members and their angels. It is interesting to see the fact that the expression בני תבל (l. 3) represents all human beings and angels, both holy and wicked, while the phrase בני שמים וארץ refers to some of them, the Community and its angels. The Community sees its members in alliance with the holy angels, as we saw the same notion in *Community Rule* above (cf. *1 En*. 104.6).

6.6.5. ʾereṣ *in* The Chariots of Glory

In *The Chariots of Glory* (4QBerᵃ⁻ᵉ [4Q286–290]) the term *ʾereṣ* appears four times. It can signify a part of *terra firma* characterized by topographical feature,

96. Cf. Chapter 2 n. 9 above.
97. Weinfeld 1992.
98. Weinfeld 1992: 433.
99. Cf. *LAB* 16.3; for the verb 'to renew', cf. 1QHᵃ 19.13; 1QS 4.25; 1QSb 5.21; 4Q215a 3.1.
100. Cf. 4Q462 1.8.
101. Cf. 4Q521 2.iii.4f.
102. Cf. 1QS 8.6, 10; 1QSa 1.3.
103. Cf. Jer. 3.19; Zech. 7.14; Ps. 106.24.
104. See Weinfeld 1992: 436; see also § 5.10.2 above and n. 264 there.

as the phrase 'a land of drought' shows (4QBer[a] 5.2). In 4QBer[a] 5.1 it is used in parallelism with *ʾadāmâ* and designates 'the earth' as the dwelling place of created beings.

The territorial use of our term can be confirmed by the occurrence of its plural form *ʾarāṣôt* (4QBer[a] 7.i.1). In 4QBer[a] 1.ii.11 there appears the phrase שבתות ארץ. This phrase usually means 'the Sabbaths of the Land'.[105] In *The Chariots of Glory*, however, there is no allusion to the Land. Rather references are made to תבל (4QBer[a] 5.7), מלכותכה 'Your sovereignty' (4QBer[a] 7.i.5), and משפחות האדמה 'the families of the earth' (4QBer[b] 5.13). Considering this universal perspective, it is preferable to render the phrase as 'the Sabbaths of the earth'.[106] If this is correct, the Community was to expect that the sabbatical years would be kept in the whole world. The worldview of *The Chariots of Glory* seems to be close to that of *Community Rule*.

*6.6.6. ʾ*ereṣ *in* Songs of the Sage

In *Songs of the Sage* (4QShir[a-b] [4Q510–4Q511]) the term *ʾereṣ* signifies 'the earth' in contrast to the heavens (4QShir[b] 3.7; 10.12). The phrase 'the foundations of the earth' occurs also in 4QShir[b] 42.6. There appears the expression 'the dust of the earth', in contrast to waters, heavens and mountains (4QShir[b] 30.4f.).

While the referent of our term in 4QShir[b] 1.2 is uncertain because of lacunae, it may connote 'the earth', since in the following lines we can read 'the seas' (l. 4). Similarly, our term in 4QShir[b] 30.1 seems to be used in contrast to heavens and abysses (l. 2).

There appears once the expression נחלת אלוהים which refers, not to the Land, but to Jacob, the people of Israel (4QShir[b] 2.i.5). In *Songs of the Sage* the Creation theology is visible, but the Land theology is not.[107]

*6.6.7. ʾ*ereṣ *in Other Qumranic Documents*

In 4QPrayer of Enosh[a-b] there appears twice a unique expression תבל ארצכה (4Q369 1.ii.2, 7//4Q499 48.2). The combination of *tēbēl* and *ʾereṣ* is known from biblical Wisdom literature (Prov. 8.31; Job 37.12).[108] The two terms are used in parallelism in 4QSapiential-Hymnic Work A (4Q426) 1.i.8-13. In this passage we can find the phrase 'the kings of the earth' (l. 13), which is employed also in 4QFlorilegium (4Q174) 1–2.i.18 (= Ps. 2.1, though in a lacuna).[109]

105. Cf. *Jub*. 50.2f., 13; 1Q22 1.iii.1; 4Q385a 45.5.

106. Thus *DSSSE*, 645.

107. *ʾereṣ* in 4QShir[b] 37.3 remains uncertain because of lacunae.

108. See BDB, 385.

109. In 4QpGen[a] (4Q252) 1.1–2.5a, retelling the Flood story (Genesis 6–8), the term *ʾereṣ* is used in the sense of 'the earth', the dry land in contrast to waters (1.3, 6, 7, 18, 21; 2.2). In

Our term can be used in territorial dimensions, as well.[110] The plural *ʾarāṣôt* appears in 4QPrayer of Enosh[a] 2.2 (though in a lacuna).[111] Mention is also made of the Land.[112] In 4QPesher on Apocalypse of Weeks a reference is made to *ʾam hāʾāreṣ* in parallelism with the Levites (4Q247 1.5).[113] The phrase *ʾereṣ yiśrāēl* occurs in 4QMMT B 63, in which it signifies the Land in relation to the law concerning fruit trees planted in the Land (cf. *TS* 58.6). Although there are further occurrences of the term *ʾereṣ* in other Qumranic scrolls, the lacunae do not allow us to determine its referent.[114]

6.6.8. Summary

Because of the fragmentary state of these documents, we cannot draw a systematic conclusion. We may deduce just a general tendency of the sectarians who produced them. What is characteristic is their universal and eschatological concern. The final judgement on nations and the wicked is expected (*Barkhi Naphshi*). An eschatological role of the sect is also depicted. *Ages of Creation*, applying the phrase בני שמים וארץ to the Community and its angels, sees its members in alliance with the holy angels. *Instruction* uses the expression כול נוחלי ארץ which seems to intend the eschatological earth possession. In *The Chariots of Glory* the phrase שבתות ארץ is employed to express the sect's hope of eschatological 'Sabbaths of the earth'. These passages show a sectarian mind.[115]

Despite general universal inclination, the territorial dimensions are not utterly absent. In *Barkhi Naphshi*[a] frag. 2 the eschatological expectation of a new Creation accords with the blessing of the Land. Similarly, *Mysteries* uses the expression ארץ צביו probably in reference to the Land, on the one hand, no less than it employs the term *tēbēl* in an eschatological expectation, on the other. Two dimensions, territorial and universal, coexist in them.

6.7. Conclusion

The uses of the term *ʾereṣ* in the Qumranic writings can be divided into two dimensions: universal and territorial. 1QS and 1QSa assign the Community members an eschatological role atoning for the earth, and 1QSb expects a messianic

Consolations quotations are made from the Isaianic passages containing our term, in which it signifies 'the earth' (4Q176 1–2.i.10//Isa. 48.9; [1–2.ii.4//Isa. 49.13]; 8–11.7//Isa. 54.5; 8–11.11// Isa. 54.9) or 'the ground' (8–11.1//Isa. 51.23).

110. 4QpGen[a] (4Q252) 2.10; 4QCatena[a] (4Q177) 12–13.i.8 (cf. Joel 2.20; 4.2).
111. See Chapter 5 n. 249 and Chapter 6 n. 66 above.
112. 4Q180 2-4.ii.2f.; 5–6.2; 4Q252 2.8; 11Q13 2.25 (cf. Lev. 25.9).
113. See DJD XXXVI, 190f.
114. 4Q174 8.2; 9–10.2; 4Q176 25.4; 4Q178 1.3; 4Q304 1; 4Q513 15.2.
115. But cf. נחלת אלוהים in *Songs of the Sage*, which seems to mean the people of Israel.

kingdom ruling over all the nations. *Hodayot* foresees an eschatological role of the Community against the rest of the people and the nations. Applying the exilic setting and employing the language of biblical Land theology, *Damascus Document* envisions the eschatological possession of the earth by the sectaries. The universal tendency is discernible also from uses of other terms *tēbēl*, *gebûl*, and *naḥalâ* in many Qumranic writings.[116] It can be ascribed to the characterization of the God of Israel as the Creator, whose sovereignty extends over the whole creation and entire history from the beginning to the end. It seems also to be in relation to the individualization of mankind revealed in uses of general terms 'man' and 'flesh' in these works. Despite the universalistic appearances, however, the sect presupposes its members being of Jewish origin. The individualization is applied only to those of Jewish descent, and the traditional biblical discrimination between Israel and nations is maintained.

The sect thus maintains a twofold discrimination; it distinguishes individualistically between the 'true Israel' and other Jews, on the one hand, nationalistically between Jews and Gentiles, on the other. The combination of universalism and individualism predicated upon Jewish nationalism engenders sectarianism, which is shared by *Community Rule*, *Hodayot*, *Damascus Document* and some other documents (e.g., *Psalms Pesher*[a] and *4QIsaiah Pesher*[a]), though with some subtle differences in nuance. The frequent universal application of the term *ʾereṣ* by these Qumranic writings is distinct from other works of the Hamonaean period when the biblical territorialism re-flourished under the political expansionism; the sectarianism is cognate to that of the Enochic corpus of the pre-Maccabaean period.[117]

However, the territorial dimensions of the term *ʾereṣ* are also discernible in some documents. While drawing the final cosmological war involving angels in heaven and all the nations on the earth, *War Scroll* envisions the Land being filled with God's glory and blessing and the safe and healthy life in it. *Habakkuk Pesher* also shows its territorial concerns along with universal perspectives. This means that the territorial concern with the Land is compatible with universalism.[118]

The universal dimensions, on the one hand, and territorial, on the other, cannot be chronologically traced, since they can coexist in a single Qumranic writing. Generally speaking, however, the pairing of universalism and individualism predicated upon nationalism is a characteristic of the Qumran sectarianism. The territorial perspectives seem to be somewhat additional for one reason or another. In other words, the Qumran sect applied the Creation theology to the universal eschatology as its soteriological scheme, while employing the Land theology according to its actual situation in which the sectaries lived (except for *Damascus Document*, which utilizes the latter as its theological scheme symbolizing universal soteriology). That is to say, the earth in their soteriology is a projection of their real

116. *Community Rule*, *Hodayot*, *Psalms Pesher*[a], *Isaiah Pesher*[a], *Instruction*, *The Chariots of Glory*, 4QPrayer of Enosh (?).

117. Cf. Nickelsburg 1992b.

118. See also *Nahum Pesher*, *Mysteries*, and 4QBark[a] 2.

life in the Land. Taking a historical overview, we can conclude that the Qumran sectarianism is an inheritance from the third century BCE onwards, and the territorial concerns reflect either the Hamonaean expansionism or the Roman conquest of Jerusalem. During approximately 200 years of its existence a shift must have happened in the sectarian life with the change of political condition around them. The change must have included the Roman conquest of Palestine and successive Herodian dynasty, which we shall see in the next chapter.

Chapter 7

Herodian and Early Roman Period

In this chapter we shall deal with the writings from the period between the Roman conquest of Jerusalem to the destruction of the Second Temple (63 BCE–70 CE). They include: (1) *Psalms of Solomon*; (2) the Similitudes (*1 Enoch* 37–71); (3) *Assumption of Moses*; and (4) Pseudo-Philo's *Liber Antiquitatum Biblicarum*.[1]

7.1. Psalms of Solomon

It is widely accepted among scholars that *Psalms of Solomon* preserved in Greek and Syriac were originally composed in Hebrew in the latter half of the first century BCE (48–40 BCE).[2] Since the Greek version shows the translator's acquaintance with the LXX, the retroversion of Hebrew *ʾereṣ* from Greek γῆ can be assured by the comparison with the relevant biblical passages, as well as general equivalence of the terms.

7.1.1. γῆ/*ʾeres *in* Psalms of Solomon

7.1.1.1. γῆ/*ʾereṣ *as Earth*

In *Ps. Sol.* 2.21 the term γῆ/**ʾereṣ* denotes 'the ground' in relation to the fall of Jerusalem.[3] In 8.7f. it signifies 'the earth' in contrast to heaven in reference to God's Creation.[4] In these passages the Creation itself is not expanded, but is related to God's judgements. The 'judgements' here refer to the Roman conquest of Jerusalem, and the psalmist regards the event as God's judgement against her leaders, villains in the psalmist's eyes. In 8.8 'the whole earth' represents 'the human world', which witnessed the event.[5] A similar statement can be found in *Ps. Sol.* 2.9-10. In 2.9 the heaven and the earth are personified representing the heavenly world and the earthly one, respectively. In 2.10 the earth represents the

1. We do not treat *Lives of the Prophets* and *Life of Adam and Eve* (or *Apocalypse of Moses*), since their original language, provenance and date are far from certain.
2. See R. B. Wright 1985: 640f.; *HJP* III, 193–5; Falk 2001: 35f. For a proposal of Herodian date (37–30 BCE), see Atkinson 1996; 1999.
3. Cf. § 2.1.2 above.
4. Cf. § 2.2.1 above.
5. Cf. Chapter 2 n. 105 above.

human world which witnesses the conquest of Jerusalem as God's judgements against her inhabitants' behaviour.[6] The idea of accounting this event as God's judgement is repeated in *Ps. Sol.* 17.10, as well.

The judgement can be expressed by obliteration of sinners 'from γῆ/*ʾ*ereṣ*', from this world of the living (2.17; 4.22; 17.7; cf. 17.2). In 2.17 those who were obliterated are Jerusalemite sinners (vv. 11-13). Nevertheless, the term γῆ/*ʾ*ereṣ* here must mean 'the earth', since the obliteration is regarded as God's righteous judgement of which 'the earth knew' (2.10). In 4.22 those who shall be uprooted are 'the profaner' sitting in the council (4.1) and 'flatterers' (4.7, 19), who are probably allusions to the Hamonaeans and the Sadducees. In this verse, too, the term γῆ/*ʾ*ereṣ* must signify 'the earth', since their death is expected (4.19f.). In 17.7 those whose seed are taken away 'from γῆ/*ʾ*ereṣ*' are identified with those who 'set up kingship equal to their hauteur, demolished the throne of David with arrogant shouting' (17.6). It is evident that the psalmist alludes to the Hamonaeans (Aristobulus II and his children), and 'a man foreign to our race' (17.7) must be identified with Pompey. Actually Pompey did not slaughter them but took them in captivity to Rome (cf. 8.21),[7] hence the verse might intend that God 'took away their seed from the Land'. In 17.10, however, God's judgements upon 'the earth' are referred to, and so the taking of the Hasmonaean family must be regarded as 'from the earth'. The expression ἡ γῆ ἡμῶν/*ʾ*arṣēnû* 'our land' in the next verse (17.11) seems to be employed in order to distinguish it from ἡ γῆ /**hāʾāreṣ* 'the earth' of v. 10. While regarding Pompey's conquest of Jerusalem as God's judgement against Jewish sinners, the scope of the psalmist(s) of these passages extends to the whole world. That is because the *intra*-national problems involved the *inter*-national issue. The event is further seen in cosmic dimensions, too, in 17.18.

Pompey's death is mentioned in 2.26-32.[8] In vv. 26 and 29 there appears a pair of 'earth and sea' which represents the earthly world in contrast to the heavenly one (v. 30). The reference to 'sea' could be in relation to a situation when the Roman imperial rule extended to the Mediterranean Sea. The psalmist contrasts the human ruler with divinity, stating that Pompey, who pretended to be 'lord of earth and sea' (v. 29), was finally despised more than 'the smallest thing on earth and sea' (v. 26), since he did not know God, the Lord of heaven. Then, the psalmist calls attention to 'the great of the earth' (v. 32), the Romans, to see God's judgement against enemies of Israel.

The idea of God being the righteous judge is repeated in other passages, too (8.23f.; 9.2; 15.12; 18.3). In these passages the judgement is related, not to the conquest of Jerusalem, but to the whole world, as shown by the reference to 'the nations/peoples of the earth' (8.23; 9.2). This judgement is expected as God's eschatological visitation to the earth (15.12).[9] The judgements are accompanied by 'mercy', which, however, is not directed to the world which is judged, but to 'the

6. Cf. Chapter 2 n. 66f. above.
7. Cf. *War* 1.157f.; *Ant.* 14.79.
8. Cf. Dio Cassius 42.3-5.
9. Cf. *1 En.* 25.3; 90.20; 1QS 3.14, 18; 4.18f.; CD 7.9//19.5f.; cf. Chapter 8 n. 33 below.

seed of Abraham, the sons of Israel' (18.1-3). That is, God judges all the nations of the earth to show his mercy to Israel. A similar statement can be found in 5.15. Here God's mercy seems to be inclined to the whole earth. In 5.18, however, God's 'goodness' is expected to be upon Israel (see 17.3).

An eschatological hope is the appearance of a Davidic messiah (17.21-46). His role extends to the whole world. The messiah 'will strike the earth with the word of his mouth forever' (v. 35; cf. Isa. 11.4). The worldwide scope of the psalmist is evident in a reference to 'the end of the earth' in 17.30f. This passage is comparable to the beginning of *Psalms of Solomon* which reminisces about the good old days of Jerusalem (1.3f.). The eschatological hope in 17.30f. is, accordingly, a restoration of Jerusalem in former times (cf. Isa. 66.18-20). Thus, the sinful kings (Hamonaeans) became arrogant because of their fame to 'the end of the earth' (1.3-8), therefore God brought a strong foreigner (Pompey) from 'the end of the earth' (8.15), but at the *eschaton* God will raise up a righteous king (messiah) whose glory will be so attractive that nations may come from 'the end of the earth' (17.31). So far, the universal dimensions of the psalmist(s) are evident in these uses of the term γῆ/*ʾereṣ*.

*7.1.1.2. γῆ/*ʾ*ereṣ *as Land*

Our term is also used in territorial dimensions. In 9.1 mention is made of 'a foreign land' in relation to the Exile. In 8.15, which tells of Pompey's attack, a reference is made to 'Jerusalem and her land'. In the next passage (v. 16) there appears a phrase 'the leaders of the land', in which 'the land' probably means 'the land of Jerusalem', and not 'the Land' as a whole, just because of the sequence of wordings. There are parallel passages in 17.11f., in which the same expression οἱ ἄρχοντες τῆς γῆς is employed (v. 12). Since 8.15f. and 17.11f. share almost identical context, the phrase must bear the comparable referent. Although the leaders of Jerusalem were actually the leaders of the Land, we need this distinction in order to clarify the referent of our term in 17.11. In the Bible and post-biblical Jewish literature the phrase ארצנו usually means 'our Land' (on Jewish lips), but in this passage most probably it refers to 'the land of Jerusalem' (cf. vv. 14f. referring to Jerusalem). The psalmist's focus upon Jerusalem is understandable since it was captured by a foreign empire after *c.* 80 years of independence.

The psalmist of ch. 17, however, does not forget to inscribe the Land theology in his eschatological hope (vv. 26-29). Here the expectation is the restoration of the twelve tribes, who shall constitute a 'holy people', 'sons of God',[10] and who shall settle in the Land, which shall be holy, hence no Gentiles will be found there. The Land here is undoubtedly identical with κληρονομία/*naḥalâ* of v. 23 (cf. 9.1);[11] hence the psalmist assumes the concept of biblical Land-promise. While this is the single portion which refers explicitly to the Land in the entire *Psalms of Solomon*, it shows well that the psalmist's nationalism contains territorial dimensions.

10. See Chapter 4 n. 128 above.
11. See Chapter 4 n. 99 above.

7.1.2. Summary

In a majority of its occurrences the term γῆ/*ʾereṣ signifies 'the human world' in relation to God's judgements. The judgements are related to the Roman conquest of Jerusalem in 63 BCE, on the one hand, to the eschatological judgements of the nations by the messiah, on the other. The worldwide scope of *Psalms of Solomon* must have been engendered by the *intra*-national problems (anti-Hasmonaean biases) involving the *inter*-national affair (Pompey's intervention). While recognizing worldwide aspects in this disaster, the psalmists were not occupied by a sectarian mind such as the one found in 1QS which connected an individual to a universal fate. Rather they maintained nationalistic sentiments. The nationalism distinguishes between Israel as a nation and foreign nations, whose final judgements are expected as mercy for Israel. The eschatological hopes, furthermore, include the restoration of the twelve tribes in the Land. The coexistence of the universal judgement and the sanctification of the Land shows some similarity to 1QM, a contemporary sectarian work.

Thus, the psalmists regard the national disaster as God's judgement against the sinful Jewish kings, but expect final judgements against the nations and establishment of the national messianic hopes. The term γῆ/*ʾereṣ plays a double role in this nationalism.

*7.2. The Similitudes (*1 Enoch *37–71)*

The Book of Similitudes, the second of the five books of *1 Enoch* (chs 37–71), is known from Ethiopic alone, but its Aramaic origin is widely accepted mainly on linguistic bases.[12] The retroversion of Aramaic *ʾara* from Ethiopic *medr* is assured by their equivalence in other Enochic writings we saw above.[13] A date around the turn of the era is acceptable.[14]

The portions 39.1-2a; 54.7–55.2; 60 and 65–69.25 are generally accepted as later interpolations, mainly from Noachic materials.[15] The insertion, however, is not a much later one, since unique uses of *yabs*/*יבשה 'the dry ground' appear throughout this work (see § 7.2.2 below). We shall, therefore, treat the present form of the Similitudes as a single work.

12. N. Schmidt 1908; Ullendorf 1960; Knibb 1978: II, 37–46.

13. See § 4.1. In this section I use the text and English translation by Knibb (1978), sometimes with modifications.

14. Greenfield and Stone 1977; Nickelsburg 1981a: 219f.; 2005: 254–6; Collins 1992; see n. 54 below.

15. Charles 1912: 64.

7.2.1. medr/*ʾaraʿ

In the Similitudes the term *medr/*ʾaraʿ* can signify the *terra firma* in contrast to the sky or to the waters.[16] Mention is made of winds blowing over the earth (41.3a), clouds remaining over the earth (41.4), and lightning flash and thunder voice 'according to the number of the regions of the earth' (60.15). The steadfastness of the earth is compared with the mountains, which, symbolizing the sinful world powers (52.2-9), will not be firm before the messiah (53.7; cf. 55.2). The earth is supported by pillars (57.2).

The term can connote 'the ground', the surface of the earth (39.5; 42.3). A reference is made to 'the dust of the earth', which is saturated by 'the secrets of the clouds and of the dew' (41.3). From the dust of the earth 'silver is produced', and 'soft metal occurs on the earth' (65.7; cf. Job 28.1f.).

Enoch travels here and there on the earth: he turned to a part of the earth where he saw a deep valley with burning fire (54.1). In a Noachic material Noah went to the ends of the earth where he found Enoch (65.2; cf. *1 En.* 106.8).

The term *medr/*ʾaraʿ* as the earth can be applied to the earthly world in contrast to the heavenly one. In 39.3 it is assumed that the end of earthly world is attached to the end of heavenly world (cf. *1 En.* 14.8f.; 18.12-14).[17] The close relationships of the heavenly world and the earthly one are described in 52.2 and 57.2 (cf. Hag. 2.6f.). The heavenly judgement is an eschatological hope of the author (47.1). The sinners, therefore, can find their place neither in heaven nor on the earth (45.2). From a Noachic material the story of fallen angels, 'who came down from heaven on to the earth', is employed (64.2; cf. *1 Enoch* 6–11).

When his eyes turn to the earthly world, the author speaks repeatedly of the rulers of the earth: 'those who possess the earth' (38.4; 62.3, 6); 'the kings of the earth and the strong who possess the dry ground' (48.8); 'the kings and the powerful of this earth' (53.5). The *medr/*ʾaraʿ* in these expressions certainly means 'the earth', since there are parallel uses of *yabs/**יבשה', as 48.8 shows.[18] It is evident that the mighty kings who possess the earth/dry ground are accused by the author of being sinners, who shall be thrown into the deep valley with burning fire (54.1f.). They are depicted as denying the dwelling of the holy ones (45.1), the Lord (45.1f.; 46.6f.) and His messiah (48.10); they have raised their hands against the Most High, and have trusted in the gods which they have made with their hands (46.7); they have done wrong to His children and to His chosen ones (62.11) and have shed their blood (47.1f.). While R. H. Charles insists that the princes are Jewish rulers, the Hamonaeans and the Sadducees, and finds no allusion to the Romans, M. Black exclusively views them as foreign rulers.[19] The expression 'those who possess the earth/dry ground' itself connotes an imperial power. It is also said that they 'led astray the world (*ʿālam/**עלם)' (69.28). The kings, therefore, at least

16. 54.7, 8; 60.16; 66.1; 69.17; cf. Pss. 24.2; 136.6.
17. Cf. also *1 En.* 18.5; 23.1-4; 33.1-3; 34.1-3; 35.1; 36.1-3; 75.6; 76.1-14.
18. See the next section and n. 33 below.
19. Charles 1912: 72f., note on 38.5; Black 1985: 196.

include foreign rulers, the Romans. On the other hand, Jewish rulers seem not to be excluded from these ‘kings’, since mention is made of the bloodshedding of the chosen ones, the author’s community members. If the author refers to the final days of Herod the Great (67.5-13), his antagonism must have been directed towards Jewish rulers, too. Accordingly, it is likely that the kings who possess the earth include both Jewish and foreign rulers (this fits well with the situation of the Land around the turn of the era). The author cannot accept the earthly rulers of his day, neither Jewish nor foreign, and expects the appearance of a messiah who shall rule the entire earth instead of them.[20]

The hope of their disappearance is formulated with the expression ‘(to be destroyed) from the face of the earth’.[21] Once the earth is called ‘His (God’s) earth’ in the same context (53.2).[22]

Our term is utilized in the eschatological expectations of the Similitudes: ‘He fills the earth with spirits’ (39.12; cf. Isa. 6.3). When the sinners are destroyed, ‘there will be rest on the earth’ (48.10). When the dead are resurrected, ‘the earth will rejoice, and the righteous will dwell upon it, and the chosen will go and walk upon it’ (51.5). Here the going and walking of the chosen upon the earth may be an application of the biblical Land theology to the eschatological earth (cf. Gen. 13.17; *Apocr. Gen.* 21.13).[23]

In 51.1f. the idea of resurrection of the dead is described. Here the resurrection of all mankind (not only of the righteous) seems to be assumed, since the righteous will be chosen among them. The earth will return bodies, and ‘Sheol’ and ‘destruction’ will return souls of the righteous and of the wicked, respectively. In other verses, however, the resurrection only of the righteous seems to be expected (61.5; 62.15). At any rate, the concept of the earth as depository of the dead and the existence of the netherworld under it are assumed.[24]

The term *medr*/*ʾaraʿ can refer to a certain land. ‘That land’ in 67.6 is where lie the mountains of metals (67.4; 52.2) and a deep valley (53.1) in which the wicked angels will be judged.

There is a single reference to the Land in the entire Similitudes: ‘the Land of my chosen ones’ (56.6ab).[25] The expression ‘chosen ones (of the angel of peace)’ might mean the whole people of Israel, since its combination with the Land (and Jerusalem) can express a nationalistic sentiment. Another expression ‘the community of the righteous’, however, suggests the righteous and the chosen in the author’s mind being his sectaries (38.1; 53.6; 62.8; cf. Ps. 1.5).[26] Then, the expressions ‘the Land of my chosen ones’ (56.6) and ‘the city of my righteous ones’ (56.7) might be the sectaries’ claim to the Land and Jerusalem to be their possession. The distinction, however, between the sectaries and the remaining people of Israel is unclear. The

20. 46.3-5; 52.4; 55.4; 62.1-3, 6.
21. 45.6; 52.9; 69.27, 28; cf. 38.1; 67.3.
22. See Chapter 6 n. 33 above.
23. See Black 1985: 214.
24. Further references to *medr* ‘the earth’ in Noachic materials: 54.10; 65.1, 3, 4, 6, 9, 10.
25. Ms. Tana 9; other mss: ‘his/their land’.
26. See Black 1985: 194.

absence of further reference to the Land is rather significant. This means that the Land no longer forms a part of the author's eschatological hopes, though its special status as God's gift is presupposed.

7.2.2. yabs/*יבשה

The term *yabs*/*יבשה (*yabšâ*), 'the dry ground', is frequently employed in the Similitudes. It is mostly used as a synonym of *medr*/*ʾ*araʿ*, and it is worthwhile to observe its uses. It can mean *terra firma* (60.11). The existence of a 'host which (is) upon the dry ground and over the water' is assumed (61.10). A reference is made to the sun 'upon the dry ground' (58.5). The rain is regarded as God's gift for *yabs*/**yabšâ* and its inhabitants (60.21f.).

The term *yabs*/**yabšâ* can refer to the earthly world in contrast to the heavenly one where angels abide. Of the angel Yequn it is said: 'this (is) the one who led astray all the children of the holy angels; and he brought them down on to the dry ground, and led them astray through the daughters of men' (69.4). Thus, it can represent the earthly world where living beings dwell (see also 67.2-3).

There are frequent occurrences of the expression 'those who dwell upon the dry ground'.[27] It is a unique locution appearing throughout the Similitudes (22 times),[28] while another rather well-known phrase 'those who dwell upon the earth' is used only once (62.1). The addressee of the vision Enoch saw are 'those who dwell on the dry ground' (37.2, 5; cf. *1 En.* 92.1). They are the inhabitants of the world including the righteous (38.2), the wicked powerful kings (55.4) and other ordinary men (40.6f.; 48.5; 53.1; 54.6; 70.1). In Noachic portions the expression frequently hints at the wickedness of human beings (54.9; 55.1; 60.5; 65.6, 12; 66.1; 67.8).[29] In the Bible and post-biblical writings up to the first century BCE mention is rarely made of 'the inhabitants of the earth'.[30] From the first century CE on, however, references to the earth's inhabitants increase very much, frequently with negative connotations.[31] This may reflect the social climate of first century CE Palestine when universal eschatologies pertaining to all human beings prevailed.[32]

27. 37.2, 5; 40.6, 7; 48.5; 53.1; 54.6; 55.4; 70.1; in Noachic portions: 54.9; 55.1, 2; 60.5, 22a; 65.6, 12; 66.1; 67.7, 8; 69.1, 7.

28. For *1 En.* 92.1, ms. BM 485: *yabs*; other manuscripts: *medr*.

29. See Charles 1912: 70 note on 37.5.

30. *yošbê ʾereṣ*/*hāʾāreṣ*: Ps. 33.14; Isa. 24.6, 17; 26.21; *šoknê ʾereṣ*: Isa. 18.3; *yôšbê tēbēl*: Isa. 18.3; 26.9, 18; Pss. 24.1; 33.8; 98.7; Lam. 4.12; Nah. 1.5; *1 En.* 92.1; Dan. 3.31; 6.26; Jdt. 1.11; CD 10.9; in the Bible *yošbê hāʾāreṣ* usually refers to 'the inhabitants of the Land' (cf. Chapter 2 nn. 203 and 243 above).

31. See *LAB* 2.8, 9, 10; 3.3, 4, 9, 12; 4.5, 16; 6.1; 7.4; 26.13; 28.6; *4 Ezra* 3.9, 12, 34, 35; 4.21, 39; 5.1, 6; 6.18, 24, 26; 7.72, 74, 127, 137; 8.41, 50; 9.19; 10.59; 11.5, 6, 32, 34; 12.23; 13.29, 30, 52; 14.17 (16), 20; *2 Bar.* 25.1, 3; 27.15; 48.32, 40; 51.15; 54.1; 56.15; *Apoc. Abr.* 23.11 (12); cf. Rev. 3.10; 6.10; 8.13; 11.10; 13.8, 14; 17.8; bad connotation before the first century CE: Isa. 24.6, 17; 26.21; Nah. 1.5; CD 10.9.

32. The use of 'those who dwell upon the earth' in *1 En.* 80.7 seems to represent a use typical of the first century CE Palestine (see Charles 1912: 172 n.). This may suggest that *1 Enoch* 80 was inserted in the first century CE (cf. Chapter 4 n. 3 above, and n. 166 below).

As we've seen above, mention is made of the rulers who 'possess/rule the dry ground'.[33] It is said of the kings and the powerful that 'these are they who judge the stars of heaven, and raise their hands against the Most High, and trample upon the dry ground, and dwell upon it' (46.7). At the *eschaton*, however, when the community of the righteous appears, 'the sinners will be judged for their sins and are driven from the face of the dry ground' (38.1).[34] The eschatology of the Similitudes includes the transformation of heaven and 'the dry ground' (45.4f.; cf. 67.2). At the *eschaton* the heaven and 'the dry ground' will be transformed, and all the righteous and holy, who will be chosen among the resurrected (51.1f.), 'will become angels in heaven' (51.4). They will dwell upon the renewed earth where 'the Lord of Spirits will remain over them, and with that Son of Man they will dwell, and eat, and lie down, and rise up forever and ever' (62.14). The earth, the author expects, will become like the heavenly world.

7.2.3. ʿālam/*עלם

In the Similitudes there appears relatively frequently another Ethiopic term, *ʿālam*. It is equivalent to Hebrew עולם and Aramaic עלם (and Greek αἰών).[35] Its uses in the Similitudes, however, contain a difference from those in biblical and post-biblical literature till then. In the Bible and Hebrew and Aramaic Jewish literature including the Dead Sea Scrolls we have hitherto treated, the term holds a temporal connotation, a long duration of time, in particular, eternity, infinite time, either in past or in future. It is not used as an independent subject or object (except Eccl. 3.11; 12.5), but as an adverbial accusative, often with prepositions (מעולם, לעולם and עד עולם in Hebrew), and as an adjective in construct combination with a noun, always in the second position (e.g., אלהי עולם).[36] These uses are employed in the Similitudes, as well; with prepositions (the Aramaic retroversion is tentative):[37]

laʿālama ʿālam//*לעלמין 'forever and ever'[38]
laʿālam//*לעלם 'forever'[39]
(wa)ʾeska laʿālam//*(ו)עד עלם 'unto eternity'[40]

33. 48.8; 62.9; 63.1, 12; 67.12.
34. Cf. 45.6; 52.9; 69.27, 28.
35. See 'Aramaic-Greek-Ethiopic Glossary' in Milik 1976 (pp. 388, 397, 403), which shows relevance of עלם-αἰών-*ʿālam* in *1 Enoch*. See also n. 65 below.
36. For a thorough study of the term *ʿôlām*, see Jenni 1952, 1953.
37. *עלם might be either singular or plural and either in a definite or indefinite form; see Milik 1976: 388.
38. 39.5, 6, 13; 40.4; 41.6; 43.4; 49.1, 2; 61.3, 11, 12; 62.14; 63.3, 6; 67.3, 9; 68.5ab; 69.7, 24; 71.16, 17; cf. לעלמין: 4Q534 1.i.11; 4Q536 2.ii.13; 11Q18 19.4.
39. 47.2; 58.6; 65.11; 67.13. For Ethiopic *laʿālam*, cf. *1 En.* 5.1//4Q201 1.ii.11; *1 En.* 10.3//4Q201 1.v.4; *1 En.* 10.13//4Q204 1.v.1; *1 En.* 77.1//4Q209 23.4; *1 En.* 91.16//4Q212 1.iv.25; cf. לעלם: 4Q197 4.i.14; 4Q213 1–2.ii.18; 4Q213a 3–4.6.
40. 48.6; 55.2; cf. 4Q546 12.1; 4Q246 1.i.3.

ʾemʿālam//*מעלם ‘from eternity’[41]
ʾemʿālam waʾeska laʿālam//*מעלם ועד עלם ‘from eternity to eternity’[42]
ʾemqedem waʾeska laʿālam//*מן קדם ועד עלם ‘from ancient time and forever’[43]
ʾemqedem ʿālam//*מקדם עלם ‘from eternal ancient time’[44]

in construct combination:

ḥeywat zalaʿālam//*חיי עלם ‘eternal life’[45]
labarakat waberhān zalaʿālam//*לברכה ונהור עלמא ‘eternal blessing and light’[46]
ʾegziʾa ʿālam//*מרא עלמא ‘the eternal Lord’[47]

Still, in the Similitudes we can discern another usage of the term ʿālam/*עלם, in which it conveys a sense of ‘the world (-age)’, as the Hellenistic Greek αἰών does.[48] There are three occurrences of the clause ‘before the world was created’ (39.11a; 48.6; 69.16). Similarly, there is an expression ‘from the creation of the world’ (69.17, 18; 71.15). One may suspect that these uses are due to Ethiopic (or Greek *Vorlage*); the original Aramaic might be מעלם ועד עלם, as shown by the fact that these expressions are followed by *laʿālam* ‘forever’[49] (except 71.15).[50] Yet, there are further uses of the term in which it is used in the *first* position of construct combination and as an independent object: ‘they (the holy and the righteous) have hated and rejected this world of iniquity’ (48.7);[51] ‘those who led the world astray will be bound in chains’ (69.28 [27]). In these passages the term ʿālam/*עלם cannot mean ‘eternity’ or ‘infinite time’, but represents the human world. It connotes spatial aspects, as well as temporal, hence ‘world (-age)’. That the duration of time is here definite is indicated by the demonstrative pronoun ‘this’ in 48.7.[52] Furthermore, there appears in 71.15 an expression ‘the name of the world which is to come’. The expressions ‘this world’ (48.7) and ‘the world to come’ (71.15), if the Ethiopic reflects the original Aramaic usage, can be the

41. 70.4; cf. 11Q10 3.5//Job 20.4.
42. 69.9, 19, 20, 21; cf. 4Q547 6.4f.
43. 39.10.
44. 41.4; cf. CD 2.7//4QD[a] 2.ii.7.
45. 37.4; 40.9; 58.2; cf. Dan. 12.2; 4Q418 69.ii.13.
46. 45.4; cf. 4Q542 1.ii.3; 4Q541 24.ii.6.
47. 58.4; cf. ms. Tana 9: *ʾegziʾ laʿālam.*; cf. 4Q202 1.iii.14; 4Q529 1.6, 7, 11, 12; cf. also *Apocr. Gen.* 21.2; 4Q542 1.i.1, 2; 4Q213b 6.
48. See Sasse 1978a.
49. Thus Jenni 1953: 33.
50. For 39.11b Eth. ms. Ryl reads: ‘what the world would be’ (*ment weʾetu ʿālam*); but other manuscripts: ‘what is forever’ (*ment weʾetu laʿālam*); see Black 1985: 198.
51. Cf. Gal. 1.4.
52. For the Hebrew expression ‘this world’, cf. *Ass. Mos.* 12.5; *LAB* 30.2; 51.5; 62.9; *4 Ezra* 4.27; 7.112; *2 Bar.* 21.19.

earliest uses of העולם הזה and העולם הבא well known from later rabbinic literature.[53] This new connotation of עלם/עולם emerged and developed, most likely, from the first century CE, since further evidence can be seen in *Assumption of Moses*, Pseudo-Philo, *4 Ezra*, *2 Baruch* and *Apocalypse of Abraham*, all of which date from the first to the second centuries CE.[54]

7.2.4. *Addendum:* ʿālam *in* 1 Enoch

In the Astronomical Book (*1 Enoch* 72–82), dating from the fourth or third century BCE, there are 16 occurrences of Ethiopic *ʿālam*.[55] In some of these it is certainly used in the sense of 'the world', connoting not only temporal aspects but also spatial.[56] If, then, the original Aramaic version of the Astronomical Book had used the term in this sense, the new usage of עלם would have had to date to the third century BCE at the latest. The Ethiopic text of the Astronomical Book, however, seems to represent an abridged version in comparison with the Aramaic fragments unearthed among the Dead Sea Scrolls.[57] Similarly, in the Apocalypse of Weeks (*1 En.* 93.1-10+91.11-17) where Ethiopic reads *ʿālam* in the sense of 'world', the Qumran Aramaic version has other expressions.[58] We, therefore, cannot confirm that the Ethiopic version provides us with the original use of the term עלם in the sense of 'world'. Rather, the lack of this use in the Dead Sea Scrolls must be seriously taken into consideration. While there are more than 200 occurrences of the term עלם/עולם in the Dead Sea Scrolls, no single attestation of this use has been found hitherto. If the emergence of this use had dated from the third century BCE, Qumran literature would have employed it to express their eschatological worldview. The lack of evidence from the Dead Sea Scrolls tells us that the use does not predate the sectarian literary activity. On the other hand, we have attestations of it from Jewish works of the first century CE onwards. All

53. Thus Charles 1912: 145, n. and Jenni 1953: 34.

54. Thus Jenni 1953: 34; 1997: 862; cf. Dalman 1997: 147–56. This new usage of *ʿālam*/*עלם in the Similitudes is not so frequent and shows a stage of development earlier than that in Pseudo-Philo; this may be an indication that the Similitudes predates 70 CE.

55. 72.1abc; 74.12, 17; 75.2ab, 3ab; 81.2, 3, 10; 82.1, 5, 6, 7.

56. 74.17; 75.2ab, 3ab; 82.7; cf. Albani 1994: 101–5.

57. Milik 1976: 7f., 274f.; VanderKam 1984a: 80–3. Indeed, all the passages listed in the previous note cannot demonstrate the new usage of עלם; as for 74.17 the term *ʿālam* appears only in manuscripts Eth. I, which are rejected by Knibb as his base-text (Knibb 1978: II, 21–37); all other five occurrences are found in the portions which seem to contain later redactions.

58. 91.14a: Eth. *lakwellu ʿālam*//Aram. לכול בני ארעא כלה (4QEn^g 1.iv.20); 91.14b: Ethiopic has a clause different from Aramaic; and 93.2: Aramaic is in lacuna. In 16.1 we have ὁ αἰὼν ὁ μέγας, but the original Aramaic is uncertain. In 20.2, 4 Greek has κόσμος, which, however, seems to refer to canopy, and not to 'the world (-age)'; for Gr. κόσμος in the LXX and its Hebrew equivalents, see n. 68 below. In *1 En.* 84.2 Ethiopic reads *ʾamlāk kwellu ʿālam* 'God of the whole world', but Aramaic original seems to have had a different expression (cf. Knibb 1978: II, 193f.).

in all, it is safe to conclude that the new usage of the term עלם/עולם as 'world' emerged from the first century CE.[59]

7.2.5. Summary

In its most frequent occurrences in the Similitudes the term *medr*/*'*ara*ʿ denotes the earthly world in contrast to the heavenly one. The author's universal cosmological concern is evident from the frequent reference to 'the kings and the mighty and the exalted, and those who possess the earth/dry ground', who are contrasted with the messiah who shall rule both the heavenly and earthly world forever. The earth will survive till the *eschaton* when it returns bodies to the resurrected, and then heaven and earth (*yabs*/*yabšâ) will be transformed. Although the Land is once called 'the Land of my chosen ones', the earth (*medr*/*'*ara*ʿ or *yabs*/*yabšâ) is assigned as their eschatological dwelling place. This means that the cosmological concern is so strong that the Land theology has no place to play a role, though its traditional significance as a special territory is assumed.

The universal concern is perhaps related to the expression 'those who dwell upon the dry ground' which is frequently employed throughout the work. It is probably concerning the individualization of mankind, as is discernible from the contrast between 'the righteous, the chosen ones' and 'the sinners'. The individualization characterizes the Similitudes as a sectarian work, a sectarianism which is apparent from the self-identity of the author's group as 'the community of the righteous' (38.1). The author even states that 'they have hated and rejected this world of iniquity' (48.7). The hatred and rejection of the present world that brought the community members eschatological expectations also reflect a sectarian mind. Despite its sectarian character, however, this community seems to acknowledge the survival of the ordinary people and even the Gentiles till the messianic era (48.4f.; 50.2; cf. *1 En.* 10.21; 90.38), probably because its antagonism is directed towards the world powers. The sectarianism of the Similitudes, therefore, is different from the Qumran sectaries 'who have turn[ed aside from walking in the] way of the people' (1QSa 1.2f.). The hostility of the Similitudes towards the sinful world powers is so strong that the author depicts their final judgement and the appearance of a messiah, but does not tell who the righteous are or how to be the righteous, hence it is unclear how he discriminates between the chosen and the whole people of Israel (except, of course, Jewish rulers). One can, therefore, read the Similitudes as a resistant literature employing sectarian vocabularies. It reveals the existence of the strong foreign powers in front of the author. Accordingly, we can say that the existence of Romans and their Jewish agents in the Land of the first century CE strengthened more and more eschatological expectations of God's

59. Thus, Jenni 1952, 1953.

direct intervention into 'this world', which could from then on be expressed by a new usage of the term עולם/עלם.

7.3. Assumption of Moses

7.3.1. Retroversion of the Original Hebrew Terms from Latin

Assumption or *Testament of Moses* is preserved only in Latin and in tiny Greek fragments. The Latin text is certainly a translation from Greek.[60] Hebraisms contained in it and its Palestinian provenance[61] suggest Hebrew origin of *Assumption of Moses*.[62] Since the Latin version is a translation of a translation and we have no other versions, the reconstruction of the original terminology must be difficult and hypothetical. Nevertheless, a general relevance can be established. The terms with which we are concerned are *terra*, *saeculum*, *orbis terrarum* and *region*; the first three can signify 'the earth' and/or 'world', and the first and the last can denote 'land'. In this respect, the study of M. E. Stone on *4 Ezra* is a great help. He analyses the terms *terra*, *orbis*, and *saeculum* in biblical versions (MT, LXX, Old Latin and Vulgata) and versions of *4 Ezra* (Latin, Syriac, and Armenian).[63] According to his conclusions, Latin *terra* translates Greek γῆ, which translates Hebrew *ʾereṣ* (or less frequently *ʾadāmâ*),[64] and Latin *saeculum* presupposes Greek αἰών, which reflects Hebrew *ʿôlām* (and *ʿad*),[65] and Latin *orbis* represents Hebrew *tēbēl* (Greek term is somewhat uncertain, but frequently οἰκουμένη).[66] These observations can be applied to *Assumption of Moses*, too, at least in a general manner.

Yet, instead of *orbis*, we have in *Assumption of Moses* relatively frequent uses of *orbis terrarum*, in the sense of 'world' or 'earth'. That it is a translation of Greek κόσμος is attested to by the quotation of Gelasius of Cyzicus (on 1.14).[67] This is the most difficult case for us, since there is no fixed Hebrew equivalent to Greek κόσμος in the sense of 'world'.[68] It is not a Septuagintal

60. See Tromp 1993: 78–81.

61. Tromp 1993: 117; *HJP* III, 284; Priest 1983: 921.

62. See Charles 1897: xxxvi–xlv; Wallace 1955; Priest 1983: 920; Collins 1984: 345.

63. Stone 1989: 147–84.

64. Stone 1989: 156–64.

65. Stone 1989: 165–71. The Hebrew *ʿôlām*/Aramaic *ʿālam* (total 404 times in the Bible) is translated in the LXX mostly (*c*. 95%) into αἰών (280 times) and αἰώνιος (105 times); cf. § 7.2.3 above.

66. Stone 1989: 171f.

67. For Gelasius's text, see Tromp 1993: 78.

68. The closest use in the LXX may be a translation of Hebrew צבא (usually rendered as 'host'); see Gen. 2.1; Deut. 4.19; 17.3; Isa. 24.21; 40.26. In other occasions it can be used in the sense of 'ornament' or 'adornment', translating Hebrew עדי (Exod. 33.5f.; 2 Sam. 1.24b; Isa. 49.18; Jer. 2.32; 4.30; Ezek. 7.20; 16.11; 23.40); עדן (2 Sam. 1.24a); תפארת (Prov. 20.29); תכונה (Nah. 2.9 [10]); כלי (Isa. 61.10); מעשה (Isa. 3.24); compare also the Greek version of *1 En*. 8.1 (κόσμια or κόσμους) with 4QEn^b 1.ii.27: מכונא.

Greek.[69] Furthermore, *orbis terrarum* and *saeculum* in *Assumption of Moses* seem to be interchangeable. It seems to me, then, that the Greek translator rendered his Hebrew *Vorlage*, not literally word for word, but chose relevant terms suitable to a Greek work; he might use κόσμος at times for *tēbēl* and at times for *ʿôlām* according to context. Thus, we can assume that Latin *terra* reflects Greek γῆ/Hebrew *ʾereṣ*, Latin *saeculum* Greek αἰών /Hebrew *ʿôlām*, and *orbis terrarum* Greek κόσμος/Hebrew *tēbēl* or *ʿôlām*. We shall first treat the term *terra*/*ʾereṣ*, try to restore the original Hebrew of *orbis terrarum*, then discuss uses of the terms *tēbēl* and *ʿôlām*. As for the term *regio*, which appears only twice, we shall discuss it in a relevant context.[70]

7.3.2. terra/*ʾereṣ

The term *terra*/**ʾereṣ* in *Assumption of Moses* can refer to 'the ground', the surface of the earth, on which one can run (11.12) and bend his knees (11.17), and in which one shall be buried (11.8).

It can signify the earth in contrast to heaven (3.12; cf. Deut. 4.26; 30.19; 31.28). The heaven and earth here represent what is most stable among creation. At the *eschaton*, however, when God manifests himself to the entire creation, the earth, heaven and waters will be out of order (10.4-6). In this tripartite division of the universe, the earth is further contrasted with mountains and valleys (10.4).[71]

In the eschatological vision, it is hoped, 'God will exalt you (Israel)', and 'you will look down from above, and you will see your enemies on the earth (*in terram*), and you will recognize them' (10.9f.). The *terra*/**ʾereṣ* here represents earthly world in opposition to the heavenly one, which is assigned to the eschatological habitation of Israel.

Before the final theophany, however, there will appear *regem regum terrae* 'the king of the kings of the earth' (8.1),[72] who will persecute Israel, persecution which, resembling the one at the time of Antiochian crisis, will be brought by God as punishment (8.1-5).[73]

The term can denote a 'land' territorially defined: *terram patriae suae* 'his fatherland' (3.3) and *terram alienam* 'a foreign land' (4.3), both alluding to Babylon.

Mention is made of the Land, as well. The author explains Joshua's role as: 'to lead the people into the Land that was given to their fathers' (1.8f.). The concept of the promised Land is repeated in 2.1 and 3.9. It is also called 'their (Israel's) Land' (2.3; 3.1; 4.6; 6.5).[74]

69. This cannot be a proof of a Greek origin of *Assumption of Moses*, since *2 Baruch*, too, which is certainly ascribed to a Hebrew original, contains a (mis)translation of *κόσμος (3.7).

70. In this section Tromp's English translation is used with some modifications.

71. See Tromp 1993: 232.

72. See Tromp 1993: 216f.

73. Another occurrence of *terra* in 11.18, *a faciae terrae*, can be retroverted to Hebrew *מעל פני האדמה; cf. § 2.5.1 (p. 36) and n. 351 there.

74. See Amaru 1994: 58f. For 'the land of Arabians' in 11.11, see Tromp 1993: 22.

In addition, the term *regio* occurs twice in the sense of ‘land’ or ‘region’ (4.6; 9.3). In 4.6 *regio* is employed with *terra eorum*, which could be retroverted to Greek *γῆ αὐτῶν/Hebrew *ארצם. Then, *regio* here might be the translation of *χώρα, which might be from *מדינה or *מדינתם.[75] In 9.3 *regio* is in line with *gens* and *populus*, and means ‘a land’. It could be again the translation of *χώρα, which probably renders *ʾ*ereṣ*.

7.3.3. orbis terrarum

As we have argued above, the Latin expression *orbis terrarum* renders Greek *κόσμος, which may be a translation of Hebrew **tēbēl* or *ʿ*ôlām* (or possibly *ʾ*ereṣ*). The term is used in relation to Moses in ch. 11. In vv. 8, 16 and 17 the term *orbis terrarum* probably reflects Hebrew **tēbēl*, since it appears in parallelism with *terra*/*ʾ*ereṣ* or *saeculum*/*ʿ*ôlām*.[76]

In 1.11 God is called *Dominus orbis terrarium* ‘the Lord of the world’. Since the Hebrew expression *אדון תבל is unlikely, and the same term is employed in the following passage on the purpose of the Creation (1.12, 13, 14, 17), the expression probably reflects Greek *ὁ κύριος τοῦ κόσμου and Hebrew *אדון העולם.[77] In the same manner, the expression *ab initio orbis terrarium* ‘from the beginning of the world’, which is repeated in 1.13, 14, and 17, perhaps represents the translation of Hebrew *מראשית העולם (cf. *2 Bar*. 21.4; CD 2.7; *1 En*. 41.4). The term *orbis terrarum* used in relation to the Creation seems to reflect Hebrew *ʿ*ôlām* (1.2, 12).

The term *orbis terrarum* is used in 12.4-5 three times. The first occurrence in 12.4, *Omnes gentes quae sunt in or<b>e terrarium* ‘all the nations which are in the world’, may reflect Hebrew *כל הגויים אשר בתבל.[78] The second occasion is paired with *saeculum*. The two Latin terms probably do not reflect different Hebrew words, but different Greek translations of the same Hebrew original. The Greek translator seems to have chosen the term *αἰών, rendered as *saeculum* in Latin, only when Hebrew *ʿ*ôlām* denoted, in his eyes, a temporal sense (cf. 4.2; 8.1; 11.16); when *ʿ*ôlām* denotes a space, he chose *κόσμος (1.2, 11-14, 17). In our passage (12.4) *saeculum* must connote a temporal sense because of *exitum* ‘the end’ (not geographical), while *orbis terrarum* must be a space because of reference to its ‘creation’. Thus, from the Latin translation *ab initio creaturae orbis terrarum usque ad exitum saeculi* we can reconstruct Hebrew *מראשית בריאת העולם ועד אחרית העולם or something similar to it.[79]

The expression ‘all things that were to happen in this world (*in hoc orbe terrarum*)’ (12.5) connotes simultaneously both spatial and temporal senses; it is a space where something happens, and a period which has a limitation of time (‘*this*

75. Cf. Chapter 4 n. 87 above.
76. Cf. Kahana 1969a: 324f.
77. See Kahana 1969a: 317; Schalit 1989: 125f.
78. Cf. Kahana 1969a: 325.
79. Kahana (1969a: 325): מראשית בריאת תבל ועד אחרית העולם.

world').[80] Accordingly, the expression *hoc orbe terrarum*, 'this world', here must reflect Hebrew *העולם הזה, since neither *ʾereṣ* nor *tēbēl* can imply a temporal aspect. Only *ʿôlām* can express 'this world' as a location of human activities in a definite period.[81]

7.3.4. *tēbēl *and* *ʿôlām

According to our discussion in the previous subsection, the term **tēbēl* (*orbis terrarum*) is used four times in *Assumption of Moses* (11.8, 16, 17; 12.4a). It represents the earthly human world; it has Moses as the divine prophet for itself (11.16); it is his grave (11.8); it is ruled by God with mercy and justice (11.17); and in it God has created nations (12.4a).

Another term, **ʿôlām* (*orbis terrarum*, *saeculum* and *aeternus*), appears 13 times.[82] It can express eternity: the punishment towards the impious will be 'such as there will never have been over them since eternity (*a saeculo*/*מעולם) until that time' (8.1). There appears a doxology, *Deus aeternus*/*אל(הי) עולם, 'the Eternal God' (10.7).

In 4.2 it is used in relation to God, who is said to 'rule the world' (*qui dominaris saeculo*). Here the *saeculum*/**ʿôlām* must convey a spatial connotation, since it forms a parallelism with the preceding doxology 'Lord, King of All' (cf. 11.17).[83] In 11.16 Moses is said to be 'the divine prophet for *orbem terrarum*, the perfect teacher *in saeculo*'. Admitting that *saeculum*/**ʿôlām* here can be rendered as 'this age',[84] it must contain a spatial sense since it appears in parallelism with *orbem terrarum*/**tēbēl*. The spatial aspect of the term **ʿôlām* is discernible from its uses in relation to the Creation. Years can be counted 'from the creation of the world (*a creatura orbis terrae*/*מבריאת העולם)' (1.2).[85] A place in which the books (i.e., the Pentateuch) shall be preserved is made by God 'from the beginning of the world (*ab initio orbis terrarum*/ *מראשית העולם)' (1.17). In 1.11-14 it is stated that the world was created on behalf of Israel.[86] The nationalistic sentiment is conspicuous in these lines. The people of Israel is elected and nations are condemned (1.12f.).[87] It is stated that God will manifest himself at the *eschaton* 'to punish the nations and to destroy their idols' (10.7).

That God predetermines world history is spelled out in 12.4-5.[88] The term **ʿôlām* can connote simultaneously both a space in which all things will happen

80. The demonstrative pronoun *hoc* is applied only here to *orbis terrarum*; cf. *1 En*. 48.7; *LAB* 30.2; 51.5; 62.9; *4 Ezra* 4.27; 7.112; *2 Bar*. 21.19.

81. Kahana (1969a: 325): ברחבי תבל, ignoring *hoc*.

82. 1.2, 11, 12, 13, 14, 17; 4.2; 8.1; 11.16; 12.4bc, 5, 13.

83. Cf. 1.11; 11.17.

84. Clemen (1994: 330): 'dieser Zeit'.

85. See Schalit 1989: 13–17.

86. Cf. *LAB* 39.7; *4 Ezra* 6.55, 59; 7.11.

87. See Schalit 1989: 125–54; Tromp 1993: 139–43.

88. Cf. 1QS 3.18, 23; 4.18, 20; 4QD[a] 2.i.4; *LAB* 3.10; 23.13.

(12.5) and a definite period which has an end (12.4).[89] It can convey an idea of 'history' from the creation of the world to its end.

This passage is followed by a reference to the defeat of nations by Joshua (12.8-12). The author here distinguishes the observant and sinful within Jews. The latter are ruling classes according to ch. 7, in which the author depicts the situation of his own age. A role of the nations is to punish the sinful Jews (cf. ch. 8). But at the *eschaton*, the author promises, the wicked Jews and the nations will be punished and the observant Jews will prosper. The author sees the impiety of Jewish rulers and foreign conquerors under which the people of Israel are groaning.

7.3.5. Summary

The term *terra*/**ʾereṣ* in *Assumption of Moses* can signify the promised Land. The references to the Land occur in chs 1–6, in which the history of Israel up to the author's own time is reviewed. It is, however, never referred to in the eschatological descriptions. The Land-promise is just utilized as a story setting, in which Moses makes a testament to Joshua. This means that the existence of the people in the Land is presupposed as an ordinary situation.

In contrast, the author's universal perspectives are evident from the uses of *terra*/**ʾereṣ* in the sense of 'earth' and those of *orbis terrarum* and *saeculum*. While these two Latin terms entail some uncertainty concerning their Hebrew original, some uses of them reflect a new usage of Hebrew **ʿôlām*, which can mean 'the world', connoting simultaneously both spatial and temporal perspectives (1.11-14; 12.4f.). At the *eschaton* when God's kingdom appears (10.1) the people of Israel will be exalted to heaven to live, and from above they will see their enemies on the earth (10.8-10). Israel's habitation in heaven is the author's eschatological hope, and it is predetermined from the beginning of the Creation, since the world was created on behalf of them (1.11-14).

This expectation seems to reflect the author's despair of this world which is ruled by wicked Jewish ruling classes and foreign overlords. The antagonism towards the foreign nations gave rise to strong nationalism, but the impiety of Jewish leaders deprived the author of realistic hopes. The author could just direct his readers to observe the Law perfectly and to endure the hard days without resisting the earthly powers even to death, awaiting the end of the world when God will avenge them. A sentiment of despair of the present world and strong eschatological expectations in *Assumption of Moses* would mirror a general atmosphere of Palestine of the first century CE.

89. It is one of the earliest usages of the term **ôlām* as a direct object of the verb 'to create' (1.12) and as a genitive combination with the nouns 'creation' (1.2; 12.4), 'beginning' (1.13, 14) and 'end' (12.4).

7.4. Pseudo-Philo's Liber Antiquitatum Biblicarum

Pseudo-Philo's *Liber Antiquitatum Biblicarum* is preserved in a Latin version. Although there are Hebrew fragments preserved in the *Chronicles of Jerahmeel* (*CJ*), they are medieval retroversions from the Latin.[90] The Latin version is a translation of a Greek translation of a Hebrew original.[91]

The Latin *terra* can be easily retroverted to the Greek *γῆ and the Hebrew **ʾereṣ* (partially **ʾadāmâ*), and *hereditas* to *κληρονομία/**naḥalâ*.[92] There are, however, many occurrences of *mundus*, *habitatio*, *orbis*, and *seculum* (as it is usually spelled in *LAB*'s manuscripts), all of which can mean 'the world'. Although some uncertainty remains, in many occurrences we can restore on fairly firm bases the original Hebrew for these Latin terms. We shall first treat the term *terra/*ʾereṣ*, then terms signifying the world and other related terms.[93]

7.4.1. terra/*ʾereṣ

7.4.1.1. terra/*ʾereṣ *as Earth*

The term *terra/*ʾereṣ* can mean 'the ground', the surface of the earth (18.9; 31.7).[94] It can also signify *terra firma*, dry solid land in contrast to water and celestial bodies (11.6//Exod. 20.4; cf. *LAB* 11.8; Deut. 4.16-19). The phrases *profunda terre* 'the depths of the earth' and *fundamenta habitationis* 'the foundations of the world' in 10.5 can go back to the Hebrew *תהמות הארץ and *מוסדות תבל, respectively (cf. Exod. 15.8; Ps. 18.16//2 Sam. 22.16; Ps. 71.20). *terra/*ʾereṣ* trembles as a means of God's punishment (3.9; 6.17) and as a symbol of God's epiphany (11.5; 11.14; 32.7).

*terra/*ʾereṣ* can glow by the light of the sun (26.15), and be watered by rain. While it can be destroyed by flood (3.5, 7, 8, 9; 19.11), *terra/*ʾereṣ* is productive with water. After the Deluge, the earth was divided to the sons of Noah, and then mention is made of the beginning of agriculture (4.5). Here the rain for agriculture is related to the Noachic covenant (cf. 3.11f.//Genesis 9). Similarly, the feast of Tabernacles, celebrated at the beginning of rainy season, is put in relation to the Noachic covenant (13.7).[95]

90. Harrington 1974: 1–7.

91. Harrington 1970.

92. See Chapter 4 n. 99.

93. In this section the Latin text is of Harrington *et al.* (1976: I), and the text of *Chronicles of Jerahmeel* is of Harrington (1974); the English translation of the Latin text is of Harrington (1985) with some modifications, otherwise noted. For the date, see Jacobson 1996: 199–210. The shift of uses of the terms **ʾereṣ* and **ʿôlām* suggests that Pseudo-Philo predates *4 Ezra* (i.e., pre-70 CE); compare § 7.4.2.3 and § 8.1.2.2; see also Stone 1984: 414; Mendels 1992b: 266 n. 21.

94. For 18.9, cf. Num. 22.31 and Chapter 2 n. 17 above; see Jacobson 1996: 593. For 31.7, cf. Judg. 4.21; 5.26; Jdt. 13.7, 9. In 64.6 the term *terra* certainly means 'ground', though the text is difficult; see Jacobson 1996: 1209f. In 53.9 there appears *precepi terre*, but the text must be corrupted; see Jacobson 1996: 1124f.

95. Cf. *m. Ta'an* 1.1; *b. R.H.* 16a; *tg. Jon.* Lev. 23.36.

At Moses' farewell, God revealed to him the sources of water for clouds (19.10). Here the source to water the whole earth is distinguished from that for 'the Holy Land'. In 60.2 *terra*/*ʾ*ereṣ* is depicted as productive in collaboration with the heavenly rain. In 11.9 this productivity is connected with the command to honour one's parents. The productivity of the *terra*/*ʾ*ereṣ* is included in eschatological expectations of Pseudo-Philo (3.10).

The heaven and the earth are stable, and they are called to witness at the farewell of Moses (19.4; 32.9), of Joshua (24.1) and of Jonathan (62.10).[96] That they can be witnesses par excellence is assumed in the hymn of Deborah (32.13, 15). The stability of the earth is presupposed in the expression 'all the days of the earth' (3.9).[97] The end of this earthly world is expected, however. When the appointed times are fulfilled, God will 'visit' (1.20; 26.13)[98] and 'renew' (16.3)[99] the earth, and 'there will be another earth and another heaven' (3.10).[100] The expression 'appointed times' presupposes the idea of God's foreknowledge of world history.[101]

In the eschatological vision of Pseudo-Philo the resurrection of the dead is awaited (3.10; cf. 19.12; 25.7). In Sheol (*infernus*) there are 'chambers of souls' (32.13; 40.6). The existence of the netherworld under the earth can be related to the expression 'the earth swallows up' in the story of Korah (16.2, 3, 6; 57.2; cf. Num. 16.30-32). A similar connotation may be found in the expressions 'to perish from the earth' (20.4) and 'to destroy from the earth' (58.1).

Since the earth is the space for living beings, the term *terra*/*ʾ*ereṣ* can be employed with verbs denoting their existence on it: 'to multiply' (3.1, 8, 11), 'to increase' (3.8, 11; 9.4), and 'to fill' (3.11; 4.10).[102] There are also frequent uses of the expression 'those inhabiting the earth' (*habitantes terram*/*יושבי הארץ). In many of these occurrences the expression is connected with their wickedness or sin.[103] The wickedness of the inhabitants can affect the earth. The Flood story describes how human sins involved the earth (3.6; cf. Gen. 6.13). A similar idea is expressed in an eschatological perspective, as well (1.20; cf. Gen. 5.28f.).[104] Because of its inhabitants the earth itself would be corrupted (2.8; 28.6), be cursed (3.9; 16.2) and be destroyed (3.9, 11). The wicked deeds of humans expose the existence of heaven and earth to danger (7.2).[105] Israel's sin is connected to the earth (44.6).

On the contrary, when there is a good leader, the earth is filled with God's mercy (5.2).[106] Jephtah states in his speech, 'Even if our sins be overabundant, still His mercy will fill the earth' (39.6; cf. Pss. 33.5; 119.64; Rom. 5.20).

96. Cf. Chapter 2 nn. 66f. above.
97. Cf. Gen. 8.22; Deut. 11.21; Job 8.9; 1 Chron. 29.15.
98. Cf. n. 9 above and Chapter 8 n. 33 below.
99. Cf. 4Q434 2.2f.; see also Chapter 6 n. 99 above.
100. Cf. Isa. 65.17; 66.22; *1 En.* 72.1; 91.16; *Jub.* 1.27-29; 4.26.
101. Cf. 3.9, 10; 23.13; cf. also 1QS 3.18, 23; 4.18, 20; 4QD[a] 2.i.4; *As. Mos.* 12.4f.
102. Other expressions: 9.4; 15.7; 19.16; 44.9.
103. 2.8, 9, 10; 3.3, 4, 6, 9; 4.16; 6.1; 7.4; exceptions: 3.12; 4.5; 26.13; 28.6; cf. § 7.2.2 and nn. 30f. above.
104. See Murphy 1993: 30f.
105. See Jacobson 1996: 375.
106. See Murphy 1993: 39.

The biblical story of division of the earth (Genesis 10) is reproduced in ch. 4. Verse 9 quotes Gen. 10.25 verbatim, and v. 17 makes a mixed quotation from Gen. 10.31f. In *LAB* 4.3 Japheth's portion is called 'a third part of the earth'. In accordance with the biblical narrative, Pseudo-Philo depicts the scattering of nations over the earth (7.3, 5//Gen. 11.8f.).

Since the earth was divided among nations, there appear such phrases as 'the nations of the earth' (21.5), 'every tribe of the earth' (30.2; 31.5), and 'the peoples of the earth' (35.2). All these uses emphasize the special status of the people of Israel among nations.

7.4.1.2. terra/*ʾereṣ *as Land*

The term *terra*/*ʾ*ereṣ* can refer to 'a land' territorially defined. The territorial dimensions of our term are expressed in its plural form (4.17: *in terris*; *CJ*: בארצות). A land can be defined by a proper noun: 'the land of Egypt',[107] 'the land of Canaan', etc.[108] A larger territory and a smaller region can be mentioned with our term: 'the land among the Persians and Medes' (4.3), 'the land of Tob' (39.2, 3), and 'the land of Jericho' (20.7). Once an individual estate is called 'the land of palms' (29.2).[109]

The term can be defined by a common noun: 'the people of the land' (6.4, 9, 11; 7.1); 'the inhabitants of the land' (7.5; 23.5). It can be defined by a pronominal suffix: 'his (Pharaoh's) land' (18.11); 'their (Sihon and Og's) land' (18.1). One's hometown can be called 'his land' and 'my land' (39.2, 4). There appears twice an expression 'a land (of Egypt) not their (Israel's) own' (9.3; 15.5; cf. Gen. 15.13). Egypt is also called 'a foreign land' (14.1; 43.5; cf. Exod. 2.22; 18.3).

LAB 2.1 explains 'the land of Nod' of Gen. 4.16 as follows: 'Now Cain dwelt in a land trembling' (*habitavit in terra tremens*). Here *tremens* is not a modifier of *terra*, but of Cain (not 'the land of trembling', but Cain was 'trembling' in a land). This paraphrase is a midrashic attempt to harmonize Gen. 4.16 with Gen. 4.12 in which Cain is destined to be נד בארץ.[110]

The term *terra*/*ʾ*ereṣ* can refer to the Land. In many occurrences it appears in the Land-promise with biblical styles. It is employed with such verbs as: 'to swear',[111] 'to give',[112] 'to show',[113] 'to bring into',[114] and 'to come into'.[115] A famous expression 'a land flowing with milk and honey' appears twice (15.4; 21.9).[116] A verb 'to dwell in' is applied three times in the same clause (10.2; 12.4; 21.9).[117]

107. 8.10; 10.1; 11.1, 6; 13.4; 14.1, 4. 19.5, 10, 12; 25.6.
108. 8.1, 2, 7, 9, 10; 23.5. Others: 6.1; 18.10; 23.9; 25.11; 39.9.
109. See Jacobson 1996: 823f.
110. See Jacobson 1996: 294.
111. 39.7; cf. 12.4; cf. Chapter 2 n. 193 above.
112. 8.3; 10.2; 12.4; 19.10; 21.9; 23.5; cf. Chapter 2 n. 196 above.
113. 19.7, 10; cf. Chapter 2 n. 198 above.
114. 7.4; 15.4; 23.11; cf. Chapter 2 n. 224 above.
115. 12.4; 14.2; 22.2; cf. Chapter 2 nn. 221–3 above.
116. Cf. Chapter 2 n. 265 above. A related expression 'fruits of the Land' appears twice according to biblical models (*LAB* 15.1; cf. Num. 13.26; *LAB* 20.8//Josh. 5.12).
117. Cf. Chapter 2 n. 233 above.

This clause is influenced by biblical passages (e.g., Gen. 12.7; 15.18; 17.7f.; Exod. 6.4), but not a quotation. Although these verbs appear in the sayings of the promise, they do not always describe the promise itself. Pseudo-Philo inserts the wordings of the promise into the biblical parallel passages to emphasize unfaithfulness of Israel in contrast to God's faithfulness to the covenant (10.2).[118] Similarly, verbs 'to search out' (15.1; 20.1) and 'to see' (15.1; 20.1) are employed to express the faithlessness of the searchers who 'brought a bad report about the Land' (20.1, 6).[119] It is significant to observe the fact that Pseudo-Philo applies the verb *heredito*/*ירשׁ 'to take possession of' to the Land only once just in this context (15.1).

The response of the people to this report is described in 15.4 (cf. Num. 14.3). Here, too, the language of the biblical Land-promise is inserted, and an emphasis is laid on the gap between the splendidness of God's gift and the people's unfaithfulness. Their infidelity is predicted by God in relation to the Golden Calf (12.4)[120] and at the farewell of Moses (19.7).[121] Even before coming into the Land they turned aside from God's ways; the worse their iniquities will be when they come into it; they will fall in idolatry. As these passages suggest, the verb 'to come into' plays a key role. It is again used in relation to the people's faithlessness.[122] Thus, the biblical Land promises are utilized to warn the readers against their faithlessness.

Pseudo-Philo depicts the special status of the Land. It is so special that God's eyes have been laid upon it from the Creation,[123] and that even the waters of the Flood avoided it (7.4). It is called 'the Holy Land' (*terra sancta*), for which a special place is prepared in the firmament to water it (19.10). The idea that the Land has its own source of rainfall in heaven distinguished from other lands could be derived from the expression '*his* (Israel's) heavens' which drop down dew to the Land (Deut. 33.28).[124]

The high status of the Land is closely related to the election of the people of Israel (cf. 39.7). In the Land God would establish His covenant with Abram and bless the people of Israel (7.4; cf. 8.3). Before his farewell Joshua establishes a covenant with the people and conveys God's speech (ch. 23; cf. Joshua 24). The special status of the Land and the people is dependent on their observance of the Law (23.12). Their fidelity to God will involve the fertility of the Land and a rain of blessing (13.10a).[125] The attachment of the people to the Land is manifested in 24.2: 'it is better for us to die in fear of Him than to be blotted out from the Land'.[126]

118. Cf. Exod. 14.10-12.
119. Cf. Num. 13.32; 14.36f.
120. Cf. Exod. 32.7-14.
121. Cf. Num. 27.12-14; Deut. 32.49-52.
122. 14.2; cf. Deut. 28.62; *LAB* 22.2; cf. Josh. 22.16-20; Num. 32; cf. also Exod. 34.12; Deut. 18.9.
123. Cf. Deut. 11.12; see Jacobson 1996: 381.
124. Cf. Lev. 26.19; Deut. 28.23.
125. Although Harrington and Jacobson translate the *terra* here as 'the earth', it must be 'the Land'; cf. our discussion on 19.10 above.
126. Jacobson's translation (1996: 131, 731).

Their infidelity, however, shall cause a disaster to come upon the Land. The last commandment of the Decalogue ends with a reference to the Land: 'You shall not covet your neighbor's house or what he has, lest others should covet your Land' (11.13).[127] Their faithlessness is predicted by Moses at his farewell speech (19.2).[128] Here God's departure from the Land is inserted to the biblical base text (Deut. 31.17). While God's punishment in Deut. 28.36-44 is the exile of the people, here it is God who will depart from the Land. While the restoration of Israel in Deut. 30.1-10 is dependent on the repentance, here it depends on God's faithfulness to His covenant.[129] Thus, Pseudo-Philo constantly makes a contrast between the faithful God and the faithless people.

After Moses' death the leadership of Joshua is assured by God (20.1f.) and the people (20.5). A role assigned by them to Joshua is to 'allot the Land among them' (20.9).[130] The following narrative, which paraphrases Josh. 13.1, differs from the biblical story; God states 'there is no one to apportion it' and predicts again the unfaithfulness of the people (21.1). In his response Joshua requires God to choose a dynasty to rule the people (21.4), a dynasty which probably refers to the Davidic line (21.5; cf. Gen. 49.10).[131] In the following ceremony at Gilgal the fulfilment of God's promise is celebrated (21.9). The setting of this passage is taken from Josh. 8.30-35 and the reference to the fulfilment of God's promise is made in Josh. 23.14 (cf. 1 Kgs 8.20, 56). The sequence of the narrative indicates that Pseudo-Philo again brings the contrast between the unfaithful people (21.1) and faithful God (21.9).

The apportioning of the Land is again referred to in 23.1. This passage is modelled on Josh. 18.10 and 23.1. As this connection indicates, the passages referring to the allotment of the Land are related to the foreign inhabitants of the Land (20.9; 21.1). This is natural since the Land is called 'the land of our enemies' (21.9).[132] The expression 'the inhabitants of the Land' is employed in relation to idolatry.[133] While this phrase always refers to the indigenous foreigners, the legitimacy of its possession by Israel is expressed by genitive pronouns suffixed to our term: 'their Land',[134] 'your Land',[135] and 'our Land'.[136] The Land is twice called 'the Land of Israel'.[137]

In 25.1 a reference is made to 'quiet of the Land'. This verse closes a long pre-history to the settlement of the people into the Land. From then on God's prediction which repeatedly foretells the idolatry of the people would be fulfilled.

127. Cf. Exod. 20.17; Deut 5.22.

128. Cf. *LAB* 12.4; 13.10b; 19.6f.; 21.1.

129. See Murphy 1993: 90.

130. Cf. Num. 34.17f.; Deut. 3.28; 31.7; Josh. 1.6; 11.23.

131. See Jacobson 1996: 683f.

132. The expression 'a land of enemies' in the Bible refers to a foreign land, not the Land; see Chapter 2 n. 163 above.

133. 21.1; 24.1; 25.9; 41.3. For 'those inhabiting the Land' in 39.8, see Jacobson 1996: 954.

134. 14.2; 23.1.

135. 11.13; 13.3; 19.2; 22.2b; 23.12.

136. 22.2a; 30.4; 39.8.

137. 25.1; 64.1; cf. 1 Sam. 13.19; Ezek. 40.2; 47.18; 1 Chron. 22.2; 2 Chron. 2.16; 34.7; *TS* 58.6; 4QMMT B 63.

A similar statement is employed after the death of Deborah (33.6) and at the end of the time of Judges (55.10), passages which have the same wordings: '(and) the Land was quiet for seven years'. While 33.6 follows its biblical model (Judg. 5.31), the other two (25.1; 55.10) are additions to the biblical narrative; other biblical references to the 'quiet of the Land' are omitted.[138] Accordingly, these references are deliberately made to punctuate the narrative.

7.4.2. World in Liber Antiquitatum Biblicarum

There frequently occur Latin terms signifying 'the world'. These are: *mundus* (3 times), *habitatio*/*(in)habitabilis* (5 times),[139] *orbis* (8 times), and *seculum* (36 times).[140] The first term is perhaps a translation of Greek κόσμος, of which, though, the original Hebrew is uncertain whether *ʿôlām*, *tēbēl*, or *ʾereṣ*.[141] The second and third terms are probably variant translations of Greek ἡ οἰκουμένη, which can be ascribed to Hebrew *tēbēl* (or less frequently *ʿôlām*).[142] The term *seculum* perhaps renders Greek αἰών, which reflects Hebrew *ʿôlām*. We shall first treat Latin *mundus*, considering the original Hebrew, and then investigate uses of *tēbēl* and *ʿôlām*.

7.4.2.1. mundus

Pseudo-Philo begins with the words *initio* (or *initium*) *mundi* '(in) the beginning of the world' (1.1). It is uncertain whether this phrase is the beginning of the sentence or the heading of the whole book.[143] Since 'beginning' connotes a temporal sense, Hebrew **ʿôlām* seems to fit Latin *mundus*/Greek *κόσμος better than **ʾereṣ* or **tēbēl*, both of which are spatial terms, if the original Hebrew version had contained the clause (some manuscripts omit it).[144]

In 11.1 *mundus* appears in parallelism with *inhabitabilis* and both terms represent the human world. Since *inhabitabilis* probably goes back to *ἡ οἰκουμένη/ **tēbēl*, *mundus*/*κόσμος may be ascribed to **ʿôlām* (or possibly **ʾereṣ*).

In 9.3 Amram emphasizes the endurance of the people of Israel more than the world (cf. 39.7). In this passage *mundus* is used in parallelism with *seculum*. Since *seculum* perhaps reflects *αἰών/**ʿôlām*, *mundus*/*κόσμος can be ascribed

138. Josh. 11.23; 14.15; Judg. 3.11, 30; 8.28.

139. Only those in the sense of 'world'; other uses: *habitatio* (individual's dwelling place): 4.11; 16.3; 32.8; 38.4; 55.1; 63.4; *inhabitabilis* (uninhabitable place): 3.9; 11.8.

140. Except in the sense of 'lifetime' (3.2b; 59.4).

141. Latin *mundus* is an equivalent to Greek κόσμος, which is never employed in the LXX in the sense of 'cosmos'; cf. n. 68 above.

142. Jacobson (1996: 953) indicates: '*habitabilis* is sometimes used to represent ἡ οἰκουμένη'; *orbis*, too, can be a translation of ἡ οἰκουμένη (see § 7.3.1 above), which is a translation of *tēbēl* in LXX (see § 2.5.2 above).

143. See Jacobson 1996: 281.

144. Cf. *2 Bar*. 21.4.

to Hebrew **tēbēl*. This passage attests to the cosmic scale of eschatological catastrophe expected in this work.

7.4.2.2. *tēbēl

The term **tēbēl* can be used as a synonym of **ʾereṣ* signifying the *terra firma*; 'the foundations of the world' is mentioned in parallelism with 'the depths of the earth' (10.5; cf. Exod. 15.8; Ps. 18.16). At God's epiphany on Sinai, when the earth quaked, 'all the habitable world was shaken' (11.5). Latin *omne habitabile* here probably reflects Hebrew **kol tēbēl* which is in parallelism with *terra*/**ʾereṣ*.[145] At the *eschaton*, it is expected, 'the world will sink into the immeasurable deep' (9.3).

It is employed in relation to God's Creation in 11.8. The first half is a citation of Exod. 20.11, and the second half rephrases the first. Here *universus orbis*, which can probably be ascribed to Hebrew **kol tēbēl* distinguished from the previous *terra*/**ʾereṣ*, signifies the habitable world in contrast to the uninhabitable wilderness. It is stated in 13.6 that once a year God remembers 'the entire world'. Here, too, *totius orbis* perhaps reflects **kol tēbēl* referring to the created world (in parallelism with *totius terre*/**kol hāʾāreṣ* in 13.7). A reference is made to 'the tribes of the world' (*tribus orbis*) in parallelism with 'the nations of the earth' (*gentes terre*), expressions which denote nations other than Israel (21.5). God's Creation is closely related to the election of Israel in a prayer of the people (39.7). In this passage the election connects the Creation theology and the Land theology. The term *habitabilis*/**tēbēl* is employed here to discern the following *terra*/**ʾereṣ* which refers to 'the Land'. Since the world is created for Israel,[146] the latter is more inexterminable than the former (9.3).

The election of Israel is related to the Torah (11.1f.). The Torah is a light illuminating the world and a criterion to judge it. As he enlightens God's people (11.2), the grave of Moses is also said to be 'a light for the entire world' (*totius orbis*/**kol tēbēl* [19.16; cf. *As. Mos*. 11.8]).[147] The **tēbēl* illuminated by the Torah represents the human world. It is expected that 'your (Israel's) Land will be renowned over all the world (*in omnem orbem*/**bekol tēbēl*), and your seed special among all the peoples' (23.12).

In 19.4 God's revelation of 'the end of the world' (*finem orbis*) is related to the Torah. J. Murphy regards 'the end' here as the *eschaton*,[148] but this is unlikely since *orbis*, which might reflect Hebrew **tēbēl*, does not bear a temporal sense. It is possibly something to do with God's revelation of natural mysteries to Moses in 19.10.[149]

The term *orbis*/**tēbēl* can be employed in the eschatological context. There appears an expression *visitare orbem*/*פקד את תבל 'to visit the world' (19.13).[150]

145. See Jacobson 1996: 456.
146. Cf. *Ass. Mos*. 1.11-14; *4 Ezra* 6.55, 59; 7.11.
147. See Jacobson 1996: 657f.
148. Murphy 1993: 91.
149. See Jacobson 1996: 618f.
150. Cf. 1.20; 19.12; 26.13; n. 9 above and Chapter 8 n. 33 below.

The eschatological events involved by God's visitation are described with the term *ʾereṣ* as we saw above and with another term, *ʿôlām*, which we shall see now on.

7.4.2.3. *ʿôlām

The term *seculum*/*ʿôlām* can convey a temporal connotation expressing 'eternity' as an adverbial accusative with prepositions: *in secula*/*לעולמים (3.2a; 7.1); *in seculum*/*לעולם (4.11; 53.4); *ante secula et post secula*/*מעולמים ועד עולמים (21.4).

It can also signify the 'world', the space for living beings. In 32.7 *seculum*/*ʿôlām* means a material world, which could be burned up, a synonym of *ʾereṣ*, 'the earth'. It can represent also the earthly world. There will be no idols 'in the world' (25.11; 26.4). The world can be the world of the living in which men are born (32.3) and from which men go forth at their death (50.7: *de seculo hoc*). Here the *seculum hoc*/*hāʿôlām hazeh* is contrasted with the netherworld.

The term can be employed in relation to God's Creation. It is assumed that there existed darkness and silence 'before the world was made' (60.2).[151] The *seculum*/*ʿôlām* here refers to the proto-universe, which is called *ʾereṣ* in Gen. 1.2, since the creation of heaven and earth is described a few lines below. The Creation was done by God's word (28.4).[152]

Pseudo-Philo assumes God's foreknowledge of world history (18.4; 50.4).[153] This is in relation to God's purpose of the Creation, which is manifestly uttered by God Himself in 28.4: God created the world in order to be praised by creation, and chose a 'vine' (i.e., Israel) for this purpose.[154] As the people of Israel had been chosen and the Land had been cared for from the beginning (7.4), the Torah had been prepared 'from the creation of the world' (32.7). The Torah is called 'a light to the world' (11.1).

In 28.4 it is stated in relation to the precreation that 'when man did not exist and there was no wickedness in it' (cf. *4 Ezra* 9.18). The human thoughts differed from God's purpose of Creation (35.5). The gap between God's will and human acts might be a cause to bring an end to the world. When the people made a golden Calf, Moses begged God for mercy: 'For if You indeed forsake the world, then who will do for You what You say as God?' (12.9). But the world is 'corruptible' (28.10),[155] and its end is appointed.

The end of the world is explicitly uttered by God himself: 'when the years of the world have been fulfilled ... the world will cease' (3.10); 'until the time of the world is complete' (23.13). The 'fulfilment/completion' of the 'years/time' of *seculum*/*ʿôlām* means that God predestined its end from precreation.[156] The

151. Cf. Gen. 1.2; *4 Ezra* 6.39; 7.30; *2 Bar.* 3.7.

152. Cf. Pss. 33.6, 9; 148.5; Wis. 9.1; Jdt. 16.14; *4 Ezra* 3.4; 6.38, 43; *2 Bar.* 14.17; 21.4; 48.8.

153. See also 21.2; 22.7; cf. *Ass. Mos.* 12.4f.; *4 Ezra* 6.1-6; 7.70.

154. See 12.8f.; 18.10; 39.7; cf. Ps. 80.9; Jer. 2.21; Ezek. 17.6; *4 Ezra* 9.21.

155. The corruption of the earth: 2.8; 28.6; of the people: 12.4; 22.2.

156. Cf. *Ass. Mos.* 12.4f.; *4 Ezra* 4.36f.; 5.49; 6.5; 7.74; 11.44; 13.58; 14.9; *2 Bar.* 56.2-4.

employment of the words 'years' and 'time' in these passages indicates that the term *seculum*/*ʿ*ôlām* here implies a temporal sense, a definite period, on the one hand; the expression 'the world will cease' must connote its spatial aspect, on the other. Thus, the term *seculum*/*ʿ*ôlām* can refer to the world which is a space with a definite period.

The end is implied also in the expression 'this world' (*seculum hoc*/**hāʿôlām hazeh*).[157] Seeing the transgressions of the people of Israel, God became angry and said: 'Behold I have chosen one people from every tribe of the earth, and I said that My glory would reside in this world with it' (30.2). Here again a gap between God's will and Israel's acts is contrasted. Hannah prayed in her song: 'the unjust exist in this world, but He brings the just to life when He wishes' (51.5).[158] This statement seems to connote that the wicked exist only in this world and the righteous will enjoy eternal life in the world to come (cf. 34.3).[159] The idea of the two worlds is manifested in Jonathan's saying to David: 'For yours is a kingdom in this world, and from you is the beginning of a kingdom which will come in its own time' (62.9; cf. 1 Sam. 24.21). The kingdom of David will be both in this world and in the world to come. The same idea seems to be assumed in 19.7 (cf. Deut. 32.52; 34.4). This passage implies that Moses will be resurrected and enter into the Land in the world to come. The evanescence of this world is explicitly stated by God (19.13; cf. *4 Ezra* 6.20).[160]

The end can be expressed also by the clause 'until I (God) remember the world'.[161] When He remembers the world, God will 'visit the world (*seculum*/*ʿ*ôlām*)' (19.12).[162] In the face of *eschaton* the celestial bodies will modify their courses, and the years and the times will be shortened (19.13).[163] While the Bible already provides the ideas of a new heaven[164] and eschatological disorder of celestial bodies,[165] this passage may be one of the earliest descriptions of the eschatological shortening of years.[166]

What will come after the end is called 'the new world (-age)' (23.8) and 'the (world-) age without measure' (34.3), along with 'another earth and another heavens' (3.10; cf. 16.3). It is also called 'immortal world that is not subject to time' (19.12). Latin *inhabitationem immortatem* probably reflects Hebrew *עולם ללא מוות or

157. Cf. *1 En.* 48.7; *Ass. Mos.* 12.5; *4 Ezra* 4.27; 7.112; *2 Bar.* 21.19.

158. Jacobson's translation (1996: 177).

159. So Jacobson 1996: 1103.

160. For a textual problem of 19.13, see Harrington 1985: 328 n. *q*; Jacobson 1996: 643f.

161. 16.3; 26.13; 48.1; cf. *2 Bar.* 4.1; 25.4; 44.8f.

162. God's visit to the earth: 1.20; 26.13; to the world (*orbis*/**tēbēl*): 19.13; cf. Chapter 8 n. 33 below.

163. Cf. 3.10; 9.3.

164. Isa. 65.17; 66.22; cf. *1 En.* 91.16.

165. Joel 2.10; 3.4; 4.15; Isa. 13.10; Ezek. 32.7; cf. *T. Levi* 4.1; *Ass. Mos.* 10.4-6; but compare with *1 En.* 2.1; 41.5-7.

166. Cf. *4 Ezra* 5.4f.; *2 Bar.* 20.1; 54.1; 83.1; Mk 13.20; the attestations of the eschatological shortening of years are found only from the first century CE on; hence we can infer that the insertion of *1 Enoch* 80 is contemporary to Pseudo-Philo (see above Chapter 4 n. 3, Chapter 7 n. 32).

*עולם אל־מוות (cf. *4 Ezra* 7.113). The new world is prepared for men: 'man is designed to take possession of the world' (32.3a), a clause which is in parallelism with '[to] take possession of life without limit and time without measure' (32.3b). Here a technical term of the biblical Land theology, ירש את הארץ, is reinterpreted in universal eschatological dimensions.[167]

7.4.3. Other Related Terms

7.4.3.1. terra/*ʾadāmâ

In 4.5 the beginning of agriculture is depicted. The *operati terram* here certainly goes back to the Hebrew *עבד את האדמה, a typical use of the term *ʾadāmâ*.[168]

In 11.9 the term *ʾ*adāmâ* seems to be used in the sense of 'the Land'. This is a quotation of Exod. 20.12, and Pseudo-Philo adds *et habitabis* to the biblical text.[169]

In 3.10 the resurrection of the dead from 'the earth (*terra*)' is mentioned. *Chronicles of Jerahmeel* reads here *ʾadāmâ*. This translation may be influenced by Dan. 12.2 (cf. Gen. 3.19). While the referent of *terra* here is quite clear, it is difficult to determine whether the original Hebrew was *ʾ*adāmâ* or *ʾ*ereṣ* (or *ʿ*āpār*). It seems to me that *ʾ*adāmâ* is somewhat likelier, since Gen. 2.7 and 3.19 are employed in *LAB* 39.5 in which the use of *ʾ*adāmâ* is certain.

LAB 37.3 refers to Gen. 3.18, hence the term *terra*, which means here 'the soil', certainly reflects *ʾ*adāmâ*.

LAB 16.2-3 connects Korah's story (Num. 16.1-3, 30-33) with Cain's story (Gen. 4.1-16). Here we have *terra* three times in 16.2. Since the passage apparently refers to Gen. 4.1-16, it is natural to suppose that the original Hebrew for *terra* would have been *ʾ*adāmâ*. As for the first instance, one may expect a wordplay between *ʾ*adāmâ* and *ʾ*ādām*.[170] The connection of the two stories, however, is related to the earth swallowing blood (i.e., soul) along with body (16.3). That is to say, God commanded the earth from Cain's incident on not to swallow up the blood. He rescinded the prohibition at Korah's rebellion, and the earth swallowed up both body and soul of Korah and his followers (16.6).[171] Then, the original Hebrew of 'the earth' with the verb 'to swallow up' in 16.2-3 must have been the same word and taken from Numbers 16, that is, *ʾ*ereṣ*. The first occurrence of *terra* in 16.3, too, is related to this verb. The clause 'I commanded the earth, and it ...' is deliberately repeated at the beginning of these two verses. Then, the first clause of 16.2 must have the same Hebrew word. God's command to the earth, indeed, to

167. Cf. *1 En.* 5.7; Sir. 36.1-22; 44.21; *Jub.* 22.14; 32.19; 4QpPs[a] (see § 6.5.1); *4 Ezra* 6.59; *2 Bar.* 14.13; 44.13; 51.3.

168. See § 2.5.1 (pp. 36f.) and n. 356 there.

169. See Jacobson 1996: 472.

170. So Jacobson 1996: 555.

171. Cf. Jacobson 1996: 557.

bring forth man reminds us Gen. 1.24. Accordingly, it is better to assume that the Hebrew *ʾ*ereṣ* underlies the *terra* of all its occurrences in 16.2-3.

In *LAB* 25.9 *terra* is clay which can be heaped, though the original Hebrew is uncertain (cf. 2 Kgs 5.17).

7.4.3.2. hereditas/*naḥalâ – hereditare/*yāraš

The term *hereditas*/**naḥalâ* is frequently used in reference to the people of Israel. It is mostly used with a possessive pronoun in the sense of 'God's portion'.[172] The single occurrence without a pronominal suffix is also related to God (39.7).[173]

The term can refer to a land as one's allotment (23.9 [cf. Josh. 24.4]; 39.9 [cf. Judg. 11.24]). It can be applied to a hereditary land allotted to families and tribes of Israel in the Land (24.3; cf. Josh. 24.28; Judg. 2.6). Once the term *חלק/*pars* seems to be used in the same sense (29.1; cf. Numbers 27; 36).

In 21.10 *hereditas*/**naḥalâ* refers to 'the Land'.[174] Here the Land is 'God's allotment', into which He brought the people 'with joy and gladness'.

It expresses, mostly with possessive pronoun, a biblical idea that the people and the Land belong to God as chosen among nations.[175]

As we've seen above, there appears an expression *in hereditatem seculi* 'in taking possession of the world' (32.3a; cf. *4 Ezra* 6.59). It probably reflects Hebrew *ירש את העולם*,[176] since the phrase ירש את הארץ is well known from the Bible through post-biblical Jewish literature; either it refers to the possession of the Land or of the entire earth.[177] The alteration of this traditional expression must reflect a climate of the first century CE Palestine, a mood of pessimism about this present world which could be a cause of the Great Revolt.

7.4.4. Summary

In *Liber Antiquitatum Biblicarum* the term *ʾ*ereṣ* can mean the tangible 'earth' as the ground, *terra firma*, and soil with productivity of plants. Productivity of the earth, in particular, is repetitiously described and is sometimes linked with the observance of God's commandments. The term can be used in relation to

172. 12.9; 19.8, 9; 21.4; 27.7; 30.4; 49.6.

173. See Deut. 32.8f. and Chapter 2 n. 210 above; cf. Sir. 23.12; 24.7-12; *Jub.* 1.19, 21; 22.9, 10, 29; 33.20; *4 Ezra* 8.16, 45.

174. See Chapter 2 nn. 210–13 above; cf. Sir. 36.13 [Gr. 33.13a+36.16b]; *TS* 62.11-16//Deut. 20.15-18; Jdt. 8.22; 1 Macc. 15.33f.; *Jub.* 49.19; 4Q179 1.i.12f.; *Pss. Sol.* 9.1; 17.23.

175. For the people, see 11.1; 20.4; 23.12; 30.4; 35.2; for the Land, see 7.4; 19.10.

176. The Latin *hereditare* must be a translation of Greek κληρονομεῖν, which is a usual translation of Hebrew *yāraš* in the LXX (98/146 times [*c*. 67%]; *nāḥal*: 13/146 times [*c*. 9%]). The verb *yāraš* appears with *ʾereṣ* 'the Land' 66 times in the Hebrew Bible, *nāḥal* 4 times (Chapter 2 nn. 206, 227). The phrase *yāraš ʾet hāʾāreṣ* must have been familiar to Jews; see the next note.

177. For the Land possession, cf. Bar. 2.34; *TS* 51.15f.//Deut. 16.20; *TS* 56.12//Deut. 17.14; Jdt. 5.15; *Jub.* 49.18f.; 4QRP[c] (4Q365) 23.4-6; for the earth possession, see n. 167 above.

God's Creation. Since it is stable, it can be a witness of history, and it holds dead bodies until the *eschaton* when they shall be resurrected. Although it is stable, it can be affected by human evil deeds, which cause it to be corrupted, cursed and destroyed. At the *eschaton* God will visit and renew the earth, and there will be another earth. Thus, the term *ʾereṣ* is employed to depict the Creation theology and eschatological hopes. It is notable that this work is the last Palestinian Jewish writing that utilizes our term as a direct object of eschatological expectations; God's visitation to the earth (*ʾereṣ*) and its renewal are never described in the post-70 CE writings, in which another term, *ʿôlām*, fills its eschatological roles.

ʾereṣ can also refer to a land territorially defined. It frequently appears in the statements of the Land-promise with biblical style. The special status of the Holy Land is stressed a few times. The promise and uniqueness of the Land, however, are not utilized to express Pseudo-Philo's expectations, but God's faithfulness to the covenant in contrast to the people's infidelity. When God is angry against the people, it is not the people but God who departs from the Land. This means that Pseudo-Philo feels no threat that the people might be scattered from the Land. Accordingly, *ʾereṣ* in the sense of the Land is never employed in his eschatology.

The term *tēbēl* is mostly used as a synonym of *ʾereṣ*. What is significant is that it is utilized in Pseudo-Philo's eschatology. At the *eschaton* God will visit *tēbēl* and judge *kol tēbēll* by the Law. Again, this work contains the last references to these expressions in Jewish eschatologies.

In addition, there are frequent uses of another term, *ʿôlām*. It can be used as a synonym of *ʾereṣ* and employed with such verbs as 'to create', 'to found' and 'to form' expressing God's Creation. The years for the world were appointed before its creation. Thus the term *ʿôlām* can convey both spatial and temporal senses. This is manifestly discernible in the relatively frequent uses of the expression *hāʿôlām hazeh*. This is a concept close to 'history'. The revelation of the new world after the *eschaton* is expected. Thus, the term *ʿôlām* expresses the Creation theology and eschatology, as our term *ʾereṣ* does. While, however, the latter cannot denote temporal aspect of the world, the former can connote both spatial and temporal. This new usage of the term *ʿôlām* reflects Pseudo-Philo's overview of history from the beginning to the end.

This work lacks sectarian motives. It is a nationalistic writing stressing God's faithfulness to the covenant and warning the readers against infidelity to Him. A main theme is leadership.[178] It was probably chosen to instruct them not to follow the revolutionaries against Romans, since there were no divinely legitimate leaders in Pseudo-Philo's eyes, and bad leaders would bring the people infidelity to God.

178. See Nickelsburg 1980.

7.5. Conclusion

The Roman conquest of Jerusalem and the successive Herodian dynasty as an agent of foreign overlords, which had been caused by the internal conflicts of Hasmonaean brothers, brought a new situation to the Palestinian Jewry. The Roman reign did not only mean the end of Jewish political independence, but also devaluated the high priesthood. The high priesthood had been traditionally lifelong and inherited (*Ant.* 20.229). Herod, however, abolished this custom, appointed the official from non-traditional priestly families and frequently changed in his favour. Roman rulers, as well as the Herods, followed this policy. Thus, the high priesthood became subject to the political rulers. The rise of new high priest families whose post was dependent on the then political ruler caused estrangement between the high priests and national mind.[179] The four works treated in this chapter reflect this situation when antagonism towards the rulers, foreign and domestic, increased, and the realization of eschatological expectations was felt to be drawing near.

In the Hasmonaean period the territorial expansionism of the Land became prevalent, though universal eschatologies were not utterly lost. From the Roman conquest of Jerusalem in 63 BCE on, however, the expansionism disappeared. True, in the four writings of this chapter there existed the concept of the Promised Land, even of the Holy Land, but its borders were no longer a matter of concern. *Psalms of Solomon* saw the conquest of Jerusalem as God's judgement. Admitting this event as a revelation of God's righteousness, the psalmists expected the eschatological judgements by a Davidic messiah of the whole earth (**kol hāʾāreṣ*) except Israel. The messianic hopes include his dominion over the earth (*ʾ*ereṣ*). The term *ʾ*ereṣ*, therefore, is mostly used in the sense of the earthly human world. The Roman conquest of Jerusalem gave them a worldwide scope, since it was caused by *intra*-national conflicts which involved *inter*-national intervention. Despite this worldwide perspective, the psalmists no longer hoped for the expansion of the territory of the Land; they expected the eschatological restoration of the twelve tribes of Israel in the Land (*ʾ*ereṣ*), in which no foreigners would sojourn. The consciousness of the Holy Land as a definite territory was probably an inheritance from the former Hasmonaean period, but the expansionism never revived in Jewish history from then on. In the other three writings the Land (*ʾ*ereṣ* /*ʾ*araʿ*) is no longer utilized in their eschatological descriptions.

Rather, cosmological eschatologies flourished in these works from the first century CE. The Similitudes expects the appearance of a heavenly messiah and his final judgement against the Roman rulers and their Jewish agents who rule the earthly world (*ʾ*araʿ*/**yabšâ*). The earth (*ʾ*araʿ*/**yabšâ*) is assigned to be the eschatological dwelling place of the messiah and the righteous who will become angels. The term *ʾ*araʿ*, therefore, frequently represents the earthly world in

179. For animosity of the people against the high priests, see *Ant.* 17.207; 20.180f., 206f., 247-9; cf. also *War* 2.409-17; 4.147-9, 153-7; 7.260; see Goodman 1987: 40–9, 109–33; Goodblatt 1994: 26–76.

contrast to the heavenly one. *Assumption of Moses* has a different eschatology, in which the dwelling of Israel in heaven is longed for. From there they will see their enemies on the earth (*ʾ*ereṣ*). The term *ʾ*ereṣ*, therefore, can represent the earthly world in contrast to the heavenly one. *Assumption of Moses*, however, employs another term, *ʿ*ôlām*, frequently more than *ʾ*ereṣ*, to express the world. It can connote simultaneously a space and a definite time, the world history which should come to an end; hence it can be utilized in the Creation theology with its end in perspective. Pseudo-Philo also utilizes the terms *ʾ*ereṣ* and *ʿ*ôlām* (and **tēbēl*) in the Creation theology and eschatology: *ʾ*ereṣ*/**tēbēl*/*ʿ*ôlām* was created; it will be visited; there will be another *ʾ*ereṣ* and a new *ʿ*ôlām*. Pseudo-Philo applies the biblical promise of the Land (ירש את הארץ) to the promise of the world (ירש את העולם*).

Palestinian Jews of the first century CE gave the term *ʿ*ôlām*/*ʿ*ālam* a new usage. It expresses the consciousness of the 'end' of this world; but not only the eschatological time understanding of one's own age. It expresses a view surveying all of history, from its creation to the end. In other words, it expresses a view retrospecting the Creation from the end and expecting the new Creation. This new usage is probably influenced by Greek αἰών (and/or Latin *saeculum*). Since αἰών is employed as a translation of Hebrew ʿ*ôlām* in the LXX, its other sense 'age' could easily be applied to *ʿ*ôlām*.[180] Furthermore, by the first century CE αἰών became a synonym of κόσμος in Hellenistic Jewish writings (cf. Wis. 13.9; 14.6; 18.4). This use of αἰών frequently appears in the New Testament in such expressions as 'this world',[181] 'the present world',[182] 'the end of the world',[183] and 'the world to come'.[184] Since Hebrew and Aramaic had had no equivalent to Greek κόσμος, the term *ʿ*ôlām*/*ʿ*ālam* was to connote both αἰών and κόσμος. Thus it could connote both temporal and spatial aspects of the 'world', and was favoured by Palestinian Jewry.[185]

It is noteworthy to see the fact that this new use is found in the three writings which had different provenance, while unknown to the Qumran Community.[186] Thus, it was not a sectarian usage, but rather was prevalent among the people. This means that the new usage reflects a general atmosphere of the first century CE Palestine when eschatological expectations became widespread. The messianic hopes accounted in *Psalms of Solomon* and in the Similitudes formed a part of such expectations. In the pre-Roman period messianic expectations were not so

180. Thus Dalman 1997: 152f.

181. Mt. 12.32; Mk 10.30//Lk. 18.30; Lk. 16.8; Rom. 12.2; 1 Cor. 1.20; 2.6ab, 8; 3.18; 2 Cor. 4.4; Eph. 1.21; 1 Tim. 6.17; 2 Tim. 4.10.

182. Gal. 1.4; Tit. 2.12.

183. Mt. 13.39, 40, 49.

184. Mt. 12.32; Lk. 20.35; Eph. 1.21; 2.7; Heb. 6.5.

185. There are parallel expressions between κόσμος in Wisdom and *ʿ*ôlām* in *Assumption of Moses* and Pseudo-Philo; compare Wis. 9.3; 13.2 and *Ass. Mos.* 4.2; Wis. 9.9; 11.17 and *Ass. Mos.*1.12; Wis. 11.22 and *LAB* 19.13 (cf. *4 Ezra* 6.20); Wis. 17.20 and *LAB* 11.1f.

186. In Qumranic writings another term, קץ, is frequently employed; cf. e.g., 1QpHab 7.2; 4Q180 1.1; 1QS 11.8f.

popular (only in the Book of Dreams, 4Q521 and the Qumran Community). From the Roman conquest on various messianic concepts were developed in *Psalms of Solomon*, the Similitudes, *4 Ezra*, *2 Baruch*, and *Apocalypse of Abraham*, to say nothing of the New Testament, all of which date from the Roman period.[187] The eschatological expectations of the new world and the messiah, however, reflect despair of the actual present world, which was governed by the wicked kings and high priests. We may say that this general sentiment to the present world gave rise to a new use of the term *ʿ*ôlām* in the first century CE.

The authors of these writings, which we've seen in this chapter, awaited God's direct intervention into history, depicting the eschatological hopes with the terms *ʾ*ereṣ* (earth), **tēbēl* and *ʿ*ôlām*. While positing the traditional significance of the Promised Land, they were virtually giving up on the real Land. They contrast with those rebelling against Rome in the same period, who were trying to wrest it by force from Roman rule.[188] The resignation from the present world, on the one hand, and the strong desire for liberation, on the other, fermented a disquieting atmosphere towards the Great Revolt.

187. See VanderKam 1998; see also the next note.

188. Also rebels of the Great Revolt seem to have had a kind of messianism; cf. *War* 6.312f., Tacitus, *Historiae* V, 13.2 (Stern 1974–84: II, no. 281, see note in pp. 61f.), Suetonius, *Divus Vespasianus* 4.5, *Nero* 40.2.

Chapter 8

Responses to the Destruction of the Second Temple

In this chapter we shall discuss works from the period between 70–132 CE. These include: (1) *4 Ezra*, (2) *2 Baruch*, and (3) *Apocalypse of Abraham*.

8.1. 4 Ezra

4 Ezra is preserved in Latin, Syriac and other languages. It is widely accepted that these versions are translated from Greek, which was made from a Hebrew original, which originates in Palestine towards the end of the first century CE.[1]

We need to make some comments regarding pertinent terms: Latin *terra*/Syriac ܐܪܥܐ is certainly a translation of Greek γῆ, which in turn is a rendering of Hebrew ארץ or less frequently אדמה. We can find the terms *orbis*/ܬܒܝܠ (or ܬܐܒܝܠ) in the sense of 'world' and *saeculum*/ܥܠܡܐ in the sense of 'world' or 'world-age' (or 'age'). The former probably renders Greek ἡ οἰκουμένη (or possibly κόσμος) which may be taken from Hebrew תבל, and the latter from αἰών and עולם. These three terms in *4 Ezra* are studied by M. E. Stone, as we saw above (§ 7.3.1). Latin *regio*/Syriac ܐܬܪܐ or ܐܪܥܐ, which is used in the sense of 'land', is probably a translation of the Greek χώρα, which is another frequent translation of ארץ or less frequently מדינה in the LXX.[2] Other related terms will be discussed briefly in relevant contexts. As for the text, we shall mainly follow the Latin version, and supplement our argument with the Syriac and other versions when necessary.[3]

8.1.1. *ʾereṣ *in* 4 Ezra

8.1.1.1. terra/ܐܪܥܐ/*ʾereṣ *as Earth*

The term *terra*/**ʾereṣ* in *4 Ezra* can mean *terra firma* contrasted with the sea (4.19, 21a; 6.42; cf. Gen. 1.9-10). It can be quaked and shaken as a response to God's acts

1. See Stone 1990: 1–11; Nickelsburg 2005: 270–7; *HJP* III, 294–306; Longenecker 1995: 13–16.
2. See Chapter 4 n. 87; § 7.3.2 above.
3. In this section I use the English translation of NRSV with modifications, otherwise noted.

(3.18f.; 10.26). It is expected that at the *eschaton* 'the foundations of the earth'[4] will tremble and be shaken (6.15f.), and be terrified (12.3).[5] It is assigned as a place holding dead bodies until it gives them back at the *eschaton* (7.32; cf. *1 En*. 51.1; *LAB* 3.10).

terra/*ʾ*ereṣ* is regarded as Mother Earth (5.48, 50), which can bring forth 'cattle, wild animals, and creeping things' (6.53), 'Adam' (7.116; cf. 6.54), 'mind' (7.62), and 'gold, silver, bronze, iron, lead and clay' (7.55; cf. 8.2). On the earth there are forests and trees, which are employed as a metaphor of nations (5.23f.).[6] In the image of mother *terra*/*ʾ*ereṣ* can be personified (7.54, 62; 8.2; 10.9). The personification culminates in its mourning over the perdition of its products (10.9-14). The earth as the mother of all mourns over the death of all living beings on her;[7] she herself is said to grow old (5.50-55; cf. 14.16).[8]

It is assumed that the earth was created by God (10.14; 11.46) by speech (3.4; 6.38, 43).[9] The Creation of heaven and earth was done on the first day (6.38; cf. Gen. 1.1; *Jub*. 2.2). Before the creation of the world the Paradise was planted by God's right hand (3.6; cf. Gen. 2.8; Ps. 80.16). The Paradise in *4 Ezra* functions not only as the Garden of Eden at the beginning of the world, but also as an eschatological reward for the righteous (7.36, 123; 8.52).[10] The idea that God prepared things pertaining to the *eschaton* before the Creation is manifested in 6.1-6 (similarly in 7.70).[11] Here the original phrase of Latin *terreni orbis* 'the terrestrial world' (6.1) is uncertain. Syriac reads ܐܪܥܗ ܕܬܒܠ. Possibly it might be taken from עפרות תבל (Prov. 8.26) or ארץ ותבל (Ps. 90.2), both biblical passages which refer to 'before' the Creation.[12] It is interestingly stated that the foundations of the earth themselves know their own fate at 'the end' (6.14-16).

The term *terra*/*ʾ*ereṣ* is employed in line with its inhabitants (6.24). In the vision of chs 11–12 the sovereignty of the eagle is to extend to both the earth and its inhabitants (11.5, 32, 34; 12.23f.). Its reign over 'the (whole) earth' (without reference to its inhabitants) is also mentioned, and in these cases the term represents the earthly human world (11.2, 12, 16, 41, 46). The repetitious reference to its sovereignty over the earth emphasizes the arrogance of the wicked kingdom (11.38-46) and the universal scale of the eschatological events.[13]

4. Cf. Chapter 2 n. 50 above.
5. See also 6.14; 9.3; cf. Mk 13.8 and Chapter 2 nn. 61–4 above.
6. See 8.4 (Latin alone); 9.34, in both of which *terra* is used with seeds, though the Hebrew original is uncertain whether ʾ*ereṣ* or ʾ*adāmâ*; see Stone 1990: 276.
7. See Stone 1990: 322; for the mourning of earth (ʾ*ereṣ*), cf. Isa. 24.4; Jer. 4.28; of the Land (ʾ*ereṣ*): Isa. 33.9; Jer. 12.4; 23.10; of the soil (ʾ*adāmâ*): Joel 1.10.
8. For the predetermination of the times of this world, see 4.36f.; 5.49; 6.5; 7.74; 11.44; 13.58; 14.9; in all these passages the term *saeculum* is used, but never *terra*; cf. also *Ass. Mos*. 12.4f.; *LAB* 3.10; 23.13; *2 Bar*. 56.2-4.
9. Cf. Pss. 33.6; 148.5; *LAB* 28.4; *2 Bar*. 14.17; 21.4; 48.8; see Stone 1990: 67, 183.
10. See Stone 1990: 68f.
11. See Stone 1990: 158 (and see below).
12. So Kahana 1969e: 622; Licht (1968: 34): ארץ תבל.
13. See Stone 1990: 348f.

Our term can represent the earthly world in contrast to the heavenly one (4.21; cf. 8.20f.). It can represent the world of the living on which living beings are dwelling (5.48). Human beings, therefore, can be called 'the inhabitants on/of the earth' (3.12, 35; 4.21, 39; 5.1, 6; 6.18, 26;[14] 7.72;[15] 8.17;[16] 10.59; 13.30), and 'those who are on the earth' (13.29, 52; cf. 11.6; 7.127). Mention is made of kingdoms on the earth, as well (12.13). At the *eschaton* 'unrighteousness and unrestraint shall increase on the earth' (5.10; cf. 14.17 [16]). The preposition Latin *super*/Syriac ܥܠ attached to *terra*/ܐܪܥܐ sometimes connotes a contrast with the heavenly world explicitly (4.21; 11.6) or implicitly (6.18, 26; 8.17; 12.13; 13.29, 30, 52), and once it contrasts with the netherworld (4.39, 41); at any rate these phrases involving the reference to *ʾereṣ* express the author's universal perspectives.

8.1.1.2. terra/regio/*ʾereṣ *as Land*

In *4 Ezra* the term *regio* appears eleven times, of which nine times Syriac has its equivalent; six times ܐܬܪܐ and three times ܐܪܥܐ. It is probably a translation of Greek *χώρα, which can go back to Hebrew **ʾereṣ*.[17]

Latin *regio*/Greek *χώρα represents another sense of Hebrew **ʾereṣ*, 'land', territorially defined. References are made to: 'one's own land' (13.33), 'that land' (5.3), and 'the land of their exile' (5.17). Once there appears a phrase *regionem vel locum* referring to the place from which the mountain in the vision was carved (13.7). *regio*/ܐܬܪܐ can be personified (5.11). It seems that once the Land is called 'the land of faith', which is said to be barren at the end of days (5.1).[18]

Along with *regio*, the term *terra* can refer to a 'land'. Its territorial dimension is manifested in its plural form. The phrase *omnibus terrarum orbis*/ ܠܟܠܗܝܢ ܐܪܥܬܐ ܕܬܒܝܠ 'all the lands of the world' in 5.24 may be ascribed to Hebrew *כל ארצות תבל.[19] The original expression of *foveam*/ܚܕ ܐܬܪܐ (pit/one region) at the end of this verse is unknown,[20] but the referent is certainly the Land of Israel. The Land is mentioned in 14.31: 'Then land was given to you for a possession in the land of Zion'. The implication of 'the land of Zion' is uncertain. It might be a reapplication of the fictional setting of the exile to the real historical situation of the author, who continues: 'And since He is a righteous judge, in due time He took from you what He had given' (14.32). What was taken from the people in 70 CE is not the Land as a whole, but 'Zion'.

14. Latin 6.26 lacks 'earth'.
15. Latin 7.72: *commorantes sunt in terram* instead of usual *inhabitant super terram*; Syriac: usual ܥܡܘܪܝܗ ܕܐܪܥܐ.
16. See Stone 1990: 267.
17. See Chapter 4 n. 87 above.
18. See Stone 1990: 106 n. d, 109.
19. So Kahana 1969e: 620; Licht 1968: 31.
20. See Stone 1990: 125 n. d.

The vision described in 13.12f. is interpreted in 13.39-50, in which the two terms *terra* and *regio* are used in the sense of land (*terra*: v. 40ab; *regio*: vv. 41, 42, 45).[21] This section expresses a traditional hope of the eschatological restoration of the twelve tribes by describing the fate of the lost ten tribes after the exile to the end (vv. 40-46a), their return (vv. 46b-47a) and the salvation of the remnant within 'My holy territory' (vv. 48-50). This expression probably reflects Hebrew *גבול קודשי (cf. Ps. 78.54). The salvation in 'My Land/territory' is repeated in 9.7-8 and 12.34, too. An eschatological role of the Land is depicted in 7.26, as well. The land here most probably refers to the heavenly Land of Israel, which is prepared from precreation, as suggested by 'hidden'.[22]

These four passages (13.48; 9.7f.; 12.34; 7.26) connect closely the survivors and the Land, though the connection is not congruous. It is stated in 13.48 that the survivors are the remnant of those who dwell in the Land, that is, a part of the Jews living in the real earthly Land of Israel. The remnant in 12.34 are also the dwellers of the earthly Land, since they are said to be saved in it. In 9.7f., however, the survivors are said to see God's salvation in the Land. Here it is ambiguous whether the Land is earthly or heavenly but hidden, both of which could be sanctified from the beginning (cf. 5.24; *LAB* 7.4; 19.10). Since the 'salvation' refers not to the survival itself, but to what the survivors will see, the Land here probably connotes the messianic one. The Land in 7.26 refers certainly to the heavenly one, as we've just noted. An image given by these passages is that faithful Jews living in the present Land will survive and enjoy the messianic kingdom in the eschatological Land. Then, the Land (***ʾ*ereṣ* or **gebûl*) conveys a double sense, the earthly and heavenly, or present and eschatological. By 'hidden', the author does not think of another spiritual land different from the present material Land.[23] What is hidden is not a tangible aspect, its location or border, but its essential status or order as the divine messianic territory. This double conception of the Land was perhaps caused by a gap between ideal and real: the Land must have been holy, sanctified from the beginning in ideality, but it was in reality ruled and oppressed by Romans; its true figure ought to have been disclosed at a proper time. This eschatological hope concerning the Land has some similarity to those in the Book of Dreams and *War Scroll* we saw above, but *4 Ezra* is nationalistic much more than they since it does not allow foreigners to survive; only faithful Jews in the Land and the remnant of the ten tribes of northern Israel who shall come back to the Land will enjoy the eschatological messianic kingdom (cf. 7.37). The nationalism and the double conception of the Land are in close connection with *4 Ezra*'s idea of the two worlds, which we shall see below.

21. The *terram aliam* 'another land' (13.40b) and 'Arzareth' (13.45) are likely translations of Hebrew *ארץ אחרת; see Stone 1990: 405; Kahana 1969e: 650 n. Retroversion of other occurrences: *terra sua* 'their land' (13.40a, 42): *ארצם; *ulteriorem regionem* 'a more distant region' (13.41): *ארץ רחוקה.

22. So Stone 1989: 102f.; 1990: 214.

23. See Stone 1989: 211–14, 222–5.

8.1.2. Related Terms

8.1.2.1. orbis/ܬܒܝܠ/*tēbēl

In 3.18 *orbis*/ܬܒܝܠ/**tēbēl* represents the 'inhabited world' in line with heaven, earth (*terra*), depths, and universe (*saeculum*).[24] In 5.23f., too, it is used in parallelism with *terra*. Here *orbis*, as well as *terra*, represents the earthly world on which lands and nations (= 'flowers') exist. In 9.20 the term *orbem meum*/ ܬܒܝܠ ܕܝܠܝ is used in parallelism with *saeculum meum*/ ܥܠܡܝ (cf. 6.25), both phrases which mean 'My (God's) world', denoting the human earthly world which is lost and in peril. These two expressions may be a unique development of the biblical idea that the earth is God's.[25] Here the cause of the loss and peril of the world is ascribed to human sinful actions, as in Gen. 6.11f. In 11.40, too, *orbis* is employed in parallelism with *saeculum*, representing the human earthly world which is held sway over with terror and grievous oppression by the wicked kingdom (the eagle).

The term *orbis*/ܬܒܝܠ/**tēbēl* is always used in parallelism with *terra*/ ܐܪܥ/*ʾ*ereṣ* and/or *saeculum*/ܥܠܡ/*ʿ*ôlām*; hence is a synonym of these two words. It is, however, never used in tangible senses of *ʾ*ereṣ*, nor in temporal senses of *ʿ*ôlām*. **tēbēl* is a cosmological term representing the earthly world.

8.1.2.2. saeculum/ܥܠܡ/*ʿôlām

The term *saeculum*/ܥܠܡ/*ʿ*ôlām* originally represents a temporal concept, but it can convey a spatial connotation from the first century CE on (Chapter 7 above). This spatial aspect can be discerned in its uses in *4 Ezra*, too. It can be used in line with heaven, earth (*terra*/*ʾ*ereṣ*), inhabited world (*orbis*/**tēbēl*) and the depths, all of which reacted to God's epiphany at Sinai (3.18; cf. *LAB* 32.7).[26] An earthquake *in saeculo*/**bāʿôlām* is expected as a sign of the *eschaton* (9.3f.). It can be reigned and held sway over by a human kingdom, as are *orbis*/**tēbēl* and *terra*/*ʾ*ereṣ* (11.38-42), hence represents the earthly world. It can represent the space on which human beings live. The death, therefore, can be expressed '(to) pass from the world' (4.24; 7.132; cf. *LAB* 50.7). It is stated that 'the world was made for them (those who exist now) to dwell in' (9.18). Accordingly, there are references to 'the inhabitants of the world' (3.9, 34; 7.74; 8.41, 50; 14.20). Since *saeculum*/*ʿ*ôlām* is a limited space, it cannot 'hold at one time those who have been created in it' (5.44).

It can also connote a temporal sense, as NRSV reads 'this age' in 4.27. This does not mean, however, that its spatial aspect diminishes whenever it connotes temporal aspects.[27] The term in 4.27 takes in view temporally all ages from Adam to the end, spatially – human actions in it. Conveying both spatial and temporal connotations, the term expresses a history of the earthly world. Concerning the temple cult, it is stated, 'there were three thousand years in the world (*in saeculo*/**bāʿôlām*) before any offering was offered in it' (10.45). Here the endurance of the world

24. For the translation of *saeculum* here as 'universe', see Stone 1990: 72.
25. Cf. Chapter 2 n. 91; Chapter 6 n. 33 above.
26. For the spatial connotation of *saeculum* here, see Stone 1990: 72.
27. See Stone 1989: 179, 275 n. 433; 1990: 90.

is presupposed in a manner somewhat similar to the biblical expression ‘the days of the earth’.[28] A consciousness of history is discernible in such passages as 9.5 and 14.22. Even times of precreation are imagined: ‘there was a time in this age (*saeculi*/**bā*ʿ*ôlām*) when I was preparing for those who now exist, before the world (*saeculum*/**hā*ʿ*ôlām*) was made for them to dwell in’ (9.[17-]18). Although the exact sense of *saeculi* translated here as ‘this age’ is unclear, it seems to me to connote something like ‘(world-) history’, which expresses continuous times with affairs in them.[29] The reference to the ‘end’ of *saeculum*/**hā*ʿ*ôlām* (6.25; 7.113; cf. *Ass. Mos*. 12.4) certainly conveys temporal as well as spatial connotations distinct from ‘the end of earth (ʾ*ereṣ*)’ which is geographical or spatial alone.

As the latter half of 9.18 shows, the term can be used in relation to God’s Creation.[30] In this passage the purpose of Creation is said to be ‘for those who now exist’, all creation (cf. 8.44; *2 Bar*. 14.17-19), while in other passages it is specifically connected to the people of Israel.[31] In this respect Ezra asks God, ‘If the world has indeed been created for us, why do we not take possession of our world?’ (6.59). Then the answer of angel Uriel is given in 7.11-13. In this passage two ideas are expressed: (1) a nationalistic sentiment that the Creation of the world is for the sake of Israel; (2) human sins because of which God prepared another world. The ideas depicted here are not easily compatible with other passages in which a different soteriology appears. As for (1) there is a more general universalistic view of human beings, such as ‘the righteous’ and ‘the ungodly’ (e.g., 7.17f., 51). In respect to (2) mention is made of predetermination of the two worlds before the Creation (e.g., 6.1-6; 7.70). Thus, there are two contradictory ideas in *4 Ezra*’s eschatology: national or universal soteriology, and the world to come as God’s predetermination or as a result of human sins. It is not our task to discuss the problems in full scale;[32] we must satisfy ourselves with limited treatment of them as far as our terms are concerned. We shall begin with the second issue.

The idea of the ‘two’ worlds is most explicitly stated in 7.50. This idea can be expressed by the reference to the end of this world and the beginning of the world to come. It is stated that the survivors ‘shall see My salvation and the end of My world’ (6.25; cf. 9.20; 11.39). At the end ‘the Most High is about to visit the world that He has made’ (9.2; cf. 11.44).[33] The end of this world is the beginning of the world to come (7.112f.).[34] The details of the end and the beginning are described in 7.30f. The corruption of this world is manifestly expressed in 4.11 as ‘the corrupt

28. Cf. Chapter 2 n. 68 above and *LAB* 3.9. Hebrew ימים ‘days’ is close to ‘history’, as shown by the expressions אחרית הימים and קץ הימים.

29. See the previous note; cf. Holtz (1980: 110), who proposes ‘Geschichte’ as a translation of Greek αἰών; see also Stone 1989: 179, 275 n. 435; 1990: 298f.

30. 6.1, 55, 59; 7.11, 70; 8.1; 9.2.

31. 6.55, 59; 7.11; cf. *Ass. Mos*. 1.12; *LAB* 39.7.

32. See Stone 1990: 193–5, 204–6, 299f.

33. Cf. God’s visit to *ʾ*ereṣ*/*ʾ*ara*ʿ: *1 En*. 25.3; 90.20; 1QS 3.14, 18; 4.18f.; CD 7.9//19.5f.; *Ps. Sol*. 15.12; *LAB* 1.20; 26.13; to **tēbēl*: *LAB* 19.13; to *ʿ*ôlām*: *LAB* 19.12; *4 Ezra* 9.2; *2 Bar*. 20.2.

34. For textual problems of this passage, see Stone 1989: 59f., 246f. nn. 75–82; 1990: 247f.

world'.[35] The corruptibility of this world can be expressed in its personification: 'The world (*saeculum*/*ʿ*ôlām*) has lost its youth, and the times begin to grow old. For the world-age (*saeculum*/*ʿ*ôlām*) is divided into twelve parts, and nine of its parts have already passed, as well as a half of the tenth part' (14.10-12; cf. 5.49-55; 4.44-50).[36] Although the reading 'twelve' is uncertain (Eth.: 'ten'), the general idea that the world is passing away is discernible from 4.26 and 6.20.[37] The old age of the world affects its inhabitants (14.17 [16]; cf. 5.54f.). That the world has fixed time assumes that God predetermines the existence of the two worlds. God's preparation of the final judgement before the Creation is explicitly stated in 7.70 (cf. 6.1-6). The number of those destined to be created is predetermined, as well (4.36). If the existence of the two worlds is predestined, it is God's plan unaffected by human actions.

As we've seen above, however, there is another view that because of Adam's sins this world was to be judged (7.11-13). A similar understanding is repeated in 9.17-22. In this passage it is explicitly stated that although the world had been created good enough, it was lost because of human actions (cf. *LAB* 28.4). Thus, the two ideas of the cause of the end of this world, God's predetermination and human sins, coexist in *4 Ezra* without being systematized. Even in a single section these two can coexist (4.26-32). Since human sins play an important role throughout *4 Ezra* and God's predestination is explicitly stated here and there, it is not wise to choose the one as essential and the other as insignificant.

Beneath the coexistence of contradictory ideas there might be different issues of the author of *4 Ezra*. His central concerns must be the destruction of Jerusalem in 70 CE. Admitting a cause of the disaster to be the sins of Israel (3.25-27), he is not ready to accept the event simply as God's punishment through a foreign nation, unlike the biblical prophets (e.g., Jeremiah 25), probably because the destroyer, Rome, is worse, and probably because Israel is no longer a monolithic religious community in his eyes (see below). He, therefore, has Ezra ask God 'Is Babylon better than Israel?' (3.28). This question requires the author to consider human sins, sins of Israel and of nations, both of which root in Adam (3.7, 8, 12, 20, 21f.). The answer to the problems the author gives is eschatological reward of 'the world to come' for the righteous. It presupposes a theodicy that God must be just. On the other hand, Jewish theology includes God's almightiness being beyond human knowledge. God's ability contains his perfect foreknowledge. Then, the reward for the righteous must be prepared from the outset. Thus, the two ideas, human sins as the cause of disaster and God's predestination of the two worlds, must coexist in one book. The author does not try to systematize the two ideas, no more than did Rabbi Aqiva ('all is foreordained but free will is granted' [*m. Abot* 3.15]), but pursues his central concerns legitimating Jewish theological presuppositions.

The first problem, that is, the contradiction of national and universal soteriology, is also related to the two worlds eschatology. We have mentioned above that there

35. Cf. 7.15, 96, 111; 8.34; 14.13.

36. For *saeculum* here, see Stone 1989: 179f.

37. Cf. *Apoc. Abr.* 29.1f.

are two ideas on the purpose of the Creation; for the sake of Israel (7.11) and for the sake of humans generally (9.18; cf. 8.44). In addition to these passages we must consider the passages contrasting 'many' with 'few' (7.45-61; 8.1, 3). The crucial point is who the 'few' are. To obtain a good insight it is beneficial to discuss the expression 'the inhabitants of the earth/world' which occurs frequently throughout *4 Ezra*.[38]

This expression refers to all ungodly human beings except Noah at the Flood (3.9), and all but Abraham after it (3.12). It can denote all sinful nations other than Israel (3.34, 35). It is used in contrast to heavenly existence, expressing the limitation of human ability (4.21; 13.52).

Many other occurrences are found in the eschatological context. In the vision of the evil king the expression refers to all human beings living at the end time (5.1, 6; cf. 14.17 [16]). No redemption is depicted. Similarly in the vision of God's visitation (6.18-28) the expression refers to all human beings without discrimination (vv. 18, 24). In 6.26, however, 'the earth's inhabitants'[39] are equated with 'whoever remains' who 'shall be saved and shall see My salvation and the end of My world' (v. 25). The wording 'and shall see My salvation' is exactly the same as in 9.8, in which the salvation in the Land is described (see p. 176 above).

In the fifth vision the expression signifies all human beings whom the eagle will reign over and oppress in the last days (10.59; 11.5, 6, 32, 34). Since the eagle (= Rome) is condemned by the lion (= messiah), the 'inhabitants of the earth' are somewhat sympathized with by the author.

In the interpretation of the sixth vision the expression appears twice (13.29, 30). Its referent in these two verses must be different. The former are delivered, while the latter are bewildered. As is indicated by the next verses, that refer to their making war, 'those who dwell on the earth' of v. 30 can be identified with 'all the nations' (v. 33, cf. v. 31) and 'assembled nations' whom 'My Son will reprove for their ungodliness' (v. 37). In contrast, 'those who are upon the earth' of v. 29 are identical with the survivors 'who fall into peril, who have works and faith towards the Almighty' (v. 23) and the ten tribes of Israel and the survivors in the Land (vv. 39-48). The passage 13.29f. is actually rephrased in 13.49: 'Therefore when He destroys the multitude of the nations that are gathered together, He will defend the people who remain.' Then 'those who are upon the earth' who will be delivered in v. 29 are almost identical with 'those who are upon the Land' (Hebrew *ʾereṣ* can mean both). While the expression itself keeps universal appearances, the connotation can be nationalistic. Although the text is at first glance ambiguous, one who reads the chapter through will understand this implication.

In 9.19 there appears the expression 'those who have been created in this world'. The context rushes from the precreation to the *eschaton* (9.17-22). Before the Creation, no one opposed God since no one existed; but now the created humans have corrupted; therefore God saved 'one grape' and 'one plant' (v. 21; cf. *LAB*

38. Cf. Chapter 7 nn. 30f. above.
39. The 'earth's' according to Syriac; Latin lacks it.

28.4). The following verse clearly identifies the 'those who have been created' of v. 19 with 'the multitude born in vain', all humans but 'My grape' (v. 22); the imagery of 'grape' denotes Israel (cf. 5.23).

In 8.41, 'those who have been sown in the world will not all be saved', the 'those' refers to all human beings in the entire history. Here the few–many contrast is evident. Similarly, in 8.50f. a distinction is made between 'those who inhabit the world' who 'walked in great pride' and 'those who are like you (Ezra)'.

In 7.72-74 the expression is related to the 'Law'. In this passage the use of 'iniquity', 'commandments' and the 'Law' must indicate the Torah observance, and 'those who live on earth' are all human beings in the history of the world. The Torah is given not only to Israel but also to Gentiles in *4 Ezra*.[40] It is evident that all who are disobedient to the Torah, without discrimination between Israel and Gentiles, will be punished. The angel states: 'this is the significance of the contest that all who are born on earth shall wage: if they are defeated they shall suffer what you have said, but if they are victorious they shall receive what I have said' (7.127f.). The struggle which all mankind must wage is the one against evil thought within one's own heart (7.92). Here the stress is laid on free will and human responsibility for deeds. The angel's responses are contrasted to the assumption of Ezra, who asks him, 'who among the living is there that has not sinned?' (7.46; cf. 3.20-22, 26; 4.38). Ezra accounts himself within 'those who inhabit the earth' who have sins (4.39; but see 7.76; 8.47). Thus, Ezra considers that mankind cannot escape from sins (cf. Rom. 5.12). The angel, however, rejects the idea and tells him that men should conquer the evil thought.[41] A similar argument continues in 7.132–8.3; Ezra insists that 'if He did not make His compassions abound, the world with those who inhabit it would not have life' (7.137), and then the angel answers him: 'the Most High made this world for the sake of many, but the world to come for the sake of only a few ... Many have been created, but only a few shall be saved' (8.1, 3). The angel's response is decisive; this world and many who inhabit it shall not have life in the world to come.

The expression 'the inhabitants of the earth/world' (and related expressions) is ambiguous. While its universal appearances are definite, sometimes it can be nationalistic. Is there indeed a contradiction between universalism and nationalism? The answer seems to me to be 'no'.

The universalistic character may be found in the 'many–few' distinction. Its criterion is ungodly or righteous in the light of Torah obedience. Then, the Gentiles have no hope for salvation from the outset, except some individuals who voluntarily keep the Law (3.36).[42] But if so, what does the generalized expression intend? Generalization, in my opinion, does not mean de-nationalism, but individualization of the people of Israel. Although the author of *4 Ezra* admits the sins of Israel as a cause of the destruction of the Second Temple, he presupposes ungodliness of the

40. Cf. 3.32-36; 7.21-24, 46, 79, 81, 83, 89, 94, 127f., 133; 14.20f.

41. See Stone 1990: 257, 259f.

42. The author may have 'proselytes' in his mind; see *2 Bar*. 42.5; cf. *Ant*. 20.75-96.

nations. If Israel must be judged, how much more the nations. In reality, however, Jerusalem is plundered and the Roman Empire prospers. Here arises the matter of theodicy; God shall bring great salvation to Israel, annihilating the ungodly nations. Then, the author reconsiders that the disaster is not God's punishment against Israel but an ordeal for salvation (7.12-16). Jews who remain in the Torah even in this hard situation shall be saved; but if they abandon it, they shall be judged. The nationality of Israel is no longer a guarantee of salvation; each Jew must choose of his own free will whether to remain faithful to the Torah or not, whether to follow the ways to salvation or the ways to destruction. If they leave the Torah, they will be regarded the same as the Gentiles. Thus the 'many' who shall be judged represents the Gentiles and disobedient Jews, and the 'few' who shall be saved refers to obedient Jews (and proselytes?),[43] who are the 'survivors' in the Holy Land.[44] The eschatological visions pertaining to the Land and to the world to come are systematized in 7.26-44: the heavenly Land shall appear and the messiah shall establish his kingdom in it for 400 years; then after seven days' silence, the world to come will be awake, the dead will be resurrected and judged.

Accordingly, we do not have to assume a nationalism–universalism contradiction in *4 Ezra*. There is a kind of individualism predicated upon nationalism. The individualism requires generalization since it is in relation to human free will, which distinguishes the righteous and ungodly. The generalization results in a universalism, which involves worldwide catastrophe, since the foreign nations must be annihilated. The universalism based on the nationalistic individualism gains historical scope over all human beings from Adam to the last survivors, on the one hand, over cosmology from this world to the world to come, on the other. The world is no longer a spatial concept alone, but also historical; a new concept which requires a new term, **ʿôlām*.

The individualism of *4 Ezra* is similar to the sectarianism of the Qumran Community. Both do not admit salvation to the people of Israel as a whole. They distinguish Jews and nations, on the one hand, faithful Jews and sinful, on the other. In *4 Ezra*, however, sectarian consciousness is inconspicuous. The distinction within Jews is dependent on one's free will, and who will be the 'few' or the 'many' seems not to be predestined. *4 Ezra* does not require his readers to separate from the people. Rather Ezra is a leader of the people (5.16-18; 12.40-45), and encourages them (12.46-50; 14.13-48). *4 Ezra* does not represent an individualism without ethnic distinction, a universalism promising salvation to all humans, a nationalism pursuing political independence, or a sectarianism separating from others; but it does represent a Juda-*ism*, Jewish individualism, pursuing the Torah oriented ways of life in a perfect manner. It is a response to the national disaster with cosmological theodicy.

43. See the previous note.
44. The 'survivors' may doubly connote the survivors of the war and of the faith.

8.1.2.3. hereditas/*naḥalâ – hereditare/*yāraš

The term *hereditas*/ܝܪܬܘܬܐ is highly probably a translation of Greek *κληρονομία which is an equivalent to Hebrew **naḥalâ*,[45] and its verbal form *hereditare* and *hereditatem possidere* (both ܝܪܬ in Syriac) render Greek *κληρονομεῖν which reflects Hebrew **yāraš*.[46] The noun is employed to refer to the people of Israel (8.16, 45).

hereditas/**naḥalâ* is applied through the metaphor of 'allotment' of a city in 7.9. This parable is sandwiched between Ezra's question, 'why do we not take possession of our world? (6.59), and the angel's answer, 'So also is Israel's portion (*pars*/**ḥēleq*)' (7.10), which is followed by the explanation of the two worlds (7.11-16). The nouns 'allotment' (**naḥalâ*) and 'portion' (**ḥēleq*) and the verb 'take possession of' (**yāraš*) are technical terms in the biblical Land theology.[47] They are here reapplied to the eschatological possession of the world to come by Jews who remain in the Torah. The biblical expression ירש את הארץ is reinterpreted as *ירש את העולם (6.59; cf. *LAB* 32.3).[48] The alteration of this biblical traditional expression may reflect a disappointment in this world in the face of the national crisis.

8.1.3. Summary

The term *terra*/ܐܪܥܐ/**ʾereṣ* in *4 Ezra* frequently refers to the tangible 'earth'. It can represent the space created by God for living beings. It is frequently personified as Mother Earth, and as the earthly world terrified by the last wicked kingdom. In many occurrences the term is utilized in relation to eschatological events; earthquake at the *eschaton*, Mother Earth to be now 'old', and the earth as a depository of dead bodies until the end. The term expresses the universal scale of eschatological events. Accordingly, the term **ʾereṣ* represents both the beginning and the end of creation. In other words, *4 Ezra* utilizes the traditional biblical Creation theology in its cosmological eschatology. Nevertheless, **ʾereṣ* in the sense of 'earth' itself is never applied to be a direct object of the eschatological hopes.

Instead, another term, *saeculum*/ܥܠܡܐ/**ʿôlām*, plays a significant role in *4 Ezra*'s eschatology. It can be used as a synonym of **ʾereṣ* and **tēbēl*, hence it connotes a spatial aspect of the world. It can, however, also convey a temporal connotation, though with limitation. Accordingly, the expression 'the end of **hāʿôlām*' is applicable and signifies 'the end of the world'. The 'end of this world' does not mean the beginning of the 'spiritual world', as scholars of earlier generations assumed, for the earth (**ʾereṣ*) must be continually existing in order to give back the dead bodies

45. See Chapter 4 n. 99 above.
46. See Chapter 7 n. 176 above.
47. For the same use of this verb, see 7.17 and 7.96; cf. Chapter 2 nn. 204–10 above.
48. Cf. Chapter 7 n. 167 above.

for resurrection after the world to come awakes (7.30-32). This makes a difference between *ʾ*ereṣ* and *ʿ*ôlām*. The latter can connote a temporal sense and can utterly pass away (4.26); the former, while it can grow old (5.50-55) and 'be changed' at the end (6.16), cannot cease to exist as far as the resurrected will have their own bodies. Thus, the semantic fields of the two terms partially overlap, but *ʾ*ereṣ* lacks the temporal connotation of *ʿ*ôlām*. If the earth (*ʾ*ereṣ*) continues to exist in the realm of salvation, it would not be enough to express the complete newness of the eschatological world to come. This can be a reason that a soteriological expression ירש את הארץ, which expresses a traditional hope either of the Land possession or of the eschatological possession of the earth, is replaced by *ירש את העולם.

The term *ʾ*ereṣ* (*terra*/*regio* and ܐܪܥܐ/ܐܬܪܐ) can be used in the sense of a land, territorially defined. Its occurrences are not very many, but on some occasions it plays a significant role in *4 Ezra*'s eschatology. The Land is called 'My holy territory' and those who shall be saved are 'the survivors of the Land'. A reference is made to 'the hidden land', which is the heavenly Land assigned to the locale of the messianic kingdom, in which the twelve tribes of Israel shall be restored.

The eschatological views concerning the world to come and the Land are systematized. Then, the terminological confusion of *ʾ*ereṣ* disappears; it represents the Land, while *ʿ*ôlām* expresses the world, in the eschatological expectations. The two traditional Jewish hopes, the possession of the Land and of the world, both of which have been expressed by the same term *ʾ*ereṣ*, can now be formulated in distinct terms. While such uses of *ʿ*ôlām* as 'this world' and 'the world to come', 'the end of the world' and 'to take possession of the world' are known from the pre-70 CE writings (the Similitudes, *Assumption of Moses*, and Pseudo-Philo), *4 Ezra* is one of the earliest works to make a clear distinction on the terminology of *ʾ*ereṣ* and *ʿ*ôlām*.

8.2. 2 Baruch

2 Baruch, known from a Syriac version, is a translation from Greek, which must have been translated from Hebrew.[49] Palestine around 100 CE is widely accepted as its composition.[50] The Syriac ܐܪܥ is equivalent to Hebrew *ʾereṣ* and ܥܠܡ to *ʿôlām*.

49. Hebrew (or Semitic) as the original language is favoured by Charles 1913: 472–4; Kahana 1969d: 364; *HJP* III, 753; Klijn 1983: 616; Nickelsburg 2005: 283; Greek origin is favoured by Bogaert 1969: I, 378–80.

50. Bogaert 1969: I, 272–80, 294–319; *HJP* III, 753; Klijn 1983: 616f.; Stone 1984: 410; Sayler 1984: 103–10; Nickelsburg 2005: 283. The text of *2 Baruch* in this section is of The Peshitta Institute (1973); the English translation is of Klijn (1983) with modifications, otherwise noted.

8.2.1. ܐܪܥ/*ʾereṣ *in* 2 Baruch

8.2.1.1. ܐܪܥ/*ʾereṣ *as Earth*

The term ܐܪܥ/**ʾereṣ* in *2 Baruch* can signify the *terra firma*, in which the dead are sleeping (11.4, 6; 21.24) until it gives them back at the *eschaton* (50.2; cf. 42.8).[51] The earth holds the dead bodies intact until the end, and when they are resurrected, their shape will be changed (ch. 51). It is also assigned to keep the sacred things till the end (6.6-10; cf. 2 Macc. 1.18–2.18; *LAB* 16.12-15).[52] This passage utilizes the call to *ʾereṣ* in Jer. 22.29, in which the term probably refers to 'the Land'. Here, however, the tangible and stable aspect of 'earth' is taken up, and the biblical expression 'the earth opened its mouth and swallowed them up' (Num. 16.32) is employed.[53]

The term is twice used with a demonstrative pronoun in the sense of 'this earth' (76.2f.). The demonstrative pronoun here makes a contrast, not between this earth and a new earth,[54] but between the earth on which living beings exist and another place where Baruch shall be kept until the end.[55] The term ܐܪܥ/**ʾereṣ* here is materially perceived as a space in which habitable world (ܬܒܝܠ/**tēbēl*), mountains, depths and rivers exist. In this passage the farewell scene of Moses in Deut. 34.1-3 is imitated, but Moses goes up to the mountain to see 'the Land' (*hāʾareṣ*), while Baruch goes to see 'the earth' (**hāʾāreṣ*).

The productivity of plants of ܐܪܥ/**ʾereṣ* is presupposed (10.9; 22.5), and it is expected that the earth will yield fruits ten thousandfold in the messianic age (29.5),[56] though it is unclear whether the original Hebrew was **ʾereṣ* or **ʾadāmâ*.[57]

The term ܐܪܥ/**ʾereṣ* can be employed in relation to God's Creation (21.4, 8). The pair 'heaven and earth' can be called as a witness (19.1; 84.2).[58] An image of a cloud and rains with various colours in it over the earth is applied to describe a vision, in which the rains metaphorically denote the fate of the earthly world from the beginning to the end (the vision in ch. 53, and its interpretation in chs 56–74). In the vision the term ܐܪܥ/**ʾereṣ* is employed to express the tangible earth in contrast to cloud, rains and lightning,[59] while in the interpretation the term ܥܠܡ/**ʿôlām* is used to depict the world (see below).

51. Cf. *1 En.* 51.1; *LAB* 3.10; *4 Ezra* 7.32.
52. See Nir 2003: 43–77.
53. Cf. Chapter 2 n. 83 above.
54. In *2 Baruch* there is no idea of 'a new earth', but of 'a new world' (e.g. 44.12; see below).
55. It may be something to do with 'the earths which have not yet come' (59.9), though the connotation of plural ܐܪܥܬܐ here is uncertain.
56. Cf. *1 En.* 10.19; Irenaeus, *Adv. Haer.* 5.33.3-4.
57. Once an expression ܡܥܪܬܐ ܕܐܪܥܐ appears in 21.1, of which, however, the original Hebrew is uncertain whether **ʾereṣ* or **ʾadāmâ*. This expression itself is unique. It may imply 'a cave under the ground', since it locates in the valley of Kidron (so Muraoka 1976: 95).
58. Cf. Deut. 4.26; 30.19; 31.28.
59. 53.2, 3, 8, 9, 10; 56.3, 5.

There are relatively frequent references to 'the inhabitants of the earth' in the eschatological context.[60] There once appears an expression 'sinners on the earth', who have rejected the multitude of the goodness and have despised the great punishment (55.2). In these passages 'the inhabitants of the earth' represent the unrighteous who shall be judged (see below).

The earth can be personified (70.2, 10), and represent its inhabitants (13.11). It is utilized to express the universal scale of the eschatological events.[61]

Once an idiomatic phrase 'the way of the whole earth' is used in relation to human mortality (44.2).[62]

8.2.1.2. ܐܪܥܐ/*ʾereṣ *as Land*

The term ܐܪܥܐ/*ʾ*ereṣ* can refer to 'a land', territorially defined: 'the land of Egypt' (58.1). Babylon is once called 'O land that which is happy' (12.1), though the declaration of its decline follows immediately thereafter (12.2-4).

Mention is made of the Land several times. In the interpretation of the vision of coloured rains the Land of the time of David and Solomon 'was praised above all lands' (61.7). In the retelling of Hezekiah's time it is stated that 'all those who were in the Holy Land (ܐܪܥܐ ܡܩܕܫܬܐ/ *הארץ הקדושה) rejoiced' (63.10). Josiah is praised on account that 'he purified the Land from the idols' (66.2; cf. 2 Kgs 23.4-25). These passages express the highest status of the Land above all lands and its holiness and purity.[63]

The Land is mentioned in relation to the Exile at the beginning and towards the end of *2 Baruch*, in which the fate of Zion and the Land is connected with the Torah observance of the people (3.5f.; 77.8-10, 15f.). In the letter to the nine and a half tribes (chs 78–87) Baruch again reminds them of Zion, the Land and the Torah (84.8). Baruch appeals to the importance of the Law by comparing the former generations to his age (85.1-4). *2 Baruch* emphasizes the Torah observant life till the *eschaton*.

The Land is also mentioned in the eschatological context. The eschatological events will happen not only in one place but 'on the whole earth' (ܒܟܠܗ̇ ܗ̇ܝ ܐܪܥܐ), but the inhabitants 'in this Land' (ܒܗܕܐ ܐܪܥܐ) will be protected (28.7–29.2). Similarly, we can see a contrast between 'the whole earth' and 'the Holy Land' in 70.10–71.1,[64] and so the frequent expression 'the inhabitants of the earth' we've seen above is also distinguished from 'the inhabitants of the Land'.

The devastation of the real Land, which forms a framework of the entire *2 Baruch* (3.5; 77.9), is contrasted with the eschatological protection of the Jews in the Holy Land. In other words, the author expects an eschatological reversal of fate; Jews in the Land are now afflicted by foreign nations, but in the end the devastated

60. 25.1, 3; 27.15; 48.32, 40; 54.1; see also 51.15; 56.15.

61. 25.4; 28.7–29.1; 73.2.

62. Cf. Josh. 23.14; 1 Kgs 2.2.

63. Cf. 71.1; 84.8; 2 Macc. 1.7; *LAB* 19.10; *4 Ezra* 9.7f.; 13.48.

64. Therefore, Syriac ܕܝܢ in 29.2 and 71.1 should be translated as 'but', not 'for' or 'and' as Charles (1913) and Klijn (1983) have.

Land shall be holy and Jews in it be protected, while the 'inhabitants of the earth' shall perish. The same idea of eschatological protection is repeated in 40.2, too.[65] In 32.1 the protected are designated as the observant of the Torah. This does not contradict the idea of protection by the Land. Torah observance is a main theme throughout *2 Baruch*, and the author requires his readers in the Land to do so. Thus, the Torah observant in the Land will be protected at the eschatological disturbance; the author encourages Jews in the Land to keep the Law.[66] Concerning those who will be saved, it is stated that the apostates have only this world, but the proselytes will have eternal life (42.4-8).[67] As for the Gentiles, *2 Baruch* permits some foreign nations to survive in the messianic age, though to be subjected to Israel (72.4f.); a view different from other Jewish literature from the first century CE, in which all the foreign nations are expected to be annihilated by a messiah.[68]

8.2.2. ܥܠܡ/*ʿôlām *in* 2 Baruch

The term ܥܠܡ/*ʿ*ôlām* can be used in a spatial sense as well as a temporal one in *2 Baruch*, as in *4 Ezra*.[69] It can refer to the world of the living, into which one comes (3.1; 48.15), and which one leaves when he dies (14.2, 13a). Mention is made of 'the beginning of the world' (21.4) in relation to God's Creation by word (cf. 14.17; 48.8).[70] It was in silence before the Creation (3.7).[71] The 'length (or duration) of the world' is fixed from the beginning (56.2-4).[72] God's foreknowledge of world history is assumed (54.1: 'the days of the world').[73]

The 'world' is a place created for its inhabitants (14.17-19; cf. *4 Ezra* 9.18). The phrase 'Your world' in 14.18 expresses the idea that this world is God's.[74] Concerning men for whom the world was created, a further statement is made: 'the world has come on their (the righteous ones') account, yes, also that which is coming is on their account. For this world is to them a struggle and an effort with

65. Cf. *LAB* 7.4; *4 Ezra* 13.48f.

66. *Pace*: Bogaert (1969: I, 335–52) who argues that *2 Baruch* was written for a diaspora Jewry. The addressee of *2 Baruch*, however, must have been in the Land; those who will be protected have to be in the Land 'at that time' (29.2; 71.1), and the author of *2 Baruch* seems to expect the end drawing near (20.1; 23.7; 83.1; 85.10); then, they cannot be saved if living in diaspora. Nevertheless, the author does not require 'the nine and a half tribes', the addressee of the letter, to return to the Land (cf. 77.6; 78.7).

67. Cf. *4 Ezra* 3.36 and n. 42 above.

68. Cf. Charles 1913: 518 n.

69. We do not discern between spatial and temporal uses, since the term connotes both simultaneously; for uses in the purely temporal sense of 'forever', see 5.2; 6.9; 32.4; 40.3; 43.1; 44.12; 59.2; 66.6; 78.6; for the plural ܥ̈ܠܡܐ with *seyame*, 'ages', see 48.2; 54.3; 59.8.

70. Cf. Pss. 33.6, 9; 148.5; Wis. 9.1; Jdt. 16.14; *LAB* 28.4; *4 Ezra* 3.4; 6.38, 43.

71. Cf. *LAB* 60.2; *4 Ezra* 7.30.

72. Cf. *Ass. Mos.* 12.4f.; *LAB* 3.10; 23.13; *4 Ezra* 4.36f.; 5.49; 6.5; 7.74; 11.44; 13.58; 14.9.

73. The text ܪܘܡܘܗܝ ܕܐܪܥܐ must be a corruption of ܝܘܡܘܗܝ ܕܐܪܥܐ; this expression shows a unique development of the biblical ימי הארץ.

74. Cf. 56.2; 83.2; *4 Ezra* 9.20.

much trouble. And that accordingly which will come, a crown with great glory' (15.7f.; cf. 21.24).

This world, it is said, is filled with 'judgment, condemnations, contentions, revenges, blood, passions, zeal, hate, and all such things' (73.4f.), and 'those who pass away will be polluted by the great wickedness in this world' (21.19). It is called 'the world of corruption' (40.3),[75] 'this passing world' (48.50), and 'this world of affliction' (51.14). It is stated that 'the youth of this world has passed away' (85.10),[76] and that 'the days are coming and it will happen when the time of the world has ripened' (70.2). References are made to 'the end of the world' (54.21; 69.4; 83.7);[77] 'there is one Law by One, one world and an end for all those who exist' (85.14). As for this corruptible world, 'everything will pass away which is corruptible' (44.9). Although the corruptible world will pass away, 'the world will not be forgotten' (4.1), that is, what is not corruptible in the world will survive.

At the *eschaton* God will 'visit the world' (20.2),[78] and 'judge those who are in His world' (83.2; cf. 56.2). At the end the world will be renewed.[79] The renewal is applied to 'the whole world' (69.1). It will happen in the messianic age (73.1).

The renewed world is variously called: 'the world which You promised' (14.13); 'the undying world which is promised' (51.3); 'that world which has no end' (48.50; cf. *LAB* 34.3); 'that world which is now invisible to them' (51.8); 'that world' (51.10); 'the new world' (44.12; cf. *LAB* 23.8); and 'the world to come' (44.15; cf. *4 Ezra* 7.47). Mention is once made of 'both worlds' (83.8). The righteous in the new world 'will live in the heights of that world and they will be like angels and be equal to the stars' (51.10; cf. *1 En.* 51.4), and the world is the one 'that does not make those who come to it older' (51.16). Baruch explains to the people the significance of the future in 44.8-15. The world to come is conceived both spatially ('enter into' [44.12]) and temporally ('the promised time' [44.13]). It is worthwhile to note that the verb 'to take possession of' (ܝܪܬ/*ירש) and the noun 'allotment' (ܝܪܬܘܬܐ/**naḥalâ*) are applied to 'the time' in v. 13 (cf. *LAB* 32.3). The term 'promise' can be used with 'time' (44.13), as well as 'world', as we've seen above (14.13; 51.3). This means that the spatial connotation of the term *ʿ*ôlām* becomes manifest, and the purely temporal term ܙܒܢܐ/*זמן gains a theological significance of 'promise'.[80] In addition, the verb 'give' is employed with 'the world to come' (44.15). These terms, apparently derived from the biblical Land theology, are reapplied in *2 Baruch* to the eschatological hope of *העולם הבא.

75. Cf. *LAB* 28.10; *4 Ezra* 4.11.

76. Cf. *4 Ezra* 5.50-55; 14.10-16.

77. Cf. *Ass. Mos.* 12.4; *LAB* 9.3; *4 Ezra* 6.25; 7.113.

78. See n. 33 above.

79. 32.6; 49.3; 57.2; cf. chs 29–30; 51; 74.

80. *2 Bar.* 27.1 presupposes the division of 12 parts of this world-age, as in *4 Ezra* 14.11f., but the latter uses *saeculum*, whereas the former has ܙܒܢܐ ܗܘ.

There appears the term ܬܒܝܠ/**tēbēl* in 76.3. It represents the inhabited world in line with 'the mountains, and the depths of the valleys, and the depths of the seas, and the number of rivers' all of which are found in the earth.

In 3.7 the Syriac text has ܨܒܬܐ 'ornament', which must be a mistranslation of Greek *κόσμος. Since it appears in parallelism with ܥܠܡ/*αἰών/*ʿ*ôlām*, its original Hebrew is probably **tēbēl* (cf. *Ass. Mos*. 1.14).

8.2.3. Summary

The term ܐܪܥ/*ʾ*ereṣ* in *2 Baruch* expresses the tangible and cosmological earth. It represents a half part of what is most stable among creation; hence it can survive the eschatological disasters. Its eschatological roles, however, are very limited. It is assigned as the location of the universal eschatological events, which will involve its inhabitants, and as the depository of the dead bodies intact until the end. It is never employed in eschatological hopes.

In contrast, another sense of the term, the Land, plays a significant role. In the review of Israel's history its special status above all lands is emphasized. It is called the Holy Land, of which its inhabitants alone shall be protected from the eschatological catastrophe. The earth (*ʾ*ereṣ*) represents the location of judgement of the unrighteous Gentiles, on the other hand, the Land (*ʾ*ereṣ*) is chosen as a site of the eschatological salvation.

In the eschatological visions of *2 Baruch* another term ܥܠܡ/*ʿ*ôlām* plays a significant role, as in *4 Ezra*. There is a clear idea of 'this world' and 'the world to come'. The 'world' is not only a location of eschatological events, but an object of universal soteriology. The two traditional soteriologies expressed by the term *ʾ*ereṣ*, the one universal and the other territorial, are now expressed by two distinct expressions, *העולם הבא and *הארץ הקדושה, respectively.

Universalism and territorialism thus coexist in *2 Baruch*. The two ideologies are predicated upon nationalism, hence they are compatible. The nationalism contains an individualism, which makes a distinction between the righteous and the sinful in terms of the Torah observance and extends beyond ethnic distinction to a degree. *2 Baruch* regards apostate Jews as like Gentiles and the proselytes as like faithful Jews, and shows a positive attitude towards proselytes more than *4 Ezra*. Nevertheless, the individualism does not lead the author to de-nationalism generalizing all mankind or sectarianism separating from the people. His eschatological hopes include Israel's dominion over all nations, a dominion in which the Holy Land shall take the central position. *2 Baruch*'s soteriology contains universalism and territorialism predicated upon nationalism including individualism, a worldview which represents a Judaism very close to that of *4 Ezra*.

8.3. Apocalypse of Abraham

Apocalypse of Abraham is preserved in Slavonic recensions and a Romanian version. The Slavonic version is probably made from a Greek text, which in turn is a translation of a Hebrew original.[81] We can fairly certainly restore the original Hebrew terms from Slavonic; Slavonic *zemlja* is perhaps taken from Greek γῆ which certainly renders Hebrew *ʾereṣ* (or *ʾadāmâ*), Slavonic *vselenaja* from Greek ἡ οἰκουμένη/Hebrew *tēbēl*, and Slavonic *věkŭ* from Greek αἰών/Hebrew *ʿôlām*. Since the Slavonic text contains obscurity and difficulty,[82] the following investigation of our terms in *Apocalypse of Abraham* is to be tentative.[83]

8.3.1. zemlja/*ʾereṣ *in* Apocalypse of Abraham

The term *zemlja/*ʾereṣ* in *Apocalypse of Abraham* can refer to the 'ground', upon which Abraham fell face down (10.2, 3; cf. 17.3, 5). Its productivity of fruits as soil is assumed (7.4; 21.3).

The term can mean *terra firma*. An earthquake is enumerated as an eschatological turmoil (30.6, 8). *zemlja/*ʾereṣ* is compared with the waters and the sun in ch. 7 (vv. 5f., 11; cf. Gen. 1.9).[84] It can be used in relation to God's Creation. God is called 'the Creator of heaven and earth' (10.6).[85] The created universe can be divided into the heavens, the earth, the sea, the abyss, the lower depths, the Garden of Eden and its rivers (12.10). Mention is made of 'the elements of earth' which obey the natural orders (19.9).

The pair of heavens and earth can denote the heavenly world and the earthly one. It is stated that Abraham's glory[86] is in heaven whereas the wicked angel Azazel's is on earth, and God has made Azazel a dweller on earth (13.7f.).[87] The angel Iaoel will revile Azazel 'who has scattered about the earth the secrets of heaven' (14.4). Abraham ascended with the angel to heaven (15.4), and after his heavenly journey

81. Philonenko-Sayar and Philonenko 1981: 23f.; *HJP* III, 289; Nickelsburg 1981a: 299; 2005: 288; Stone 1984: 416; Kulik 2004: 61–4. Rubinkiewicz (1983: 682f.; 1987: 33–7) suggests the possibility that the Slavonic version may be translated directly from a Hebrew original.

82. For possible Christian interpolations, see Rubinkiewicz 1987: 63–9.

83. In this section the Slavonic text and the verse number are of Rubinkiewicz (1987), and the English translation is of Rubinkiewicz and Lunt (*OTP*) with modifications, otherwise noted; in cases where the verse number of Rubinkiewicz's Slavonic text is different from that of *OTP*, the latter is put in brackets (note that the verse numbering of Rubinkiewicz is utterly different from that of Philonenko-Sayar and Philonenko 1981).

84. According to Rubinkiewicz, ch. 7 is an insertion from Palaia (*OTP* I, 684).

85. Rubinkiewicz and Lunt literally translate the Slavonic as 'creator of heavenly and earthly things' (*OTP* I, 694; cf. Rubinkiewicz 1987: 129), but the original Hebrew probably had **šāmayim wāʾāreṣ*, as Philonenko-Sayar and Philonenko (1981: 59) render.

86. Philonenko-Sayar and Philonenko (1981) and *OTP* emend 'honor, glory' to 'part, portion', while Rubinkiewicz (1987: 144f.) reads as the text has.

87. For the translation of this passage, see Kulik 2004: 69f.

(chs 15–29) he found himself 'on the earth' (30.1), that is, returned to the earthly world.

zemlja/**ʾereṣ* is a space for living beings. Abraham saw a picture of the Garden of Eden, in which a man, a woman and a serpent appear (23.1-8). God explains that they are Adam, Eve and Azazel, and that Eve symbolizes '(men's) avarice on the earth' (23.9 [10]).[88] As for Azazel, it is said, 'through his works he could ruin humankind on earth' (23.11 [12]). Because of men's corruption God 'will bring upon all creation of the earth[89] ten plagues through evil and disease and the groaning of the bitterness of their souls' (29.15). This impious world age endures twelve periods (29.2),[90] and the ten plagues are said to have been prepared against the heathen 'beforehand in the passing of the twelve hours on earth' (30.2).

The existence of Hades and hellfire under the earth is presupposed. Mention is made of 'the furnace of the earth' and 'the untrodden parts of the earth', into which Azazel is commanded to go (14.5; cf. *1 En.* 10.4-6). The hellfire for those who desire fornication is prepared 'in the lower depths of the earth' (24.7 [6]). As the eschatological punishment of those who have mocked and ruled over the chosen people God had 'prepared them (to be) food for the fire of Hades, and (to be) ceaseless soaring in the air under the earth' (31.3; cf. 10.11).[91]

The term *zemlja*/**ʾereṣ* can refer to a 'land', territorially defined. The land of Egypt is once called 'an alien land' (32.2; cf. Gen. 15.13). The Land is referred to only in one passage (10.13 [-14]): 'I (the angel Iaoel) am sent to you (Abraham) now to bless you and the Land which He (God) whom you have called the Eternal One has prepared for you. For your sake I have indicated the way to the Land.'[92] While this passage refers to the preparation of the Land by God, its precreation is not explicitly articulated (compare with *LAB* 7.4; *4 Ezra* 7.26). The paucity of reference to the Land in *Apocalypse of Abraham* is surprising, considering its main character Abraham, who represents one of the most important figures in the biblical Land theology (it is possible that passages pertaining to the Land theology were omitted by the Bogomils who transmitted the text).[93]

88. As for Adam's symbol the text is unclear; Philonenko-Sayar and Philonenko (1981): 'le penchant des hommes'; *OTP*: 'the world of men'; Rubinkiewicz (1987) 'la lumière, le soleil'. Kulik (2004: 84) proposes that here Adam and Eve respectively symbolize 'reason' and 'desire', suggesting a similar allegorical interpretation of Philo of Alexandria.

89. Slavonic is literally 'all earthly creation', but adjective use of Hebrew **ʾereṣ* is unlikely.

90. Cf. *4 Ezra* 14.11; *2 Bar.* 27.1.

91. The translation of Rubinkiewicz (1987); *OTP* reads the Slavonic literally, 'the air of the underworld (regions)'.

92. 'The way to the Land' (*lit.*, 'the earthly way') according to the emendation by Rubinkiewicz (1987). *OTP* reads literally 'the way of the land' and misguidedly suggests it reflecting Hebrew *drk ʾrṣ* 'manners (or morals)' (I, 694 n. 1; cf. Rubinkiewicz 1987: 133 note on v. 13).

93. Rubinkiewicz points out the possibility that the absence of mention of resurrection in *Apocalypse of Abraham* is due to the Bogomils (*OTP* I, 685).

8.3.2. vselenaja/*tēbēl *in* Apocalypse of Abraham

The term *vselenaja/*tēbēl* can be used in parallelism with *zemlja/*ʾereṣ* (7.7). A reference is made to 'the fullness of the world' at the end of a list of created things (12.10).[94] It is interestingly stated that the 'inhabited-world' lies upon Leviathan, and his motion causes the destruction to it (21.4; cf. 10.10).[95]

The term can represent the habitable world in which human beings live. In a song which the angel Iaoel taught Abraham God is praised as 'redeemer of those who dwell in the midst of the impious and the unjust, of those who are dispersed in the inhabited-world (*vselenaja/*tēbēl*) in the corruptible world (*věkŭ/*ʿôlām*)' (17.21 [17]).[96] Among the ten plagues at the *eschaton* 'famine of the inhabited-world' is enumerated (30.5).

8.3.3. věkŭ/*ʿôlām *in* Apocalypse of Abraham

The term *věkŭ/*ʿôlām* can mean spatially the created world. God introduces himself to Abraham as 'I am before the world[97] and the Mighty God who in the beginning created the (two) lights of the world' (9.3).[98] God created not only one world, but (two) worlds. God said to Abraham, 'I will show you the worlds (pl., *věky*) which were by My word made and firmed, created and renewed' (9.9).[99] Mention is made of 'this world' and 'the world to come' in a single passage (31.2).[100] The idea of the two worlds implies that this world has a limit of time from the beginning to the end;

94. Cf. Pss. 50.12; 89.12; Isa. 34.1.

95. For a similar idea in rabbinic sources, see Ginzberg 1998: V, 43–6, n. 127, esp. p. 45.

96. Different translations are proposed by Philonenko-Sayar and Philonenko (1981), *OTP*, and Rubinkiewicz (1987); here I present a modified translation.

97. *OTP* and Philonenko-Sayar and Philonenko (1981) translate Slavonic literally as 'Before-the-World' and 'antérieur au Siècle', but Rubinkiewicz (1987) renders it as 'l'Eternel'. Kulik (2004: 44f.) retroverts this Slavonic phrase into Greek ἕως εἰς τὸν αἰῶνα/Hebrew עד עולם meaning here 'forever'. It seems to me, however, that the literal translation of Slavonic (i.e., 'before the world') might, rather, reflect the original Hebrew (probably *מקדם העולם), since *Apocalypse of Abraham* usually has another Slavonic phrase for 'the Eternal One' in other occurrences (10.13, 14; 12.3; 13.8, 10; 14.2; 16.3; 17.7, [16, 18]; 18.11; 22.3; 23.8, 11, 13; 26.1, 4; 27.4, 6, 9; 28.1; 29.1, 7; 30.1). In our passage probably God's pre-existence is affirmed (cf. 20.1), as noted by Philonenko-Sayar and Philonenko (1981: 55).

98. My translation. For translating 'two lights' as the object of the verb 'create', see Kulik 2004: 45f.

99. My translation from Philonenko-Sayar and Philonenko, who observe the parallelism of the four verbs (1981: 57, v. 8). *OTP*'s translation does not make sense; Rubinkiewicz in his French translation (1987: 125) proposes a reading of 'les serments' (instead of the verb 'affirmed'), which, according to him, corresponds to Hebrew שבעה. In *Apocalypse of Abraham*, however, God's promise to Abraham is not renewed (cf. 17.25 [21]), but the world (17.22 [18]). The plural 'worlds' (or 'ages') appears also in 9.5, but the text is uncertain; cf. *OTP* I, 693 n. 9 c; Rubinkiewicz 1987: 125 n. v. 5. For God's Creation by word, see n. 70 above.

100. 'The world to come' according to ms. S; the reading of mss ABCK, 'present', which is chosen by Rubinkiewicz (1987) does not make sense.

hence the term *věkŭ/*ʿôlām* maintains its temporal sense together with spatial. The 'end of the world (age)' is indeed referred to (22.4), and this world is divided into twelve periods (29.1f., 9).[101] The temporal aspect of our term is distinctive in 28.7 (5).

This world is characterized as evil. It is called 'the corruptible world' (17.21 [17]), and 'the impious world' (29.2, 13; 32.2 [3]). In contrast, the world to come is designated as 'the world of the just' (17.22 [18]) and 'the world of justice' (29.14, 18). The world to come is prepared (21.1) and renewed (17.22 [18]; cf. 9.9).

At the *eschaton* God's judgement will come upon 'the heathen' (29.14) and the apostates who 'abandoned the Lord' (31.6-8). After the ten plagues God will send His chosen one, the messiah, to summon God's people (31.1), who 'will live, being affirmed by the sacrifices and the gifts of justice and truth in the world of justice' (29.18). Thus the eschatological expectation includes the appearance of a messianic figure and the restoration of the temple cult.

8.3.4. Summary

The term *zemlja/*ʾereṣ* in *Apocalypse of Abraham* means the tangible earth, the created earth, the earthly world in contrast to the heavenly one, and much less frequently a land territorially defined. Along with the Creation theology and the Land theology, it is utilized to express the universal scale of eschatological disasters, though its significance is minute. The term *vselenaja/*tēbēl* is used as a synonym of *zemlja/*ʾereṣ*, signifying the space where human beings live. The term *věkŭ/*ʿôlām* can denote the world in spatial and temporal dimensions. It is utilized in the Creation theology and in cosmological eschatology. The significance of the term **ʿôlām* increases and that of the term **ʾereṣ* decreases, in particular, in the eschatological description, as in other post-70 CE Jewish literature.

Apocalypse of Abraham lacks any sectarianism. It is a nationalistic writing, summoning the readers to remain faithful to the one true God by instructing their eschatological salvation and the final judgement against the foreign overlords and the apostates.

8.4. Conclusion

The destruction of the Second Temple gave rise to three apocalypses. Although they admitted this fatal event was God's punishment of Israel for its sins, the authors of these writings could not accept this explanation as enough to clear away all scepticism about theodicy caused by the disaster. If Israel must be punished, all the more, the other nations, the Romans in particular, should be chastened; if Jerusalem must resign herself to her fate of ruination, all the more, the foreign nations should

101. For 29.1, see Rubinkiewicz 1987: 191f. n. v. 1.

be annihilated, since they are ungodly much more than Israel. The solution should be decisive and universal in the light of Israel's bitter experience. The eschatology requires references to God's Creation activity, since it is cosmological. Thus the beginning is retrospected from the perspective of the end; an overview of world history is given, and the appearance of a new world is expected.

This eschatological perspective of history can be expressed only by the term *ʿôlām, which has recently gained a new usage. This is an eschatological term; it will be visited and renewed by God, and be possessed by the survivors. Even when employed in reference to the first Creation, it is retrospectively viewed in the light of its end. Therefore, the idea of העולם הזה cannot stand in its own right, but is complementary to the concept of העולם הבא. Since, however, it can bear a spatial connotation, its uses penetrate the semantic field of the term *ʾereṣ. It can be a synonym of *ʾereṣ and *tēbēl, but it is distinct from them in its temporal aspects. It was surprisingly quickly developed in the first century CE and speedily obtained popularity among the Palestinian Jewry.

The earth (*ʾereṣ) is created to be the scene and witness of world history. It provides human beings with the stage setting. Since it is the locale of creatures, it cannot come to an end but exists in the age of salvation. The earth (*ʾereṣ), therefore, is no longer utilized as an eschatological term. The significance of the term *ʿôlām increases and that of *ʾereṣ (earth) decreases in eschatological dimensions.

The Roman victory over the Jews gave a new significance to another sense of the term *ʾereṣ, the Land. It is the Holy Land, the scene of the eschatological salvation, in which the traditional twelve tribes of Israel shall be restored; it is the location of the messianic kingdom, and it will protect its inhabitants. The eschatological roles of the Land in *4 Ezra* and *2 Baruch* are distinct from pre-70 CE Jewish eschatologies (except 1QM and *Psalm of Solomon* 17 reflecting the Roman conquest in 63 BCE). The Land, however, is not a direct object of promises; it is not used with such verbs as 'to give' and 'to possess'. The eschatological promises are connected to *ʿôlām. Rather, the Land is frequently connected to the Torah observance. It is still a present Jewish dwelling place in which the people should remain faithful to the Torah in order to receive the eschatological rewards. This may reflect the situation of Palestine in 70–132 CE; despite the defeat of the Great Revolt, many Jews remained in the Land. The issue caused by the war was not abandonment of the Land, but of the Torah, the Jewish way of life, Juda-*ism*. The emphasis on the Torah observance in all the three writings we've treated in this chapter suggests the probability of the existence of such Jews as does also the growth of Christianity in this post-Destruction generation. The frequent references to 'apostates' in *Apocalypse of Abraham* can be an attestation to this if it reflects the original text.[102] The issue of abandonment of the Land is a post Bar-Kokhva problem which the rabbis would have to face.[103]

102. Analysing a rabbinic text (*t. Shab.* 15 [16].9), Schäfer (2003: 147) suggests the existence of the Hellenized or Romanized Jews before the Bar-Kokhva revolt.

103. See Gafni (1997: 58–78), who insists that there is a shift of the rabbinic attitudes towards the Land after the failure of the Bar-Kokhva revolt.

8.5. Appendix 3: ʾaraʿ *in Jewish Palestinian Papyri from the Second Century* CE

In this appendix we shall supplement our discussions with papyri from the Judaean Desert from the beginning of the second century CE collected in *TJD*.

Among the findings from the Judaean Desert, there is a gift deed from Naḥal Ḥever dating 120 CE (*TJD* Naḥal Ḥever 7 [A: 96f.; B: 45]). The term *ʾaraʿ* appears in line 4. Its precise referent is unclear (field?), but it consists of a part of personal property. The gift is expressed in line 5 with the verb 'to give' (יהב) and with the adverb 'in perpetuity' (עלם).[104]

In the same document there appear phrases ארע וערת 'the craggy land' (lines 6, 37) and ארעא חורתא 'the white land' (line 10, the meaning uncertain).

104. In *TJD* Naḥal Ḥever 6 (A296; B97) there appears twice the phrase ארעא הי 'that land' which may refer to the land-estate of an individual.

Chapter 9

Conclusions

In this chapter we shall first give an overview of the shift of usages of the terms and summarize our findings. In this context, then, we shall synthesize a transformation of Jewish worldviews over time.

The Hebrew term ʾ*ereṣ* and Aramaic ʾ*araʿ* can signify a tangible dry solid part of the earth, which allows for the productivity of plants. Maintaining this essential connotation, its uses can be largely divided into two: references to the earth as a whole and to a land as a definite territory, especially to the Land of Israel (= the Land). The former can be utilized in the Creation theology, 'God created the earth', while the latter is important in Land theology, 'God promised Israel to give/take possession of the Land'. Both theologies can be applied to soteriologies, especially in eschatological perspectives. In the following we shall focus upon these two soteriologies, universal and territorial, as far as they are concerned with the term ʾ*ereṣ*/ʾ*araʿ* and other related terms.

9.1. Shift of Usage of the Term ʾereṣ/ʾaraʿ

In the Bible, as we saw in Chapter 2, the uses of ʾ*ereṣ* as the earth are expressions for the greatness and distinctness of the Creator, the God of Israel, on the one hand, and for the uniqueness of the people of Israel among nations, on the other. The special relationships between God and Israel are manifested in the promise of ʾ*ereṣ*, the Land. The history of Israel begins with the journey to the Land, and its salvation history ends with the return to the Land. The blessed life of Israel in the Land is the ultimate concern for the biblical writers and compilers. The fate and hope of Israel cannot be told without referring to the Land, and the Land loses its special status as ʾ*ereṣ YHWH* 'the Lord's Land' without Israel, the observer of God's law. The two concepts, Israel and the Land, are ideologically an inseparable pair, forming a central biblical theology. Whether universal or territorial usage, the term ʾ*ereṣ* expresses Israel-centrically the relationships between the God of Israel and the world, and between the people of Israel and nations of the world (God-Israel-nations relationships). In other words, the term plays a role in placing their national history within the world history.

The borders of the Promised Land, however, are variously defined in the Bible. There are chiefly three types of territory of the Land in the Bible: the Lord's Land (the western side of Jordan), the Land of the twelve tribes of Israel (including

Transjordan), and the Greater Israel (to the River Euphrates). In some passages, furthermore, the Land-promise extends to the ends of the earth (the maximal Israel). In this case the two meanings of *ʾereṣ*, Land and earth, tend to overlap.

Some Aramaic papyri from Elephantine may suggest a background of the terminology in the biblical Land theology, such as יהב = נתן 'to give' and עד עלם = לעולם 'forever', terms which are frequently employed in the context of Land-promise. The biblical implications of the term *ʾereṣ*, therefore, can be placed in the broader cultural contexts of the ancient Near Eastern world, as we saw in Chapter 3. The terms *ʾereṣ* and *ʾaraq*/*ʾaraʿ* in non-Jewish inscriptions and papyri can be used in cosmological dimensions and in Creation theology.[1] They can represent the earthly world in relation to an imperial power, providing an idea parallel to the biblical expectation that a (messianic) king of Israel may rule over the entire world.[2]

The terms can represent a territorial 'land', as well. Some inscriptions reveal that non-Jewish kings or governors were also strongly concerned with the possession and expansion of their territories. Their dominion of the territory is legitimated either by a deity or their good deeds. A Moabite inscription from the ninth century BCE (*KAI* 181) provides us with a background of the use of the terms ירש 'to take possession of' and ישב 'to dwell' in the biblical Land theology. Two New Punic inscriptions from the first to second centuries CE show the inhabitants' attachment to their land as the 'fatherland' (*KAI* 121; 126).

It is interesting to see the fact that these uses of the term *ʾereṣ*/*ʾaraʿ*/*ʾaraq* in the ancient Near Eastern world contain nationalistic implications both in universal and territorial dimensions.

In Enochic literature from the Hellenistic period before the Maccabaean uprising (*1 Enoch* 1–36; 72–82; 91–107), as we saw in Chapter 4, there are no uses of the term *ʾaraʿ* (Ethiopic *medr*) in reference to the territorial Land, but dominantly to the universal earth. It shows its calendrical concerns about the cosmic order in relation to the Creation, on the one hand (*1 Enoch* 72–82), and about world history in relation to eschatology, on the other (*1 Enoch* 1–36; 91–107). While its cosmological soteriology seems universalistic, it actually intends the realization of maximal Israel (*1 Enoch* 10) or the eschatological earth possession of the righteous Jews (*1 Enoch* 5). The former is an expression of a nationalistic sentiment, while the latter is that of sectarianism. It is remarkable that the idea of the eschatological possession of 'the earth' (*1 En.* 5.7) is a reinterpretation of the biblical phrase 'to take possession of *ʾereṣ*', a central representation of the Land-promise in the Pentateuch.

Ben Sira, too, shows his concerns about cosmic order in relation to Wisdom. His employment of the term *ʾereṣ*/γῆ tends to be universal. In his reinterpretation of the Land theology, Ben Sira expects Israel's dominion over the entire world (Sir. 44.21). He did not, however, forget the biblical significance of the Land as Israel's

1. *KAI* 26A+B, III.18; 27.13-15; 129.1; 202B.25f.; 222A.26; 244.3; 266.1f.
2. *KAI* 215.14; 216.4; 217.2.

allotment, and expected the restoration of the twelve tribes in the Land (Sir. 36.13). Thus, in Sirach's soteriology coexist two Land theologies, the maximal Israel and the Lord's Land as Israel's allotment.

The persecution of Antiochus IV Epiphanes brought gradually but drastically the significance of the Land back into Jewish religion, as we saw in Chapter 5. Under the persecution the book of Daniel and the Book of Dreams (*1 Enoch* 83–90) sharpened the cosmological eschatology, which included a belief in the resurrection of the (righteous) dead. At the same time, they remembered the special status of the Land as 'the Land of Beauty' (Dan. 11.16, 41) and 'a pleasant and glorious Land' (*1 En.* 89.40). In the time of ceasefire, employing a fictional setting of the Exile and repeating the biblical Land theology, the author of Baruch instructed his compatriots to return to their God, the Creator of the earth (Bar. 3.24-38), in order to live a peaceful life in the Land (Bar. 2.29-35). Thus the book of Baruch revived the two biblical theologies concerning the term γῆ/*ʾ*ereṣ*, Creation theology and Land theology, both of which expressed nationalistically God-Israel-nations relationships. After the Maccabaean revolt, *Temple Scroll*, a composition of laws concerning the Temple and its city, and lives of the people outside the Temple city, presented anew the idea of the Holy Land in which the holy people should live the Torah-oriented life.

Under the Hasmonaean dynasty the author of Judith employed the Creation theology to make a contrast between the true one and only God and a foreign king who pretended to be the one and only god. He also shows his consciousness to the Land as a defined territory by other terms: κληρονομία/*נחלה 'allotment' (Jdt. 8.22) and ὅριον Ισραηλ/*גבול ישראל 'the territory of Israel' (Jdt. 14.4; 15.4; 16.4). 1 Maccabees applied these terms to express the religious significance of the Land and to legitimate the Hasmonaean policy of territorial expansionism (1 Macc. 2.46; 9.23; 15.33f.). *Jubilees* theologically promoted this policy and legitimated Jewish possession of the land of Canaan (*Jubilees* 8–9). At the same time, it retained the eschatological Land theology extending to all the earth in relation to the Creation theology (*Jub.* 1.29; 4.26; 22.11-15; 32.19; 50.5). *Jubilees* is the first work which utilized the two Land theologies with a distinction between the one concerning Israel's possession of the Land (*medr*/*ʾ*ereṣ*) in this world and the other regarding that of the earth (*medr*/*ʾ*ereṣ*) in the world to come. When the political expansionism reached its peak under the king Jannaeus, *Genesis Apocryphon* expected the realization of the Greater Israel and theologically legitimated that policy (col. 21).

When separating from the people, as we saw in Chapter 6, the Qumran Community was occupied by sectarianism similar to the Enochic one from the pre-Maccabaean period. The terms *ʾereṣ* 'earth' and *tēbēl* 'world' were applied to a cosmic scale soteriology, on the one hand; the terms *naḥalâ* 'allotment' and *gebûl* 'boundary' were spiritualized in such ways as the former meant an individual's talent for understanding the sect's truth while the latter designated the Torah's fence, on the other. The sectaries identified themselves with a counterpart to 'the sons of heavens', and assigned to themselves an eschatological role of 'atoning for the earth (*ʾereṣ*)'

(1QS 8.6, 10; 1QSa 1.3). But they also showed their territorial concerns with the Land in terms of eschatological soteriology (esp. 1QM 12.12//19.4).

As we discussed in Chapter 7, the Roman conquest of Jerusalem and the successive Herodian dynasty as an agent of foreign overlords brought back the eschatological soteriology of cosmic scale which was known from the third century BCE onwards. At the same time, the concept of the Holy Land was not utterly lost, but continued to be an important assumption which was inherited from the Hasmonaean period.

Psalms of Solomon expected both the appearance of a Davidic messiah whose dominion should extend over all the earth (γῆ/* *ʾereṣ*) and the restoration of the twelve tribes of Israel in the Land (γῆ/* *ʾereṣ*). The two biblical Land theologies, the maximal Israel and the Holy Land, were united in *Psalms of Solomon*'s eschatology in a manner similar to Sirach (*Ps. Sol.* 17.21-46). Pseudo-Philo also posited the concept of the Holy Land (*LAB* 19.10), but its soteriology was much more universal (*LAB* 3.10; 19.12). The Similitudes (*1 Enoch* 37–71) and *Assumption of Moses*, too, show their strong concerns with the fate of the world at the *eschaton*. The terms *medr* (Eth.)/* *ʾaraʿ* and *terra* (Lat.)/* *ʾereṣ*, therefore, tended to be used cosmologically in contrast to the heavenly world. The frequent employment of other terms – *yabs*/*יבשה (Similitudes) and *orbis terrarum*/*mundus*/*תבל (*Ass. Mos.* and *LAB*) – shows the same tendency.

From the first century CE on there arose a new usage of the Hebrew term *עולם and Aramaic *עלם (Eth. *ʿālam*/Lat. *saeculum*). It could now express simultaneously the world as a space and the world-age as a definite time, the world history which should come to an end. The term replaced the terminology of the biblical Land theology; Pseudo-Philo employed the expression 'to take possession of the world (*saeculum*/* *ʿôlām*)' instead of the biblical 'to take possession of the Land (*ʾereṣ*)' (*LAB* 32.3).

The destruction of the Second Temple, as we saw in Chapter 8, gave rise to three apocalypses (*4 Ezra*, *2 Baruch*, and *Apocalypse of Abraham*). A cosmic scale soteriology was dominant, and the world to come was expected. The eschatological significance of the Holy Land was posited, too. Thus, universalism and territorialism could coexist in their eschatological soteriology, as in *Psalms of Solomon* of the first century BCE. The three apocalypses of post-70 CE, however, could express now these two ideologies with two distinct terms, * *ʿôlām* and * *ʾereṣ*. While the term * *ʾereṣ* did not lose its tangible senses and cosmological implication of the earth in contrast to heaven, it was no longer utilized as an object of worldwide eschatology; this role was replaced by * *ʿôlām*. Instead, the territorial designation of * *ʾereṣ* as the Land became clearer.

4 Ezra applied such expressions as 'to take possession of the world (*saeculum*/* *ʿôlām*)' and '(God will) visit the world (*saeculum*/* *ʿôlām*)' in the cosmic scale eschatology, on the one hand (*4 Ezra* 6.59; 9.2); it contained the biblical idea of 'the Lord's Land' and the Lord's 'holy territory', on the other (9.7f.; 12.34). *2 Baruch* also presumed the concept of the Holy Land (*2 Bar*. 63.10), while it applied such verbs of biblical Land theology as 'to give' and 'to promise' to 'the world (* *ʿôlām*)' and even to 'the time (**zemān*)' (14.13; 44.8-15; 51.3). *Apocalypse* *of Abraham* shows similar usages of the terms *ʾereṣ and *ʿôlām. It is remarkable that all these three apocalypses contain a messianic expectation.

The failure of the Bar-Kokhva revolt, and the Hadrian persecution after it, deprived Jews of hope for political national independence and for tense realization of messianic and apocalyptic expectations. The problems caused by the revolt included reduction of Jewish population in the Land and emigration of at least some important personalities. From the post-Bar-Kokhva period tannaitic sources began to emphasize the importance 'to live in the Land of Israel' itself (e.g., *t. A. Z.* 4.3).[3] The special significance of the Land brought about a new expression, חוץ לארץ 'outside of the Land', which was well-known from rabbinic literature, but unknown from literature preceding it. While messianic expectations and a hope for העולם הבא 'the world to come' as a reward were not utterly abandoned, the idea of the Land of Israel in a real life gained a special significance in rabbinic Judaism.[4]

9.2. *Transformation of an Aspect of Jewish Worldviews: A Historical Synthesis*

The Hebrew Bible is the holy scriptures of the national religion of Israel. It is, therefore, full of nationalistic ideologies. The Land theology is typical of biblical nationalism. The Creation theology is also an expression of nationalism, despite its cosmological universal appearances. Nationalism is an assumption and a goal of the Bible: it is an assumption because the Bible speaks of the God of Israel; it is a goal because the Bible aims to establish the national identity by describing the special relationships between God and the people by means of the Law, namely, the covenant. Accordingly, we can dare to say that there is in the Bible no universalism which generalizes all human beings who are living under various cultures.[5]

This explains a characteristic of the biblical universalism. The worldwide soteriology is related to the Creation theology which depicts the God of Israel as the Creator, the one and only Lord of the whole universe. It expects, therefore, the Gentiles' acceptance of the God of Israel and that nation's dominion over the entire world in religio-political dimensions. In other words, the biblical universalism, in essence, is a kind of 'imperialism' or 'hegemonism'. The Land theology can be combined with this universalism, since the Promised Land can extend to the ends of the earth. Universalism and territorialism, which are normally presumed as contradictory ideas, can be integrated under nationalism, a biblical assumption. The realization of this unity is, at least in part, due to a double-meaning of the term

3. See Gafni 1997: 58–78 with further reference to rabbinic passages.

4. For the Land theology in rabbinic literature, cf. Gafni 1997; Thoma 1970; Primus 1986; Sarason 1986.

5. I must hasten to add that there are some exceptions in narrative pieces and episodes in the Bible. I also admit the possibility or probability that the *original* intention of some biblical traditions may have contained some universalistic essence free from any nationalism. Nevertheless, when integrated into 'the holy scriptures', such pieces were to be constituents of biblical nationalism; this accords with our methodological presupposition which we've defined at the beginning of this book: 'we shall treat the Bible as a whole' (§ 1.4).

ʾereṣ, the earth and the Land. In this sense the term is a nationalistic expression, and we can here observe its significance in the Bible and in post-biblical literature. We must remind ourselves, however, that this nationalistic sentiment concerning our term is not exceptional; nationalism of this kind is discernible among other cultures of the ancient Near Eastern world. The Bible just provides us with its most explicit example.[6]

As long as the Jewishness was defined by one's descent, the idea of Juda-*ism* had no room to be born. The encounter with Hellenism enabled Jews to define 'themselves as "Judaists," adherents of "Judaism"'.[7] Then the question of Jewishness arose; who was a Jew? The matter of Jewishness, which had discriminated between Jews and Gentiles, became the discrimination within the Jewish descendants. This question was sharpened from the third century BCE onwards and brought about various sectarian movements, which characterized an aspect of Second Temple Judaism.

Enochic circles from the third to the beginning of the second centuries BCE made a distinction within Jews between the righteous and sinners, positing a biblical discrimination between Jews and Gentiles. Despite their domestic concerns, they applied the biblical Land theology to a cosmic scale eschatology (*1 En.* 5.7). The combination of intra-national discrimination and cosmic soteriology characterizes their sectarianism, which is a kind of particularism. Their sectarianism does not mean de-nationalism generalizing all mankind indifferent to nationality, as some scholars suggest. Nationalism was an assumption from the outset: their particularism was a result of conflict with their compatriots; the cosmic eschatology was an attempt to cope with the internal opposition by the vision of God's direct intervention in the world.

Universalism predicated upon nationalism was also assumed by Ben Sira, who hoped for the realization of the maximal Israel, along with the restoration of the biblical Land. Before the Maccabaean period a universalistic tendency is evident. This is probably due to the influence of Persian and Hellenistic imperialism and of Hellenistic culture in general. The universalistic tendency is a reflection of the condition of the Land in reality which is projected on the earth in soteriology. We can here observe an interesting role of a double meaning of the term *ʾereṣ*/*ʾaraʿ*, the Land and the earth.

The Antiochian persecution and its aftermath recalled to the second century BCE Jews a traditional significance of the Holy Land as a defined territory. The recognition of its importance to the Jewish way of life promoted the religious and political restoration of the biblical *ʾereṣ yiśrāēl*. The terms *naḥalâ* and *gebûl yiśrāēl* regained their Pentateuchal implication of the Promised Land, and the term *ʾereṣ* took back its territorial connotation. While nationalistic sentiments increased under the Hasmonaean dynasty, there were also active sectarian movements motivated by

6. Admitting questions applying the term 'nationalism' to antiquity, problems which have been claimed by social scientists, we can, I believe, discern a kind of nationalism in ancient worlds; for this issue in the Bible and in the ancient Near Eastern world, see e.g., Grosby (2002) with further literature; for the Second Temple Judaism, see Goodblatt 2001.

7. Schwartz 1992: 11.

anti-Hasmonaean feelings. The Qumran Community inherited particularism from the pre-Maccabaean Enochic circles and sharpened it. The Qumran sectarianism was characterized by dualistic worldviews: dividing world history into this present world and the world to come and individuals into 'the Sons of Light' and 'the Sons of Darkness', they expected the eschatological salvation of the sectaries.

The Roman overlordship stimulated the Jewish national mind. It engendered hopes for a messiah who would judge nations, and for the realization of God's Kingdom. The strong expectation in eschatological soteriology with cosmic upheavals was the reverse of their disappointment in the present world. The stronger the disappointment was, the acuter the eschatological hopes became. The burning expectation of cosmological eschatology gave rise to a new usage of the term *ʿôlām*. The disappointment in the present world provided Jews with a view to regard the world history as corrupted from the Creation, and to survey it as an epoch. Because of this worldview, they could apply the term *ʿôlām*, which might be taken from Greek αἰών designating an epoch, to the whole world history from the Creation to the *eschaton*. This new usage, therefore, was an expression of disappointment with God's sovereignty in reality, which was projected on the hope for the world to come in soteriology. The connotation of *ʿôlām* is close to the traditional expression ימי הארץ 'the days of the earth'. But the latter sees world history as an accumulation of events, whereas the term *ʿôlām* represents a view which surveys world history as a totality. It reflects the consciousness of 'the end' of this present world. It was, therefore, employed in the singular form to express 'the world' connoting simultaneously its spatial and temporal aspects. Despite its universal denotation ('world'), the term *ʿôlām* did not represent universalism which generalized all mankind irrespective of nationality. Its new usage emerged as a response to Roman rule. Accordingly, the eschatological hopes expressed with the term *ʿôlām* were motivated by nationalism. In other words, the new usage was an answer to the question of theodicy, which was caused by the contradiction between the existence of the Jerusalem Temple which symbolized God's sovereignty and the fact of foreign lordship.[8]

The issue of theodicy was further sharpened by the destruction of the Temple. The answer to this disaster was twofold: God's judgement by means of a messiah should be revealed to the entire world (*ʿôlām*) and the salvation should appear in the Land (*ʾereṣ*). Universalism and territorialism coexisted in the eschatological soteriology; and these two ideologies could now be expressed by two distinct terms, *ʿôlām* and *ʾereṣ*. The Land was no longer merely the Holy Land, but was now assigned as the location of the eschatological salvation. The survivors of salvation were to be perfect Torah observant in the Land. The ideas of the final judgement on the world and the salvation in the Land were seemingly based on nationalism. The nationalism, however, did not regard the people as a whole to be worthy for salvation; only those who remained faithful to the Torah would be saved. Thus Jews were individually evaluated. This individualism, however, was different from

8. See Schwartz 1992: 9f.

particularism of the Qumran sectaries. In the latter, those who would be saved were predetermined, whereas in the former, each Jew would choose of his own free will whether to follow the ways to salvation or the ways to destruction. The doctrine of free will could be also applied to individual Gentiles, the proselytes, who voluntarily chose the Torah-oriented life.[9] This doctrine, which had been known from *Psalm of Solomon* 9, was employed in the post-70 CE Jews, and symbolized the end of sectarianism current in the Second Temple period.[10] The doctrine of free will, however, did not focus on de-nationalism generalizing all mankind. The priority of Jewish nationality was still an assumption, but each Jew was required to make the decision to be a 'Judaist' or a heathen. Proselytes were only exceptionally accepted.

The Hebrew Bible, especially the Pentateuch, was composed to establish a national identity of Judaeans. The biblical religion, therefore, had a nationalistic tendency from the outset. The encounter with Hellenism brought about a question of Jewishness. The answers to this question contained nationalism expecting the realization of the maximal Israel, and sectarianism limiting salvation particularistically to those Jews who lived according to a certain way of life. Nationalism reached its peak under Roman rule and caused the Great Revolt and the Bar-Kokhva revolt. The destruction of the Jerusalem Temple required individual Jews to decide of their own free will whether to be Judaist or heathen. Jewish nationality provided them a privilege, but it no longer assured them salvation. The national religion of Judaeans transformed into Juda-*ism* after various attempts to define Jewishness, a Judaism which would result in rabbinic Judaism.

9. For proselytism, see e.g., Goodman 1989; 1992; 1994; S. J. D. Cohen 1999.

10. See Neusner 1972; S. J. D. Cohen 1984.

Bibliography

Abegg, M. G. (1994) 'Messianic Hope and 4Q285: A Reassessment', *JBL* 113: 81–91.

Academy (1973) *The Book of Ben Sira: Text, Concordance and an Analysis of the Vocabulary* (Jerusalem: The Academy of the Hebrew Language) (Hebrew).

Aharoni, Y., M. Avi-Yonah, A. F. Rainey, and Z. Safrai (2002) *The Carta Bible Atlas* (Jerusalem: Carta, 4th edn).

Albani, M. (1994) *Astronomie und Schöpfungsglaube: Untersuchungen zum astronomischen Henochbuch* (WMANT 68; Neukirchen-Vluyn: Neukirchener Verlag).

Alexander, P. S. (1999–2000) 'A Reconstruction and Reading of 4Q285 (4QSefer ha-Milhamah)', *RevQ* 19: 333–48.

Amaru, B. H. (1981) 'Land Theology in Josephus' Jewish Antiquities', *JQR* 71: 201–29.

—— (1986) 'Land Theology in Philo and Josephus', in Hoffman (ed.) 1986: 65–93.

—— (1994) *Rewriting the Bible: Land and Covenant in Postbiblical Jewish Literature* (Valley Forge: Trinity Press International).

Anderson, B. W. (ed.) (1985) *Creation in the Old Testament* (Philadelphia: Fortress Press).

Applebaum, S. (1986) 'Hasmonean Internal Colonization: Problems and Motives', in Kasher, Oppenheimer and Rappaport (eds) 1986: 75–9 (Hebrew).

Atkinson, K. (1996) 'Herod the Great, Sosius, and the Siege of Jerusalem (37 B.C.E.) in Psalm of Solomon 17', *NovT* 38: 313–22.

—— (1999) 'On the Herodian Origin of Militant Davidic Messianism at Qumran: New Light from Psalm of Solomon 17', *JBL* 118: 435–60.

Avi-Yonah, M. (1984) *Historical Geography of Palestine: From the End of the Babylonian Exile up to the Arab Conquest* (Jerusalem: Mosad Bialik, 4th edn) (Hebrew).

Bar-Deroma, H. (1960) 'The River of Egypt (Nahal Mizraim)', *PEQ* 92: 37–56.

Bar-Kochva, B. (1989) *Judas Maccabaeus: The Jewish Struggle Against the Seleucids* (Cambridge: Cambridge University Press).

Bauer, W. (2000) *A Greek-English Lexicon of the New Testament and Other Early Christian Literature* (F. W. Danker rev. and ed.; Chicago, London: The University of Chicago Press, 3rd edn).

Baumgarten, J. M. (1990) 'The Qumran-Essene Restraints on Marriage', in Schiffman (ed.) 1990: 13–24.

Beckwith, R. T. (1981) 'The Earliest Enoch Literature and its Calendar: Marks of their Origin, Date and Motivation', *RevQ* 10: 365–403.

Bergman, J. and M. Ottosson (1977) 'ארץ', in *TDOT* 1: 388–405.

Betz, O. (1970) 'Israel bei Jesus und im Neuen Testament', in Eckert, Levinson and Stöhr (eds) 1970: 275–89.

Black, M. (1970) *Apocalypsis henochi graece* (PVTG 3; Leiden: E.J. Brill).

—— (1985) *The Book of Enoch or I Enoch: A New English Edition with Commentary and Textual Notes* (Leiden: E.J. Brill).

Bockmuehl, M. (2001) '1QS and Salvation at Qumran', in Carson *et al.* (eds) 2001: 381–414.

Bogaert, P.-M. (1969) *Apocalypse de Baruch: introduction, traduction du syriaque et commentare* (2 vols; Paris: Éditions du Cerf).

Boorer, S. (1992) *The Promise of the Land as Oath. A Key to the Formation of the Pentateuch* (BZAW 205; Berlin: W. de Gruyter).

Brongers, H. A. (1975) 'Bemerkungen zu Jes 58.13-14', *ZAW* 87: 212–16.

Broshi, M. (2000) 'Acts of a Greek King', in Schiffman and VanderKam (eds) 2000: I, 5.

Brownlee, W. H. (1977) *The Midrash Pesher of Habakkuk* (SBLMS 24; Missoula: Scholars Press).

Brueggemann, W. (1977) *The Land: Place as Gift, Promise, and Challenge in Biblical Faith* (Philadelphia: Fortress Press).

Buber, M. (1952) *Israel and Palestine: The History of an Idea* (London: East and West Library).

Burke, D. G. (1982) *The Poetry of Baruch* (Septuagint and Cognate Studies 10; Chico: Scholars Press).

Carson, D. A., P. T. O'Brien and M. A. Seifrid (eds) (2001) *Justification and Variegated Nomism: Volume 1–The Complexities of Second Temple Judaism* (Tübingen: Mohr Siebeck; Grand Rapids: Baker Academic).

Charles, R. H. (1895) *The Ethiopic Version of the Hebrew Book of Jubilees* (Oxford: Clarendon Press).

—— (1897) *The Assumption of Moses* (London: Adam and Charles Black).

—— (1902) *The Book of Jubilees* (London: Adam and Charles Black).

—— (1908) *The Greek Versions of the Testaments of the Twelve Patriarchs* (Oxford: Clarendon Press).

—— (1912) *The Book of Enoch or 1 Enoch* (Oxford: Clarendon Press, 2nd edn).

—— (1913) 'II Baruch', in R. H. Charles (ed.), *Apocrypha and Pseudepigrapha of the Old Testament in English* (2 vols; Oxford: Clarendon Press) 2: 470–526.

Clemen, C. (trans.) (1994) 'Die Himmerfahrt Moses', in *APAT* 2: 311–30.

Cohen, S. A. (1990) *The Three Crowns: Structures of Communal Politics in Early Rabbinic Jewry* (Cambridge: Cambridge University Press).

Cohen, S. J. D. (1984) 'The Significance of Yavneh: Pharisees, Rabbis and the End of Jewish Sectarianism', *HUCA* 55: 27–53.

—— (1999) *The Beginnings of Jewishness: Boundaries, Varieties, Uncertainties* (Berkeley: University of California Press).

Collins, J. J. (1984) 'Testaments', in Stone (ed.) 1984: 325–55.

—— (1990) 'Was the Dead Sea Sect an Apocalyptic Movement?', in Schiffman (ed.) 1990: 25–51.

—— (1992) 'The Son of Man in First-Century Judaism', *NTS* 38: 448–66.

—— (1993) *Daniel* (Hermeneia; Minneapolis: Fortress Press).

Craven, T. (1983) *Artistry and Faith in the Book of Judith* (Chico: Scholars Press).

Crawford, S. W. (2001) 'The Meaning of the Phrase עיר המקדש in the Temple Scroll', *DSD* 8: 242–54.

Dalman, G. (1997) *The Words of Jesus: Considered in the Light of Post-Biblical Jewish Writings and the Aramaic Language* (trans. D. M. Kay; Eugene: Wipf and Stock Publishers).

Davies, E. W. (1989) 'Land: Its Rights and Privileges', in R. Clements (ed.), *The World of Ancient Israel: Sociological, Anthropological, and Political Perspectives* (Cambridge: Cambridge University Press): 349–69.

Davies, P. R. (1983) *The Damascus Covenant: An Interpretation of the 'Damascus Document'* (Sheffield: JSOP Press).

Davies, P. R. and D. J. A. Clines (eds) (1998) *The World of Genesis: Persons, Places, Perspectives* (JSOTSup 257; Sheffield: Sheffield Academic Press).

Davies, W. D. (1974) *The Gospel and the Land: Early Christianity and Jewish Territorial Doctrine* (Berkeley: University of California Press).

—— (1982) *The Territorial Dimension of Judaism* (Berkeley: University of California Press).

Dearman, J. A. (1989) 'Historical Reconstruction and the Mesha Inscription', in Dearman (ed.) 1989: 155–210.

Dearman, J. A. (ed.) (1989) *Studies in the Mesha Inscription and Moab* (Atlanta: Scholars Press).

Delcor, M. (1966) 'Les attaches littéraires, l'origine et la signification de l'expression biblique "prendre à témoin le ciel et la terre"', *VT* 16: 8–25.

Diepold, P. (1972) *Israels Land* (BWANT 95; Stuttgart: Kohlhammer).
Dimant, D. (1984) 'Qumran Sectarian Literature', in Stone (ed.) 1984: 483–550.
—— (1995) 'The Qumran Manuscripts: Contents and Significance', in D. Dimant and L. H. Schiffman (eds), *Time to Prepare the Way in the Wilderness* (Leiden: E.J. Brill): 23–58.
Douglas, M. C. (1999) 'The Teacher Hymn Hypothesis Revisited: New Data for an Old Crux', *DSD* 6: 239–66.
Duhaime, J. (ed. and trans.) (1995) 'War Scroll', in *DSSHAG* II, 80–203.
Dupont-Sommer, A. (1959) *Les écrits esséniens découverts près de la Mer Morte* (Paris: Payot).
Eckert, W. P., N. P. Levinson and M. Stöhr (eds) (1970) *Jüdisches Volk-gelobtes Land* (München: C. Kaiser).
Edelman, D. (1988) 'The Asherite Genealogy in 1 Chr 7:30-40', *BR* 33: 13–23.
Elgiven, T. (1999) 'Renewed Earth and Renewed People: 4Q475', in D. W. Parry and E. Ulrich (eds), *The Provo International Conference on the Dead Sea Scrolls: Technological Innovations, New Texts, and Reformulated Issues* (Leiden: E.J. Brill): 576–91.
Emerton, J. A. (1982) 'The Origins of the Promises to the Patriarchs in the Older Sources of the Book of Genesis', *VT* 32: 14–32.
Endres, J. C. (1987) *Biblical Interpretation in the Book of Jubilees* (Washington, D.C.: Catholic Biblical Association of America).
Evans, B. and G. Cusack (eds) (1987) *Theology of the Land* (Collegeville: Liturgical Press).
Even-Shoshan, A. (ed.) (1990) *A New Concordance of the Bible: Thesaurus of the Language of the Bible: Hebrew and Aramaic Roots, Words, Proper Names, Phrases and Synonyms* (Jerusalem: "Kiryat Sefer" Publishing House).
Falk, D. K. (2001) 'Prayers and Psalms', in Carson *et al.* (eds) 2001: 7–56.
Fitzmyer, J. A. (1967) *The Aramaic Inscriptions of Sefire* (Rome: Pontificial Biblical Institute).
—— (1971) *The Genesis Apocryphon of Qumran Cave I: A Commentary* (Rome: Biblical Institute Press, 2nd rev. edn).
Fowler, M. D. (1982) 'The Israelite *bāmâ*: A Question of Interpretation', *ZAW* 94: 203–13.
Fulco, W. J. (1976) *The Canaanite god Rešep* (New Haven: American Oriental Society).
Gafni, I. (1981) 'Reinterment in the Land of Israel: Notes on the Origin and Development of the Custom', *The Jerusalem Cathedra* 1: 96–104.
—— (1997) *Land, Center and Diaspora: Jewish Constructs in Late Antiquity* (Sheffield: Sheffield Academic Press).
García Martínez, F. (1992) *Qumran and Apocalyptic: Studies on the Aramaic Texts from Qumran* (Leiden: E.J. Brill).
—— (1994) *The Dead Sea Scrolls Translated: The Qumran Texts in English* (trans. W. G. E. Watson; Leiden: E.J. Brill).
—— (2000) 'Temple Scroll', in Schiffman and VanderKam (eds) 2000: II, 927–33.
García Martínez, F. and E. J. C. Tigchelaar (1989–90) 'The Book of Enoch (1 Enoch) and the Aramaic Fragments from Qumran', *RevQ* 14: 131–46.
Garnet, P. (1977) *Salvation and Atonement in the Qumran Scrolls* (Tübingen: Mohr).
Geyer, J. (1970) 'קצות הארץ – Hellenistic?' *VT* 20: 87–90.
Gibson, J. C. L. (1971–82) *Textbook of Syrian Semitic Inscriptions* (3 vols; Oxford: Clarendon Press).
Ginzberg, L. (1998) *Legends of the Jews* (7 vols; Baltimore: Johns Hopkins University Press).
Goldingay, J. E. (1989) *Daniel* (Word Biblical Commentary 30; Dallas: Word Books).
Goldman, M. (trans.) (1969) 'The Book of Jubilees', in Kahana (ed.) 1969: I, 216–313.
Goldstein, J. A. (1976) *I Maccabees. A New Translation with Introduction and Commentary* (AB 41; Garden City: Doubleday).
—— (1979–80) 'The Apocryphal Book of I Baruch', *PAAJR* 46–47: 179–99.
Goodblatt, D. M. (1994) *The Monarchic Principle* (Tübingen: J.C.B. Mohr).
—— (2001) 'Judean Nationalism in the Light of the Dead Sea Scrolls', in D. M. Goodblatt, A. Pinnick and D. R. Schwartz (eds), *Historical Perspectives: From the Hasmoneans to Bar Kokhba in Light of the Dead Sea Scrolls: Proceedings of the Fourth International Symposium*

of the Orion Center for the Study of the Dead Sea Scrolls and Associated Literature, 27-31 January, 1999 (Leiden: E.J. Brill): 3–28.
Goodman, M. (1987) *The Ruling Class of Judaea: The Origins of the Jewish Revolt against Rome A.D. 66-70* (Cambridge; New York: Cambridge University Press).
—— (1989) 'Proselytising in Rabbinic Judaism', *JJS* 40/2: 175–85.
—— (1992) 'Jewish Proselytizing in the First Century', in J. Lieu, J. North and T. Rajak (eds), *The Jews among Pagans and Christians in the Roman Empire* (London; New York: Routledge): 53–78.
—— (1994) *Mission and Conversion: Proselytizing in the Religious History of the Roman Empire* (Oxford: Clarendon Press).
Grabbe, L. L. (1992) *Judaism from Cyrus to Hadrian* (2 vols; Minneapolis: Fortress Press).
Green, W. S. (ed.) (1980) *Approaches to Ancient Judaism. Vol. II* (Chico: Scholars Press).
Greenfield, J. C. and M. E. Stone (1977) 'The Enochic Pentateuch and the Date of the Similitudes', *HTR* 70: 51–66.
—— (1979a) 'The Books of Enoch and the Traditions of Enoch', *Numen* 26: 89–103.
—— (1979b) 'Remarks on the Aramaic Testament of Levi from the Geniza', *RB* 86: 214–30.
—— (1993) 'The Prayer of Levi', *JBL* 112: 247–66.
Grintz, Y. M. (1986) *The Book of Judith: A Reconstruction of the Original Hebrew Text with Introduction, Commentary, Appendices and Indices* (Jerusalem: Mosad Bialik, 2nd edn) (Hebrew).
Grosby, S. (2002) *Biblical Ideas of Nationality, Ancient and Modern* (Winona Lake: Eisenbrauns).
Gunneweg, A. H. J. (1983) 'ʿAM HAʾAREṢ–A Semantic Revolution', *ZAW* 95: 437–40.
Habel, N. C. (1995) *The Land is Mine: Six Biblical Land Ideologies* (Minneapolis: Fortress Press).
Hanhart, R. (1983) 'Das Land in der spätnachexilischen Prophetie', in Strecker (ed.) 1983: 126–40.
Hanson, P. D. (1977) 'Rebellion in Heaven, Azazel and Euhemeristic Heroes in 1 Enoch 6-11', *JBL* 96: 195–233.
Harrington, D. J. (1970) 'The Original Language of Pseudo-Philo's Liber Antiquitatum Biblicarum', *HTR* 63: 503–14.
—— (1974) *The Hebrew Fragments of Pseudo-Philo's Liber Antiquitatum Biblicarum Preserved in the Chronicles of Jerahmeel* (Missoula: Society of Biblical Literature).
—— (1985) 'Pseudo-Philo', in *OTP* 2: 297–377.
—— (2000) 'Sapiential Work', in Schiffman and VanderKam (eds) 2000: II, 825–6.
Harrington, D. J., J. Cazeaux, C. Perrot and P.-M. Bogaert (eds and trans.) (1976) *Pseudo-Philon, Les Antiquités Bibliques* (SC 229-30; 2 vols; Paris: Éditions du Cerf).
Harvey, G. (1996) *The True Israel: Uses of the Names Jew, Hebrew and Israel in Ancient Jewish and Early Christian Literature* (Leiden: E.J. Brill).
Hatch, E. and H. A. Redpath (1989) *A Concordance to the Septuagint and the Other Greek Versions of the Old Testament (Including the Apocryphal Books) in Three Volumes* (Grand Rapids: Baker Book House, 4th edn).
Healey, J. P. (1992) "am ha'arez', in *ABD* 1:168–9.
Heinemann, I. (1948) 'The Relationship between the Jewish People and Their Land in Hellenistic-Jewish Literature', *Zion* 13: 1–9 (Hebrew).
Hezser, C. (1997) *The Social Structure of the Rabbinic Movement in Roman Palestine* (Tübingen: Mohr Siebeck).
Hoffman, L. A. (ed.) (1986) *The Land of Israel: Jewish Perspectives* (Notre Dame: University of Notre Dame Press).
Hollander, H. W. and M. de Jonge, (1985) *The Testaments of the Twelve Patriarchs: A Commentary* (Leiden: E.J. Brill).
Holtz, T. (1980) 'αἰών', in von H. Balz and G. Schneider (eds), *Exegetisches Wörterbuch zum Neuen Testament* (3 Bd., Stuttgart-Berlin-Köln-Mainz: Kohlhammer) 1: 106–11.
Horgan, M. P. (1979) *Pesharim: Qumran Interpretations of Biblical Books* (CBQMS 8; Washington: Catholic Biblical Association of America).

Jackson, K. P. (1989) 'The Language of the Mesha Inscription', in Dearman (ed.) 1989: 96–130.
Jackson, K. P. and J. A. Dearman (1989) 'The Text of the Mesha Inscription', in Dearman (ed.) 1989: 93–5.
Jacobson, H. (1996) *A Commentary on Pseudo-Philo's Liber Antiquitatum Biblicarum with Latin Text and English Translation* (2 vols; Leiden: E.J. Brill).
Janzen, W. (1992) 'Land', in *ABD* 4:143–54.
Japhet, S. (1983) 'People and Land in the Restoration Period', in Strecker (ed.) 1983: 103–25.
Jastrow, M. (1903) *A Dictionary of the Targumim, the Talmud Babli and Yerushalmi, and the Midrashic Literature* (Jerusalem: Chorev).
Jenni, E. (1952) 'Das Wort 'ôlâm im Alten Testament', *ZAW* 64: 197–248.
—— (1953) 'Das Wort 'ôlâm im Alten Testament', *ZAW* 65: 1–35.
—— (1997) 'עולם', in *TLOT* 2: 852–62.
Johnson, D. (1988) *From Chaos to Restoration: An Integrative Reading of Isaiah 24-27* (JSOTSup 61; Sheffield: JSOT).
Johnston, P. and P. Walker (eds) (2000) *The Land of Promise: Biblical, Theological and Contemporary Perspectives* (Downers Grove: InterVarsity Press).
Kahana, A. (1969a) 'Ascension of Moses', in Kahana (ed.) 1969: I, 314–25.
—— (1969b) 'The Book of Baruch (1 Baruch)', in Kahana (ed.) 1969: I, 350–61.
—— (1969c) 'The Books of Maccabees 1-2', in Kahana (ed.) 1969: II, 72–231.
—— (1969d) 'The Vision of Baruch 2', in Kahana (ed.) 1969: II, 362–407.
—— (1969e) 'The Vision of Ezra', in Kahana (ed.) 1969: II, 607–53.
Kahana, A. (ed.) (1969) *hasefārîm haḥiṣônîm* (2 vols; Jerusalem: Maqor, 2nd edn).
Kallai, Z. (1975) 'The Boundaries of Canaan and the Land of Israel in the Bible', *Eretz Israel* 12: 27–34 (Hebrew).
—— (1997) 'The Patriarchal Boundaries, Canaan and the Land of Israel: Patterns and Application in Biblical Historiography', *IEJ* 47: 69–82.
Kasher, A. (1988) *Edom, Arabia and Israel: Relations of the Jews in Eretz-Israel with the Nations of the Frontier and the Desert during the Hellenistic and Roman Era* (332 BCE–70 CE) (Jerusalem: Yad Izhak Ben Zvi) (Hebrew).
Kasher, A., A. Oppenheimer and U. Rappaport (eds) (1986) *Man and Land in Eretz-Israel in Antiquity* (Jerusalem: Yad Izhak Ben Zvi) (Hebrew).
Klijn, A. F. J. (trans.) (1983) '2 (Syriac Apocalypse of) Baruch', in *OTP* 1: 615–52.
Knibb, M. A. (1978) *The Ethiopic Book of Enoch* (2 vols; Oxford: Clarendon Press; New York: Oxford University Press).
—— (1983) 'Exile in the Damascus Document', *JSOT* 25: 99–117.
—— (1987) *The Qumran Community* (Cambridge; New York: Cambridge University Press).
Kottsieper, I. (1998) *Zusätze zu Ester und Daniel* (ATD Apokryphen Band 5; Göttingen: Vandenhoeck & Ruprecht).
Kugler, R. A. (1996) *From Patriarch to Priest: Levi-Priestly Tradition from Aramaic Levi to Testament of Levi* (Atlanta: Scholars Press).
Kulik, A. (2004) *Retroverting Slavonic Pseudepigrapha: Toward the Original of the Apocalypse of Abraham* (Atlanta: Society of Biblical Literature).
Kutscher, E. Y. (1954) 'New Aramaic Texts', *JAOS* 74: 233–48.
—— (1957) 'Dating the Language of the Genesis Apocryphon', *JBL* 76: 288–92.
—— (1958) 'The Language of the Genesis Apocryphon: a Preliminary Study', in Ch. Rabin and Y. Yadin (eds), *Scripta Hierosolymitana IV: Aspects of the Dead Sea Scrolls* (Jerusalem: Magnes Press): 1–35.
Kvanvig, H. S. (1988) *Roots of Apocalyptic: The Mesopotamian Background of the Enoch Figure and of the Son of Man* (WMANT 61; Neukirchen-Vluyn: Neukirchener Verlag).
Lacocque, A. (1979) *The Book of Daniel* (Atlanta: John Knox Press).
Leaney, A. R. C. (1966) *The Rule of Qumran and its Meaning* (London: SCM).
Leslau, W. (1989) *Concise Dictionary of Ge'ez (Classical Ethiopic)* (Wiesbaden: O. Harrassowitz).

Levine, B. A. (1978) 'The Temple Scroll: Aspects of its Historical Provenance and Literary Character', *BASOR* 232: 5–23.
Licht, J. (1968) *Sefer Ḥazon ʿEzra* (Jerusalem: Mosad Bialik) (Hebrew).
—— (1996) *The Rule Scroll: A Scroll from the Wilderness of Judaea: 1QS, 1QSa, 1QSb: Text, Introduction and Commentary* (Jerusalem: Mosad Bialik, 2nd edn) (Hebrew).
Lichtenberger, H. (1980) 'Atonement and Sacrifice in the Qumran Community', in Green (ed.) 1980: 159–71.
Lipinski, E. (2004) 'קָנָה', in *TDOT* 13: 58–65.
Littmann, G. (trans.) (1994) 'Das Buch der Jubiläen', in *APAT* 2: 31–119.
Löhr, M. (trans.) (1994) 'Das Buch Judith', in *APAT* 1: 147–64.
Lohse, E. (1971) *Die Texte aus Qumran Hebräisch und Deutsch* (München: Kösel, 2nd edn).
Longenecker, B. W. (1995) *2 Esdras* (Sheffield: Sheffield Academic Press).
Lyons, W. J. (1996) 'Possessing the Land: The Qumran Sect and the Eschatological Victory', *DSD* 3: 130–51.
—— (1999) 'Clarifications Concerning 4Q285 and 11Q14 Arising from Discoveries in the Judean Desert 23', *DSD* 6: 37–43.
Maier, J. (1960) 'Zum Begriff יחד in den Texten von Qumran', *ZAW* 72: 148–66.
—— (1995) *Die Qumran-Essener: Die Texten vom Toten Meer*, Bd. 1 (München: E. Reinhardt).
McCready, W. O. (1982–4) 'The Sectarian Status of Qumran: The Temple Scroll', *RevQ* 11: 183–91.
Mendels, D. (1987) *The Land of Israel as a Political Concept in Hasmonean Literature* (Tübingen: J.C.B. Mohr).
—— (1992a) 'Baruch, Book of', *ABD* 1:618–20.
—— (1992b) 'Pseudo-Philo's Biblical Antiquities, the "Fourth Philosophy," and the Political Messianism of the First Century C.E.', in J. H. Charlesworth (ed.), *The Messiah: Developments in Earliest Judaism and Christianity* (Minneapolis: Fortress Press): 261–75.
Michel, O. (1978) 'ἡ οἰκουμένη', in *TDNT* 5: 157–9.
Milik, J. T. (1951) 'Manuale disciplinae', *VD* 29: 129–58.
—— (1955) 'Le Testament de Lévi en Araméen', *RB* 62: 398–406.
—— (1972) 'Milkî-Sedeq et Milkî-Resa dans les anciens écritis juifs et chrétiens', *JJS* 23: 95–144.
—— (1976) *The Books of Enoch: Aramaic Fragments of Qumran Cave 4* (Oxford: Clarendon Press).
Miller, P. D. Jr (1980) 'El, The Creator of Earth', *BASOR* 239: 43–6.
Mink, H. A. (1987) 'The Use of Scripture in the Temple Scroll and the Status of the Scroll as Law', *SJOT* 1: 20–50.
Moore, C. A. (1974) 'Toward the Dating of the Book of Baruch', *CBQ* 36 (1974): 312–20.
—— (1977) *Daniel, Esther and Jeremiah: The Additions* (AB 44; Garden City: Doubleday).
—— (1985) *Judith. A New Translation with Introduction and Commentary* (AB 40; Garden City: Doubleday).
—— (1992a) 'Jeremiah, Additions to', in *ABD* 3:698–703.
—— (1992b) 'Judith, Book of', in *ABD* 3:1117–25.
Muraoka, T. (trans.) (1976) 'Syriac Apocalypse of Baruch', in S. Yagi (ed.), *Seisho Gaiten-Giten, vol. 5* (Tokyo: Kyobunkwan) 69–154 (Japanese).
Murphy, F. J. (1993) *Pseudo-Philo: Rewriting the Bible* (New York: Oxford University Press).
Murphy-O'Connor, J. (1974) 'The Essenes and their History', *RB* 81: 215–44.
—— (1977) 'The Essenes in Palestine', *BA* 40: 100–24.
—— (1985) 'The Damascus Document Revisited', *RB* 92: 223–46.
Neusner, J. (1972) 'Judaism in a Time of Crisis', *Judaism* 21: 313–27.
Newsom, C. A. (1980) 'The Development of 1 Enoch 6-19: Cosmology and Judgment', *CBQ* 42: 310–29.
Nickelsburg, G. W. E. (1977a) 'Apocalyptic and Myth in 1 Enoch 6-11', *JBL* 96: 383-405.
—— (1977b) 'The Apocalyptic Message of 1 Enoch 92-105', *CBQ* 39: 309-28.

—— (1978–9) 'Riches, the Rich, and God's Judgment in 1 Enoch 92-105 and the Gospel According to Luke', *NTS* 25: 324–44.
—— (1980) 'Good and Bad Leaders in Pseudo-Philo's *Liber Antiquitatum Biblicarum*', in J. J. Collins and G. W. E. Nickelsburg (eds), *Ideal Figures in Ancient Judaism* (Chico: Scholars Press): 49–65.
—— (1981a) *Jewish Literature Between the Bible and the Mishnah* (Philadelphia: Fortress Press).
—— (1981b) 'Enoch, Levi, and Peter: Recipients of Revelation in the Upper Galilee', *JBL* 100: 575–600.
—— (1982) 'The Epistle of Enoch and the Qumran Literature', *JJS* 33: 333–48.
—— (1984) 'The Bible Rewritten and Expanded', in Stone (ed.) 1984: 89–156.
—— (1992a) 'Enoch, First Book of', in *ABD* 2:508–16.
—— (1992b) 'The Qumranic Transformation of a Cosmological and Eschatological Tradition (1QH 4:29-40)', in J. T. Barrera and L. V. Montaner (eds), *The Madrid Qumran Congress: Proceedings of the International Congress on the Dead Sea Scrolls Madrid 18-21 March, 1991* (Leiden: E.J. Brill): 649–59.
—— (2001) *1 Enoch 1: A Commentary on the Book of 1 Enoch, Chapters 1-36; 81-108* (Minneapolis: Fortress).
—— (2005) *Jewish Literature Between the Bible and the Mishnah* (Minneapolis: Fortress Press, 2nd edn).
Nir, R. (2003) *The Destruction of Jerusalem and the Idea of Redemption in the Syriac Apocalypse of Baruch* (Atlanta: Society of Biblical Literature).
Nitzan, B. (1986) *Pesher Habakkuk* (Jerusalem: Mosad Bialik) (Hebrew).
—— (1993–4) 'Benedictions and Instructions from Qumran for the Eschatological Community (11QBer, 4Q285)', *RevQ* 16: 77–90.
Orlinsky, H. M. (1986) 'The Biblical Concept of the Land of Israel: Cornerstone of the Covenant between God and Israel', in Hoffman (ed.) 1986: 27–64 (originally *Eretz Israel* 18 [1985]: 43–55).
The Peshitta Institute (ed.) (1972) *The Old Testament in Syriac According to the Peshitta Version* (Leiden: E.J. Brill).
Philonenko-Sayar, B. and Philonenko, M. (1981) 'L'Apocalypse d'Abraham', *Sem* 31.
Plöger, J. G. (1977) 'אדמה', in *TDOT* 1: 88–98.
Priest, J. (trans.) (1983) 'Testament of Moses', in *OTP* 1: 919–34.
Primus, C. (1986) 'The Borders of Judaism: The Land of Israel in Early Rabbinic Judaism', in Hoffman (ed.) 1986: 97–108.
Rabin, Ch. (1958) *The Zadokite Documents* (Oxford: Clarendon Press, 2nd edn).
Rappaport, U. (1967) 'The Hellenistic Cities and the Unity of Eretz-Israel in the Hasmonean Period', in S. Perlman and B. Shimron (eds), *Doron: 18 Mechqarim Mugashim le-Proph. B. Z. Katz* (Tel-Aviv: Tel-Aviv University): 219–30 (Hebrew).
——(1986) 'The Land Issue as a Factor in Inter-Ethnic Relations in Eretz-Israel during the Second Temple Period', in Kasher, Oppenheimer and Rappaport (eds) 1986: 81–6 (Hebrew).
Reiterer, F. V. (1980) *'Urtext' und Übersetzungen: Sprachstudie der Sir 44, 16-45, 26 als Beitrag zur Siraforschung* (St. Ottilien: EOS Verlag).
Rendtorff, R. (1975) *Israel und sein Land* (München: C. Kaiser).
Reventlow, H. G. and Y. Hoffman (eds) (2002) *Creation in Jewish and Christian Tradition* (JSOTSup 319; Sheffield: Sheffield Academic Press).
Rost, L. (1965) 'Die Bezeichnungen für Land und Volk im Alten Testament', in L. Rost, *Das kleine Credo und andere Studien zum Alten Testament* (Heidelberg: Quelle & Meyer): 76–100 (originally in *Festschrift Otto Procksch zum sechzigsten Geburtstag am 9. August 1934* [Leipzig: A. Deichert & J.C. Hinrichs, 1934]: 125–48).
Rubinkiewicz, R. (1987) *L'Apocalypse d'Abraham en vieux slave* (Lublin: Société des Lettres et des Sciences de l'Université Catholique de lublin).
Rubinkiewicz, R. and Lunt, H. G. (trans.) (1983) 'Apocalypse of Abraham', in *OTP* 1: 682–705.

Russell, D. M. (1996) *The "New Heavens and New Earth": Hope for the Creation in Jewish Apocalyptic and the New Testament* (Philadelphia: Visionary Press).
Rüterswörden, U. (1993) *Dominium terrae. Studien zur Genese einer alttestamentlichen Vorstellung* (BZAW 215; Berlin: Walter de Gruyter).
Safrai, Z. and Ch. Safrai (1993) 'The Sanctity of Eretz Israel and Jerusalem', in I. M. Gafni, A. Oppenheimer and M. Stern (eds), *Jews and Judaism in the Second Temple, Mishnah and Talmud Period: Studies in Honor of Shmuel Safrai* (Jerusalem: Yad Izhak Ben-Zvi): 344–71 (Hebrew).
Sarason, R. S. (1986) 'The Significance of the Land of Israel in the Mishnah', in Hoffman (ed.) 1986: 109–36.
Sasse, H. (1978a) 'αἰών', in *TDNT* 1: 197–208.
—— (1978b) 'γῆ', in *TDNT* 1: 677–81.
Sayler, G. B. (1984) *Have the Promises Failed? A Literary Analysis of 2 Baruch* (Chico: Scholars Press).
Schäfer, P. (2003) *The History of the Jews in the Greco-Roman World* (London: Routledge).
Schalit, A. (1989) *Untersuchungen zur Assumptio Mosis* (Leiden: E.J. Brill).
Schiffman, L. H. (1980) 'The Temple Scroll in Literary and Philological Perspective', in Green (ed.) 1980: 143–57.
—— (1988) 'The Law of the Temple Scroll and its Provenance', *Folia Orientalia* 25: 85–98.
—— (1990) 'The Impurity of the Dead in the *Temple Scroll*', in Schiffman (ed.) 1990: 135–56.
—— (1994) 'The Theology of the Temple Scroll', *JQR* 85: 109–23.
Schiffman, L. H. (ed.) (1990) *Archaeology and History in the Dead Sea Scrolls: The New York University Conference in Memory of Yigael Yadin* (Sheffield: JSOT Press).
Schiffman, L. H. and J. C. VanderKam (eds) (2000) *Encyclopedia of the Dead Sea Scrolls* (2 vols; New York: Oxford University Press).
Schmidt, F. (1990) 'Jewish Representations of the Inhabited Earth during the Hellenistic and Roman Periods', in A. Kasher, U. Rappaport and G. Fuks (eds), *Greece and Rome in Eretz Israel: Collected Essays*, (Jerusalem: Yad Izhak Ben-Zvi–The Israel Exploration Society): 119–34.
Schmidt, N. (1908) 'The Original Language of the Parables of Enoch', in R. F. Harper, F. Brown and G. F. Moore (eds), *Old Testament and Semitic Studies in Memory of William Rainey Harper* (Chicago: University of Chicago Press) 2: 329–49.
Schmidt, W. H. (1967) *Die Schöpfungsgeschichte der Priesterschaft* (WMANT 17; Neukirchen-Vluyn: Neukirchener Verlag, 2nd edn).
Schwartz, D. R. (1986) 'The End of the ΓΗ (Acts 1:8): Beginning or End of the Christian Vision?', *JBL* 105: 669–76.
—— (1990) 'On Two Aspects of a Priestly View of Descent at Qumran', in Schiffman (ed.) 1990: 157–79.
—— (1992) *Studies in the Jewish Background of Christianity* (Tübingen: J.C.B. Mohr).
Schweid, E. (1985) *The Land of Israel* (trans. D. Greniman; Madison: Fairleigh Dickinson University Press).
Segal, J. B. (1983) *Aramaic Texts from North Saqqâra* (London: Egypt Exploration Society).
Segal, M. Z. (1958) *Sefer Ben-Sira Ha-Shalem* (Jerusalem: Mosad Bialik, 2nd rev. edn) (Hebrew).
Shatzman, I. (1996) 'The Army of the Sons of Light in the War Scroll (1QM)', in I. M. Gafni, A. Oppenheimer and D. R. Schwartz (eds), *The Jews in the Hellenistic-Roman World: Studies in Memory of Menahem Stern* (Jerusalem: Merkaz Zalman Shazar): 105–31 (Hebrew).
Shemesh, A. (1999–2000) 'The Holiness According to the Temple Scroll', *RevQ* 19: 369–82.
Simon, M. (trans.) (1969) 'Judith', in Kahana (ed.) 1969; II, 348–76 (Hebrew).
Smend, R. (1983) 'Das eroberte Land', in Strecker (ed.) 1983: 91–102.
Sokoloff, M. (1979) 'Notes on the Aramaic Fragments of Enoch from Qumran Cave 4', *Maarav* 1/2: 197–224.
—— (1990) *A Dictionary of Jewish Palestinian Aramaic of the Byzantine Period* (Ramat-Gan: Bar Ilan University Press).
Stadelmann, L. I. J. (1970) *The Hebrew Conception of the World: A Philological and Literary Study* (Rome: Biblical Institute Press).

Steck, O. H. (1993) *Das apokryphe Baruchbuch: Studien zu Rezeption und Konzentration 'kanonischer' Überlieferung* (Göttingen: Vandenhoeck & Ruprecht).

—— (1998) 'Das Buch Baruch', in O. H. Steck, R. G. Kratz, and I. Kottsieper, *Das Buch Baruch, der Brief des Jeremia, Zusätze zu Ester und Daniel* (ATD Apokryphen Band 5; Göttingen: Vandenhoeck & Ruprecht): 10–68.

Stegemann, H. (1963–4) 'Der Peßer Psalm 37 aus Höhle 4 von Qumran (4QpPs 37)', *RevQ* 4: 235–70.

—— (1983) '"Das Land" in der Tempelrolle und in anderen Texten aus den Qumranfunden', in Strecker (ed.) 1983: 154–71.

Stern, M. (1972) *The Documents on the History of the Hasmonean Revolt* (Tel-Aviv: Hakibuts Hameuhad, 2nd edn) (Hebrew).

—— (1974–84) *Greek and Latin Authors on Jews and Judaism* (3 vols; Jerusalem: Israel Academy of Sciences and Humanities).

—— (1981) 'Judaea and her Neighbours in the Days of Alexander Jannaeus', *The Jerusalem Cathedra* 1: 22–46.

Stone, M. E. (1978) 'The Book of Enoch and Judaism in the Third Century B.C.E.', *CBQ* 40: 479–92.

—— (1984) 'Apocalyptic Literature', in Stone (ed.) 1984: 383–441.

—— (1989) *Features of the Eschatology of IV Ezra* (Atlanta: Scholars Press).

—— (1990) *Fourth Ezra: A Commentary on the Book of Fourth Ezra* (Minneapolis: Fortress).

Stone, M. E. (ed.) (1984) *Jewish Writings of the Second Temple Period* (Assen: Van Gorcum; Philadelphia: Fortress Press).

Strecker, G. (ed.) (1983) *Das Land Israel in biblischer Zeit* (Göttingen: Vandenhoeck & Ruprecht).

Strugnell, J. (1969–71) 'Notes en marge du Volume V des "Discoveries in the Judaean Desert of Jordan"', *RevQ* 7: 163–276.

Swanson, D. D. (1994) '"A Covenant Just Like Jacob's": The Covenant of 11QT 29 and Jeremiah's New Covenant', in G. J. Brooke (ed.), *New Qumran Texts and Studies* (Leiden: E.J. Brill): 273–86.

Talmon, S. and Y. Yadin (1999) *Masada VI: Yigael Yadin Excavations 1963-1965, Final Reports* (Jerusalem: Israel Exploration Society).

Thoma, C. (1970) 'Das Land Israel in der rabbinischen Tradition', in Eckert, Levinson and Stöhr (eds) 1970: 37–51.

Tov, E. (1975) *The Book of Baruch also Called I Baruch (Greek and Hebrew)* (Missoula: Scholars Press).

—— (1976) *The Septuagint Translation of Jeremiah and Baruch. A Discussion of an Early Revision of the LXX of Jeremiah 29-52 and Baruch 1:1-3:8* (Missoula: Scholars Press).

—— (1997) *The Text-Critical Use of the Septuagint in Biblical Research* (Jerusalem Biblical Studies 8; Jerusalem: Simor, rev. and enlarged 2nd edn).

Townsend, J. L. (1985) 'Fulfillment of the Land Promise in the Old Testament', *BSac* 142: 320–34.

Tromp, J. (1993) *The Assumption of Moses: A Critical Edition with Commentary* (Leiden: E.J. Brill).

Ullendorf, E. (1960) 'An Aramaic "Vorlage" of the Ethiopic Text of Enoch?', in *Atti del Convegno Internazionale di Studi Etiopici* (Rome: Accademia nazionale dei Lincei): 257–69.

VanderKam, J. C. (1973) 'The Theophany of Enoch I 3b-7, 9', *VT* 23: 129–50.

—— (1977) *Textual and Historical Studies in the Book of Jubilees* (Missoula: Scholars Press).

—— (1981) 'The Putative Author of the Book of Jubilees', *JSS* 26: 209–17.

—— (1984a) *Enoch and the Growth of an Apocalyptic Tradition* (Washington, D.C.: Catholic Biblical Association of America).

—— (1984b) 'Studies in the Apokalypse of Weeks (*1 Enoch* 93:1-10; 91:11-17)', *CBQ* 46: 511–23.

—— (1989) *The Book of Jubilees* (2 vols; CSCO 510-511; Lovanii: E. Peeters).

—— (1994a) DJD XIII.
—— (1994b) 'Genesis 1 in Jubilees 2', *DSD* 1: 300–21.
—— (1994c) 'The Theology of the Temple Scroll: A Response to Lawrence H. Schiffman', *JQR* 85: 129–35.
—— (1997) 'The Origins and Purposes of the Book of Jubilees', in M. Albani, J. Frey and A. Lange (eds), *Studies in the Book of Jubilees* (Tübingen: Mohr Siebeck): 3–24.
—— (1998) 'Messianism and Apocalypticism', in B. McGinn, J. J. Collins and S. J. Stein (eds), *The Encyclopedia of Apocalypticism* (New York: Continuum) 1: 193–228.
—— (2001) *The Book of Jubilees* (Sheffield: Sheffield Academic Press).
Vermes, G. (1997) *The Complete Dead Sea Scrolls in English* (London: Allen Lane/The Penguin Press).
—— (1999) *An Introduction to the Complete Dead Sea Scrolls* (London: SCM Press).
von Rad, G. (1936) 'Das theologische Problem des alttestamentlichen Schöpfungsglaubens', *ZAW* 66: 138–47 (= in von Rad 1961: 136–47).
—— (1943) 'Verheißenes Land und Jahwes Land im Hexateuch', *ZDPV* [1943]: 191–204 (= in von Rad 1961: 87–100).
—— (1961) *Gesammelte Studien zum Alten Testament* (München: C. Kaiser).
von Waldow, H. E. (1974) 'Israel and Her Land: Some Theological Considerations', in H. M. Bream, R. D. Heim and C. A. Moore (eds), *A Light unto My Path* (Philadelphia: Temple University Press): 493–508.
Wallace, D. H. (1955) 'The Semitic Origin of the Assumption of Moses', *TZ* 11: 321–8.
Weber, H. R. (1971) 'The Promise of the Land', *Study Encounter* 7: 1–16.
Weinfeld, M. (1983) 'The Extent of the Promised Land – the Status of Transjordan', in Strecker (ed.) 1983: 59–75.
—— (1984) 'Inheritance of the Land – Privilege versus Obligation: The Concept of the Promise of the Land in the Sources of the First and Second Temple Periods', *Zion* 49: 115–37 (Hebrew).
—— (1991–2) 'God versus Moses in the Temple Scroll: "I Do Not Speak on My Own But on God's Authority"', *RevQ* 15: 175–80.
—— (1992) 'Grace after Meals in Qumran', *JBL* 111: 427–40.
—— (1993) *The Promise of the Land: The Inheritance of the Land of Canaan by the Israelites* (Berkeley: University of California Press).
Wentling, J. L. (1989–90) 'Unraveling the Relationship between 11QT, the Eschatological Temple, and the Qumran Community', *RevQ* 14: 61–73.
Wernberg-Møller, P. (1957) *The Manual of Discipline: Translated and Annotated with an Introduction* (Leiden: E.J. Brill).
Westermann, C. (1971) *Schöpfung* (Themen der Theologie 12; Stuttgart: Kreuz-Verlag).
White, S. A. (1990) '4QDt^{n}: Biblical Manuscript or Excerpted Text?' in H. W. Attridge, J. J. Collins and T. H. Tobin (eds), *Of Scribes and Scrolls: Studies on the Hebrew Bible, Intertestamental Judaism and Christian Origins, Presented to John Strugnell on the Occasion of his Sixtieth Birthday* (Lanham: University Press of America): 13–20.
Whitelam, K. W. (1989) 'Israel's Traditions of Origin: Reclaiming the Land', *JSOT* 44: 19–42.
Wilken, R. L. (1992) *The Land Called Holy: Palestine in Christian History and Thought* (New Haven: Yale University Press).
Wintermute, O. S. (trans.) (1985) 'Jubilees', in *OTP* 2: 35–142.
Wise, M. O. (1990) *A Critical Study of the Temple Scroll from Qumran Cave 11* (Chicago: University of Chicago).
Wittenberg, G. (1991) 'The Significance of Land in the Old Testament', *Journal for Theology in South Africa* 77: 58–60.
Wright, C. J. H. (1990) *God's People in God's Land: Family, Land and Property in the Old Testament* (Grand Rapids: Eerdmans).
Wright, R. B. (1985) 'Psalms of Solomon', in *OTP* 2: 639–70.

Yadin, Y. (1962) *The Scroll of the War of the Sons of Light against the Sons of Darkness* (trans. Ch. Rabin; Oxford: Oxford University Press).
—— (1965) *The Ben Sira Scroll from Masada with Introduction, Emendations and Commentary* (Jerusalem: Israel Exploration Society).
—— (1983) *The Temple Scroll* (3 vols; Jerusalem: Israel Exploration Society).
Ziegler, J. (1965) *Sapientia Iesu filii Sirach* (Göttingen Septuaginta XII, 2; Göttingen: Vandenhoeck & Ruprecht).

Index of Ancient Sources

Apocrypha

Pseudepigrapha

51.15 148, 186
51.16 188
53 185
53.2 185
53.3 185
53.8 185
53.9 185
53.10 185
54.1 148, 166, 186, 187
54.3 187
54.21 188
55.2 186
56–74 185
56.2 123, 187, 188
56.2-4 165, 174, 187
56.3 185
56.5 185
56.15 148, 186
57.2 188
58.1 186
59.2 187
59.8 187
59.9 185
61.7 186
63.10 186, 199
66.2 186
66.6 187
69.1 188
69.4 188
70.2 186, 188
70.10 186
70.10–71.1 186
71.1 186, 187
72.4-5 187
73.1 188
73.2 186
73.4-5 188
74 188
76.2-3 185
76.3 189
77.6 187
77.8-10 186
77.9 186
77.15-16 186
78–87 186
78.6 187
78.7 187
83.1 166, 187
83.2 123, 187, 188
83.7 188
83.8 188
84.2 185
84.8 186
85.1-4 186
85.10 187, 188
85.14 188

4 Ezra 151, 153, 158, 172, 173, 174, 175, 176, 177, 178, 179, 180, 181, 182, 183, 184, 187, 189, 194, 199
3.4 165, 174, 187
3.6 174
3.7 179
3.8 179
3.9 148, 177, 180
3.12 148, 175, 179, 180
3.18 177
3.18-19 174
3.20-22 181
3.21-22 179
3.25-27 179
3.26 181
3.28 179
3.32-36 181
3.34 148, 177, 180
3.35 148, 175, 180
3.36 181, 187
4.11 178, 188
4.19 173
4.21 148, 173, 175, 180
4.24 177
4.26 179, 184
4.26-32 179
4.27 150, 156, 166, 177
4.36 179
4.36-37 165, 174, 187
4.38 181
4.39 148, 175, 181
4.41 175
4.44-50 179
5.1 148, 175, 180
5.3 175
5.4-5 166
5.6 148, 175, 180
5.10 175
5.11 175
5.16-18 182
5.17 175
5.23 181
5.23-24 174, 177
5.24 175, 176
5.44 177
5.48 174, 175
5.49 165, 174, 187
5.49-55 179
5.50 174
5.50-55 174, 184, 188
5.54-55 179
6.1 174, 178
6.1-6 165, 174, 178, 179
6.5 165, 174, 187
6.14 174
6.14-16 174
6.15-16 174
6.16 184
6.18 148, 175, 180
6.18-28 180
6.20 166, 171, 179
6.24 148, 174, 180
6.25 177, 178, 180, 188
6.26 148, 175, 180
6.38 165, 174, 187
6.39 165
6.42 173
6.43 165, 174, 187
6.53 174
6.54 118, 174
6.55 156, 164, 178
6.59 133, 156, 164, 167, 168, 178, 183, 199
7.9 183
7.10 183
7.11 156, 164, 178, 180
7.11-13 178, 179
7.11-16 183
7.12-16 182
7.15 179
7.17 183
7.17-18 178
7.21-24 181
7.26 176, 191
7.26-44 182
7.30 165, 187
7.30-31 178
7.30-32 184
7.32 174, 185
7.36 174
7.37 176
7.45-61 180
7.46 181
7.47 188
7.50 178
7.51 178
7.54 174
7.55 174
7.62 174
7.70 165, 174, 178, 179

Greek and Latin Authors

Index of Modern Authors

0 1341 1526377 1

RECEIVED

OCT 3 1 2013

GUELPH HUMBER LIBRARY
205 Humber College Blvd
Toronto, ON M9W 5L7